Getting Out

Getting Out

Your Guide
to Leaving America

Updated and Expanded Edition

Mark Ehrman

process self-reliance series

Getting Out: Your Guide to Leaving America
Updated and Expanded Edition © 2012 by Mark Ehrman
All rights reserved.

Getting Out is the second volume of the Process Self-Reliance Series

Process Media
1240 W Sims Way #124
Port Townsend WA 98368

www.processmediainc.com
www.gettingoutofamerica.com

Associate Editor for Updated Edition: Cletus Nelson
Researcher: Elizabeth Kotin
Additional Research: Amanda Wilson
Editorial Assistance: Laura Smith Guerrero
Editorial Assistance: Leslie Reed

Design by Gregg Einhorn

ISBN 978-1934170298
ISBN 1934170291

10 9 8 7 6 5 4 3 2 1

America, love it or...

Contents

At some point during the coming years, due to an array of factors, with energy scarcity foremost among them, the economic system of the United States will teeter and fall, to be replaced by something that most people can scarcely guess at, and that even those who see it coming prefer not to think about.
—Dmitry Orlov, *Reinventing Collapse*

We have been gradually disempowered by a corporate state that, as Huxley foresaw, seduced and manipulated us through sensual gratification, cheap mass-produced goods, boundless credit, political theater and amusement. While we were entertained, the regulations that once kept predatory corporate power in check were dismantled, the laws that once protected us were rewritten and we were impoverished. Now that credit is drying up, good jobs for the working class are gone forever and mass-produced goods are unaffordable, we find ourselves transported from *Brave New World* to *1984*. The state, crippled by massive deficits, endless war and corporate malfeasance, is sliding toward bankruptcy. It is time for Big Brother to take over from Huxley's feelies, the orgy-porgy and the centrifugal bumble-puppy. We are moving from a society where we are skillfully manipulated by lies and illusions to one where we are overtly controlled.
—Chris Hedges, "2011: A Brave New Dystopia"

The greatest irony in modern American may well be that while argument and discord prevail in the edifice of American Democracy, the best and most thoughtful citizens have already left the building.
—John R. Wennersten, *Leaving America: The New Expatriate Generation*

Foreword: What Are You Waiting For?

Back in 2006, when the first edition of this book came out, the bubbles were still inflating, the economy hadn't yet crashed and despite the mounting evidence to the contrary, the mythology of America as the best of all possible worlds still lingered via some mysterious inertia. Those who were paying attention knew better, but sounding the alarm, saying that the USA was a place you wanted to leave, was a message that the public at large wasn't yet ready to hear. Oh sure, moving abroad could be accepted as a delightful, purely elective and perhaps even frivolous lark. And of course, it can be that, as well. But there was a growing sense among people of "uh oh, maybe it's time to get out." Some of them never before imagined they would one day feel the need to flee. They didn't know where to begin. "Leave? And go where? How? What would I do?"

My idea was to create an easy-to-use manual that could walk anyone through the process of looking for and finding a new life abroad. Regardless of whether a person was a fundamentalist Christian, left-wing radical or apolitical hedonist, the book would have to help them identify what they like and don't like, need and don't need, tolerate and can't tolerate, and figure out how those applied to countries around the world and their respective costs of living, available employment and entry requirements. For such a thing to be useful for any American contemplating getting out, I needed to reach out beyond my own experience and research and tap into the expertise of Americans all around the world, from all walks of life, from every race, creed, color, age group, sexual preference and just about any other dimension that I could think of, and ask them to share their experiences moving and living abroad and their advice for others who wanted to do the same.

They were liberals creeped out by the Bush Adminstration's sinister antics. Conservatives and libertarians alarmed by the soaring deficit. Muslims who no longer felt comfortable under the hostile and suspicious gaze of post-9/11 America, Jews who felt their Jewishness needed to be practiced in their ancestral homeland, and Christians who believed the U.S. didn't allow them to freely invoke God whenever they had the urge. Some were lonelyhearts in search of love...or wanted to be united after they'd found it. Others sought adventure. Still others, jobs. Many could no longer "afford" America and moved to a place where their money would stretch further. More than likely, they were driven by a combination of factors. Each one was testament to the fact that there is no "typical American expat." They operated under different, though often overlapping, criteria when evaluating where they should go. Likewise, they employed strategies both unique and tried-and-true for making it happen. Some were lucky. Others clever. And many simply persevered. Regardless of their level of education, expertise, or how articulate they might or might not be, each one offered, if only by their successful example, invaluable information as well as inspiration. Their suggestions and experiences could then be not only integrated into the general structure and focus areas of the book, but also shared directly with the readers themselves. Their support, encouragement and enthusiasm kept me going through the arduous days, weeks and months it took to put the whole thing together.

The result was *Getting Out: Your Guide to Leaving America*.

Upon release, *Getting Out* was pretty much either ignored or ridiculed by the mainstream media. Those who did deign to notice it found the material to be useful but thought the tone and attitude to be unnecessarily alarmist. Nevertheless, *Getting Out* found its audience. Independent bookstores all over the country displayed copies in their window…or it wound up in front of mega stores in the "Employee Picks." Many blogs took notice. Word of mouth carried it the rest of the way. My inbox filled with countless emails from strangers, expressing their desire to leave the United States. For many of them, *Getting Out* represented the first affirmation that they were not alone—that what they were thinking and feeling was shared by a diffused and nearly invisible multitude.

That was then, as they say, and this is now. While our politicians played musical chairs, and pundits argued about what it all meant to the viewers at home, *Getting Out* has gone from being radically chic to desperately obvious. The State Department estimates that over five million of your fellow citizens (who are non-military or otherwise unaffiliated with the U.S. Government) have already made their exit, and the true figure is probably a lot higher given the huge numbers of Americans who leave and don't bother to register their presence anywhere they can be counted. Network news and major newspapers now regularly report on how Americans by the droves are seeking opportunities in China or India, or moving to Canada and other countries with a saner healthcare system—or to Mexico, Costa Rica or the Philippines where decent lifestyles can still be led for pennies on the ever-shrinking dollar. *Getting Out*, as it were, had made it to prime time.

Needless to say, it was time for a facelift. We didn't just replace old information with new, however. We also tweaked the format and cleaned up the design, making it easier to use. New countries have been added. In addition to presenting the most up-to-date visa, residency and citizenship information available, we've beefed up the information about taxes and finance, energy and employment, business and environmental policies, and food, drug and gun laws. We've located dozens of new contributors. This new edition of *Getting Out: Your Guide to Leaving America* is cleaner, meaner, more current and ready to help you meet the new realities. Many thanks to Cletus Nelson who researched, updated and sourced much of the information and data within.

Nowadays, it hardly needs to be pointed out anymore that the American Dream has been bankrupted—morally, politically and, without a doubt, economically. Our infrastructure rots, healthcare costs metastasize, and political discourse has turned into a World Wrestling Federation-like spectacle. Corruption has seeped into every capillary of our body politic. Powerful megabanks responsible for plunging the country into recession have been lavishly rewarded. Transnational corporations are given greater rights than a living, breathing U.S. citizen. Military adventurism marches ever onward while the fiat dollars that finance it are being Quantitatively Eased into oblivion.

The only question left is when is it all going to blow. And the answer is, it's already started. And so should you.

All right, you had your little "fling" with hope. Now it's time to get real.

Getting Out is a way for you to vote with your feet, outsource yourself or drop out of the rat race, off the grid or simply out of harm's way. It's the one power that still undeniably rests with every individual. Use it. Time is running out.

Mark Ehrman
Berlin, Germany

About This Book (a.k.a.: *the fine print*)

Every effort was made to ensure the accuracy of the information in the book at the time it was published. The world, however, is in rapid flux. Prices and currency values fluctuate (something to keep in mind particularly when amounts are quoted in U.S. dollars). Laws, regulations, visa classifications and requirements—even entire governments—are often changed, modified, or disappear completely. On more than a few occasions, extremely complex procedures, regulations/requirements or systems have been boiled down to their most relevant points, since to do otherwise would mean this book would never end. And then of course there's the inescapable reality that the information herein was compiled by humans, and subject to such shortcomings thereof.

Before finalizing any plans, you would be advised to check current conditions and the most up-to-date and detailed list of requirements.

With respect to sources used in this book: In most cases, mainstream sources and research organizations are used and these are, whenever possible, identified. Recognize that a) any rating or ranking cannot possibly give a complete picture of the situation of any complex society comprising of millions to hundreds of millions of individuals, and that b) these sources often have inherent biases and agendas and that their perceived reliability is often contingent on the particular ideological orientation of the reader (to gauge your particular level of agreement with the source in question, it is often sufficient to look up how they rank the U.S.). They are only presented here as a generalized guide to conditions in the area in question and to alert the reader to dimensions of life abroad that they otherwise might not consider.

As with everything else, you are encouraged to do as much additional research as possible and to consult sources you believe would be most consistent with your personal tastes and ideological leanings. Obviously, before committing, a scouting trip to your desired location to suss it out for yourself beforehand is more than advisable.

Introduction
Enter The Matrix...
And Get Out!

Expatriate, Know Thyself

So you want to get out? Well, the world is a big place. Some parts are easy to move to but lack opportunities for work. Others have onerous laws but have jobs for the asking. There are places you can live for a year on a month's salary and others you'll need millions in the bank just to consider. There are nanny states and police states. And some people believe those two are one and the same. After all, one person's hell is another's paradise.

And then there are all those questions: How do you get permission to live in another country? What does it cost to live there? What will I do? What if I want to buy property, open a business, look for work?

A little overwhelming, isn't it? A successful Getting Out strategy is best conceived of as a matrix, where your goal is to try and find the best fit between all the variables that make up you the individual and those that make up life in foreign country. So, where do you begin? With the person closest to you—yourself. Before you examine life in other countries, take a good look at your situation. This will bring the world into better focus.

Here are a few things to consider:

Your Age: Some countries, like Canada, have laws favoring immigration by younger people with their entire working life ahead of them. Other countries, such as Panama, make it easy for seniors to retire there. Students and recent graduates can avail themselves of a host of programs that facilitate transfer overseas, and even arrange work permits. Younger folks are probably more willing to take a few months or years doing odds jobs than someone in midcareer.

Income: How long can you live off your savings? Some countries offer residencies at a price, whether through investment or straight cash transaction. Can you afford to "buy" your way in? Many visas are contingent on proving you make a certain amount of money, or have a minimum bank balance. Indeed, few countries will let you in without you somehow demonstrating that you have sufficient income/savings on which to live.

Skills: Having the right skill set makes a big difference. There isn't a nation on the globe that doesn't need for nurses, for instance. Information technology professionals, engineers, and business and marketing professionals tend to have the run of the globe.

Preferences: Why are you leaving the U.S. and what do you expect from life abroad? Do you prefer fast-paced urban excitement or lazy days on sunny beaches? Do you want good governance, economic liberty, or cheap living? Easy entry or guaranteed healthcare? And if you can't get everything you want, what difficulties and restrictions are you willing to tolerate?

Your Family Tree and your Relationships: Having a parent or even grandparent who is or was a citizen or resident of a country can facilitate citizenships and residencies that would be more difficult or even unavailable to others. Likewise, children and blood relatives. Spouses of foreign citizens generally have it relatively easy, and often even domestic partners and engaged couples. Needless to say, just knowing someone there can make a world of difference in helping you through the myriad details of transitioning to a new culture and make the process far less alienating than having to go it alone.

And of course, if you have a spouse or children, then you must factor in their situation, preferences, etc., as well.

Armed with this self-knowledge, you're ready to explore the nuts and bolts of *Getting Out of America*. The remainder of the book is divided into the following areas:

Part I: The Basics: Living And Working

Getting In...and Staying In:
Visas, Residencies, Work Permits and Citizenship

Before you can choose a place to go, you need to understand the system of how to legally reside there. The section gives you the lowdown on Visas, Residencies and Work Permits and covers the basic procedures of being allowed to enter, remain, and work in a given country, as well as a few common tricks and tips to getting the paperwork you need. For those keen on going all the way, the Foreign Citizenship section lays out the rules and what your best chance of obtaining a foreign passport would be, and what that means as far as your U.S. citizenship is concerned.

Getting By: Jobs and other Hustles

Addresses the vital question of how you will earn a living—will you go where you can find work, or find work where you want to go? For some, having some kind of employment is a prerequisite for any kind of move; others have access to money from home and are simply looking to live as easily and as cheaply as possible. In "Getting By," we explore the common gigs and hustles of American expats overseas.

Part II: For Your Consideration...The Rest of the World

Is it Any Better There? Choosing the Country That's Right for You

While legal residency and means of support will form the backbone of your Getting Out strategy, there are many issues—from the level of taxation to the care of the environment, sovereign debt to crime and safety — that affect the experience of life in another country. This section offers a host of different questions to consider, and the tools and resources you need to match the place to your preference...or vice versa.

May We Suggest? The Getting Out 61+1

All things considered, you have over 60 countries that offer the most attractive overall package to the would-be American exile: ease of immigration or long-term stay, availability of work, affordability and overall desirability. Then we give the lowdown on what it takes to set up a life there. Of course you don't have to pick just one. With the globe transforming so quickly in terms of climate, political stability, and economic health, more and more people are configuring their lives so they don't stay anywhere for very long.

Part III: Doing It

Getting Real: The Transition and Beyond

From moving your stuff to staying in touch, there's lots of details to deal with once you put a plan into action. Insuring your health, paying your taxes, schooling your kids and driving your car are all covered here.

A World Wide Web of Resources

Obviously, a single book will only get you so far. It cannot possibly contain every answer to all questions that any person might have. But we don't just leave you high and dry. To get even more specific and individualized questions answered, we point you to voluminous additional resources, user forums and links to many of our contributors around the world.

Of course, no matter where you go, what you do, and for how long you do it, you'll need to have a few essentials.

Money: While all-inclusive packages provided by corporations for their transfers or Peace Corps for their volunteers take care of most of the moving costs, unforeseen expenses always arise. The consensus is that having three months' living expenses should be considered the absolute barest minimum. Scrape together what you can, sell what you don't need, or beg from anyone who will listen. It's a rare breed of expat adventurer who drops into a country penniless and is able to make a go of it. For the rest of us, in the early going especially, count on dipping generously into your savings. If you don't have any, then start putting some aside. You'll need it.

Time: Processing visas, applying for jobs, and arranging myriad other details necessary to pave your way to your new life doesn't happen overnight. Depending on your choice of destination and job prospects, the process can take weeks, months, and in some cases, even years. Start now.

Patience: Bureaucratic delays are unavoidable and can often be maddening. Try to remember you'll be dealing with another culture that may involve an entirely different way of doing things. The greatest asset you can have is the ability to wait without losing your head.

And finally...

The Passport: Even if your ultimate goal is to give yours up, you're not going anywhere unless you first have one. Only 28 percent of Americans—85.5 million—currently possess this little blue book. You'd better be among them. "Stateless" individuals, the official term for people who possess no internationally recognized citizenship, are even lower on the bureaucratic totem pole than destitute refugees, since not even pity will help you.

If you plan on relocating to Canada, Mexico, the Caribbean, or Bermuda, the State Department is now issuing Passport Cards which are less expensive than a traditional passport, though hardly that much less to make it worthwhile. These wallet-sized cards will let you reenter the U.S. by land or sea but cannot be used if you return by plane.

Passport: $135 for adults, $105 for children under 16
Passport card: $55 adults, $40 for children under 16
You can apply at your nearest post office.
Applications can be downloaded at **travel.state.gov**

I Got Out

Jude Angione, Age 60
Rochester, NY ➡ Toronto, Canada

I'm a lesbian and have been out for 40 years. I came out here on a student visa in 1970 to go to the University of Toronto. I stayed because of politics, family reasons and because Toronto in the 1970s was the center of the universe.

Cara Smiley, 40
New Haven, VT ➡ Oaxaca, Mexico

The USA had become unbearable after 9/11. The self-imposed ignorance and refusal to discuss the issues became more and more difficult for me to deal with on a daily basis. In December 2001, I decided to live permanently in Mexico. I love and respect the deep-rooted Mexican culture.

I came here as an organic food inspector, working for a company back in the States before eventually starting my own company in Mexico City. I also met a man here and fell in love.

In December 2006, my fiancé and I moved from Mexico City to Oaxaca City, Oaxaca because Eugenio's family lives here and because it is a beautiful colonial city. In November 2007, Eugenio and I got married.

We purchased 1.25 acres of land about 20 minutes south of Oaxaca City. In November 2008, we started building our house. We have 11 table grape plants, over 30 (baby) fruit trees and a very diverse vegetable and herb garden.

There has been and continues to be a great deal of social unrest in Oaxaca which has, on occasions, led to violence. Every once in a while, Eugenio asks me if I would like to live in the USA again. The answer is always no. I like the life we have created here—our home, our friends and our work. I do not plan to return. While the USA has an incredible cultural diversity, there is nothing like living, immersing oneself entirely, in another country, culture, language, etc. Viva Mexico!

Name Withheld by Request, Age 60
Chicago, IL ➡ San Miguel de Allende, Mexico

I was an advertising art director for 22 yrs, financial layoff after financial layoff...the industry is in horrific shape and no one over 50 is being hired. I freelanced after the last layoff but no one has a budget for freelancers so that went away too. I decided I had to cut my cost of living or I'd tear thru my savings way too fast.

I had started painting in 2003 and that had gone really well. I had several solo shows. So, tired as I was of Chicago's endless winters and too humid summers, I moved to San Miguel de Allende, in Mexico's high central desert. It is an "artist's town."

I can now concentrate on painting and see how far I get with it. I love it, and every day is a pleasure now.

It would take a huge change, a huge financial change for me to be able to afford to live in the States again. I'm not a suburban type and the big cities are too expensive with no income...not to mention the cost of health insurance when you are self-employed. I have cut my cost of living in half (at least) by living here.

Sharon Hiebing, Age 46
Oakland, CA ➡ San Ignacio Town, Belize

I never thought I'd be "that person" who would stay in her hometown her entire life, but slowly, that was what my life was beginning to look like. I realized I did not want that, and since I wasn't getting any younger, I needed to act. So, in January, 2010, I put my pool and spa business on the market. Eight months later, I was on a plane to Belize.

I chose Belize for its wonderful climate (average temperature is around 80 degrees year-round), proximity to the United States (so I could travel back home easily—it's only a 2 ½-hour flight to Texas), low cost of living (most folks can live quite well on $1500–2500 USD a month), and access to wonderful oceans, rainforests, rivers, ruins, and fresh produce. Lastly, the people were marvelous—some of the friendliest I've ever met.

Kelly Kittel, Age 49
Portsmouth, RI ➡ Tamarindo, Costa Rica

I have been leaving the U.S. all my life—starting in college with study abroad and then the Peace Corps where my husband and I met. We have lived outside the U.S. three times—one year in Portugal and this is our second time in Costa Rica and we now own property here.

I have never been enamored of our consumer-oriented narcissistic culture nor of the military-industrial complex. I never wanted my kids to think the rest of the world lived like they do in the U.S. We have exposed them to travel and other cultures and languages as much as possible and wanted them to see how the rest of the world lives. They all speak at least two languages now. They see how unsustainable American culture is. We expect them to change the world.

For me, it wasn't a matter of dissatisfaction with American government or society, though I do have complaints. Nor did I make the move in anticipation of the spike in unemployment that would hit just a year after my move abroad. I wish I could boast that kind of insight.

Frank, Age 37
Orlando, FL ➡ Orosi, Costa Rica

Most of my career, I built furniture for hotels and bars around the world. I'd done a lot of really neat stuff. And I started building out nightclubs in Central Florida and I started doing events, too. I was pretty successful. Then they started to shut the scene down. In 2000, they passed an anti-rave law that it's against the law to dance in public after 2 a.m. And I thought, "This is insanity. The Constitution says we have a right to gather. It doesn't say we can't gather if we're going to dance." Then they put cameras on every corner, the taxes are out of control, and I started feeling like it's not a free country.

I wanted to go to Costa Rica for a while. In 2005, I had a girlfriend and she got pregnant. I didn't see a future for me in the U.S. and I certainly didn't see any aspect of the U.S. that would be good for raising a child. So we moved to Costa Rica because it's a better place to raise a kid.

Not just your cost of living goes down here, but your stress level. You don't have the stress of trying to pay crazy bills and the stress of always trying to get someplace. Being in this environment and being around these people, I don't miss the States at all. I was over it before I even left the States, and now I don't go back even for a visit.

Name and address withheld, Age 49
San Antonio, TX ➡ David/Panama City, Panama

I have lived close to Latin America and worked in Mexico, Central, and South America for almost 30 years. My company only manufactures products for use in Latin America and I traveled almost every country extensively. I am in road paving so I see a lot about government, local customs, and quite a bit of countryside.

I realized we were paying welders and fitters $65,000/year in San Antonio with health insurance, taxes, and all the loser programs required. I also found out I could not get the number I wanted nor get them to come to work.

Here, I pay no income taxes. I have no government prying into my technology. If my customer is injured by my machine, no court will judge that he can own my children's inheritance. I employ a few more people...I have that luxury.

I'm glad I'm here. I wish we didn't have dollars...and I wish we didn't have to do biz with the U.S.

James Lindzey, 43
Ft. Lauderdale, FL ➡ Medellín, Colombia

I'm an ex-dot-com guy, not one of those that made millions, just decent money for a few years, far from Silicon Valley. Making about 90K a year before I just realized I was feeling empty and in the Miami area I felt like an aunt next to the celebs—flashy people driving around with Lamborghinis and pulling up to nightclubs in yachts, or maybe it was the after-hour parties at $5 million penthouses.

Something clicked. I had to get out. I was worried about security at first. Everybody reassured me that Colombia was OK, so in 2005, I just sold everything and came down here, sight unseen. I went to Bogotá. At first, I supported myself by doing tech support via cable modem at 500k out of Bogotá back in 2005. After months of rain, I took my friend's advice and booked a flight to Medellín, "the city of eternal spring."

I don't like overstressed fast-paced cities, they just burn everyone out. Well, Colombian people like to work but they like to be social, and take time to talk to you as well. In the States, I felt like the run of the mill apple pie American but here I get special attention, and people treat me much better.

Josh Plotkin, Age 20
Huntington Beach, CA ➡ Vitória, Brazil

I'm a 20-year-old college dropout turned English teacher who until recently was living in Medellín, Colombia, but I just moved to Vitória, Brazil. A main factor in my decision to leave the U.S. was that I fear what is coming next over there. I don't want to be around for it. Fourteen trillion dollars in debt is a time bomb that is going to explode and my generation is going to get the short end of the stick.

Bob Hand, Age 76
Colorado Springs, CO ➡ Rio Grande do Sul, Brazil

I moved to Brazil not to escape the United States but to begin a new life with my wife, Cidinha.

I like Brazil, its culture, and the Brazilian people very much. My first trip to Brazil was as a tourist in 1973 when I visited Manaus, Brasilia, Salvador, Rio de Janeiro, the historic cities of Minas Gerais, and ended at the home of a friend in São Paulo. We kept in touch over the years as I moved about the USA and settled in Colorado. Then in 2000, I encountered on the Internet a person in a small town in Minas Gerais.

As our friendship developed, my friend told me about the situation with street kids in her town and she wanted to do something to help them become self-sufficient. I liked the idea and offered to help with a project, especially since it would be based on freedom and prosperity, and not on a victim mentality. I made my first trip to that small town in 2001 and thereafter founded a nonprofit organization called BizKidz of Brazil. We launched the project in Minas Gerais in 2004 and I made annual visits to Brazil to support it personally. While there in 2007, I got to know Cidinha, we fell in love, and after I returned to Colorado we kept in touch via Skype every night. On subsequent trips, in 2008, Cidinha and I travelled to Salvador, historic cities of Minas Gerais, then to the south and Curitiba, Nova Petropolis, and Florianopolis. We knew by then that we wanted to be together permanently, and we chose to live in Nova Petropolis, since we liked the city and it would be more difficult for her to part with her family and move to the USA.

I knew nothing about Rio Grande do Sul until we moved here. What I found was a spirit of liberty that has deep roots in the culture of the Gaúcho. Being a libertarian-minded person, I was very interested in learning more about this local mentality, quite different from other parts of Brazil. Last year, I attended the Forum of Liberty in Porto Alegre, and will attend again in April of this year.

David Morrill, Age 61
Ft. Lauderdale, FL ➡ Cuenca, Ecuador

I had spent years pursuing the Great American Dream but came to understand that the pursuit was keeping me in the Great American Rut. I had visited a number of Latin American countries, many of them with my father on bird-watching tours, and came away from Ecuador with the best feeling. I liked the people, landscape and the cities and the fact that it's only a four-hour flight back to see family and friends in Florida. One of my criteria for choosing Ecuador was the standard of living. A number of other countries were attractive to me, but the level of poverty and sense of desperation was extreme and I decided I would not feel comfortable living with this.

Ande Wanderer
Denver, CO ➡ Buenos Aires, Argentina

I feared I was becoming too complacent with my relatively comfortable life in the U.S. I had my reporting job at a newspaper, a good stable of friends, regular activities and a pretty good life.

But while living in Denver, I also seemed to keep having experiences that made me feel I was living in a punitive nanny state without the nanny (i.e., healthcare). I would walk or ride a bike in an effort to be 'eco-friendly' and racked up hundreds of dollars of tickets for having an 'abandoned automobile' parked on the street.

One time I was stopped at an alcohol checkpoint. While waiting in line, I took off my seat belt (which I used religiously) to reach in the glove box for my car's documentation and promptly received a ticket for 'no seat belt.' I put an old couch on the porch of my apartment building in a gentrifying neighborhood. It made a nice place for neighbors to gather and keep an eye on the unattended children playing in the street. We got a ticket for 'unsanctioned porch furniture.'

All this was during the mortgage boom and acquaintances were trying to convince me to look at buying a property even though I knew there was no guarantee of gainful employment for the next 30 years of my life. It seems like I dodged a bullet—getting ensnarled in 'the American dream' and working for the rest of my life to pay off my debts, if I even could.

It was also a personal goal to become fluent in a second language and knew that my weekly Spanish conversation group wasn't cutting it—for me immersion would be the best way to accomplish it.

I accomplished a lot of what I set out to do living in Argentina. I've thought about returning to the U.S. or Canada, and have even perused job ads, but thoughts of getting up on cold, dark mornings and trudging to a 60-plus-hour-a-week job have kept the idea dormant.

Vina Rathbone, Age 24
Boise, ID ➡ Buenos Aires, Argentina

After graduating college in 2009, I was unable to secure full-time employment. I looked for months and worked as a temporary contractor for various corporate companies. I started to research teaching English abroad as a possible next step.

As a student of anthropology, other cultures fascinated me. I had already traveled extensively in Europe and I wanted to push myself out of my comfort zone. I knew next to nothing about South America, but I did know some Spanish. Buenos Aires has a reputation as a very European and cosmopolitan city, which appealed to me. I knew I wouldn't be able to make much money here, but I was seduced by ideas of tango tradition and cheap wines, so I came anyway. Had I known more about South America, I probably would have chosen to move to Chile, which has a much more stable economy and political structure, but once I got sucked into the Argentine 'locura' (craziness), there was no way out.

Bud Smith (and Sumana Harrison), late 60s
Colorado/Arizona ➡ Jujuy, Argentina

When I retired to Boquete, Panama in 2004 I figured I had found my pot of gold at the end of the rainbow. But after four years of living in that very small country, I became a little claustrophobic and decided to do some traveling. I rented my home and property, sold or gave away most of my belongings and bought an airline ticket to Ecuador.

My first day there I met a wonderful lady, another American expat who had lived in Oaxaca, Mexico for many years before moving to Cuenca a few years before. She also was ready once again to move on, and after a few months spent traveling around Ecuador, we hit the road south.

Traveling by bus, we made it slowly through Peru and on into Argentina and Chile, then back north through Peru and Ecuador and north to Colombia, moving with the seasons. As the southern summer began, we would travel south again through Peru and Bolivia and once again into Argentina. A total of 2 ½ years!

We have settled into the far northwestern part of Argentina in the province of Jujuy, about 1000 miles west of Buenos Aires and at the foothills of the Andes. The climate here has four seasons but is mild year-round, the cost of living is reasonable, the local wines are world-renowned as well as inexpensive and the Argentine steaks are to die for!

Tim, 29
Los Angeles, CA ➡ London, U.K.

I left America for the United Kingdom in 2008 to pursue a Ph.D. in London. I really needed a change and job prospects were looking terrible in a tanking economy. My healthcare costs for even basic allergy and asthma were extortionate and I found myself going down to Mexico every few months to stockpile medicine at less than half the price. Frustrated and broke, I not only wanted to go back to school, I wanted to get out of the country. London was an easy choice: amazing options for postgraduate education, one of the most cosmopolitan cities in the world, socialized healthcare and a shared language. I'm planning to stay through 2012. If it weren't for the restrictive visas, I'd live here permanently.

Serena Page, Age 36
Los Angeles, CA ➡ Paris, France

I left for Paris in 2002, shortly after graduating college with a minor in French. It was my intention to stay three months, to take French classes and improve my language skills. I liked it so much that I never managed to leave. Three months turned into a year, and then I met my husband who is a dual French-American citizen, and now we are here indefinitely. I'm a "lifer," you might say.

Bruce Epstein, Age 46
New York, NY ➡ Orsay, France

I was 38 years old, married, with a seven-year-old daughter when we moved to France in 1995, not so much as to escape the U.S. (though now we're glad we did), nor because of some lifelong aspiration, but simply because the opportunity arose. We're still here 16 years later.

Laura, Age 40
Baltimore, MD ➡ Rome, Italy

I worked for Corporate America for 15 years, was burnt out, not married and wanted to change. I moved in 2004. The reason I chose Rome is that I wanted to live in a place that was completely steeped in history. Not like, "Let's go see the ruins," and then there is the rest of the town. But someplace where, in your daily life, you're in constant contact with the ghosts of the past. For historical/documentary filmmaking, which is what I was doing, London is perhaps the best place to be, so a "career move" would have taken me there. As far as languages go, I knew French, not Italian. But defying logic and practicality, I decided to go for the place where I most wanted to live, and try and make it work there. And I figured if it doesn't, I could fall back on the more practical choices or go back home.

After two years, I let go of 15 years as a filmmaker in favor of being...a tour guide! I had never ever contemplated this job path, but now that I am doing it (nearly 5 years), it is obviously the best job in the world for me as I wanted to be immersed in history and art, and now that is also my job. I'm also living with my Italian boyfriend.

Bryn Martin, 31
Chicago, IL ➡ Lausanne, Switzerland

I left the U.S. for adventure. After finishing my Ph.D. in engineering, I was offered a post-doctoral research position at the U.S. National Institute of Health and also at the Swiss Federal Institute of Technology in Lausanne (EPFL). My wife and I considered the possibilities and decided to take the risk. I am also a musician, and I thought it would be interesting to explore the European scene. The decision was also influenced by the fact that the standard post-doc pay at NIH in Bethesda, MD was $36,000 while in Switzerland it was over $80,000. At the time we were expecting our first baby and I was concerned that my wife would not be able to stay home for the first few months after the birth due to lack of money if I took the post-doc position at NIH. Work at EPFL is paradise. I think there is no comparison to any university in the United States in terms of work environment, funding, facilities, and quality of research.

€ric D. Clark, "Age is just a number; I am experienced"
San Francisco, CA ➡ Lisbon, Portugal

I have lived in the E.U. since 1987, in Paris for 12 years, then Cologne, then Berlin... and now lovely Lisboa. As a Black/Cherokee classical pianist, I was not interested in rap/r&b/jazz or any of the other genres associated with people of the ethnic order in the States at that time. That was very limiting.

The thing about the E.U. I love is being able to visit the different cultures in a mere matter of minutes from some places: I am privileged in the fact that when I said "I hate this country" (around 19 years old), meaning the States, I actually had been to every state in the union except Hawaii before "getting out." Hence my decision—that, and there was the fact that there was no real outlet for me then made it easy: this coupled with the fact I studied music written while the country was still in its infancy made it obvious to me.

I visit the States often and find the level of stupidity frightening! I sincerely doubt I could live there again.

Jennifer and Doug St. Martin, Age 33
Greenville, SC ➡ Lisbon, Portugal

There were many things that pushed us to leave the U.S. For one, Doug is a chiropractor, and we wanted to take the healing powers of chiropractic to a country that had few. The last place we lived, in South Carolina, we loved, but it was difficult to practice there as it was near a school and had a high concentration of chiropractors. When the economy took a plummet, there were less people able to afford maintenance care, so they would only come in when they were hurting. Chiropractic is about being proactive with your health, not reactive, and so it didn't turn out to be the kind of practice that Doug had envisioned.

We decided to sell and use the money to move where chiropractic was relatively new. Doug was offered a great opportunity to run a satellite clinic in Lisbon, which is owned by a Canadian chiropractor that attended the same school as he did. When opportunity like that knocks, you pack your bags and fly!

I had been in love with the European lifestyle since I had visited a few times. It just seems to fit us better. It is tough bringing money over here because the dollar is plummeting so rapidly and you lose a lot in the exchange. However, it is nice to be making Euros and have it be worth so much more going back Stateside.

We were also disgusted with the direction that food was taking in the U.S. With it becoming illegal in some states to purchase raw milk and raw honey, organics getting watered down by big agribusinesses, and a host of other healing foods under fire, we were pretty much fed up. Here, in Portugal, the food is grown the way it is meant to be grown—untainted by chemicals and GMO engineering. This is an old-time farming country, and people are not ready or willing to change—thankfully!

Finally, we were not happy with the direction the government was going. Let's just say, it was time to leave and take our usefulness elsewhere. We know the political situation in Portugal is not great right now either, but we are willing to take their mischief over the U.S.' malevolence right now.

Alessandra
New York, NY ➡ Porto, Portugal

I first became interested in living outside the United States during the summer of 2008, while on a study abroad graduate program in Barcelona, Spain. Although New York City had been a wonderful place to live, I had a feeling there was a different place out there for me. I had spent many years searching for the perfect U.S. city to call home. I saw many beautiful places, but I couldn't find the right fit. Once I arrived in Spain, I felt a great sense of openness and adventure, and something bigger than just wanting to feel at home. I absolutely loved it. I thought, why couldn't I live here?

Last summer, I began a serious relationship with a Spanish writer and musician that I met while traveling in Portugal. After living in Italy for eight months, I moved to Porto, Portugal to be with him and have an experience together out of our native countries. We will live here for a while, then we plan to move elsewhere in the E.U. I hope that the two of us will eventually settle in Spain to have a family.

Bill Agee, 50
Philadelphia, PA ➡ Copenhagen, Denmark

Growing up in New Jersey and then living in New York City for 10 years, I figured that living in Europe was just a dream. But the reality of living in a quaint yet modern European city has been an amazing and, needless to say, life-changing experience for me. It is an entirely different way of leading one's life. Life here in Copenhagen is just so much more livable than any place I've experienced in the U.S. I take a train and a boat to work. I ride my bike to buy groceries and go to the cinema. I have a balcony where I can sit and watch the rides at Tivoli Gardens, the amusement park in the center of Copenhagen that inspired Walt Disney. And when Copenhagen is not enough, I take a one hour flight to London, Paris, Amsterdam or Prague for the weekend. This is what I left the U.S. for—to experience a way of life that just doesn't exist in the United States.

Easton West, Age 27
Pineland, FL ➡ Berlin, Germany

I originally left the U.S. for Vancouver because I wanted to finish design school, smoke weed, make hip hop beats and do art. When I finished school, I was bored of all that and moved permanently to Berlin. I figured that if I am going to have to live and work, I would rather do it in a place that supports arts and culture, but is not a complete hippie let's-smoke-a-bong culture. I like money but I want to enjoy where I am while I'm making it. I don't feel like there's much of a corporate vs. anti-corporate vibe going on here like there is in the States or even Canada. Whether corporate or independent, everybody seems to keep a pretty home-y feel and there's a nice balance between work and hanging out and enjoying your life. Here, you can still be an alternative-stoner-slacker-whatever, if you want, but there's more to life here than just that.

Camille Moreno, Age 25
New York, NY ➡ Berlin, Germany

The first time I visited Europe was on a three-week vacation to Berlin in November of my junior year of college. My whole life I hadn't given a second thought to Germany, only that the language sounded so much like English that I thought I could probably learn it one day. Upon arriving back in the States, I said to my mother, "mom, I think Europe likes me." After graduating from college, I decided I would move to Spain to regain my Spanish, which was lost after I moved from Costa Rica to the U.S. as a small child. I decided Spain was hot, and I probably couldn't get any jobs teaching English until the autumn anyway, so my first summer was spent in Berlin, falling in love with the city and learning German. In mid-September, I carried on to Spain, where I lived first in Granada in the south. That didn't seem to rock my boat so after about a month I joined WOOF (World Wide Organization of Organic Farms) and found myself working on an apple farm in the Basque in the north of Spain. That is until the farmer and I had our differences and I moved on yet again to Vitoria-Gasteiz, not far from the farm. By Christmas I could tell that Spain just was not for me, as well as the fact that I couldn't seem to get a visa in Spain without first returning to the States. The whole time I was in Spain I had been on my German visa. So I decided to return to Berlin and make it happen. I have now been here three years.

Sarah Madole

New York, NY ➡ Athens, Greece

I left the U.S. for graduate school reasons. If you're a scholar of antiquity writing your dissertation, you don't get proper street cred until you've lived in an ancient country. I went to Athens because the American School of Classical Studies at Athens was best suited to my research, which is based in Turkey. Rome would've been my first choice, but my area is the Greek-East. Anyway, the scholarly community in Athens is singular.

Tinuola, Age 33

New York, NY ➡ Prague, Czech Republic

New York City was the only home I had known since immigrating to the U.S. with my family from Nigeria. I went to high school and college in the city, and after graduation worked there as well. I could not imagine living anywhere else. But by the early 2000s I felt "stuck" in almost all aspects of my life; I was uninspired, frustrated/angry, and unhappy. I wanted a change, but wasn't sure how it would happen.

The flexibility of my job—though I had become bored and often felt isolated—was too comfortable to give up. The real estate boom was in full swing, and my income was no match for the astronomical prices of apartment rentals or sales in NYC.

In 2006, I moved to Prague.

Maybe the most surprising aspect of moving to the Czech Republic is the subtle shift in my identity as a black person. Before moving to the USA, I grew up in Nigeria. I was black—yes, that was the color of my skin—but that was not my identity and certainly not the basis for which I was judged or perceived by others. So imagine the contrast when I moved to the States and discovered that being black came with a host of "issues" and expected behaviors and mindsets.

In Prague, where clearly I am a minority, my blackness suddenly doesn't carry the same connotation. On the trams, old women, with a twinkle in their eyes, reach out to touch my dreadlocks. "To je moc krasna." Very beautiful, they say in soft, lyrical voices. The children just tug from behind, and I exchange a smile with their very apologetic mothers. There are few who look like me, so when I walk around people stare. But in my awareness of being the object of attention I don't feel or get defensive—unless provoked, and there have been a very few unsettling comments or encounters.

I'm a black woman, yes that hasn't changed, but I'm having or living a human experience much as I did as a child growing up in Nigeria.

Gary Lukatch, Age 67
St. Louis, MO ➡ Budapest, Hungary

In 1999, I decided, after nearly 30 years in the financial business in the USA, that I was tired of the continuing intrusive presence of Big Brother in my life. Merely having a 'choice' of two bad candidates for President every four years was no choice at all. There were accumulative restrictions on personal liberty being enacted by the federal government and throughout the States, including: seat belt laws, no smoking laws, kid helmet laws, etc. I am perfectly capable of taking care of myself, thank you, and do not need a government to legislate my personal responsibility.

So, at age 55, I quit my job, sold my house, sold my car, sold my stuff and began to plan for my future outside of America. I decided my work would be English teaching, so I took a TEFL class (Teaching English as a Foreign Language) and moved to Budapest, Hungary, to begin my second life.

One will never get rich in this field, but all I wanted was to live a happy (happier) life, to travel and to enjoy whatever time I had left. In many respects, I have had a richer, more fulfilling life than in the past. My horizons have broadened considerably, and my quality of life has become...well, true quality.

To all those stay-at-home, squeamish, fearful Americans, I say, "Take the plunge and make your life so much better than just sitting in a tract house and hoping you can make your house payments and feed your kids for the next year or two." I did, and I've never looked back. And never will. Best damn move I ever made.

Chris Jacobs, Age 24
Pensacola, FL ➡ Tartu, Estonia

I chose Estonia for three reasons. The first reason was that I had been here before as an exchange student and knew how things worked here. Second, my girlfriend lived here and I wanted to be with her. Third, I came here once in 2010 to complete an internship with a company that offered me a current job here after my U.S. graduation in Dec. 2010. I lived in Tallinn for a little while, but actually moved to Tartu where my work is located, got an apartment in Old Town part of Tartu, near the University and have enjoyed my life here since.

J.M., Age 33
Portland, OR ➡ Pushkin, Russia

Originally, it was just the new opportunity. I had been traveling to Russia since early 2003 for work (I was with a major American truck-builder). It took me all of two weeks there to recognize it as a place and a people with genuine potential. Traveling back periodically to visit, we've been able to see the U.S. with fresh eyes, and have decided it's no place to raise kids or a family—to say nothing of the economic and political problems there. Furthermore, the environment in Russia is so much more civil, open, and generally free than in the U.S., that it made for an easy decision.

Even in big cities (with the exception of Moscow, which is like any other megapolis anywhere on the planet), the small-town attitudes of civility and neighborliness are nearly ubiquitous. Russia is an immigrant country for the last 1000+ years, and it shows in the way they take to new people and the ease with which they help them fold into their society. We're not planning on returning. In fact, we're working on arranging things so that my wife's and my parents will be able to come over here when they are ready to retire.

Name withheld by Request, Age 29
Jacksonville, FL ➡ Dubai, UAE

From an American perspective, people really don't understand why someone would get up and leave America for somewhere else. For me, when I graduated college, I knew I wanted to try something different and have opportunities to see the world. Staying in the U.S. would have hindered me. I've been here seven years, met my wife here, and we are still enjoying the tax-free lifestyle. I don't know if we will be here forever, but it was definitely a good place to ride out the economic crisis.

Scott, Age 50
Oklahoma ➡ Riyadh, Saudi Arabia

I prefer the lifestyle here overall as it provides many things for me. First is a good income which is stable and guaranteed by my employment contract. It allows me to take paid vacations with airfare (while my previous employment allowed only one week off per year until three years of employment). Most contracts in KSA allow one month per year with airfare plus time off during Ramadan and Hajj. I also now have the ability to support my family due to the money I am earning and lack of significant expenses here—no taxes, no utility cost, and cheap gas for my car. And finally, I feel part of the global community, not just someone in a small town in Oklahoma. I have made friends with all types of people and professions, which I would not have the opportunity to do living Stateside.

Paul Schuble, Age 25
Laurel, MD ➡ Hyogo Prefecture, Japan

I attended the Villanova School of Business and was required to study a foreign language. I wanted something different—to stand out from the legions who study Spanish or Italian. I liked sushi and video games, so Japanese seemed a good choice.

Every year a representative from the Japanese Consulate in New York would visit Villanova to give a presentation on the Jet Programme—an initiative sponsored by the Japanese government that seeks to recruit college graduates of various nationalities and academic backgrounds to come to Japan and teach foreign languages and act as cultural ambassadors. So really from my freshman year I knew I wanted to come to Japan and teach English.

During my time at university, I studied abroad in Japan twice and made many Japanese friends both in Japan and in America, further strengthening my resolve to get into the JET Programme. I did, and left for Japan in July, 2008. I never regretted my decision.

Marshall Creamer, Age 25
Chicago, IL ➡ Hong Kong

I left the United States because I had a deep desire to continue my travels around the world (I studied abroad in Italy my junior year of college, that experience changed my life) and to experience something new. I had a lot of things motivating me to leave the U.S.: money, the opportunity to travel, and the ability to be in a different political situation. I am a Libertarian, so Hong Kong has a lot that appeals to me.

Edna Vuong, Age 31
New York, NY ➡ Beijing, China

I had been out of school for about two years and found that working as an architect was very different from studying architecture. Working was more technical than creative and I missed designing. It just happened that it was right before the Olympics and at the time there was lots of work in China. The projects they were working on were totally unrealistic and would never get built in the U.S. but the Chinese government was intent on impressing the rest of the world so developers were willing to spend the money to make things happen.

I was getting comfortable with my life in New York and was afraid if I didn't make the move right then, then it would never happen at all. I quit my job and got a one-way ticket and moved there in February, 2008.

China attracts a lot of young architects who are still in school or fresh graduates who are unable to get jobs at home. Basically, I was bored and I've always wanted to live overseas. The work in China was exciting and there are tons of jobs for foreign-educated architects.

Jennifer Ashley, Age 29
Los Angeles, CA ➡ Chengdu, China

I left because I thought that I should experience life outside the U.S. Since I'd just graduated college, it seemed like a good time, before I tied myself down to a career, relationship, property, etc. Much of Asia, but China in particular, was/is a haven for native English speakers to find work teaching English. I figured one year would be a good length of time. It wasn't nearly enough, I realized, when that year was up. Seven years later, I'm still here.

Paul Tenney, Age 31
San Francisco, CA ➡ Singapore

I had serious misgivings about the direction of the U.S. as a country. Personally, I was finding it difficult to imagine getting ahead financially there, but the notion of becoming an "expat" always struck me as something of a cop-out. I hadn't ever seriously considered living in another country. I had never even left North America prior to taking the opportunity to move to Singapore. As much as I thought of myself as cosmopolitan and globally-minded, I see now that I was very much, like most Americans, fearful of leaving the U.S.

As far back as 2008, a year and a half before I was ultimately given an opportunity to move to Singapore for work, my company announced its intention of opening an Asia Pacific office that would be based in Singapore. "Singapore," I thought. "That's on the other side of the world, not to mention a backwards police state."

The post remained open.

In early 2009, amidst a crumbling U.S. economy, my career wasn't going the way that I hoped. My job was becoming overwhelming with no sign of relief. I found myself bored in San Francisco with no real sense that things were going to pick up, and some elements of my personal life were not going particularly well either. May 29th, 2009, I got a call from one of my biggest clients—they were moving their business away from our company. The writing was on the wall. There was still an opportunity for someone in the company to relocate to Singapore, and I made up my mind that I would volunteer for the job.

I really knew very little about Singapore or what exactly expatriation would be like. Once I did arrive, I had absolutely no regrets. It was remarkably easy to adapt to my new environment, and for the most part I hardly even think about the fact that I'm living "in a foreign country." With minor exceptions, all my travels through Asia and Europe since I'd left the U.S. have hammered home the point—life isn't really all that different wherever you go. Don't be afraid.

Tyler Watts, Age 29
Riverside, CA ➡ Ho Chi Minh City (Saigon), Vietnam

I left the U.S. in 2005 as I had become interested in Vietnam and its culture and people and wanted to spend some further time working and living there. I originally anticipated staying for two years and then coming back to America, but have since extended until now.

I chose Vietnam initially as I had traveled here as a student twice and found the people and the country pulling at me like a magnet. I would say this has to do with Vietnamese culture and its welcoming nature, its curiosity, and the people's extreme kindness. It also has to do with the young population (the figures are astounding with some saying about 60% of population under 30) and the sheer energy of a country that is developing so fast. It's an exciting place to be and it's a useful time to be here in helping Vietnamese attain their ambitious goals.

Art F., Age 65
Silicon Valley, CA ➡ Sihouanoukville, Cambodia

In August of 2001, the company I was working for went into a financial crisis, and laid off many workers, including me. My termination package wouldn't last long with a $2000 monthly rent. Things were getting really slow in the Valley, and when 9/11 happened the job market collapsed. I sold what I could, moved the rest into storage, put my Harley in my son's garage, took myself and my cat to Puerto Vallarta, a town that I had been to many times. This was the first time I retired.

About one year later, I moved back to the U.S., and got a very low-paying job in a printing plant, to help pay my credit card bills. This job I kept from 2003 until I could not stand working for idiots anymore. I retired again in April of 2008.

I set my sights on Asia. I was there in 1967—1968, courtesy of the U.S. Air Force and was able to take several R & R's (five-day vacations) to Bangkok. I fell in love with the country, and the people. I went back to Thailand in 2005, and again in 2006 and did some investigation into the cost of living, and found it very low. I also have a friend there. In 2009, I contacted him again, and he told me that he had moved to Cambodia—much cheaper than Thailand. I decided to take the plunge. I sold everything I could, packed the rest and stored it at my son's house, put everything else into two suitcases, and bought a one-way ticket here.

Now I have a three-bedroom, four-bath house, $300 a month. I have no car, and therefore no car payment, though I am planning on buying a moto (scooter) soon. I'm renting one now for $80 an month. Once the women in this town find out that you are staying in Cambodia, and don't have a girlfriend, you will be swamped. It didn't take long before I found one and it seems to be working out.

Ted Hung, Age 29
San Francisco, CA ➡ Melbourne, Australia
I didn't leave the U.S. for a better job, I left for a better life.

People were so focused on making money that they forgot about what was really important in life. It felt like success was measured by how much money you made, how fast of a car you drove, how much plastic surgery you've had, and how hot your wife/husband is. It just seemed like such a fake society. Here in Melbourne, the culture is really laid back and it permeates all aspects of life and work. Melbourne was and still is one of the most livable cities I have ever been in. Australians are friendly, the culture is diverse, and there are so many beautiful natural wonders here.

Macaela, Age 29
Waldoboro, ME ➡ Wellington, NZ
I originally came to New Zealand to do a one-year backpacking tour. I was 23 at the time and in a job I couldn't stand and there was absolutely nothing stopping me from heading overseas! NZ was the only English-speaking country I could get a year-long work visa. Anyway, I got over here and realized I guess I wasn't cut out for backpacking, and have been in Wellington for the entire six years I've been here. But seeing the country is so small geographically it's pretty easy to do long weekends all over. Plus this place makes road-tripping and camping a breeze—plentiful backpackers and campgrounds! I'm (finally) getting around to applying for residency. It's pretty unheard of for someone who has been here for as long as I have to still be on a visa, but it's do-able.

Part I
The Basics:
Living and Working

Getting In...And Staying In: Visas, Residency, Work Permits and Citizenship

 For many people, the first question that comes to mind when considering moving abroad is "Will they let me live there?" Countries tend to be like country clubs and the particularly affluent and desirable ones are picky about who they let in. By contrast, other nations, usually poorer, have a much more open-door policy. Latin American and Southeast Asian countries are magnets for expats in part because being able to legally reside there is so easy. Western Europe tends to be more difficult and much of Scandinavia, as well as Iceland, pretty much a pipe dream for most people. Unless of course you have lots of money. Or a job offer. Or needed talent. Any number of factors can add to the odds or the ease with which you establish legal residency.

For just about anyone who moves abroad, regardless of the length of time they've been away and how many times they've been through it before, applying for and waiting for approval of their visas and permits is the most stressful and nerve-racking aspect of life in a foreign country.

An almost universal residency requirement for any functional state, unless you qualify for refugee status or as an asylum seeker (these categories are seldom if ever applicable to Americans and other Westerners, and are not covered in this book), is that you be able to demonstrate that you can support yourself. Often this is calculated as a function of the subsistence wage in that country—thus in the poorer countries, you might find requirements as low as a few hundred dollars a month. While this requirement might seldom exceed $2000 a month in more affluent countries, in practice, without a compelling reason to grant you permission to stay (e.g. a spouse), your actual requirement can be many times higher. For most of the nations on earth (who aren't choosing to isolate themselves for political, religious or ethnic reasons), having sufficient wealth means you'll find few obstacles to extended residency even among the most selective and exclusive nations of Europe. Should you invest money into the economy, or better yet, hire local labor, then your entry obstacles evaporate even further.

Doing business can also be an "in." In some cases, like in Mexico, just setting up a company that only exists on paper is sufficient. More often, you'll be required to demonstrate (through accounting records, business licenses, etc.) that you are engaged in real and legitimate business. Freelancers, too, can also sometimes squeeze in under this rubric.

Arriving somewhere with a job offer (where the employer has received permission or is otherwise allowed to hire or contract foreign labor) means not only will you have proof of self-sufficiency, but generally speaking, you should find getting your visas, permits and residency to be little more than bureaucratic formalities and paperwork—most of which your employer will do for you. Countries whose industries are short of certain skills or background (construction, IT, etc.) may relax visa requirements as a way to attract people with those qualifications. Often, these categories are posted on the country's visa/immigration website.

Students have a pretty easy time getting permission to study in almost any country. Academics get easy treatment, too. Artists, particularly established ones, can often get special visas in many parts of the world as do journalists and religious and volunteer workers. And of course, if you have a relative, spouse or even a fiancé in that country, there's likely a special path in for you, as well.

Only a tiny percentage of Americans who leave make it all the way to foreign citizenship. In fact, it's possible to live your entire lifetime abroad and never become more than a guest of your adopted country. Even if citizenship is your goal, and even if you can place yourself into one of those fast-track categories, you're still going to enter on a visa, and often you're going to have to establish years of legal residency before you're sworn in and given your new passport. And certainly, if you're only planning a few-month reconnaissance trip to your prospective homeland, or just want to take a short "America break" for a year or so, the visa game is all you need to know.

Visas: What Are They Good For?

Although the word visa is commonly used generically to refer to all documents that govern your stay in the country, in some places a visa merely allows you to cross the border and enter the country. To remain there for any realistic length of time, non-citizens must have a residency permit. These are often coupled with the visa. Other times, they must be applied for separately and in different places (one, say, at the consulate in the U.S. and the other at a police station in your new country). Often approval for the former renders approval for the latter a mere formality (indeed, having the former is a condition of getting the latter) but in some cases, you might feel like you're starting again from scratch. Some are rubber-stamped into your passport; others are affixed with a sticker or issued as a separate document. Each government has devised its own diabolically confusing system by which visas can either have names, letters or numbers, or some combination of all three. Some are given out freely, with only the barest of formalities, while others involve a lengthy bureaucratic process. Sometimes you're required to state the purpose of your visit (immigration, retirement, business, tourism, university study, work, etc.) and stick to it. Other times, you can arrive as a tourist (often without any kind of application beforehand) and switch to another type of visa/residence permit after you arrive.

You must get the specific requirements for your particular visa from the consulate of the country concerned and it's critical that your information be current because these requirements can often change like the seasons. Rules can often be long and complicated, and while Canada and the U.K., for instance, have moved much of the immigration and registry process to the Internet, you will most likely wait in lots of lines and in some cases be better off hiring an attorney. In Southeast Asia and Latin America, where expats are considered an industry, there are armies of these competing paper-pushers who will, for as little as a few hundred dollars, navigate the bureaucracy for you, leaving you little to do except show up and sign the papers. In first-world countries, this type of help is as expensive as what you would imagine any kind of qualified legal advice and assistance to be.

Generally your visa has three important components:

Length of Stay/Re-entry Allowance

All visas state how long you are allowed to remain in the country. You can be issued a three-day transit visa, good for simply crossing the country on your way to somewhere else, or one that's good for the rest of your life. Typically, once you graduate past tourist status, your permit will allow you to enter and leave the country as often as you like, but some do require that you reapply if you leave the country. Because visas are, strictly speaking, the document that allows you to enter the country (as opposed to a resident permit which technically allows you to remain, although in practice these two are often lumped together), they often have a "validity period." Although confusing, this usually does not refer to the length of time you can stay, but the window of time in which you must enter the country—which is to say, after the validity period, your visa will have "expired" and if you haven't entered the country already, you likely won't be allowed in the country even if you have a valid resident permit (obviously, this is only pertinent to visas not issued at the border, upon entry).

Prohibited Activities

This usually means work. Sometimes no employment is allowed at all. Other times, you are allowed to work in a specific industry or at a specific place of employment. Other common restrictions include the ability to take advantage of social services, buy/own property or a business, or occasionally live outside a designated region or regions.

Renewability/Changeability

How many times can your visa be extended, if at all? Can you apply for a different class of visa while you hold your current one? Renewable visas are the surest path to permanent residency and citizenship.

Important Note:

Not all visas are issued within the destination country. Some must be applied for in advance at an embassy or consul and still others can only be issued while you're still in your home country. Be sure you know the terms before you leave. For example, if you were to arrive in Spain on a tourist visa and decide to change your status, you could find yourself having to return to the United States before your visa can be changed—a pretty significant detour. At the very least, you will have to leave the country or the region before your new paperwork is sorted out.

Depending on the country and the type of infraction, violating the terms of your visa can lead to repercussions as mild as a small fine and as severe as jail and deportation. In some countries, such as Argentina, overstaying your allotted time is part of some expats' strategy, since they regard the fine as simply the price of staying in-country. In most cases, however, violating your terms (of

length of stay, employment or other proscribed activities) is risky business…
and should be avoided.

Applications for visas can require a host of documents:

Police Report

Because most countries are not interested in accepting criminals, particularly those on the lam, you may be asked to present yourself at your local police precinct and request a document which states that you're not wanted for any crimes in the United States. The document will also list your police record, if any. In some cases, you're required to get this from the FBI, a process which involves being fingerprinted and having the results sent to Washington D.C. before a letter is issued clearing your name.

Evidence of Sufficient Funds

Bank statements, pay stubs, pension plans or other documents that demonstrate you have enough funds or income to live on for the specified period of the visa. Sometimes these even must be certified by an accountant. The amount is usually calculated to be slightly above the local minimum wage. In cash-strapped nations, you probably won't encounter more than a cursory nod at these requirements. But the higher up the food chain you go in terms of per-capita GDP, the more deeply you can expect your solvency to be scrutinized.

Proof of Health Insurance

Likewise, many countries want to be certain that should you fall ill or meet with a life-threatening accident, someone other than the State will pick up the bill.

AIDS Test

More countries are requiring a certificate stating that you have been recently (usually within the past six months) tested and have been found to be HIV-negative.

Vaccinations

Unless you've traveled through some infested area, which, for the time being anyway, won't be the case if you're coming from the U.S., you do not need vaccinations to travel anywhere on the planet.

Depending on what kind of residency or citizenship status you are seeking, birth certificates, marriage licenses, separation agreements, divorce decrees, and death certificates might all be required. Start collecting those today. There will be applications to fill out, photos to submit, and finally, money: excepting most tourist class visas, you will be Euro'd and Yen'd to death. In Cambodia, you might pay as little as $25, while a Swiss residency permit (depending on where you settle) can go as high as €1500. If you're looking to relocate to a large European country, costs can easily run into the thousands of dollars before you reach permanent residency or citizenship. Again, poorer countries treat these visa fees as revenue generators and unless you present yourself as a truly undesirable specimen, they aren't in the habit of peering into the paperwork too closely, as long as legal tender is being ponied up. The greater the affluence of the country, however, the tinier role your ability to pay the administrative fees will play in the decision to approve a visa or residency. In any case, you'll need to factor these additional costs into your overall budget.

You don't have to expect much in the way of language or cultural literacy requirements in the early going, but should you attempt to reside in a country permanently or acquire citizenship then these will likely be put to the test. There is also the not-insignificant factor that few countries will provide you with the necessary forms and instructions in English.

So, where do you find out more?

In most cases, to get the requirements for a particular visa, you'll need to contact the embassy or consulate of the country in question. You can usually visit their websites and find the info under "Consular Affairs." Also check the country's Ministry of Foreign Affairs or Immigration Bureau website. It's becoming rarer and rarer for information on these sites not to be presented in English. A comprehensive list is maintained online at **www.gettingoutofamerica.com**.

Apostilles:
When sifting through the requirements for visas, residency or citizenship, you'll often come across the word "apostille." This is something akin to an international notarization in countries that are signatory to the Hague Apostille Convention ("Convention of 5 October 1961 Abolishing the Requirement of Legalisation for Foreign Public Documents") as a simplified method of certifying documents that might be required by a foreign government, in cases where it's impractical or impossible to submit the original document (say, a passport). In the United States, the certifying (apostille) agency is the office of the state's Secretary of State in which the document was issued (i.e., birth certificate), though depending on the document (court

documents, military documents, etc.) and the state in question, different procedures may apply. Further information about apostilles can be found in the "Specialised section" on the Hague website www.hcch.net and through the Secretary of State (usually, this information is posted on their website) of the relevant state.

The following countries are signatory to the Hague Apostille Convention (note: the list of Hague signatories can differ depending on the particular Convention in question):

Albania
Argentina
Australia
Austria
Belarus
Belgium
Bosnia & Herzegovina
Bulgaria
China, People's Republic of
Costa Rica
Croatia
Cyprus
Czech Republic
Denmark
Ecuador
Estonia
Finland
France
Georgia
Germany
Greece

Hungary
Iceland
India
Ireland
Israel
Italy
Japan
Latvia
Lithuania
Luxembourg
Macedonia
Malta
Mauritius
Mexico
Monaco
Montenegro
Morocco
Netherlands
New Zealand
Norway

Panama
Peru
Poland
Portugal
Romania
Russia
Serbia
Slovakia
Slovenia
South Africa
Spain
South Korea
Suriname
Sweden
Switzerland
Turkey
Ukraine
United Kingdom
USA
Venezuela

Field Guide to Common Visas

Visas come in all shapes and sizes. Visas granted to refugees don't really apply to the U.S. expat, although the way things are going, that may change. Ditto, asylum seekers. The Transit Visa (allowing you to cross a country's territory on your way to somewhere else) or Medical Visa (allowing you to visit for the purposes of medical treatment), are too specific to bother considering. Some countries issue specific visas for every application category, while in other places they are lumped into three or four overall types, with multiple possibilities for acquiring each one. Eligibility for any visa or permit is seldom 100% clear-cut and can be subject to legal hairsplitting and the caprice of random bureaucrats. Still, most people who succeed in staying on long after all the holiday-makers are back home, generally do it via the following types of visas. Again, names, terms and availability vary widely from country to country.

Permanent Resident

The equivalent of the U.S. Resident Alien or "Green Card." The Permanent Resident Visa usually allows you to do almost anything a citizen can do except vote and travel under that nation's passport, though there are more than a few exceptions to this rule. Often, you are also required to spend a certain percentage of your time residing in that country. After a given number of years, you can usually qualify for citizenship. The rules for obtaining permanent residency often don't veer too far from rules for citizenship. In other cases, they're not really "permanent" at all, but simply allow for longer-term stays than other permits offered by that country.

Temporary Resident/Settlement/Long-Stay Visa

Often a stepping stone to permanent residency, this sort of visa has a specific designation (three, five, or 10 years) and can come with none, some or all of the restrictions placed on other visas.

The following visas are sometimes issued on their own and at other times are used as a consideration for offering one of the residency permits outlined above:

Family Reunion/Marriage/Relative Visa

In the interest of keeping families together, governments often make allowances for family members of citizens or residents to come over and stay. Sometimes these require that you actually live with your family or that your family make a pledge to financially support you while you are in the country. In any case, should you have family living there, you're more than likely to be fast-tracked into residency.

Marriage/Spouse Visa

Marry a citizen or permanent resident and you're granted one of these, usually on your way to permanent residency or citizenship. In countries like

New Zealand, these privileges extend even to fiancés and domestic partners, though eventually you'll be expected to tie the knot or get out. Many progressive governments (Canada, Holland, Germany, etc.) recognize same-sex partnerships for visas and immigration.

Visas for Dependents

In many cases, if a family member is granted any residence visa, there will be some accommodation for family and spouse (though financial self-sufficiency requirements will be adjusted accordingly). Work or business visas often come with visas for spouses/dependents (generally children under 18, but if you can make a case that you have to take care of your old mother, that can sometimes fly). With investment and retirement visas, there is usually an additional amount added to the minimum investment or stipend (much lower than the original amount) for each additional dependent. Malta, for instance, requires an additional $2,500/year over and above the minimum required income, per dependent. In the case of Hong Kong, though, once you've sunk $1.2mil into their economy for their investment visa, the wife and kids are on the house.

Pension/Retirement Visa

The Pensionado, as most people know it, is how countries attract people who will spend money, won't make trouble, and won't enter the job market. If you can prove you have a guaranteed income, usually in the form of some kind of pension (in Costa Rica, $1,000 a month; in Thailand approximately $2,100), and are over a specified age (as low as 45, as high as 60), this is the option best worth taking. Often your Social Security benefits are enough. Though also aimed at retirees, the rentista visa offers similar terms with no minimum age limit. In Mexico and Panama, for example, anyone who can provide evidence of a guaranteed income of approximately $1,000 a month (plus a few hundred for each additional family member) can qualify for a visa.

Investment Visas

Few countries say no to money. If you have deep pockets and are willing to invest in a given nation's economy, you shouldn't encounter too many obstacles obtaining residency. For example, Vanuatu's five-year residency is yours with an investment of around $200,000. In Australia, you wouldn't get by without sinking over $600,000 in a designated investment in the national business economy. The U.K. would like to see you pony up around $360,000 if you're actually going to be working in your business (you must also hire at least two full-time employees), $1.35 million if you're just going to sink money into the country and do nothing else ("passive investment'). In the low-rent countries of Latin America and Southeast Asia such visas are within middle-class means, especially since in many cases, real estate qualifies as an investment. Panama will allow you in if you simply deposit $300,000 in a savings account. If your politics are as green as your bank account, investing a mere $60,000 in Panama's rainforest reforestation program ($100,000 in Costa Rica) gets you in, too.

Working With Your Visa

For many people, moving abroad without being allowed to work is a nonstarter. How easy or difficult it is to get permission to make a living depends on where you go, what you do, and most importantly, who you work for (i.e., yourself, a local company, a foreign company). These permits can be issued as stand-alone visas or as an addition to your residency visa. Generally, they fall along the following lines:

Work Permit

Few nations have any incentive to allow foreigners to take jobs that could possibly go to locals. Typically you have to beg, cajole or otherwise convince a local employer to sponsor you. That means he vouches that he couldn't find a qualified candidate domestically. Usually, the government's ministry of labor or equivalent bureau must approve the request. If you truly have mad skills in what you do, then somebody might be motivated to do that on your behalf. Many of the finest restaurants in the world for instance, have their meals cooked by foreign-born chefs. Obviously, the bar tends to be lower with highly technical and specialized skills but quite high if you just want to tend bar or wash dishes. Jobs requiring native English speakers are usually allowed (including of course, English teaching, where the school can be expected to handle the details for you). Work permits can sometimes restrict you to one location, one job, one company. If you're fired or you quite, you're back to square one, unless there is some allowance to seek other work. Some even allow your husband or wife to work, too. In almost all cases, a permanent residency allows you the right to seek employment just like any other citizen. Spousal visas, too, often allow unrestricted employment. For further information on work issues, see Jobs Chapter.

Overseas Employee Visa

If a U.S. company sends you to work at the São Paulo office, often you'll get one of these from the government and moving expenses from the firm. In many cases, you can simply set up a company or corporation in the U.S. and declare your new home to be a "branch office," with yourself, of course, as the main employee, since immigration officials often recognize "branch offices" as a valid visa category.

Business Visa

Sometimes these are issued to businessmen and aren't much different from ordinary tourist visas. Others are geared toward people who will stay and conduct business for stays of one to five years or more. People who export local goods, buy and sell real estate, or work in the tourist trade often operate under one of these. Sometimes solo freelancers must file for these (other times, there is a separate self-employment visa). In many countries, it's possible to set up an empty holding company and get one. In other places, you might be required to actually demonstrate that business is being conducted. Such places usually generate armies of immigration attorneys and consultants who charge a fee to process the pro forma paperwork. If you actually do have a company AND you hire local labor, your chances of being welcomed with generous visa terms increases dramatically.

Self-Employment Visa

Freelancers who can take their game overseas usually aim for one of these. You'll usually be asked to present documents—bank statements, business invoices, etc.—that you really do have a career and that it earns you income so that you won't be hitting up the local job market. The Internet, social networking, cloud computing, online videoconferencing and other virtual tools have spawned countless possibilities for independent contractor types to conduct their business wherever they are. Because expatriates tend to be independent-minded to begin with, a large percentage of non-retirees of ordinary means fall into this category.

Needed Skill/Expert Visa

This kind of visa allows you to surf the job market like any other local. The catch is, you have to match certain designated skills and occupations that the government would like to attract. Canada, New Zealand, and Australia post their current needs on their websites.

Canada: www.cic.gc.ca   New Zealand: www.govt.nz
Australia: www.immi.gov.au

Working Holiday/Travel and Working Visa

Ireland, U.K., Australia, New Zealand and Canada all offer some kind of short-term work scheme for recent college grads under the age of 30. Ireland gives you a stingy four months; Canada and New Zealand give you a year. The U.K. has a slightly different "scheme," as they call it, which lets you work for six months. If you're a skilled networker, you can use this time to make the necessary connections that will allow you to stay on more permanently. For Americans, these visas are managed through a private foundation, usually BUNAC, www.bunac.com, which will take care of all the paperwork for you for $400–$750, depending on the country. You'll arrive with permit in hand, and have some resources at your disposal, but finding an actual job is up to you.

Other types of visas...

Artist/Performer Visa

For the struggling creative geniuses so they can contribute something to the local color and culture.

Instructor or Academic Visa

For English teachers and college professors. It's a pretty cushy way to go. Austria even offers a special legal mechanism whereby prominent academics can be granted citizenship.

Journalist/Media Visa

Freelancers can try it, but it works better if you have an accredited media organization behind you. These visas, however, tend to be issued for short-term (30–90 days) assignments, geared toward journalists working in-country to cover a particular event. Long-haul journos will probably need to apply for a work or self-employment visa.

Religious/Missionary Visa

If you're willing to spread the Good News about Him (usually through some established evangelical organization), bring your Bible and get your visa. This is also good if you want to retreat to an overseas monastery for a couple years.

Student Visas

They're recognized almost anywhere there are universities. They usually expire when your studies do. Canada and Australia allow you to hold a part-time job. The U.K. offers employment schemes for students in their "gap year" before college and some even allow employment for up to two years after graduation. Expect to provide documentation that you've been accepted and enrolled at an approved university/course of study, that you have sufficient funds and other basic requirements, though the typical student that has been accepted and enrolled at a foreign university or other institution should not experience too much trouble in landing one of these. In most cases, the university will help guide you through the process. Be aware: often these visas must be applied for BEFORE you enter the country, though some countries do allow you to convert a tourist or visitor visa to a student visa after you arrive.

Volunteer Visa

If you're working for a humanitarian or even missionary program or for recognized organizations, you will probably be issued one of these, usually through the organization you work for. While these don't allow you to take employment, anyone who wants to make a career of helping the less fortunate of the world will find this a valuable stepping stone—as this is how all the contacts are made.

Tourist Visa

Aside from a transit visa, which allows you nothing more than direct passage through a country, this is the bottom rung on the visa pole. Since almost all countries depend to some degree on tourism, they tend to be given out like candy, usually free, often right at the point on entry—especially to Americans, who still have a reputation as reckless spenders. These visas are usually loaded with restrictions, the primary ones being that you can't work and you must leave when it expires. Often, tourist visas cannot be renewed and require that you leave the country before you can return. Still, many people manage extended stays either by overstaying and paying the fine, or making the (usually) 90-day "visa run"—stepping over the closest border just before your visa expires, then getting it stamped on the way back. In Thailand, visa buses make daily trips to the Cambodian border and back, while twilight operations, typical in many Third World countries, actually allow the lazy to have someone else ferry your passport to the border and back. Be warned: letting your passport out of your sight and control is risky business. U.S. passports are worth their weight in gold on the black market.

The Schengen

Twenty-six European nations are signatories to a treaty that allows for one single border. The good news is that Americans can travel through the entire Schengen zone without a visa (though it's generically referred to as a Schengen Visa). The bad news is that it's only for a maximum of 90 days during any 180-day period, meaning you have to essentially leave the entire

Schengen area for at least the same amount of time as you had stayed. Some countries, Germany for instance, will allow you to "convert" to a residency permit after you arrive. Others, such as Spain, will not. This makes settling down tricky but not impossible. Note that residency and work permits are only valid in their respective countries and these are NOT valid in the entire Schengen zone, though in the case of residency at least, the absence of border checks and passport control within the zone makes such a distinction difficult to enforce. In 2011, Denmark reinstalled customs controls within the Schengen, though it's not clear that this will have any effect on passport, visa and residency issues.

Be aware that the Schengen countries, while located in Europe, are NOT synonymous with the E.U. (European Union) countries, nor are they synonymous with the Eurozone (which refers to all the countries that use the Euro as a form of currency). For a list of Schengen countries and other European treaty organizations, see pp 190–191.

NOTE: Regardless of the human rights situation in the country you choose, as a non-citizen (and likely non-permanent resident, as well), you can be certain to enjoy less rights than a national. Caprice can play a large role in whether your application is approved or denied and your recourse options are likely to be few to none. Also, while most countries might tolerate some low-grade misbehavior by its citizens, you'll likely have no such luxuries. Political rabble-rousing (or even being caught at a political demonstration in some of the more, uh, sensitive countries) can be grounds for deportation as can even misdemeanor criminal activity.

What's Your Visa Story?

Barbara Warwick
Visa Exempt
Germany

I don't need a visa because I am a U.S. military employee dependent. But when I first came I found a job teaching English at the VHS Heidelberg, which allowed me to get a special visa for English teachers that was valid for the duration of the class(es) I was teaching. I had to get that visa renewed with every new class.

Ted Hung
Permanent Resident
Australia

My journey to gaining permanent residency was a long and involved process. When I was working in Australia, I really wanted to find a way to stay in the country without having to be sponsored by a company. I really loved the lifestyle that living in Australia gave me, but the work was not as fulfilling as I had hoped. The company that I was currently working for offered to sponsor me for permanent residency here, but they required that I stay with them for a minimum of four more years or pay all the fees myself. Thus, I set out to apply for permanent residency on my own using a migration lawyer. The migration lawyer roughly doubled the cost of applying for the permanent resident visa, but I feel it was worth it given the fact that during my application period I needed to move back to the U.S. If I were to do it again, knowing what I know now, though, I would probably do it myself and save the money.

The migration lawyer provided counseling, document certification services, and a local point of contact for the government during my application. One of the surprising things during the application process that I encountered was that Australia did not recognize any of my degrees from the U.S. Ironically, even though I was being sponsored to work as a computer professional in Australia, they still needed evidence that I was certified to be a computer professional in Australia. In order to do this, I needed to contact all of my employers from the last four years and have them write a letter certifying that I worked as a computing professional. This took the most time of the entire application process—a year just to get in touch with the companies (many of which only keep records for four years). Once I was certified as a computing professional in Australia, I was able to apply for permanent residency and within three months I was granted the visa.

In terms of sponsoring my partner for permanent residency, Australia is one of the countries that recognize de-facto spouses (i.e. non-married couples of either gender) for sponsored permanent residency. The main proof the Australian government needed for this was that my partner and I lived together for one year. Since we were aware of this before we started living together, we needed to keep thorough documentation of our ongoing relationship through pictures, bills, personal statements from friends, and shared flight tickets. The main difficulty for us was that we planned on moving to Australia together when we had only lived together for six months. During that period, she was able to stay in Australia for three months at a time on a tourist visa. She needed to leave twice during that period in order to renew it. Australia is very strict about their tourist visas only being used for tourist purposes, so it was always a tricky process for her to come back in. In fact, the first time, we arrived in Australia together, and a large angry woman interrogated her for 10 minutes. We had to emphasize that my partner was only "visiting." We eventually made it through one year living together, and once we submitted the application, there were no issues and my partner was granted a de-facto spouse visa within a few months. After being de-facto spouses for around one year, we decided to make it official and get married.

Bob Hand
Permanent Resident
Nova Petrópolis, Rio Grande do Sul, Brazil

I came to Brazil on a Business (VITEM II) Visa which does not permit me to receive pay and only allowed me to stay 180 days maximum out of the year.

In order to be married, both Cidinha and I had to assemble various documents. I needed a birth certificate not more than 90 days old. I needed a certificate of divorce, and a certificate of that marriage, so I had to obtain these from New Jersey (birth), Illinois (marriage), and Colorado (divorce). Then each certificate had to be authenticated by the Brazilian consulate nearest each of those states. I also had to obtain an authenticated certificate of my Social Security income, my passport, and my visa. Cidinha had to obtain similar documents from her sources. Any discrepancy noted by the cartorio (recorder's office) would have further delayed the process. Fortunately, my attorney guided us well.

Of course, for each document obtained, a fee was charged by the issuing office and the consulate, and for each step of the procedure a fee was charged by the Brazilian bureaucracy, including the Federal Police.

After the marriage was finalized, we took that certificate to the Federal Police who then created an application for a Permanent Certificate due to marriage. I received that certificate in January 2011. The certificate is not the final document. Some day I'll receive a card with ID number as a Resident "Estrangeiro." That comes from Brasilia and can take a couple of years to be issued.

Meanwhile, I can stay here indefinitely with the certificate that I have.

Frank
Permanent Resident
Costa Rica

We came here when my girlfriend was six months pregnant. A year after my daughter was born, we had a son. If you have kids in this country, you still have to apply for residency but they cannot deny it to you. You have a child and the child has rights and the government can't tell a child that her parents are no longer welcome in the country. I'm a permanent resident. I can stay. I can legally work. I can hire people.

Bill Agee
Permanent Resident
Denmark

If one has the opportunity, I absolutely recommend moving out of the U.S. with a company, or at least a job offer. The company takes care of all your residency and work permit, finds you a place to live for the first couple of months, and moves your stuff. It is not easy to get residency as an American. There are no special exceptions for the U.S. of which I am aware, so as an American you stand in line with people from all corners of the world. I moved here with a company which gave me the work and temporary residency, and then later married my Danish partner. We were married in the Copenhagen city hall by the mayor in 1999. After we were married, I received a residency permit, which needed to be renewed the first three years, and then became permanent. The process for gaining residency through marriage has become a bit tougher in recent years for non-E.U. nationals, but I think the biggest matter is that you must be 24 years old.

Libby Hansen
Permanent Resident
Denmark

When I came in 1993 it wasn't all that difficult to gain residency here. Because my husband is a Danish citizen, I applied and submitted the necessary information about my background and received both residency and work permit. Because the lax residency requirements have been abused by too many immigrants who have managed to bring their families to Denmark once they have secured residency for themselves, now the rules have changed to make it harder to gain residency in the first place.

Noemi S.
Permanent Resident
New Zealand

I started at the bottom of the barrel as a student on a "Working Holiday" visa when I first arrived as a nanny. I never knew about these visas until I was 28 years old and on vacation, so I quickly returned to the U.S., saved my pennies and returned to New Zealand 10 months later so I'd still be eligible for the working holiday visa prior to the cut-off age of 31. The immigration website is super simple to use and the application took no time to submit. There is a limit for each country as to how many they'll accept under this working holiday visa program, so it's best to apply early in the cycle. After leaving my nanny job, I obtained a job for a web company who helped me get a work permit. A work permit is attached to the place of employment and as much as I liked working there, I knew I needed more employment flexibility so started the process for permanent residency. This process can be time-consuming and expensive but many people do it so it's not all that daunting. After gathering all your education and work history, getting a medical check, X-rays, and the police check, I submitted it all with my application and money to the immigration services who took about three months to process and grant me permanent residency. After being an employed permanent resident, you are eligible for indefinite permanent residency, which means no matter how long you leave NZ for, you'll always have residency. You have to be a permanent Resident for five years in order to earn citizenship. I plan on doing this in the next two years as it's always good to have options and I've grown quite fond of this little set of islands in this corner of the world.

D. Richard Carlson
Permanent Resident
Philippines

Anyone can stay in the Philippines as a tourist for up to two years. After that s/he would have to leave the country for at least 24 hours. I came on a tourist visa designated as 9(a) for two and a half years and later with Resident Visa by Marriage, known as 13(a). Just completed 13(a) Probationary stage and have been approved as a Permanent Resident since Dec. 12, 2010.

James Lindzey
Spouse Visa
Colombia

Visas, well, I actually did the opposite of what most people do as I was married to a Colombian woman in Fort Lauderdale before I came here. Her family lost a petition for asylum, and from the American side of things, if you are already in Immigration Court, then getting married is not going to guarantee that the foreign spouse can stay. Besides having a baby, living overseas for a year or two can prove you have a real relationship. I came into Colombia on a Spouse visa. We did everything at the consulate in Miami before we came over, although you can actually do this in Colombia on a tourist visa. Current rules have made it harder, but not that much. The first marriage visa must be applied for in person in Bogotá or at a consulate. Yes, just like everywhere else in the world, the spouse visa is used as an easy method to migrate to Colombia.

Just don't stay in the country after you get divorced, AND THINK because your visa says you have two or three years that you're OK. Many people that get stuck in this situation call me (I run ColombiaVisas.com), and you can get kicked out for two or three years, requiring a visa to reenter the country. Fines are not too bad, and you should pay before you leave the country or your six months will turn into two or three years, easily.

I had a divorce drag on for about 1.5 years or so, and my ex-wife didn't get me the divorce papers quickly after they were filed. She was living in another city so the final divorce papers took months to show up. DAS (departamento administrative de Seguridad) made me file a report and come back the next day to pay a fine, which could have been up to 4,000 USD, but luckily it was just 250 USD. Luckily, in that time I had started a vacation rental company, Paradise Realty, and met a beautiful young woman who I had married. I did not have to leave the country, but standing in lines for three days was not any fun. Luckily, I have messengers that work for me in Bogotá now.

MOST POPULAR VISAS: Retirement, Business, Spouse, Business Owner. No consular fees for retirement, business, business owner visas for U.S. citizens. Generally speaking, visas are much easier than other former hot spots like Costa Rica, where they examine papers and require large sums of money in a bank account for many years. Maybe one day Colombia will get there. Right now there's a great window of opportunity. Pension earners just have to show about 850 USD a month, or small entrepreneurs starting up or buying an existing business at just 30,000 USD can qualify for a residency visa. Business visas for foreign companies allow people to stay six months at a time, with financial supporting letters from a host company in Colombia and a foreign company, along with business licenses of course. Retirement is the easiest because the first application can be done with a power of attorney. No presentation in person is necessary.

Many people also come to Colombia and get married, the only hangup is that they must prove they are single, and come with a birth certificate, and they can get married in Colombia. Of course usual rules apply to getting documents legalized and translated before taking them to the local notary. Civil marriages have a five-day cooling-off period before you can marry. After that you get your official marriage certificate issued in one to three days on average and you are qualified to get married. Women with children must prepare other paperwork re child support before getting married. After three years with the same wife you can get a permanent foreign residency card.

Michael Luksetich
Self-employment Visa
Amsterdam, Holland

Getting a permit in the Netherlands is a lot like a Catch-22. You need a job to get the permit and a permit to get the job. However, there are some ways around this requirement. Anyone getting work with a major/international company will probably have access to in-house lawyers familiar with the immigration system so not too many problems involved there. Also people with special skills, IT work, healthcare and such can get legal without too much difficulty at all. Another way is with a partnership permit. Basically what this mean is if your boy- or girlfriend (either one, they don't care here) is a resident of the European Union and has a full-time job paying more than €1400 a month after taxes then you can get a permit to live and work as well.

Of course, I did none of these things. One other option if you're from the USA is the Friendship Treaty of 1948. Among its many provisions is a statement saying that any person from the USA that wants to invest in or start a business in the Netherlands must invest 10,000 guilders. In 1948 that may have been a lot of money but now days that's not even €5,000. So if you have a business idea that you wish to try there is basically no barrier to immigrating. I started Mike's Bike Tours, Amsterdam and I used the local accounting firm Van Noort Gassler and Co. They are extremely qualified and have helped me out with my paperwork to such a degree that I don't even think about it anymore.

Art F.
Business Visa
Sihanoukville, Cambodia

Upon entering the country, I got a 30-day business visa ($40). After 30 days, I applied for a one-year business visa ($295). There is no permanent visa being issued at this time. Residence permits are available, but you have to have connections, and it will cost thousands of dollars. Khmer government is really greedy, and corrupt. So people just stay here on Business Visas for year after year. Doesn't seem to be a problem as long as the local gov't gets its $295 a year. Border runs are not needed if you have the business visa. It allows you multiple entries and exits.

Jim Cotner
FM2 Business Visa
Baja California, Mexico

There are many ways of becoming a legal resident in Mexico, some easy, some difficult. How I did it was I formed a corporation called Chongo Bravo. You go to a Notary Public or Notario Publico as it's called here. A Notario in Mexico is a lawyer that's been granted by the state the function of certifying business deals. And their seal gives these deals official approval. They also do property titles, as well. So you get one of these Notario Publicos to file the paperwork with the government of Mexico for a permit to open up a foreign business. Then you can start a 100% foreign-owned business in Mexico as long as they are not fishing concerns or various extraction industries like oil, but in all those other things like real estate property, trade or manufacturing, retail or anything else you can imagine, a 100% foreign-owned company is A-OK. It's been this way since 1992.

The Notario Publico gets approximately $1500 to set this corporation up. It comes in little parts, you know, fees here and there. Then after about a month, you come back to the Notario and you enter the country with a visa—a regular tourist visa, usually—and you sign the corporation into law.

You assign yourself president in the articles of the corporate constitution and if you come in with a partner, you can grant that partner full Power of Attorney so they can do any activity on the corporation's behalf.

Now, here is the trick. In order to engage in any business activity in Mexico you have to already have a business visa or you have to be a Mexican citizen. In order for this plan to work, the business has to request that the government issue the company's president or any other employee, for that matter, a business visa. So how does an American get around this Catch-22? What you do is grant a Mexican accountant (many of whom specialize in this sort of thing) the rights to perform certain duties within your corporation. One of those duties is to file on your behalf the request for a FM2 business visa, which can be renewed annually. It looks like a passport. The accountant submits the paperwork to the Mexican IRS which they call the Hacienda and to the Bureau of Immigration. Expect to pay an additional $1,000 for this service.

With that visa you get your Mexican driver's license and with that you engage in all the other activities as a Mexican citizen (including renewing your own visa) besides voting and holding a Mexican passport. So in essence the company is legally regarded as a Mexican citizen; they call it a persona morale, a moral entity.

You have to forego your rights to sue in U.S. court. You have to pay taxes, but for that you get an accountant. The accountant has to file every month for this Mexican corporation (I pay around $75 a month for this service. Others can try and do it alone, if they feel bold enough). They just put in zeros. Zero income and zero expenses and then every year you have to file an annual report, but it's kind of like an EZ form. And then you have to file the same form with the Office of Foreign Affairs or Foreign Businesses. Potentially, after two or three years, you have to show that you are conducting business. This could be something like you say the place that you purchased or rented was leased to an American for three months in holiday season, and they gave you cash and you spent cash. The government is not what you'd call aggressive about looking into these things, so in reality you don't actually have to earn any income. You just have to create this shell company and you're in.

Of course, you can conduct real business, which I intend to do. Through Chongo Bravo, I purchased some land in Baja, and I will soon develop it into a surf camp.

Edna Vuong
Work Visa
China

I moved to Beijing on a tourist visa since I didn't have a job at the time. It is possible to secure a job before moving, but I felt that it would be easier to get a job if I was already in Beijing. I also wanted to actually visit the offices and see the work environment and get a sense of what I would be working on before committing to any one office. The office I eventually decided on is a U.K.-based firm and was not registered with the Chinese government at the time. So I worked on a tourist visa for about six months before getting a work visa. The longest tourist visa I could get at the time was a three-month L visa. Every time the visa ran out I would have to leave the country and reapply. Since the office was not registered, they paid for these visa runs.

Visa runs are pretty easy and are a good excuse for more travel. Most people go to Hong Kong, but Korea, Singapore, and Japan are also good options. It is important to make sure you don't stay past your visa date. The fine is pretty hefty.

For a work visa, I had to have a health check, which consists of X-rays, ultrasounds, EKG, and giving blood to test for HIV, syphilis, and drugs. You also have to provide a copy of a diploma from a university and a formal invitation letter from your employer. It isn't cheap, but your employer should pay for all of this. The visa has to be renewed yearly, but the health check only needs to be done the first time.

Marshall Creamer
Work Visa
Hong Kong

I had to fill out a work visa application form, send a copy of my résumé, copy of my passport, and send a few reference letters. It was a very simple process for me, but that might be because I was able to transfer with my company. I don't know any of the steps my company had to go through.

Paul Schuble
Three-year Work Visa
Japan

As a member of the JET Programme [Japan Exchange and Teaching Programme], I wasn't required to do very much. After being accepted, my visa was taken care of for me. The only real paperwork I've had to do has been while in Japan. Is when I take a trip away. In order for someone who's not a permanent resident to leave the country and come back, one must apply for a reentry permit.

Cara Smiley
FM2 Work Visa
Mexico

From 2002 to 2004, I worked part-time for an American organic certification agency and I represented their company in Mexico. I simultaneously worked as a consultant to a certified organic processing facility located in Northern Mexico, traveling four to six times a year to visit the operations. My FM3 work visa was the category of "visiting non-immigrant non-lucrative company representative." This allowed me to work in Mexico and get paid in the USA. I obtained the work visa when I represented a U.S.-based organic certification agency in Mexico.

In 2004, I struck out on my own and created my own business. I own my own company, Integrated Organic Services, Inc., which is incorporated in the USA. I am an employee of my company. I have had an FM2 Immigrant work visa for the last five years. My visa states that I am authorized as the Company Representative and as an Organic Inspector. Although I: 1) am contracted by U.S. organic certification agencies to perform on-site inspections in Mexico and Latin America, 2) am contracted by U.S. organic certification agencies to perform desk audits of certified organic operations and 3) am contracted by Mexican companies to perform consulting work, for the sake of simplicity, I ONLY report the first to Immigration.

Once a year, I complete a two-page Application that is on the Instituto Nacional de Migracion (INM) website. I present copies of the three months' most recent USA bank statements (my personal bank account and my business bank account) with translations into Spanish. All documents that are in English must be translated into Spanish and the Spanish translation (which I do) must be "certified" by a INM recognized translator. I present a letter from SAGARPA (equivalent of the USDA in Mexico) clarifying that I am allowed to practice my profession (inspect organic operations in Mexico) in Mexico. I present a letter stating my desire to continue living and working in Mexico. I present a letter stating that I continue to be the owner, company representative and employee of my company here in Mexico. I present a payment of approximately $250.00 USD. In previous years, I have been required to present Apostiled and translated (into Spanish) USA birth certificate, USA certificates of training as an organic inspector and USA business incorporation certificate and a notarized Mexican marriage certificate. Every year, in addition to the regular stated requirements, INM always requires something "extra" which is not a stated requirement.

Of the 10 times that I have requested and obtained a Work Visa, I have only hired a lawyer once. Frankly, it was not worth the expense. I ended up having to invest the same amount of time, stress and anxiety as when I have requested it on my own. I find that I generally have to go to the INM office (there is one in Oaxaca City) about four times: once to get the "current" list of requirements, once to turn in the required documents and for them to identify what "extra" previously unspecified documents will be required this year, once to turn in the "extra" documents and once to pick up the Visa.

Being married to a Mexican does not help one obtain a Work Visa.

This year, I will apply for Mexican citizenship. The paperwork required is relatively simple—Apostiled birth certificate, Mexican State and Federal penal checks, marriage certificate, etc. and a written test on Mexican culture, history, politics, etc. It took me about three months to compile the documents and the government will take about three months to review and reject/approve my citizenship.

Name Withheld by Request
FM3 Residence Visa and Work Permit
Mexico

I got an FM3, which looks like a U.S. driver's license, by using a "facilitator" here. It was so easy. In order to move your possessions across the border you need an "FM3" so that you don't pay duty on anything. Many people try to fill out the forms themselves and wind up frustrated and having it take way too long. I took people's advice and hired someone to do the paperwork for 75 USD, and he got my FM3 for me in 6 days. The cost was around $200.

I did not have time to get a work permit when I got my FM3 as I was leaving too soon to return to Chicago to pack and sell things to prepare for the move. When I got down here permanently, I went back to the same person who then filed "work permit" papers for me that just get added to my FM3. You must choose only ONE specific occupation. I chose "painter"—though I wish it could have included graphic design, it does not.

Karen (and Jack) Dague
Work Visa—Residency Permit
Poland

My husband started the process to get his work visa in Oct. 2010. This ended up taking about five months to do. The paperwork was finally together but he then had to take the paperwork and his passport to the Polish Embassy in Washington DC, USA. Since he began his job here officially Jan. 1, 2011, it was impossible for him to take off the time to go to the States in January or February...so the middle of March my husband arrived in the States and went to the embassy and finally received his official work visa. Part of the reason this process took so long was that they kept transferring his case to several different people in different countries.

With the work visa finalized now it was time to move on to the residency cards... different documents had to be acquired and that has taken over two months. Again, our case has been transferred to different people and we finally have someone local who is supposed to be helping us get them done. I went to the immigration office with passport, marriage certificate, five passport photos, Jack's work permit, our lease agreement and finally got my residency card finished.

Doug and Jennifer St. Martin
Work Visa and Family
Lisbon, Portugal

When Doug was offered the associate doctor position, he immediately set to work acquiring a work visa, with the hiring doctor's sponsorship. By default, the family is allowed to come and live. He has a work visa, and temporary residency here. It only took about two months from the start of the process to acquire the work visa, because his job (chiropractor) is unique here, and he was being hired by someone with Portuguese citizenship. However, there were some complications to get fiscal numbers and everything for tax purposes straightened out, and that took us six weeks from the time we arrived to complete (and that was with a connection in the Social Security office). It requires a lot of patience. However, after two years here, I am still not 100% finished with my process of acquiring residency, and am currently consulting with a lawyer to move it along a little faster.

The only trick is to be extremely patient. Go a couple times to the immigration office if you don't like one person's answer there, as the next person will probably tell you something different. It is a process that requires a cool head. They also don't mess with lawyers from this country much, and they can speed the process along, and do not charge outrageous fees. Definitely come with time and money on your hands.

David Morrill
Residency Visa
Ecuador
I have a residency visa, which is relatively easy to get in Ecuador. The two most popular ones are the pensionada, or retirement, visa (9-I) which requires an "income for life" of $800 (Social Security, a pension or trust income qualify); or, the investor visa (9-II), which requires an investment in Ecuador of $25,000 or more, which can be in real estate or a CD. My university retirement qualifies me under the retirement visa.

Scott
Work Visa (resident visa)
Saudi Arabia
I've been here since 2009 but I've spent a total of 18 years in Saudi Arabia. A work/residency card (*Iqama*) is mandatory—failure to have one can lead to deportation. The company/sponsor provides the visa and maintains it.

Paul Tenney
Work Visa
Singapore
You must have a job, initially, to get a work visa, and I already had that as I was coming here on a work assignment. I really marveled at the process, it felt like applying for college all over again—they wanted detailed work history, college transcripts and a copy of my diploma, etc. They want the best, the brightest, and the most productive people in the world to come to Singapore so that they will contribute to the country's prosperity. It is the exact opposite of U.S. immigration policy. "Give us your tired, your poor, your huddled masses" is replaced with a critical evaluation of each prospective immigrant to ensure that they will become a positive factor in their society.

Dealing with the bureaucracy in Singapore is like taking a shortcut compared to just about anywhere in the world. Efficient, predictable service is their goal and they achieve that with great success.

If I remain in Singapore, I would likely elect to become a resident alien, but Singapore does not allow dual citizenship. I would have to give up my U.S. citizenship.

Turner Wright
E2 (English Teacher) Visa
Bugu, South Korea

I am on an E2 visa [English Conversation Teacher], which required extensive paperwork—a copy of my university degree and transcript, a criminal background check (soon to be federal), passport photos, and a few documents issued by the recruiting agency. For Korea, in-person interviews at a consulate or embassy are required to receive a visa. I made a special trip to Houston and interviewed during the final World Cup match.

Tinuola
Residency Permit
Czech Republic

I have my "long-term" residency permit and work visa through my employer. (That Czech immigration uses the word "long-term" to describe both documents is quite funny because they have to be renewed annually.) For work, almost all the international companies in Prague help their non-Czech employees through the residency/work permit process. I can't think of any that don't—unless they only hire Czechs. Even the podunk language schools offer some level of assistance. This was a key factor in my decision to move to the Czech Republic—that companies are open to do this. I was extremely fortunate that my firm—an American multinational—hired a consulting company to handle all immigration issues for its employees, thus I did not experience any difficulty with my status.

Chris Jacobs
Residency Permit
Estonia

As an American, you can be in Estonia up to three months without a visa. After that, you need a residency permit. A residency permit can be issued for several reasons. I received one first as an exchange student, and again as an employee. The entire process of obtaining residency is pretty simple. It took two months for student residency, and four months for working residency because I ran into a few problems along the way.

J.M.
RVP—Temporary Residence Permit
Pushkin, Russia

We started out on yearly business visas (me and my wife) and 'accompanying family' visas (the kids). However, in 2009, the rules for visas changed—and it got to be too much of a pain in the ass to work around them—that we moved into the "RVP"—a temporary residence permit that is good for three years at a time.

Getting a business visa is as easy as finding one of the thousands of "visa-obtaining" Russian companies, having them apply for an official invitation permit from the Russian immigration authorities, filling out the forms available online, and dumping it all (and money, naturally) with a Russian consulate for a couple days.

The biggest hassles with business visas:

First, one can only have a single Russian visa at a time, and visas can only be obtained outside Russia. This means staying to the end of a visa, leaving the country on the old one, then being stuck out of the country for at least three or four days (it used to be possible to do in a single day, but that changed in 2009) while you get your new one issued. At least the easiest way to avoid getting stuck in lines at the consulates is to get your visa in a country whose citizens have the right to travel to Russia visa-free. We tended to get ours in Kiev; only non-Ukrainians need Russian visas, so these were the only visas they had to process all week.

Second, while the multi-entry visa is technically valid for a year, it only grants permission to be in Russia for six months out of that year—in two three-month parts. This is a potentially serious problem, although we never had a problem since they're just not tracking compliance with that particular aspect of the rules very closely.

As for the residence permit, it IS obtainable and extendable inside Russia, so there's no need to leave every year. Getting it, however, is a year-long process, with interviews, collection of a vast number of documents, including birth and marriage certificates, police records from other countries you've lived in (or documents confirming that you have no police record), proof of income, etc, etc.—all translated into Russian by a notarized translation service. Permits are granted on a quota system, with no regard given for the nationality of the applicant. This means that an American waits in the same line for one of the same couple-thousand (in Saint Petersburg, they issue 1500 a year; in Moscow somewhat fewer; out in the eastern provinces, it varies) permits as do the numerous Uzbek, Kazakh, Tajik, etc. migrant workers.

One of the best things about Russia, however, is that there is practically no problem which cannot be solved. In this case, it took a chat with a policeman, the application of a couple hundred rubles (six USD or so equivalent) and a visit to a scanner and printer later on to gin up a new registration doc.

Name Withheld by Request
Residence Visa
Dubai, United Arab Emirates

They have what they call a residence visa that the company pays for and is sorted through them. It's an interesting system because you usually have to work for the employer before a year and if you want to change you have to have a "no objection letter." If you do not have this, your company can place a ban on you and you will be forced to leave the UAE for six months. I have changed employers and most are pretty flexible with this.

As for citizenship in this country, you are not eligible unless you stay for 20 years and speak Arabic. For me, it's not really an issue.

Tyler Watts
Temporary Resident
Vietnam

All foreigners living in VN for a prolonged period must apply for a work permit and thereafter a work visa or residence card. To receive a work permit, one must submit notarized degrees, and complete a criminal background check and a health check. Vietnam seeks highly skilled workers so a bachelor's or higher is expected at least. Many expats here did visa runs to Cambodia or nearby countries but the government has cracked down and the possibility of extended runs has decreased, though it is still possible.

I initially came here single and as a recent grad and I met my wife after about a year and a half of living and working here. She is Vietnamese and her hometown is in a rural area of the Mekong Delta. We both taught at the same university in the Mekong Delta (An Giang University). It is certainly helpful to have her assistance in doing all manner of paperwork here but my legal status with work permit, residence card, etc. is unrelated to our marriage. It's possible to get a temporary residence card based on marriage, however each province seems to look at the law differently (this is true for most documents and processes).

If you have a work permit then getting a visa is usually no trouble. However some companies are reluctant to get the work permit for foreigners and in that case it seems one can still do visa runs across the border but it's a risky option. If you have a work permit the process for getting a temporary resident card seems not too difficult.

I have had various visas but have always gone through my organizations and companies here. I did get my own visa with a letter from the ministry of education for about a year when I was working with a nonprofit volunteer organization as their in-country representative. Never had any big issues except when a 'friend' was to pick up my completed visa and passport in Hanoi and mail it to me and he never did (saying it was lost). The visa department never let me know they had the passport so I went through the process of getting a new one only to find it was sitting in their office the whole time.

Overall I have found the government employees to be helpful. There is loads of bureaucracy but the people in the cogs of it all can't help being in such a red-tape-littered system. I have given a bribe or two to get things done quickly (though in the States this is called the "expedited fee" so I don't have too many qualms about it). I have had kindly people who have turned bribes down as well. I find that attempts at the language, respectable dress, a patient attitude and a kind heart go a long way. I make an effort to remember the names of those working in government offices (particularly in places I frequent) and it is certainly appreciated.

Sharon Hiebing
Retirement Visa (Qualified Retirement Program)
Belize

I didn't just move to Belize sight unseen. I made a preliminary "research" trip, and during that trip I met with an attorney to review which of the three immigration choices that Belize has to offer was right for me. I decided on the Qualified Retirement Program (QRP). You must be 45 years or older and have a monthly pension of at least $2,000 USD to qualify. One of the perks is that you only need to live in Belize one month out of the year, and they let you bring all of your household goods and either a car, boat or airplane over duty-free! Some of the cons are you are not allowed to work for pay (although you may buy or start a business), and none of the time in the QRP counts toward permanent residency, if you ever decide to go that route.

The process was very straightforward—simply fill out an application, provide copies of various documents (birth certificate, passport, etc.), a police report, two reference letters, and a physical exam, along with your fees. I did it all via FedEx prior to moving to Belize. All in all, getting into the program and paying for the attorney cost about $3100 USD (it's about half that without an attorney, and you need to add another $750 USD for your spouse and each dependent/child). Every year I must renew.

Belize has two other immigration options—Tourist Visa or Permanent Residency. They are both quite straightforward, and each of the three options has its pros and cons. I think Belize's immigration process is one of the easiest of any country I've seen.

Camille Moreno
Resident Permit (Student)
Germany

I am now on my second student visa. To get the student visa I had to provide bank statements and display an interest in studying in Germany. I had told the Office of Foreign Relations that I would study in Berlin, and they had allotted me two years to learn German and get accepted to a university. I continued to learn German at school and later by doing some internships in art galleries around town. I took the C1 language test and failed. I did some more internships, took it again, passed, and within a month or so had been accepted to one of the art universities. Having done what I said I would do within the first two years, getting the visa the second time around really just involved providing a new photo and giving them €60.

Tim
Student Visa
United Kingdom

I am in London on a student visa, working on a Ph.D. in the humanities. I've been here for a few years, working part-time and subsidizing my stay with a few student loans. I came here with my partner, who enrolled in a two-year Master's degree program in art. School seems expensive but luckily I won a studentship at the last minute and tuition was waived for the first three years of my four-year program. For most people, it is still actually cheaper than paying full price for art schools in the States, so if you are trying to make a decision, don't discount London just because it sounds expensive.

Technically, I can work 20 hours a week on my student visa, but the current administration seems to be making it harder and harder for students to use their visas as a way into U.K. society. The Conservatives in the U.K. are trying to cut net immigration in half and they have identified the student visa as the most abused category of immigration. On top of closing down an armada of bogus language and business schools running out of offices in central London, they are getting rid of legitimate opportunities, like the post-study work visa, which allows graduates to apply for a two-year extension. Despite all this, it is still the best and easiest way to get into the country other than marriage.

Vina Rathbone
Tourist Visa
Argentina

I am an illegal resident, unfortunately. It is very easy to do this in Argentina. Many people come here on three-month tourist visas, and then renew their visas every three months by taking a short ferry trip across the river to Uruguay. You can do this several times without being questioned. If you overstay your tourist visa and it expires, the next time you leave the country, you must pay a 300 peso (U.S. $75) fine.

Kelly Kittel
Tourist Visa
Costa Rica

I have a tourist visa so I have to leave every three months. It stinks and is a pain in the, um, passport. Rumor has it that CR is finally realizing they are sending all this income out of the country every three months and hopefully someday soon you will be able to pay right here to extend your three months instead of leaving the country.

Getting Out to the Max: Foreign Citizenship, Second Passports and Renunciation

To live under the most hassle-free status in a foreign land often means going all the way and becoming a citizen. Your right to live there would become unquestioned, as is your access to all the perks—health insurance, the right to work, and the ability to collect unemployment benefits, where available.

Will the feds snatch your passport out of your ungrateful hands once they discover that you're taking your citizenship elsewhere? Not likely. To get your U.S. passport revoked, you have to do more than just live somewhere else. A lot more. On the other hand, your adopted country may not allow you to hold two passports, in which case you'll have to decide which one you'd prefer to keep (see Dual Citizenship section).

Of course, for most people, foreign citizenship is far from an absolute necessity. Many long and happy lives are lived by Americans abroad on far weaker documentation. Others can't wait to escape the U.S. government, particularly the IRS.

Many people interested in opening offshore accounts where large sums of money can be discreetly stashed seek passports from less inquisitive governments. The web of international rules and by-laws you would need to navigate without running afoul of any powers-that-be are complex. Assuming you have an asset portfolio that makes this worthy of consideration also assumes you have some spare change left over to hire an international legal team to sort it all out for you. It is not a game for do-it-yourselfers. Using the offshore banking system for money-laundering, financial hijinks or other criminal activity will land you in trouble with just about every law enforcement organization on the planet. We don't recommend it.

Seven Paths to Citizenship

Despite what many people believe, only in a small minority of cases in a minority of countries is national identity given away "automatically." Returning exiles, particularly in certain cases of political upheaval, secession and/or displacement, exiles are given the opportunity to reclaim their citizenship. In this, as in many cases having to do with birth and descendancy, it is often not so much a question of being "granted citizenship" as merely getting the government to recognize what has always been a legal fact.

Immigration laws change frequently, are applied capriciously, and are full of contingencies and exceptions. A criminal record in the U.S., undesirable political activity, or simply a lack of visible means of support might cause your prospective government to spurn your petition. This is not to say that there aren't a few tried and true methods that you can count on to work most of the time. Before making your move, however, you are encouraged to contact the appropriate embassy to find out the most current immigration laws and how they apply to your particular situation.

By Birth

If you were not born in the United States, ask your land of birth if you could have citizenship. Chances are, they'll say yes. Not every country recognizes anchor babies (or *jus solis*). And those that do may require that you can produce one parent that was a citizen, as well. If the country in question gained independence or radically transformed its government (e.g., the former Soviet Bloc) after you were born, things get trickier. In other cases, the laws acknowledge in some way that birth, while not automatic, constitutes a valid reason to petition the government for your papers and sets a lower bar than it does for other would-be citizens.

By Ancestry

Where's your daddy from? If he was a citizen of the country you want to move to, you're often in better shape than if you were born there to non-citizen parents. If it's just your mother who's the citizen, it's usually, but not always, just as good (unless you were born out of wedlock or your father is unknown, in which case a mother counts like a dad). Indeed, ancestry is usually the fastest track to citizenship, often demanding no other requirements (i.e., language proficiency, residency, etc.). In some rare instances, it takes both parents to lock in citizenship. Since this is known as *jus sanguinis* (citizenship by blood), there's also a preference for native-born parents over the naturalized kind. Ireland, Greece and Croatia, for instance, will even grant citizenship to grandchildren. Germany will grant citizenship to descendents of citizens who were expelled or lost their citizenship during the Nazi period. This is worth knowing even if you don't want to live in those countries, because you'll receive E.U. citizenship and passport entitling you to live and work anywhere among the 27 member states. Likewise, having a parent or sometimes grandparent from any member state (as well as Switzerland, Norway, Iceland and Liechtenstein) can be your key to living and working just about anywhere on the continent. While it seldom puts you on the express lane to citizenship the way a native-born parent would, even the merest drop of the motherland's blood in your veins—or a close relative who still lives there—can grease the wheels of your return.

Marry In

Many who journey to foreign citizenship take the marriage path, either from love or by other means. There will be other demands besides the usual ones that go along with having a spouse—continuous residency in the country, proving cohabitation, etc. Some countries, particularly conservative Latin American and Islamic countries, grant citizenship to women marrying a male citizen, but not male outsiders marrying that country's women. Other governments recognize marriage in a way that lowers or waives other requirements for a prospective citizen. In either case, you will likely be granted residency while your paperwork moves through the system, a process that can take years. Even in the cases where you're not going to be granted citizenship, you're usually allowed to stay there as a permanent resident, which is almost the same thing. Marriage in a foreign country subjects you to another legal apparatus. In conservative Catholic and Muslim countries, those laws favor men.

Gay Marriage/Civil Union

The following countries allow immigration based on same-sex partnerships: Australia, Belgium, Brazil, Canada, Czech Republic, Denmark, Finland, France, Germany, Iceland, Israel, the Netherlands, New Zealand, Norway, South Africa, Spain, Sweden, and the U.K.

Wait For It

This is known as "Naturalization" and involves a long protracted slog. Getting a government to grant an outsider the rights to become a member of their particular country club, as it were, often requires fulfilling a mosaic of requirements that vary greatly from country-to-country. You will, with few exceptions, be required to put in years of residency and to stay out of trouble and not be a pain or burden. And there's the rub, since living and working are difficult (though far from impossible) without the privileges of citizenship or at least permanent residency. If you get your toehold and can put in the years, you'll only have to face the battery of tests on the language, history, and culture of your new land, submit a stream of letters of recommendation, pay outrageous fees and grind away hours in bureaucratic red tape before you obtain your prized new passport. If family ties, adoption, and marriage aren't specifically acknowledged in the laws of that country, they can still lower the residency bar, making employment and living permits easier, as well as being considered as part of the case as to why you should be naturalized.

Earn or Beg For It

Often known as "citizenship by petition," this method involves demonstrating to immigration authorities that you have performed some great service to that country and thus deserve to be accepted as one of them, or that you would become a great asset to that country. In 2005, the former World Chess Champion Bobby Fischer (now deceased) was granted Icelandic citizenship under article 6 of the Icelandic Nationality Act that allows the Althingi (Icelandic Parliament) to bestow citizenship by statute. Fischer's "in" was that he put the country on the map in 1976 when he played Soviet Chess Champion Boris Spassky in a widely-watched match held in Reykjavik. This earned Fischer the affection of Icelanders. This method also works well for distinguished scientists, artists and celebrities whose mere presence can be said to confer prestige upon the nation. Unless there's a Nobel prize or something similar among your important papers, this method is probably not an option for you.

Buy It

Economic citizenship, as it's called, where a passport is issued to anyone who makes a "significant investment" in a given country, was once a big revenue generator for nations in the tax haven business. Post-9/11 arm-twisting by the U.S. government shut down the majority of these mills, most notably Grenada's where citizenship and cheap tropical surroundings were for sale for a mere $40,000. Nowadays, only the Caribbean nations of St. Kitts and Nevis (that's one country) and Dominica (pronounced "dah-min-EEK-uh" and not to be confused with the Dominican Republic) remain in the citizenship mill business. St. Kitts has a rather pricey program, costing as little as $200,000 (for an individual) as a straight-up payment or around $350,000 if it goes to a long-term (minimum five years) designated real estate investment. Dominica is the Wal-Mart of economic citizenship, allowing you to snap up a passport for $75,000–$100,000. In the case of Dominica, it's truly an "economic" citizenship (more about getting your money out of the USA than your actual person) since they don't even require that you actually live there.

But for the truly rich, this is of little consequence, as there are myriad ways that money buys citizenship or at least long-term residency (which in many cases makes you eligible for citizenship). In Austria, for instance, this is not spelled out in law, but it does occur in a few cases per year. Investment visas can easily be issued until residency requirements are fulfilled. A well-paid attorney can petition the government on your behalf. Only the most blindly Marxist or paranoid totalitarian regimes shut the door to rich people.

BE WARNED: Much of what is being offered as a "Second Passport," particularly if it's over the Internet or of the "pay a guy in a back room" kind of deal, is a scam. If you're not a diplomat, then you'd better not be in possession of a diplomatic passport, regardless of who sold it to you and how. If you're not required to be physically present at some government office(s) in the country in question, what you'll receive is likely bogus—if you receive anything at all. If you are caught traveling with any kind of forged or otherwise sketchily-acquired passport, you could easily find yourself in jail. If you've used it to open up an offshore bank account, your assets can be seized.

Play the Race Card

In less than a handful of countries, your ethnicity is your ticket. The African nation of Liberia still offers citizenship to any person of "Negro-African descent." Perhaps the most famous and often-used ethnic entry is Israel's

Law of Return, which basically grants any Jew, whether by descent or conversion, automatic Israeli citizenship.

Wikipedia has decent, though occasionally confusing or inaccurate, explanations of the general terms of nationality laws (the laws that determine who is, isn't, can and cannot be a citizen of a given country). A better bet is to contact the embassy or consulate of the country you're interested in or see if they post their nationality laws online (many do).

Second Passport Without Citizenship

A few countries, such as Panama and Uruguay, offer a "passport" that confers no rights of citizenship. Panama allows foreigners (usually retirees) to deposit enough money in a five-year interest-bearing (4%) CD with a designated (state) Panamanian bank. As long as the monthly interest exceeds around USD $850 (meaning a balance of over $260,000 or so) you are considered a "retiree" and offered a passport valid for five years and renewable as long as you keep fulfilling the requirements of the program. Unlike the citizenship-for-sale deals in the Caribbean, the money is not paid but deposited and thus, it's still yours. Obviously, you'll be making less interest than other banks might pay, plus you'll be paying a few thousand to a lawyer to push the paperwork, but it's still the most achievable method of obtaining a second passport. Because the document does NOT make you a citizen, it is essentially a travel document and is of limited use for American citizens, particularly in relation to the cost.

Join the French Foreign Legion

Believe it nor not, the French Foreign Legion, that last-ditch repository of misfits, ne'er-do-wells and adventurers, still offers a chance to leave your old name and country behind. If you're between the ages of 17–40, are in good health and don't mind quelling a Third World upheaval should you be called upon to do so, France needs you. Pay starts at €975 a month (roughly $1,285) and room, board and medical benefits are included. After three years of a five-year contract, you are eligible for French citizenship. On October 12, 2000, the legion was ordered to accept women into its ranks. As of this writing, compliance has not yet begun.

Dual Citizenship

Does acquiring a foreign citizenship require that you give up your American one? Probably not. While the United States government does not officially encourage you to share allegiance with another land, or even recognize it, it does not outlaw the practice of dual citizenship and likely won't outlaw it in the foreseeable future. The reason for this has a lot to do with the needs of multinational corporations in the global marketplace, but implications can accrue to the benefit of the disgruntled citizen.

As a dual citizen, you would still be allowed to vote in U.S. elections, but conversely, you would still be liable for income tax—see The IRS and You. And should the draft be reinstated, you'd still be eligible. Then again, you might be drafted into the military services of your new country.

In some cases, however, a foreign government will not grant you citizenship until you give up yours. The necessity to renounce citizenship in order to become a citizen of another country is getting rarer and rarer. Almost 100 countries and territories recognize dual citizenship. And the list grows by the year, the latest being Chile and Portugal.

Countries Which Do Not Recognize Dual Citizenship

Brunei	Kenya	Peru
China	Kiribati	Poland
Denmark	Kuwait	Romania
Ecuador	Malaysia	Saudi Arabia
Fiji	Mauritius	Singapore
Indonesia	Myanmar	Solomon Islands
Japan	Nepal	Turkey
Kazhakstan	Papua New Guinea	Venezuela

(some restrictions apply in Austria, Egypt, Germany, Iran, Latvia, Norway, Pakistan, Peru and Spain)

Freeing yourself of the IRS certainly has appeal, and for many wealthy people, it's almost a no-brainer, but before taking such a drastic step, think hard. The U.S. will not release you of financial obligations incurred prior to renunciation, nor of any military service you are obligated to fulfill and certainly won't let you off on any criminal charges (quite the opposite: you'd be considered a fugitive from justice). You will likely still have to file returns for many years afterwards. Your Social Security payments would still be paid, but you would forfeit any military pension. Of course, one day you might want to return to the U.S. As a non-citizen you will be subject to the same requirements and humiliations as the average foreigner now endures. In some cases, this means long application processes in American embassies overseas, fees, long lines, and various other frustrations. You can be turned away at the U.S. border simply because a Customs agent doesn't like the way you look. In fact, depending on the country you adopted, considerably worse things can happen. 'Nuff said.

Jude Angione
Dual Citizen, U.S. + Canada

I became a Landed Immigrant in 1972 and a Canadian citizen in 1977. It was dead simple in the '70s. All you had to do was show up at the border with a job offer in Canada. It's much more expensive and time-consuming now, somewhere in the neighborhood of $4,000 to get through the landed immigrant process.

Alessandra
Dual Citizen, U.S. + E.U.-Italy
(lives in Porto, Portugal)

I started looking for visa options and a way to legally live and work in Spain. While securing a Spanish visa seemed difficult, through online research, I discovered I was eligible for Italian citizenship through blood (*jure sanguinis*). My great-grandparents on my father's side of the family had all immigrated to the United States from Italy in the late 1800s, after laws had been passed in Italy allowing the right to citizenship to be passed on to future generations. As an Italian citizen, I would be able to travel, live and work throughout the E.U., which sounded like a dream to me.

I made an appointment to file the citizenship application with the Italian consulate in New York City, where I was still a resident. The application preparation required a great amount of determination, paper shuffling, and help from my family to locate old birth, death and marriage records for my Italian relatives from the Italian govenrment and U.S. offices at the Federal and State level. I prepared and completed the application on my own, but there are agencies or law offices that will prepare the documents for you, if you prefer to pay someone. The process from start to finish took about 18 months, and required a great amount of determination, paper shuffling, and help from my family to locate old birth, death and marriage records for my Italian relatives.

After receiving my approval letter, I filed for and received a passport.

Seven Ways to Lose Your Citizenship

Revocation of U.S. citizenship is rare, and despite the erosion of citizens' rights and much talk about revoking citizenship by executive fiat, it is highly unlikely that you'll lose your citizenship unless you make a conscious choice to do so. The following are the seven ways Americans can have their birthright legally revoked:

1 Being naturalized in a foreign country, upon the person's own application made after reaching 18 years of age;
2 Making an oath or other declaration of allegiance to a foreign country or division thereof, again, after reaching 18 years of age;
3 Serving in the armed forces of a foreign country if those armed forces are engaged in hostilities against the U.S., or if the person serves as an officer;
4 Working for the government of a foreign country if the person also obtains nationality in that country, or if to work in such a position an oath or other declaration of allegiance is required;
5 Making a formal renunciation of U.S. citizenship before a U.S. consular officer or diplomat in a foreign country;
6 Making a formal written statement of renunciation during a state of war, if the Attorney General approves the renunciation as not contrary to U.S. national defense; and
7. Committing an act of treason against the U.S., or attempting by force or the use of arms to overthrow the government of the U.S.. Renunciation by this means can be accomplished only after a court has found the person guilty.
Source: www.visalaw.com

Those required to renounce or otherwise gung-ho to give up their American passport for political reasons or taxation purposes will likely make use of option #5. And if you choose to go through with it, you have to go to a U.S. embassy or consulate abroad (it cannot be done in the United States) and formally renounce your citizenship. U.S. consular officials often take umbrage at such requests and the experience of relinquishing your passport is likely to be unpleasant. For some, this renouncement becomes the opportunity to make the ultimate political statement...or at least an interesting blog post.

It can't be stressed often enough that this is a big step, and careful thought should be given before doing something as irrevocable as renunciation.

Renunciation of U.S. Citizenship

IMMIGRATION & NATIONALITY ACT

Section 349(a)(5) of the Immigration and Nationality Act (INA) (8 U.S.C. 1481(a)(5)) is the section of law that governs the ability of a United States citizen to renounce his or her U.S. citizenship. That section of law provides for the loss of nationality by voluntarily performing the following act with the intent to relinquish his or her U.S. nationality:

"(5) making a formal renunciation of nationality before a diplomatic or consular officer of the United States in a foreign state , in such form as may be prescribed by the Secretary of State" (emphasis added).

ELEMENTS OF RENUNCIATION

A person wishing to renounce his or her U.S. citizenship must voluntarily and with intent to relinquish U.S. citizenship:

1. appear in person before a U.S. consular or diplomatic officer,
2. in a foreign country (normally at a U.S. Embassy or Consulate); and
3. sign an oath of renunciation

Renunciations that do not meet the conditions described above have no legal effect. Because of the provisions of section 349(a)(5), Americans cannot effectively renounce their citizenship by mail, through an agent, or while in the United States. In fact, U.S. courts have held certain attempts to renounce U.S. citizenship to be ineffective on a variety of grounds, as discussed below.

REQUIREMENT—RENOUNCE ALL RIGHTS AND PRIVILEGES

In the case of Colon v. U.S. Department of State, 2 F.Supp.2d 43 (1998), plaintiff was a United States citizen and resident of Puerto Rico, who executed an oath of renunciation before a consular officer at the U.S. Embassy in Santo Domingo. The U.S. District Court for the District of Columbia rejected Colon's petition for a writ of mandamus directing the Secretary of State to approve a Certificate of Loss of Nationality in the case because the plaintiff wanted to retain one of the primary benefits of U.S. citizenship while claiming he was not a U.S. citizen. The Court described the plaintiff as a person, "claiming to renounce all rights and privileges of United States citizenship, [while] Plaintiff wants to continue to exercise one of the fundamental rights of citizenship, namely to travel freely throughout the world and when he wants to, return and reside in the United States." See also *Jose Fufi Santori v. United States of America*, 1994 U.S. App. LEXIS 16299 (1994) for a similar case.

A person who wants to renounce U.S. citizenship cannot decide to retain some of the privileges of citizenship, as this would be logically inconsistent with the concept of renunciation. Thus, such a person can be said to lack a full understanding of renouncing citizenship and/or lack the necessary intent to renounce citizenship, and the Department of State will not approve a loss of citizenship in such instances.

DUAL NATIONALITY/STATELESSNESS

Persons intending to renounce U.S. citizenship should be aware that, unless they already possess a foreign nationality, they may be rendered stateless and, thus, lack the protection of any government. They may also have difficulty traveling as they may not be entitled to a passport from any country. Even if they were not stateless, they would still be required to obtain a visa to travel to the United States, or show that they are eligible for admission pursuant to the terms of the Visa Waiver Pilot Program (VWPP). If found ineligible for a visa or the VWPP to come to the U.S., a renunciant, under certain circumstances, could be barred from entering the United States. Nonetheless, renunciation of U.S. citizenship may not prevent a foreign country from deporting that individual back to the United States in some non-citizen status.

TAX & MILITARY OBLIGATIONS/NO ESCAPE FROM PROSECUTION

Also, persons who wish to renounce U.S. citizenship should also be aware that the fact that a person has renounced U.S. citizenship may have no effect whatsoever on his or her U.S. tax or military service obligations (contact the Internal Revenue Service or U.S. Selective Service for more information). In addition, the act of renouncing U.S. citizenship will not allow persons to avoid possible prosecution for crimes which they may have committed in the United States, or escape the repayment of financial obligations previously incurred in the United States or incurred as United States citizens abroad.

RENUNCIATION FOR MINOR CHILDREN

Parents cannot renounce U.S. citizenship on behalf of their minor children. Before an oath of renunciation will be administered under Section 349(a)(5) of the INA, a person under the age of eighteen must convince a U.S. diplomatic or consular officer that he/she fully understands the nature and consequences of the oath of renunciation, is not subject to duress or undue influence, and is voluntarily seeking to renounce his/her U.S. citizenship.

IRREVOCABILITY OF RENUNCIATION

Finally, those contemplating a renunciation of U.S. citizenship should understand that the act is irrevocable, except as provided in section 351 of the INA (8 U.S.C. 1483), and cannot be canceled or set aside absent successful administrative or judicial appeal. (Section 351(b) of the INA provides that an applicant who renounced his or her U.S. citizenship before the age of eighteen can have that citizenship reinstated if he or she makes that desire known to the Department of State within six months after attaining the age of eighteen. See also Title 22, Code of Federal Regulations, section 50.20).

Renunciation is the most unequivocal way in which a person can manifest an intention to relinquish U.S. citizenship. Please consider the effects of renouncing U.S. citizenship, described above, before taking this serious and irrevocable action. If you have any further questions regarding this matter, please contact the Director, Office of Police Review and Inter-Agency Liaison (CA/OCS/PRI), Overseas Citizen Services, Bureau of Consular Affairs, U.S. Department of State, 4th Floor, 2100 Pennsylvania Avenue, N.W., Washington D.C. 20037. email: askpri@state.gov

Anthony D.

Madrid, Spain

Part of the process of becoming a citizen is having to get fingerprints made. The Spanish National Police made them, I sent them into the FBI, they sent them back because they weren't done right, and I had to get them done again. I got in the line to submit documents at 3 a.m. because they only let 100 people in every day to submit...or so I thought. Guys from South America sleeping in boxes come out like caterpillars from cocoons around 8 a.m. to sell their places to the highest bidder...or so I thought. Turns out that the mafias are now gone. It's just paperwork...nothing too interesting. Well, the U.S. embassy made it a bit more fun when they told me (when I expressed my concern about Spain's insistence that I "renounce" my U.S. citizenship) that if they take my passport to just come by and get another one. Just a silly game, really.

Getting By: Jobs and Other Hustles

So, once you've resolved the issue of being able to legally reside somewhere, you'll no doubt want to give some thought as to what you're going to do and how you're going to support yourself once you're there. In almost any country on earth, at least some Americans are living and working. Some methods require skill, others ingenuity and some are the result of dumb luck. Persistence never hurts. And there are even a few overseas gigs that are just about there for the asking.

Generally, your choices fall into four categories:

Non or Low-Paying:

Students, interns and volunteers get easy visas, make contacts, and begin to lay the foundation for a career abroad. The question is, can you support yourself until that career happens?

U.S. Employment:

Get hired or transferred by a U.S. based enterprise and you're paid in dollars, the visa hassles are usually handled by your well-connected employer, and there's usually a living stipend thrown in as well. While it's more than possible to leave the country while still working for the United States Government (or one of its bloated portfolio of private contractors), most people who go the Getting Out route would prefer to avoid that kind of attachment. Working for a multinational with branches all over the world (or at least elsewhere in the world) and angling for a job when one opens up overseas is probably the best strategy.

Work for a Local Company or Organization:

Landing a job abroad is a lot more difficult since it requires learning the hiring protocol of a different culture. The visa challenges are more daunting; usually this requires that a company representative vouch that no local candidate could fill the position. In the case of the E.U., a candidate must first be sought among all member nations. You are usually, for better or worse, paid in local currency. If your job is in one of the progressive democracies, you can expect a healthy benefits/vacation package as well. You might try and work for a foreign company with a branch in the U.S. while you're still living here. Then suck up to the manager who can have you transferred to their home office.

Work for Yourself

Choosing to go abroad (and more to the point, actually following through and doing it) generally requires a bit of self-sufficiency so it's not surprising that a good percentage of expatriates hustle up their living on their own, too. Working for yourself involves fewer bureaucratic hassles since governments are lenient with visitors who pay their own way and don't put a strain on the employment market. Freelance writers, photographers, designers, Internet entrepreneurs and overseas business operators form the core of America's mobile class. Yoga teachers, chefs and massage therapists do it pretty well too. Musicians can always swing a few pennies busking at the nearest Metro station, and they're used to a lifetime of starvation, anyway. More ambitious and enterprising types even start businesses abroad, typically, but not necessarily, in the tourist or expat trade. This involves a few more hassles, since that means you're usually operating under more government rules and regulations.

In this section we present a few examples of common hustles expats abroad engage in and tell you how you can be one of them. You can find additional links in the resources section in the back of the book. You'll notice that many jobs can fall into more than one category. Teaching English, for instance, can be done through any of the four methods described above. Likewise, many a successful strategy involves combining options—say, working part-time at a hotel, tutoring English on the side, and maybe even selling a newspaper or magazine article or photograph here and there. Use the elements you need and make something that works.

Studying Abroad

For students, the ticket out couldn't be simpler—continue your courses, but do it in Wales, the Bahamas, Hong Kong, Bali, Melbourne, or wherever strikes your fancy. While many expatriate options necessitate putting your career track on ice, carefully choosing your study abroad program allows you to continue your merry climb up the ladder of success while enjoying an extended absence from the United States. Most countries cast a relatively favorable eye on education-seekers, and student visas are issued more liberally than residency permits. Many allow you to hold a part-time job, too.

The simplest option is right on your own college campus. More than likely, they have a study abroad office. If your school lacks an overseas program, fear not. Certain colleges, such as the Institute for Study Abroad at Butler University (**www.ifsa.-butler.org**), specialize in semesters abroad. Most programs ferry you to English-speaking countries but not exclusively. SUNY Brockport offers semesters studying Vietnamese culture geared toward English speakers at the University of Da Nang. More are listed in the resources section. Expect to find packages that are nearly all-inclusive—tuition, housing and usually meals, books, language lessons and a bunch of culture tours thrown in for good measure. And the affiliation with a U.S. university means your credits stand a good chance of being recognized by whatever institution ends up issuing your diploma.

While costs vary, figure on paying anywhere from $8,000–$15,000 a semester. Compared to what you might be paying at a lot of U.S. private—and even public—institutions, this can be competitive or even a bargain, especially since most expenses are taken care of. For the relatively privileged, it's something Mom and Dad wouldn't feel guilty shelling out for. And for the rest of us, there's still all the usual financial aid hustles available to stateside students —loans, grants, scholarships and work/study, with a few added twists.

Most of these options top out at one year, but if you're intent on getting out for longer, or if you would care for unlimited options of curriculum and locale, you can enroll directly in a foreign university. You can take Russian language at Moscow University, Accounting at Heidelberg or simply get your dentistry degree at Montreal's McGill University. Of course, if your language skills aren't up to par, you're pretty much restricted to English-speaking programs. Other disadvantages include a greater chance that your hard-earned college credit will not be transferrable. And while financial aid options are more limited (there are student loans to some recognized overseas universities, and some scholarships do pay for study abroad), many overseas university tuitions—even for international students—are often a fraction of what they are compared to the U.S. Particularly worth checking out are colleges in Germany, Sweden, Norway, and Finland. The whole idea of tuition still hasn't fully caught on, though it is spreading. Extra fees are also sometimes charged for international students. For a good rundown of university options abroad, see **www.studyabroaduniversities.com**. Information about scholarships and other aspects of international study can be found at **www.scholars4dev.com**.

Need Financial Aid?

The David L. Boren scholarships of the National Security Education Program provide up to $20,000 a year to have students go abroad and study exotic cultures in far-off lands—Cyprus, Azerbaijan, Kenya, Vietnam. The downside is that when you're done, you have to agree to work for the U.S. intelligence community—in other words, become a spy. See here: **www.iie.org.**

Barbara Warwick
Ph.D. Student
Heidelberg University

I taught English and afterschool art and theater at a Franco-German school, took German and got my Magister at the local Uni. Now working on a doctorate and doing my at-home marketing job.

European universities are cheap (like $1000/semester) and many countries are moving toward the BA/MA system, including Germany. Anyone who is thinking about shelling out for private school in the Liberal Arts should really consider doing a degree in Europe instead. If you can pass the language test (which I did easily after a year of intensive German), you can get in. French schools have a more rigorous application process. Germany is basically first come, first serve, except for the sciences, which are competitive. Professors in Germany often allowed me to write papers in English. If you want to be a doctor or a lawyer, stick to the U.S. schools. But if you are going to study art history, sociology, or even English lit (for the truly lazy American student), do it in Germany where it won't put your parents in the poorhouse.

Bryn Martin
Post-Doctoral Fellow
Swiss Federal Institute of Technology, Lausanne (EPFL)

I am a post-doctoral fellow at the Swiss Federal Institute of Technology (EPFL) and an independent musician (bryyn.com). As a post-doc, my research field is in cardiovascular hemodynamics and craniospinal disorders/neuroengineering.

I was recommended by a personal contact for the position. I think it is nearly impossible to move to Switzerland without a direct contact with someone who can find you a job. Or you can try and work for Nestlé or Philip Morris.

Peace Corps

So you want to get out right now, have a visa, a job, a place to live and—what the hell—a new purpose in life? The easiest, cleanest ticket is Uncle Sam's own Peace Corps. Since 1960, when President John F. Kennedy conceived of the idea, the Peace Corps has been the outfit of choice for disgruntled Americans seeking to bid their country goodbye. Between 7,000 and 8,000 volunteers a year move through the Peace Corps which now operates in 77 countries—Colombia, Sierra Leone, and Indonesia being the most recent additions. Apply today, and within a year, you could be on your way to somewhere far, far away—all expenses paid.

Will they take you? If you are over 18, have U.S. citizenship and hold a college degree, chances are good. Even applicants without four-year degrees have been known to squeak in. While its roots are in agricultural development, the Peace Corps have been active in AIDS prevention and control as well as information technology, so should you have some kind of background in computers, management or agriculture, you will find yourself actively courted. Those who don't bring any particular skills to the table are most often pressed into service teaching English.

What's the deal? You serve two years plus 10–12 weeks training. Volunteers get free transportation to and from their assigned country, are provided living expenses comparable to what the locals make, and all health coverage is paid for. And when it's all over, a lump sum of $7,425 (technically that's $275 for every month you serve). So unless you have debts to pay, you can tread water financially. And if your debts happen to be of the student loan variety, relax, they're deferred and some loans may even qualify for partial cancellation once you've completed your term of service.

The downside is that the Peace Corps is a bit like the army. You go where they send you, do what they tell you. You can rank your preferences when you apply, but there are no guarantees. If you're ready to re-embrace America when your term is up, you're on a flight back to America. If that period has only whetted your appetite for the global lifestyle, you've got cash in hand and hopefully a Rolodex full of contacts to make your permanent escape a reality.

Peace Corps: Where Do They Serve?

Albania, Armenia, Azerbaijan, Belize, Benin, Botswana, Bulgaria, Burkina Faso, Cambodia, Cameroon, Cape Verde, China, Colombia, Costa Rica, Dominican Republic, Eastern Caribbean, Ecuador, El Salvador, Ethiopia, Fiji, Georgia, Ghana, Guatemala, Guyana, Honduras, Indonesia, Jamaica, Jordan, Kazakhstan, Kyrgyz Republic, Lesotho, Liberia, Macedonia, Madagascar, Malawi, Mali, Mexico, Micronesia and Palau, Moldova, Mongolia, Morocco, Mozambique, Namibia, Nicaragua, Niger, Panama, Paraguay, Peru, Philippines, Romania, Rwanda, Samoa, Senegal, Sierra Leone, South Africa, Suriname, Swaziland, Tanzania, Thailand, The Gambia, Togo, Tonga, Turkmenistan, Uganda, Ukraine, Vanuatu, Zambia.

Contact Info:
Peace Corps
Paul D. Coverdell Peace Corps Headquarters
1111 20th Street, NW
Washington, DC 20526
800-424-8580
www.peacecorps.gov

Name Withheld by Request, 23
Peace Corps Volunteer
Kirovograd region, Ukraine

Right now, I'm an English teacher, living in a village of about 4000 people. I've been in Ukraine since September 2010 and at my work site since December. My days are mostly spent preparing lessons, teaching a couple classes of resolutely silent teenagers or squirming children, walking around the village, writing copious and irrelevant poems and essays for myself, talking to the elderly lady with whom I live.

I think for everyone who applies to Peace Corps, the paperwork and the wait seem endless. I began my application during my senior year of college, two years ago now. I was passed over for the first round—the recruitment officer who I worked with in Chicago was very encouraging throughout the long process. Once you are nominated to a region, your application then goes on to Washington. Then it's a lot more paperwork, particularly of the medical sort. This took months for me to complete.

I had first been assigned a position in either Jordan or Morocco. By the time I had completed my mountain of medical paperwork (the application process can be a Kafka-esque nightmare of bureaucracy), those positions had filled up, so I was asked to serve in Ukraine instead. Even though Ukraine may not seem quite so foreign or mystical a country compared to my imagined Arabian nights, it really has an exoticness of its own.

It's warm now and I have honestly never seen a more beautiful spring. Apricot and cherry trees have burst into white blossoms, and there are baby goats, baby ducklings, and baby cows everywhere. Little children greet you, *Zdraste*, hello, on the street, riding two to a bicycle and grinning at you. Everyone is outside now, working in their plots in the fields or in their kitchen gardens. Ukrainians don't have a great reputation of welcoming foreigners, but once you're in, they will shower you with delicious selections from these gardens: fresh produce, infinite potatoes, jams they preserved themselves.

Out here, there are no restaurants or even a supermarket, just a couple run-down, creepy bars. We have a few small stores. These sell mostly dry goods, but the big store by my school (by "big" I mean the size of a large-ish living room) has some produce like carrots and apples. To get to a supermarket, I take a 20-minute bus or electric train into the next town. In this town there's also the bazaar, which every decently-sized town or city will have—on weekends they are bigger, with stall after stall of beautiful farm produce, eggs, milk, fish still flopping in tubs, giant bloody slabs of meat, preserves, as well as clothes, electronics, kitchenware, etc.

As for visas, the Peace Corps arranges that for you, as well as your living accommodations, three months of language and technical training, and a monthly stipend. I have no idea how I would survive in this country on my own, or without having taken Ukrainian lessons for four hours a day for weeks on end. I get on OK on the Peace Corps stipend, and while I can't afford to go to bars or movies every weekend, I also don't have very many temptations.

Volunteer Organizations/NGOs

If you've got time and the urge to help, there are plenty of organizations that will take you on. Many may offer at least some kind of perk, such as travel expenses, a stipend or at least college credit, particularly when you bring a valuable skill set to the table. Of course, it's important to know who you're working for. The Peace Corps (and USAID) operates under the auspices of the U.S. State Department, though even the hippie-hearted tend to see the work that they do as benign. And they offer more pay and benefits than you're likely to find anywhere else under the rubric "volunteer." Other government programs that take on volunteers pursue a more palpable foreign policy agenda.

Some Christian organizations do feed and clothe the needy; others take a heavier hand and try to evangelize the natives under the guise of humanitarian aid, often in countries where such activity is against the law. Most of the heavy lifting in the humanitarian world is done by NGOs—or non-governmental organizations. Regardless of their mandate or activities, if any organization is large enough, there will be some paying positions. For an extensive list of major volunteer organizations and their affiliations, organizational partners, etc., see the Resources section. Many organizations, such as Volunteer Global (**www.volunteerglobal.com**) are there to promote volunteerism in general and act as portals to affiliated programs, matching willing volunteers to needy causes. You can also browse ads for job and volunteer positions in the humanitarian and international development world at **devnetjobs.org**. You'll find more listings online at **www.gettingoutofamerica.com**.

Tyler Watts
Volunteer → Paid Employee
Ho Chi Minh City, Vietnam

I came here in 2005 with an American volunteer organization, Volunteers in Asia, and was with them for the first three years in VN. As part of my volunteer term with VIA, I worked with an NGO charity organization, Friends of Hue Foundation, and also connected with several NGOs as part of my work. I primarily taught English.

As I had come before as a student to Vietnam, I asked about volunteer organizations that supplied teachers to Vietnam. One foreigner mentioned to me about ELIC (a Christian organization), WUSC (Canadian organization) and VIA (Stanford-based nonprofit volunteer organization). After looking at all of them, it seemed VIA was the best fit, primarily because of cost (it was the cheapest) but I liked the philosophy of the group a bit more as well. Due to the downturn of the economy VIA has had to scale back operations so it's an organization that I appreciate greatly, but alas they have a very small presence in Vietnam now. Teachers for Vietnam (www.teachersforvietnam.org) has teachers in more rural areas in Vietnam, which I think is the most exciting place to be for an educator. Other high-profile programs here include UN Volunteers and ones operating through the Fulbright Program.

I think having an organization that supports you is valuable (especially if you haven't traveled abroad before), but not essential. There are lots of opportunities to get involved in all sorts of projects informally here and they are not difficult to find. However, for access to more rural areas, it's probably best to go with an organization.

The opportunities for volunteers to segue into something paid are large but primarily to be found in the larger cities—and the best-paying to be found in Hanoi or Ho Chi Minh City. You can certainly find teaching gigs in smaller cities and it will be highly appreciated but pay is less, though cost of living is significantly less, as well.

I now work full-time for a hospitality company. I am a trainer for staff working in five-star level hotels, apartments and restaurants, focused on English language and soft skills training. I work six days a week, 8:30–5:30 on weekdays and a half day on Saturday. I am by no means a wealthy expat but my family and I live comfortably and sufficiently above the local standard.

Retire, Slack or Slum It

 Unlike your parents, countries don't really mind if you sit around all day doing nothing, as long as you spend money and don't become a burden on the system. So if you've saved enough money, have a steady source of income, such as a pension, you can head to where the living is cheap and ride out your money in relative style. Retirees, in particular, are offered incentives by dozens of countries—many located in the tropics—who'd love a slice of the pension pie. In much of Central America and Southeast Asia, gray-haired Americans live a life of tropical luxury simply on what they get from Social Security. Boho slackers with a novel to finish might gravitate toward sophisticated and underpriced cities like Berlin and Buenos Aires. With costs low, and enough in the bank, you're living easy. If you can scare up some under-the-table work or private lessons or sell a freelance article, so much the better.

Social Security Abroad

If you are a United States citizen, you can travel and/or live in most foreign countries without affecting your eligibility for Social Security Retirement benefits. There are a few countries—Cambodia, Cuba, North Korea, Vietnam and many of the former U.S.S.R. republics—where they cannot send Social Security checks. (Exceptions to this rule are Armenia, Estonia, Latvia, Lithuania, and Russia.)

Almost 400,000 Social Security checks are mailed to beneficiaries living outside of the United States each month, and many more are directly deposited to expat recipients' U.S. bank accounts. Recipients living in Argentina, Australia, Canada, France, Germany, Ireland, Italy, Norway, Portugal, Spain, Sweden, the United Kingdom, and a handful of other countries can receive Social Security benefits from an international direct deposit service without any penalty. More details about receipt of Social Security benefits abroad can be found at: www.socialsecurity.gov

NOTE: Renouncing U.S. citizenship does not mean you forfeit your Social Security. That will only happen if and when the Social Security System (and the U.S. economy) goes bankrupt. Retired military personnel who renounce, however, do lose their retirement pay. Something to consider.

Name Withheld by Request
Artist/Semi-Retiree
San Miguel de Allende, Mexico

What do I do for work/money? Pray. Just joking. I'm living off of savings and income from the sale of my Chicago condo, which was sold "just" before the crisis hit. I moved to an apartment in Chicago for two years before moving to Mexico. I'm also painting and have already sold three paintings, am being represented by a very modern high-end store right now. I've only been here a few months.

My strategy to make my money last longer was to leave the U.S. There, it felt like my money was pouring out the door. Now I feel that the flood has become a trickle. I will be eligible for Social Security in 1½ years, which you DO get here. I want to paint and make it my life's work.

Libby Hansen
Retiree
Copenhagen, Denmark

I am living off a small pension and trying not to dip into savings too much. Social Security pension from the U.S. is payable in Denmark. I also receive small pensions from both Canada and New Zealand. I was not aware that I would qualify for a pension in either country. The Danish pension authority supplied me with applications for pensions in both countries when they found out that I had lived in those two places.

I don't work any longer but in general the work week here is shorter than in the U.S. 37 hrs/week is the norm. Vacation time is five or six weeks for most people! Maternity leave is six months with possibility to extend to a whole year with 80% pay for the mother and a couple of months 80% paid leave for the father.

This doesn't seem to be an ideal place to retire unless one has family here. The language would be difficult to learn at a late age, the cost of housing is also much higher than the U.S., not to mention the cost of goods and services. I am retired here because I already own a house without a mortgage in a place in the country that I enjoy living.

Teach English

If you're an American, chances are you speak English. A lot of people in the world don't and desperately want to learn how. It's the language of science, of business and of popular entertainment. That may explain why teaching English as a second language has become nearly synonymous with expats trying to make a go of it overseas without any special skills or knowledge. Overseas English language schools will usually arrange for visas and sometimes even accommodations. You often don't even have to know the local tongue, because classes tend to be immersion deals and often all that's required is that you converse. Other schools tend to emphasize more structured lessons, but still done entirely in English. No surprise that the real money is in teaching business English and that standards for these kinds of gigs tend to be higher.

What do you need? In some cases simply being a native speaker is enough. Many English language schools prefer that you have a university degree and some teaching experience. But if this is the way you're thinking of going, then a formal certificate in teaching English known as TEFL (Teaching English as a Foreign Language) or TESOL (Teaching English to Speakers of Other Languages) not only provides the most opportunities for jobs (many schools, businesses and organizations will not hire you without one), but schools offering these certificates will usually assist with job placement. A quality four-week program can cost around $1,300. There are scams galore, so be sure to carefully research the organization you're dealing with before turning over money and packing up.

Important criteria that you need to look for in a TESOL Certificate course include at least 100 hours of time spent in the classroom studying how to be a teacher, and at least six hours spent actually teaching actual students under the direction and supervision of a trained, experienced teacher. Of course, if you're intrepid and resourceful, you can post ads and try and scare up students yourself, whatever your certification level.

The greatest demand for English teachers is in China, Japan and particularly South Korea. Schools in these countries offer competitive salaries, frequently with room and board—and some even offer airfare. Russia and increasingly Poland offer the most opportunities in Europe.

The English-teaching scene is Germany is pretty robust and you can come on a tourist visa, get hired and have your visa extended as long as you have classes.

Generally, any non-English speaking country has some jobs for English teachers, but in areas where salaries tend to be low and there's little investment or emphasis in getting the population international business-ready, you'll find the pickings much slimmer...unless you're willing to volunteer. In which case, you'll find yourself much more in demand.

Your first stop is probably to log into all things English teaching at Dave's ESL Café (**www.daveseslcafe.com.**) More resources can be found in the Resources section.

Paul Schuble
English Teacher
Hyogo Prefecture, Japan

I'm an ALT (Assistant English Teacher) and member of the JET Programme working for the Hyogo Prefectural Board of Education. JET works as a kind of liaison that matches members with contracting organizations (usually schools or boards of education). Although you may request a specific placement during your application period, you are offered an assignment only once. This means that if you want to work in Tokyo but are offered a position in rural Hokkaido, you may not negotiate. I made three requests and was placed in an entirely different region of Japan from all three. Still, I've enjoyed my experience.

I work at two different schools. My main school is a public senior high school, and I work 8:30—4:30, Tuesday-Thursday. My main job is to prepare lessons and team teach with several different Japanese English teachers. I also play a large part in running the school's English Club and often support the English department staff by clarifying English grammar points when I can, marking papers, or whatever else they need me to do.

The other school I work at is a public part-time school, where I work Monday 1:00—9:00 and Friday 9:30—5:30. My job at this school is very similar to what I do at my main.

My salary is 3,600,000 yen ($45,000) per year. That's enough to live comfortably and send home about 50,000 yen ($625) a month to pay off my student loans, but haven't saved a whole lot of money during my time here.

I also studied in Japan twice before coming to live here. I highly recommend study abroad. For one thing, studying abroad is a good way to test the water and see if you like living in another country and how well you can cope with culture shock and all the challenges that come with being in a foreign country.

If you know where you want to live in the future, as I did in my case, studying abroad there is also a good way to do some recon, as it were, and to start learning the native language if it's not English.

Jonathan Lukacek
English Teacher
Osaka, Japan

I work as an English teacher, but am directly hired by a city's board of education. I teach in junior high schools mainly but occasionally teach a few hours in elementary schools too. Teaching is not my desired career choice but for now it supplies a stable income and gives me enough time to work on my passions. The most enjoyable aspect of the job is interacting with young people directly and getting so much inspiration from their young minds. The only advice I have for aspiring teachers is be yourself but be flexible. Use your personality and your humor as a way to interact with people; don't be just a "teacher," be an artist. Use this experience as a platform for improving your social skills in Japan.

I run a small blog about design, fashion, and vintage at www.bandanna-almanac.com. It is a side job but it keeps me making stuff and to get out and explore the country. The more things I find the more I discover about myself and what it is I am passionate about.

Leslie Reed
English Teacher
Incheon, South Korea

I had a fantastic, well-paying job at an art gallery in Los Angeles, but felt restless and creatively unsatisfied. I wanted to relocate and reinvent myself. So I started looking for work on Dave's ESL café. Combed through the posts and decided to apply with AEON to work in Japan. The interview process was funny. It consisted of two white businessmen showing videos and talking about life in Japan, their Japanese wives, and how great the sushi is. The second interview was to teach a mock lesson to your fellow interviewees, like an audition. They called me back for a third time and asked where I would prefer to work. I said near Tokyo, Osaka, Kyoto or other major city. My interviewer pulled out a map of Japan and pointed to the southernmost tip and said there was a little town there with a tiny population, nothing nearby and no other native English speakers or Western teachers. It is also isolated by a mountain range that's impassable in winter. He asked me how that sounded. I said it would be tough to be that remote, and I'd prefer to be somewhere more populated. I received a rejection letter the next week.

I started considering Korea. At first all the negative rants online turned me off, but the salary and glowing endorsements from Korean friends in L.A. convinced me. I found a good recruiter who was honest and realistic about what to expect. I chose to teach in private school versus public because of the higher salary, smaller classes, and guaranteed location. Public schools have the advantage of much more time off, but they pay less and you cannot choose your location.

After several months getting the paperwork together for the E2 visa, I hopped a plane to Incheon. FBI background check regulations add 12 weeks to the paperwork process, so it's important to allow enough time. The other option is to head over on a tourist visa, then make a visa run to Japan.

Representatives from the school were waiting at the airport to pick up the incoming teachers and drive us. Thought it was strange that they insisted on taking us by the school at 10 p.m., after we'd all been on 14-hour flights. To my great relief it was just to see the exterior and then they dropped us off at a nearby hotel. We wandered the streets just soaking up all the lights, trying random restaurants (no easy feat for a vegetarian who spoke no Korean) and laughing at all the misused English on signs.

Experienced teachers know that establishing discipline on the first day of class is crucial. I made the mistake of trying to make the first day fun, but it ended in total chaos. I was kicked, bitten, dong chimed (translates literally as poo stab), and had to call for reinforcement from the manager to handle 10 five-year-olds. I went back to my apartment, cried like a girl and thought about leaving. Then I got mad, toughened up and pulled it together. Now my kids snap to attention and line up on command. Once discipline is established, then you can have fun with the students. They will feel safer and happier knowing the rules and limits. They give me presents, draw pictures, and we have a great time together.

Turner Wright
English Teacher
Bugu, South Korea

I am an English teacher at a hagwon, which is a private English academy in Korea (as opposed to public schools). If you're trying to be an English teacher, work is not too difficult to find, especially in Korea. Anyone who's a citizen of an English-speaking country and the holder of a university degree can get a job teaching English in Asia. Period. When I applied to work for AEON in Japan, they held interviews in Austin, Texas. For Korea, I contacted the school directly after a search on Seoul Craigslist Jobs (accepted within 10 hours of applying).

Adam Lederer
Language Expert
Berlin, Germany

I'm an English language expert for a research institution. I work with scholars—from those working on their doctoral degrees to those working as full professors—on improving their writing. I help with grammar and style, plus I am familiar with how academic publishing works so I help people navigate the publication process. Much like my initial job in Germany, that I fell into, I sort of fell into this job. I bypassed most of the German bureaucracy and procedures that go with job hunting and I never actually wrote a German-style résumé.

Generally speaking, though, I would advocate that anybody moving abroad research what is appropriate for your target country. For example, if you want a job in Germany, the vast majority of people need to include information about their personal life in the résumé package that would be illegal in the United States (for example: date of birth and marital status), as well as a professional studio head shot.

The easiest job for Americans moving to Germany to find is probably teaching English—but from what I understand it's not a career choice for people hoping to live the high life. I've also heard that some of the language schools work their employees fairly hard and are not always forthcoming with payment. It'd probably be wise to investigate the school before agreeing to work for them.

Gary Lukatch
English Teacher, retired
Budapest, Hungary

For first seven years I taught English as a Foreign Language, which was my only source of income, and I supported myself well enough to live adequately and to travel extensively. Since 2007, I have been retired and living on Social Security and a small pension, but still enough so that I average about three to four times what the average Hungarian makes in a month.

When I first arrived, I did work on the black, and was paid in cash without need for receipts or other paperwork. As I got more teaching jobs on my own, companies for which I taught required official receipts, obtainable only when one is a legal resident with work permit, so I had to have official status. No bureaucratic troubles, as I used a local company to help me get my paperwork. I also set up my own company for billing purposes.

When I was teaching full-time, I taught 13 classes per week, each of 90-minute duration, which equaled 20 clock hours a week, or half-time. English teaching (I specialized in Business English) brought me a minimum of $1,500 per month when I taught full-time; since rent and utilities averaged around $400 per month, I did quite well, dining out often, partying (to excess) and traveling extensively.

I did have some savings, which I used as needed. I lived off my teaching income when I taught, and now I live off retirement income only (with a small nest egg as backup for emergencies). My retirement income allows me to live a good, if not extravagant, lifestyle, and I still travel extensively.

Vina Rathbone
English Teacher ➜ Employment Recruiter
Buenos Aires, Argentina

I work full-time as a recruiter for an American company that works remotely in Buenos Aires. We have a small office, and all of the employees are also expats. My work is all in English, and my clients are all in the USA. This makes me feel not so far from home, and it is the type of job I would enjoy doing back home.

Before that I taught English to business executives in local companies as a private teacher. I came here without a job or any connections, but have had great luck finding opportunities via Craigslist. That is how I found several English classes and my current recruiting position.

Working for Uncle Sam:
U.S. Government Jobs Overseas

How does a pay scale of $43,000–$56,000, plus medical, dental, relocation costs, 10 paid holidays and up to 45 vacation days per year sound? You'll travel to exotic destinations and meet heads of state, important business-men, and other dignitaries and, best of all, you can ignore parking tickets with impunity. The downside is, you won't have any say in where you go, who you see and what you do. But as you're the representative of the U.S. government and its policies, it's not a great escape for the politically disgruntled.

To join, there's a written exam, a background security check and a medical examination in addition to face-to-face interviews. You will be asked to choose one of the five career tracks: Management Affairs, Consular Affairs, Economic Affairs, Political Affairs, or Public Diplomacy.

Requirements vary, but generally you're expected to hold a four-year university degree. You don't have to speak a foreign language (they'll teach you), but applicants with Slavic, Middle Eastern, and Asian languages are actively sought. **www.careers.state.gov**

The kinder, gentler arm of the U.S. Foreign Service is USAID. A kind of career extension of the Peace Corps, it offers similar pay and benefits as other Foreign Service posts, but the focus is more humanitarian, at least that's what they say (**www.usaid.gov/careers**).

Also worth remembering is that U.S. military bases often hire civilian employees for administrative, IT, maintenance and other tasks. And with around 1,000 of them dotting the planet, if you have the skills, are located (or are willing to relocate) nearby, and don't mind carrying water for the empire, you can land a job there without ever having to worry about discharging a weapon. You get paid in dollars and as you'll be working on a little island of America, you don't really have to mess too much with the government bureaucracy of the host country.

You can find a list of U.S. military bases abroad at **Militarybases.com**. Most have websites where jobs are advertised. You can also find openings by visiting **www.federalgovernmentjobs.us** and typing "overseas" (or your desired country/area) in the search engine. These jobs are GS (i.e., government service), meaning you are essentially on the civil servant pay and benefit scale. Be aware that only some overseas positions are open to U.S. citizens.

Private U.S. Miliary Contractors

Civilian contractors means more than mercenaries. Military installations are like small cities, with restaurants, shopping centers, sports facilities and just about anything you'd find off-base. College campuses, even. The jobs—from flipping burgers to systems programming—are filled by civilians. The University or Phoenix (**www. phoenix.edu**) and the University of Maryland (**www.ed.umuc.edu**) hold contracts for "educational services for the U.S. military." They have openings in both academic and non-academic areas. At the burger-flipping end of the spectrum, try the job board at The Exchange (**odin.aafes.com**), the outfit which pretty much provides all the back-home consumer comforts (from retail stores to fast-food restaurants) to the men and women in uniform around the world.

Name Withheld by Request
USAID Worker
Location Withheld by Request

I'm with USAID as an Education Advisor in (undisclosed Third World location) putting such children's shows as *Sesame Street* on the air and setting up home-based schools around the country. My husband is with the State Department. We are with our two children and are having a great time. My husband and I met in the Peace Corps where we were both teaching English, and though we went back to the U.S. to start our family, we left again and have no intention of ever doing anything other than what we are doing. His job keeps us in a house, and I have the freedom to find any number of fantastic work experiences, either paid or not. It's an incredible luxury and I love it.

USAID is separate from State, but USAID direct-hire employees usually are in the embassy with State, for example, and share some services, depending on the post, like human resources, furniture pool, housing, etc. USAID is not a cabinet-level agency, so the head of USAID is called "the administrator" rather than a secretary, but he is roughly equivalent to the Secretary of State. So, you see, we are not the same agency, but very close cousins.

Ply Your Trade Overseas: Who Gets Hired and How

The overseas job market is like the domestic job market, only more difficult. The hiring protocols—from the way to behave in an interview to how to discuss salary—are different from those in America. Certainly, the higher up the education and experience ladder you are, the more likely you are to find work. Demand tends to be high for people with a background in information technology, engineering, oil and natural resource development, banking and finance, and health.

While there is a general disinclination to allow foreign workers to take jobs that could go to a locals, labor shortages do exist in some countries. Canada, Germany, Australia, New Zealand and many of the oil-producing countries of the Middle East all rely on expatriate labor. Poorer countries, as you might guess, pay poorer salaries. Matching your background to a nation's needs is a good place to start if you're looking to make a career-track move.

Internet searches will turn up hundreds of sites for overseas jobs, and only a fraction are legitimate or helpful. General job sites such as Monster.com have extensive overseas listings, but expect limited results. Craigslist.org has branches in almost every major city and their classified ads are geared toward English speakers. It's certainly worth a peek, though the want ads are a nest of tightwads. Needless to say, your chances are far better searching locally and applying locally. The job ads in the trade journals and websites of particular industries are also a better source, provided you have the skills and background in that industry.

The easiest way to get employed overseas, of course, is to be transferred there. Working for a multinational corporation is your best bet or, if not, at least a growing enterprise that opens branches in foreign countries.

College students or recent grads should also consider internships. From the U.S. State Department to the U.N. to hundreds of overseas organizations, corporations, and NGOs, the opportunities for an internship are endless. Some even pay or provide room and board. You can help design PlayStations for Sony in London or design floor space with an architectural firm in Stuttgart. Many of these internships lead to permanent positions overseas, whether as part of an established career track or as a result of networking and making contacts. Additional job resources can be found through websites listed in the Web Resources section at the end of the book.

Careers with the United Nations

Would you like to be one of the 24,000 people employed by the United Nations all over the world? Secretary General Ban Ki-moon pulls down $227,253 but entry-level jobs start at around $35K. There's added benefits for hazard assignments, and spouses. The flag and uniform are pretty snazzy, too. Competition is fierce. Junior professional candidates must have a B.A. degree and be less than 32 years old, and take the National Competitive Recruitment Examinations. Professionals need advanced degrees, and, depending on the position, must have anywhere from two to 15 years of field experience. To find out if there's a place for you inside the world's most bloated bureaucracy, visit the United Nations job vacancy board at **www. jobs.un.org.**

Marshall Creamer
Overseas Transfer
Hong Kong

I work for a global marketing research company as a project manager and it's my job to oversee our research studies. I was specifically brought to the Hong Kong office to assist my team with a new tracking study that is going to be conducted in eight European countries over the next year. In Chicago, I would work eight hours a day and if I worked more than that, at my grade level within the company, I was entitled to overtime pay. When I accepted the job in Hong Kong, I moved to a new company grade level, and am no longer entitled to overtime pay. The Hong Kong culture is very much focused on work and working long hours. Working abroad also has its perks. I was able to get a raise, a housing allowance (Hong Kong is the most expensive city in the world in terms of housing), and I will qualify for the U.S. tax exemption, so I will only be required to pay the local Hong Kong taxes.

Hailey McPherson, 20
Disneyland Performer
Hong Kong

I'm a dancer and vocalist at Disneyland. Right now we're rehearsing for the big 5th anniversary, "Celebration in the Air." I'm also training to be a Face Character. Those are the people who walk around the park as Disney characters—Belle, Cinderella, Sleeping Beauty. What I think is interesting is that it takes more training to be a Face Character than to learn all the songs and dances.

My boyfriend's friend's cousin got us in the Disney front door. We still had to audition for our separate roles. We mostly went for it as a way to escape our career ruts and because it's just totally different from anything anybody we know has ever done. Whenever I audition for anything there's really nothing to set me above the competition. Now I'll have Hong Kong Disneyland on my résumé. If nothing else, people will ask what that was like and it will give me extra time to make an impression.

My schedule varies and I work my butt off, but I actually got a vacation after just a couple of months on the job. You can't beat that.

Edna Vuong
Architect
Beijing, China

The job search process is pretty much the same for an architect no matter where you go. I basically just asked friends if their offices had Beijing branches. I also looked on the Internet. There are also a few international job sites specifically for architects and engineers. I also had friends who had worked in Beijing. Once I compiled a list, I put together a packet of work samples and a cover letter and emailed them to all the firms on my list. Employers are mainly concerned with how long you are willing to stay in China. There are a lot of expats working in architecture, but the turnover is pretty high. China attracts a lot of young architects who are still in school or fresh graduates who are unable to get jobs at home. So if you are willing to stay beyond a few months, you are more attractive to more firms.

There is a big range of firms in Beijing. There are a handful of corporate international offices, a smaller number of super famous international studios, internationally known Chinese offices, and then there are the local government offices. Kids in school usually intern in the famous Chinese offices, but they work insane hours with virtually no pay. The work is really interesting, but you burn out quickly. I worked in an international office that fell somewhere between a corporate office and a studio. I worked on anything from master planning of cities to mixed-use office/residential/malls. The scale of the work is huge and totally different from anything in the U.S. I also worked on more schematic competitions.

I have mixed feelings about my experience in China. I think it was a great experience professionally because I was exposed to a type of work that I would never have experienced at home. Things in the States are a bit limited by code and regulation. Clients are unwilling to do anything risky. In China, things are limitless and that teaches you to think a bit differently, but at the same time everything here is about getting the biggest bang for the smallest buck. No one cares about quality. If the government has a code that won't let you do something it is common to submit fake drawings to the government and simply change the design once it has been approved. It is also not uncommon to just pay someone off.

Ted Hung
Software Engineer
Melbourne Australia

Getting the job was easy...especially since people with experience in the games industry are in demand in Australia. The job market in Australia is generally quite good. Even during the Global Financial Crisis, there was still pretty low unemployment. On-the-job training and other sorts of career advancement opportunities are not as readily available in companies in Australia, and expenditures on employee retention are scarce. On the other hand, the workplace and work is significantly less stressful here (although it appears to be getting more and more stressful).

J.M.
Factory Manager
Pushkin, Russia

I run a factory that manufactures heavy trucks. My wife has an online business selling fabric and other quilting stuff. I came over to Russia already having arranged to do what I'm doing. I've met people who did it the other way around, and that also seems to be a viable option. On what I make, we've been able to take major vacations at least once a year (last year was driving to Paris so my kids could go to Disneyland); my wife has been able to fly back to the States at least twice a year. That last wasn't terribly expensive, though. Regular life in Russia is cheap enough that making even a couple grand a month is going to leave you able to sock away a goodly chunk of your income for whatever you want. We've long ago paid off any outstanding debts we had from the U.S.

Bill Agee
Marketing Professional
Copenhagen, Denmark

I came to Sweden with my job, working in marketing for an international retail company based across the sound from Copenhagen. My background was a liberal arts education followed by 10 years working on Madison Avenue in account management. By taking a position with a foreign-based company, you significantly increase your chances of getting a job abroad, since you can request a transfer or apply for a position with the company where they are based. This is usually looked very favorably upon, as experience in the home country allows the company to then transfer you back to your own home country knowing many of the business and social nuances of the company's leadership. You become a "local with credentials."

I have now been working in Sweden for 12 years, while living in Denmark. The Scandinavian way of working is consensual in most ways. Bosses don't decide, they lead. Co-workers don't follow, they provide direction. It may take longer to decide where you want to go, but once the direction is set, all are pushing very hard in the same direction and arrive together. You have to appreciate this way of working to succeed within a Scandinavian company.

If you don't have the opportunity to move here with a company, then look at your company's competitors in Denmark to see if there are any that are recruiting. Obviously your experience in the identical field will be appreciated whether you got it in the U.S or down the street. I also recommend using the specific skill/education that you have and applying for jobs in Denmark that are listed online in English. There are quite a few international companies based here or with large offices/labs, etc. here that recruit internationally. I know several people who got their jobs that way. The businesses that are big here are IT, pharma, retail, shipping, telecom, and service industries. Big names in Scandinavia are Maersk, H&M, Eriksson, Novo-Nordisk, Bang & Olufsen, IKEA, Statoil, ICI.

Correspondent/Stringer/Editor/Blogger

Do you dream about stringing for newspapers and magazines, selling overseas news and travel stories and financing your life abroad as a foreign correspondent? Well, wake up. If you're not already making your living in the writing game, your chances of achieving that lifestyle anytime soon by moving abroad are not very good. Even seasoned writers find themselves struggling unless they are part of some large news organization. Stringing gigs (freelancing stories to a newspaper's foreign bureau) are disappearing along with the publications that hire them. Only a handful of travel publications pay decently, and competition for those is stiff. Most local English language expat publications don't offer much in the way of compensation. And the Internet has driven down the rates for the written word to the point of being a virtual sweatshop.

Things are even less rosy for photographers. Often, reporters will be asked to provide photos and sometimes even video (for streaming on a website) along with their articles.

But if you have talent and perseverance, and have another avenue of income in the meantime, you can become one of a handful of lucky scribes in every foreign city who make the overseas dream a reality. Freelancing for publications in the U.S. also means you are eligible for a self-employment visa, which is far easier to obtain than a work permit. However, it can be quicker to land a job with an American newspaper and eventually request a transfer, in which case visa matters will be all but taken care of. Also, **mediabistro.com** and **journalismjobs.com** run ads from overseas news organizations looking for staff.

If you're lucky—which means being either young (recent graduate) and promising or a veteran with a hefty list of accomplishments—you can receive a fellowship to report from a foreign land, observe its culture and/or media operation, or even help set one up in a country where their media is not as well-developed. Even if the fellowships are short-term (some are as short as two weeks), you can still make contacts both in the host country and among the international journalism set that can prove invaluable toward sustaining a future life abroad. The Society of Professional Journalists (**www.spj.org**) keeps a pretty extensive list of available awards.

A more realistic and less competitive plan might be to seek out organizations and businesses that need English language copy edited. In many countries, you can simply sign up with an agency as an English-language proofreader and editor. For those willing to reach a level of bilingual fluency, there is a far less scrappy world beyond English teaching: translating. The pay tends to be far better and you usually work from home. Most translators sign up with an agency (or a few agencies), who take a percentage but ideally, keep you supplied with paying work without you having to go look for it. The sites, **www.proz.com** and **translatorscafe.com**, are good places to start to familiarize yourself with the translation world.

The more entrepreneurial expats will often start a local English-language publication where they are, particularly if one doesn't yet exist. These are usually online and require that the person also take care of the web development, advertising revenue and other aspects—or hire someone who will.

James Young
Mexico Correspondent for *Variety*
Mexico City, Mexico

While I had several journalist friends here when I first arrived to Mexico City in 2000, I never imagined I'd be writing copy for a living. After all, my bachelor's is in physics, and my first connections were largely through a painter friend with whom I had begun to seriously explore the art world.

Through hard work and sheer luck, I scored an assistant curatorship at a museum from 2001 to 2004, but I began to realize that as vibrant and fascinating a career in art is, most of the people doing it have major financial support from family, inheritance, etc.

I needed a Plan B, and when a journo friend took off to grad school, I jumped. They say that there are two ways to make it in print journalism: start at a little, local paper and work your way up to bigger and bigger ponds, or get a job at a foreign English-language paper sold to expats. Abroad, most editors for these expat papers are just looking for native speakers with good grammar and a willingness to learn.

When I found myself working for the first time in journalism as the Living editor for the *Miami Herald* International Edition's Mexico Edition in 2004, I definitely found myself in a sink-or-swim situation with a wicked learning curve.

By the time the edition folded in 2007, I had gained a certain mastery over my editorial skills and had begun one-offing the occasional article on film or art. As an editor, I was frequently required to write up blurbs and filler for pages; however, I found feature writing to be an entirely different beast—wild but ecstatically fun to tackle.

Had I been Stateside, I doubt I would have ever had the chance to grow into this profession the way I did. I'm currently the Mexican correspondent for film trade mag *Variety* and a handful of other "strings"—journo slang for regular writing gigs.

I love the fact that I live or die by my words. It's richly rewarding, giving me the creative outlet I've been searching for all my life, and it largely boils down to having had the huevos to break from my fairly comfy life in Austin, Texas, and face down the often mind-blowingly frustrating hurdles one faces living somewhere like Mexico City.

Gabriella Van Leuven
Editor, *China Daily*
Beijing, China

When I lived in Chicago I worked as an editor at McGraw-Hill (textbook publishing company). One of my co-workers there is married to a guy who is getting his Ph.D. in Chinese history. They moved to Beijing so he could work on his Chinese, and she has a lot of professors and academic big-timers in her family and knew someone who knew someone at the *China Daily* and got this job. I was traveling around the world and stopped in to visit them one cold February. Later, when they moved back to the U.S., my friend recommended me for the job. As I was kind of nomadic at the time, it was a perfect fit. I applied, was tested, tested again, tested again, interviewed, interviewed again and finally hired. I had experience working as a freelance writer and editor at McGraw-Hill (which being a "Fortune 500" has a lot of international cred). Also, most importantly, I knew someone.

As is usually the case with "Foreign Experts" in China (it's a government-given title that has to do with visa status) on top of my salary they offered to fly me out here and set me up in an apartment across the street from where I work.

Ande Wanderer
Freelance Writer/Photographer/Videographer/Webmaster
Buenos Aires, Argentina

I have two websites, Wander-Argentina.com and Wander-Argentina.org, and also do freelance writing, editing, photography and translation. I took advantage of the wonderful educational opportunities here, completing a low-cost, one-year course in documentary film at the film worker's union and now occasionally do short feature and travel videos. Thanks to my Latin American lifestyle, I had the time to figure out how to build a website and Wander-Argentina.com is now among the leading English websites about travel in Argentina. Recently I started a secondary website, Wander-Argentina.org, about work, study and volunteer here after watching the number of first-world immigrants to Argentina explode.

Nanny/Au Pair

If you're good with children, and can stand a background check, au pair/nanny is another way to go. It helps also to be female (this is one of the most reverse-discriminatory professions in the world), and young (usually under 27). Although people use "nanny" and "au pair" interchangeably, they aren't really synonymous. A nanny, strictly speaking, is someone whose career is taking care of a family's children on a live-in basis. There are even schools for nannies. Au pairs are usually of student (or slightly older) age and are brought over in the spirit of cultural exchange and generally work about 25 hours per week. Au pairs can expect room and board and a little pocket change, a simplified visa process (though generally limited to one or two years) and an opportunity to see family life abroad way up close. Nanny contracts can be more individualized and generally they get even more generous deals but there's not the same fast-track visa system, particularly if you are older than au pair age. Sites like Great Au Pair (**greataupair.com**) and Au Pair Search (**aupairsearch.com**) connect would-be nannies and au pairs with parents who need them, worldwide, while providing a variety of safeguards and protections for both au pair and the family. Also check out Interexchange (**www.interexchange.org**), which hooks up Americans with families overseas. Dozens more function within a specific country or region. You can find a searchable database at the International Au Pair Association website **www.iapa.org** (and more resources can also be found in the back of this book). Western Europe is prime nanny country, followed by Australia and New Zealand, but as the middle class expands in Asia and South America, expect more opportunities to open up in those regions as well.

Once you're in country and have references, you can begin to offer yourself as a nanny. Experienced nannies can work through a local or international agency (many of the latter are based in the U.K.), browse the classifieds, or, as is often the case, land a job through word of mouth. This usually requires permission to seek employment in that country, but the hiring of undocumented workers for childcare is not exactly an unheard-of practice just about anywhere in the world.

Noemi S.
Au Pair ➡ Web Producer/Information Architect, Student Jeweler, House-Sitter
Auckland, New Zealand

I was in NZ in 2004 traveling and did the research to figure out that my skills (IT and the like) are quite in demand. I decided to take a bit of hiatus from the advertising world and do something more chill, like nannying for a bit while I decided where in NZ I want to live when I finally decide to get back into an office. I signed up at greataupair.com and found a great family to come work for within three months. You pay $40, and then you can send messages to those you are interested in and they contact you with more questions if they are interested. The family that hired me set a time to chat via phone to see if we were a fit. After talking to three families in NZ, I decided on the family who had two little girls. Going from being a nine-to-fiver in the States to a nanny in rural NZ has taken some getting used to, but the freedom I've enjoyed was incomparable. After about seven months, I sent my CV to a job recruiter within the advertising industry in Auckland, and within a week, I had four companies interested in meeting me. Things take a bit longer here as what I do isn't a low-paid position. Companies seem to take their time in really examining who they are hiring, because firing or laying off isn't so easy here as it is in the States.

If you're in IT, medicine or any of the others in short occupations list, you should be a shoe-in. In the advertising world, no matter where in the world you are, you sometimes pull long hours but those times were definitely few and far between here in NZ compared to the U.S. As a web producer and information architect, I worked about 40 to 55 hours a week but the high end was rare as people really respect the work/life balance. The fact that we get 20 paid days leave says it all. And if I needed more, they were fine with me taking the time off unpaid and there was no risk in losing my job.

I left full-time work two years ago to fulfill a dream of becoming a studio jeweler. I am studying full-time but still dabble in my past occupation on a part-time basis for extra cash for clients both here and in the U.S. The government here is supportive of students and offers a weekly student allowance (for citizens or permanent residents) to full-time students who qualify. As much as I'm thankful for the allowance, I knew it wasn't enough to live on so the opportunity came up to house-sit a friend's house just as I was leaving full time work for school and then out of that I saw the need for house-sitters as New Zealanders are a travelling bunch. I made a website to publicize my services and have been living free as a house sitter for over two years and plan on continuing this for as long as it's viable.

Minding Your Own Business

If you've long since been priced out of the dream of opening your own restaurant, starting your own winery or managing your own seaside bed and breakfast in the United States, why not take your business elsewhere? Buy-in costs in Latin American or Southeast Asian countries are substantially lower than they would be at home—and because countries benefit from the investment (especially if you're going to employ locals) the visa bar is lowered considerably. Those with serious venture capital (in the six-figure range) will find welcome even in the more immigrant-aversive lands.

Most expats piggyback off the tourist trade—starting flat-rental services, guided tours, nightclubs, restaurants, and motels. Depending on how involved your business is, you'll likely need a local lawyer, and sorting through those in a foreign culture can be an adventure in itself. Laws (particularly if they involve food), business practices and cultural habits can differ dramatically from what you might be used to at home.

Marlane O'Neill
Owner, Narbonne Gites (guesthouse)
Narbonne, France

We have a chambre d'hote, Narbonne Gites, in the middle of the city. Sometimes we work every day, about two-three hours a day, some weeks we don't work at all.

In the chambre d'hote we do the usual cleaning and prepare breakfast too that is taken in our main dining room. We guide our guests to what they need or want in Narbonne, we market the property, take reservations.

We were living off savings before the chambre d'hote got off the ground and it looks like this year it will support us completely. The Americans and English we know all have their own businesses. One does dog breeding, others have gites (guesthouses) or home construction companies. One I know is a writer/astrologer and very successful!

Frank
Owner/Manager, Hotel Reventazon & the Hilltop Eco-Sanctuary
Orosi, Costa Rica

I own a hotel, a restaurant and a farm. When I started here, I was running a business taking people on four-wheel quad tours. In 2005, I bought a seven-bedroom hotel and a restaurant next door with a liquor license. I bought the farm at the end of 2008.

When I had employees, I used to market the hotel. For the past year, I just have volunteers.

The way they have it structured is basically, after employees work for you for about two or three years, it doesn't matter when an employee quits or gets fired. You're responsible for their unemployment. So when you take somebody on and you've had them for 90 days, you are responsible for paying their unemployment when they leave. You will pay whether they quit or get fired, but there's a difference in how much you have to pay them. If they've worked for you for a couple of years and you had to fire them, that's the worst-case scenario for an employer. They'll make more money if you fire them than if they actually show up to work. So you have employees that want to get fired and you have employers who will pay them to do nothing just because it costs more to get rid of them.

It can be a nasty situation. Here you're guilty until proven innocent. If any employee makes an accusation, they don't have to have any proof, and the government goes after the rich gringo and they are either going to have to prove their innocence or they're going to have to pay fines.

So I don't have any employees. I'm the only employee here. Anything else I have is either rented out or is run by a volunteer. Foreigners can't make money working here unless they have ticos working for them, but they can volunteer. And they can barter. They can trade labor for housing and food. My accountant deals with the other paperwork. I keep things really streamlined. The amounts are really small. I mean, my property tax for a hotel, restaurant and a house is probably less than $200 a year.

The whole time I had my farm, I haven't paid property taxes but my lawyer says it's not a big deal. It'll probably be only another $20–$30 a year.

I run a cash business. I keep a roof over my head, gas in my truck. I survive. When I had employees, I used to market the hotel, but now that it's all volunteers, I just keep things to a minimum. The people that stay here are people who just show up and they need a place to stay. When I had employees, I had a website and we were full a lot of the time, but now my focus is on the farm.

It's not like my farm is going to make a lot of money. Once I'm ready, I'm just going to live out on the farm and rent out the hotel. I don't even want to deal with that anymore.

I know I can have the government come out to my land and they'll actually plant trees and stuff, but then they'll be out there all the time monitoring things and with the kind of structures that I want to make, well, I don't need people poking around. I want to experiment and make a lot of cool structures and not have to ask permission for everything I do.

I want to get a community together but not some kind of community where we're selling land or something. I want it to be more of a barter community where money is not really an issue. I don't want to charge anybody rent. I just want to get away from everybody else's thinking and just create my own reality.

James Lindzey
Co-owner, Paradise Realty (also runs ColombiaVisas.com)
Medellín, Columbia

I have been able to maintain a very nice lifestyle, though I am working about 60–70 hours a week. Hopefully this will decrease with time. I have had my real estate business for about three years now, and the visa business for about five years. I consider myself lucky enough to have had a remote network administration job from the States which has provided the foundation and time needed to get started here. My wife manages the businesses with me, and now she has a job that earns her much more than basic salary.

Some of the biggest challenges to me have been learning how to stay up with: 1) changing laws affecting businesses in a developing country; 2) Colombian bookkeeping; 3) when and how to pay taxes correctly; 4) keeping records of international money transfers and rules therein because after all this is Colombia; and 5) cultural work habits of Colombians compared to Americans.

Minimum-wage employees are plentiful, just mediocre. Minimum wage, $300 a month, plus benefits, for a total of around 850,000 pesos, or around $450. Worker protection rights are tight, so don't try to get around that if you don't have a contract with the employee, or you may get dragged into court.

Don't expect the same returns on business in a developing country that you would get in another place. Workers can be cheap but your quality of work might not be what you expect. You get what you pay for, and with high poverty you always have to watch employees carefully for petty items. Trust is of utmost importance with our workers. Colombia along with other places has what I like to refer to as micro-economies. Lower commissions and lower prices for many service-oriented industries produce lower income, so you may have lower margins to work with.

Local authorities will come by and check your papers, visas, accounting, permits, taxes, etc, and if you're up to par on all this then you're OK, otherwise be ready to pay a $1,500 USD bribe or more to a lawyer to get you out of the mess. You should only operate storefront operations in certain zones or you will have to pay vacunas ("vaccinations," i.e. bribes).

I also started ColombiaVisas.com to share information and experiences with other expats and Colombians, as well. Over the years, ColombiaVisas.com evolved into a full-time business, handling a couple hundred visas a year, relocation services, and also helping expats set up about 50 companies a year in Medellín and Bogotá. I believe that running my businesses from the Internet has saved me from the exposure my friends have had with authorities.

Sharon Hiebing
**Owner, Wealth Ships (online relocation consulting service)
and Red Roof Property Management
San Ignacio Town, Belize**

Currently, I run two businesses in Belize. The first is an internet-based business called Wealth Ships, an expat relocation consulting service that helps others properly go through the three phases of relocation—research, preparation, and consulting. I began this business immediately upon arriving in Belize because so many people kept emailing me for help with their upcoming relocation or ongoing research process. Eventually I'd like to expand the service to countries other than Belize, via franchising opportunities. I've written one e-book in my "Follow Your Dream Compass" series on the Research phase, and plan on writing books on the remaining two phases soon.

The second business is more of a brick-and-mortar business called Red Roof Property Management. We help landlords with leasing and management of rental properties, absentee owners with caretaking and house sitting, and other miscellaneous services like utility setup or tenant locator services.

When I first moved to Belize, I initially moved to a part of the country that within three months I realized was not right for me. So I moved to a district in the Western part of the country called Cayo, in a town named San Ignacio. Upon moving there, I found it almost impossible to find a rental home. Once I did, I was appalled at the lack of formality in the process and realized there was probably a lot of landlords getting swindled due to that fact.

Since only a few realtors dabbled in property management (and only because they felt like they had to, not because they wanted to), I decided to open a company that focused exclusively on property management.

I found starting a business in Belize was actually quite simple. First, I went to the Town and/or Village board and applied for a Trade License, which I must renew annually. Next, I traveled to the capital and visited the Belize Companies and Corporate Affairs Registry, where I protected my business name by registering it. And that's it!

If someone wants to secure their business from liabilities and creditors, they can consult with a Belizean attorney to set up a partnership, LLC, or corporation, but that certainly is not a requirement in the beginning. Every year as a business owner, you must file income tax returns, and if you sell goods, every month you must file sales tax returns for any sales over $6250 bze ($3125 USD). If you have employees, you must pay a social security tax, but that is a relatively simple and straightforward venture as well from what I understand, although at this time, we have no employees.

After three months of running Red Roof Property Management, we are doing incredibly well. One of our challenges has been educating the Belizean public as to what it is we do, but they are learning. And the other realtors have welcomed us with open arms.

David Morrill
Partner, Real Estate Company/Freelance Writer/Expat Consultant
Cuenca, Ecuador

Initially, my plan was to export ceramic products from Ecuador to the U.S. Cuenca is known for the high quality of its crafts, especially handmade ceramics. Like a lot of expats considering starting a business I quickly discovered that I faced a huge learning curve. I had no experience either in exporting or retail and, in Ecuador, I faced the challenge of acclimating to the culture.

When I complained to the lady who was helping me make business contacts—the same lady who sold me an apartment when I first came to the country—she suggested that I help her sell real estate to gringos, a market she was just getting into. I did, and over several months realized I could make a much better living helping her than trying to get my export biz off the ground.

The real estate partnership has lasted for six years and is still going strong. So long as you are not taking jobs from Ecuadorians, foreign residents are allowed to have businesses here. There is the usual government red tape associated with operating a business but it's not really overbearing. Business tax rates are a little lower than in the U.S.

Combining a gringo and a local seems to be the best business model in Ecuador, especially if the business is aimed at expats and foreign tourists. I don't actually sell real estate but I talk and write to clients about living in Ecuador, adjustment issues, legal matters, immigration—stuff I understand since not only had I been a newbie asking the very same questions a few years ago, but I was also in the publishing and advertising/PR business in Miami, San Francisco and Tallahassee, Florida.

Related to real estate, I also give presentations at conferences and seminars for gringos considering moving offshore.

Unrelated to real estate, I wrote "Ecuador: The Owner's Manual" for International Living. I am also the Cuenca editor for the *Miami Herald* International Edition and pick up occasional "retranslation" work, rewriting tourist and business English written or translated by Ecuadorians for English-speaking foreigners. I´m not smart enough to do real translation work.

Cara Smiley
Organic Certification Consultant and Inspector
Oaxaca, Mexico

From 2002 to 2004, I worked part-time for an American organic certification agency and represented their company in Mexico. I simultaneously worked as a consultant to a certified organic processing facility located in Northern Mexico, traveling four to six times a year to visit the operations. In 2004, I struck out on my own and created my own business: Integrated Organic Services, Inc. which is incorporated in the USA. I am an employee of my company.

I contract my services as a consultant, inspector, and reviewer to companies in the organic industry, both in Latin America and the USA. Although I: 1) am contracted by U.S. organic certification agencies to perform on-site inspections in Mexico and Latin America, 2) am contracted by U.S. organic certification agencies to perform desk audits of certified organic operations and 3) am contracted by Mexican companies to perform consulting work, for the sake of simplicity, I ONLY report the first to Immigration.

The Mexican companies that contract my consulting services require Mexican invoices. Because my company is not incorporated in Mexico and does not pay taxes in Mexico, it cannot generate Mexican invoices. As such, my husband, who owns his own company, which does pay taxes in Mexico, bills all of my Mexican clients. He pays Mexican taxes on that income.

Laura
Independent Tour Guide
Rome, Italy

My skills as a filmmaker were all but useless here, so, after two years, all my savings gone, way into credit card debt (which I had never had in the States), I realized I needed to do something else. A lot of Americans, Canadians and Brits end up teaching English and when I realized I couldn't pay the rent, I did the same. But it wasn't enough.

I met a guy who ran one of the best tour companies in Rome. I had never considered tour guide as a job previously, but he hired me on a freelance basis. In the next few months, I picked up another freelance guide gig, learning more itineraries, then another and another.

In the beginning, I was mostly working for other people (who had already established business and websites) and had a few personal contacts inquiring for tours, but over the years, the balance gradually shifted. After two and a half years, I put up my own website and now I rarely do tours for other people, and I'm often so busy I have other people working for me.

It's funny because I recall when I first moved here, my dad grumbled to my mom, "When is she gonna stop going to museums and archaeological sites and look for a damn job?" And now going to museums and reading books and visiting archaeological sites is my job.

Unfortunately it is becoming more and more difficult for a non-citizen to be a tour guide...so if you aren't Italian or have a shot at picking up an E.U. passport, you should at least have a degree in a subject like art history, archaeology or something related, in which case you might get a license via something called the Bersani law. You have to have your transcripts translated into Italian and then the government decides if you qualify. This is how most foreigners manage it now although a lot of them still do it illegally also.

And remember, there's 3000 years of history to cover here, so my advice would be to start reading and studying.

Independent Contractors/Internet Commuters

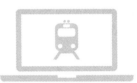 Until recently, independent contractor usually meant freelance writers and photographers and people who gave private lessons—language, yoga, etc. Thanks to the Internet, armies of workers have become geographically independent of where their labor is consumed. In plain English, they can work anywhere they can get a (usually hi-speed) connection. Transcribers, graphic designers, technical writers and a host of other digital-based careers are moving into the virtual world. Websites such as **contractjobs.com** cater to this community, matching contract workers to contract jobs anywhere on the planet, while paydays get handled by PayPal. The rise of Internet-based telephones, such as Skype and Vonage and myriad of other smaller companies allow free or low-priced international calling and other features and free videoconferencing, as well. File transfer services such as DropBox (**www.dropbox.com**) allow you to create virtual workgroups and send and receive larger files than most email servers will allow. Many providers can rent you a U.S. area code and phone number (say 212, in New York) so you can maintain a U.S. profile, but the phone will actually ring at your computer in Colombia.

Cap'n Mike
Telecommuter
Somewhere in the Caribbean
I was living in Santa Cruz, CA and working in Silicon Valley (Sunnyvale). I would commute every day over Highway 17, a notorious death alley where we drove too fast over twisting mountain passes.

On an October afternoon in 1989 (I think), the Loma Prieta (World Series) earthquake destroyed the highway. It would be closed for at least SIX MONTHS. Since I had my own development lab on my property, and the phone lines were back up in two weeks, I started telecommuting. This was enormously successful, and when the highway was reopened, we saw no reason for me to resume physically commuting.

Meanwhile, my wife and I split up (amicably). She hates boats as much as I love 'em, so since she was the boss, boats were out of my life during the marriage. With her out of the way (so to speak) my boating life resumed.

At a drunken sojourn at a conference in Newport Beach, CA, I gazed out at all the pretty sailboats and said "ya know, I could move aboard a boat and the boss would never know." This was in '96, I think. By 1999 I had sold my house (at an obscene profit) and bought *Island Flyer*, my Lagoon 37 catamaran, in West Palm Beach Florida. I left the States on April Fools Day, 2000.

I've been telecommuting ever since. At first with dinghy trips to Internet cafés, then via my Globalstar satellite phone (small data files), and now mostly through Wi-Fi services which are found on most islands. I have a booster kit to increase my range.

My payment is wired to an account in California. I do enjoy a tax break because my workplace (the boat) is located outside the U.S.

David Herrick
Digital Ilustrator
Phuket, Thailand

I'm a freelance digital illustrator. I send and receive correspondence with clients via email, and deliver my digital files as attachments. I don't have clients within Thailand. My customer base is all Stateside so I don't have a conflict with Thai laws, taxes or work permits. I make a modest living by American standards, but my money goes a lot further here in Thailand.

Alessandra
Freelance Graphic Designer
Porto, Portugal

I have met many Americans living abroad that receive financial support from spouses or family, but I've supported myself. I work as a freelance graphic designer for companies based in the U.S., which I have done since 2006. This has allowed me to travel, work from the road, and live in any location with an Internet connection.

While I am still freelancing remotely, I mostly work at home in a space I've set up for myself. I work as a graphic designer for web and mobile applications, so all of the work can be done by sending files and communication over the Internet. I use Skype and Internet conferencing to present designs and have design reviews with the clients. I have a Wi-Fi connection here, and I keep an Internet key as a back-up in case the Wi-Fi connection goes down or I need to work on the road. I use Skype and online chat to keep in touch with my clients, which right now are two companies based in New York City. Since I worked for them while I lived in NYC, they know me well.

I work on a project basis, which means that work is inconsistent. There are times during the year when I work full-time and other periods where I am not on an active project. Being flexible is essential to being a freelancer. I always meet my deadlines, do work within the set budget, and make sure I put in extra time if needed to make sure the client is happy with the work. For me, missing a deadline or a phone call is not an option.

Odd Jobs and Working Off the Books

 A hallowed tradition. Pubs, restaurants, and night-clubs are the popular picks among the permitless masses. Laws are sometimes more lax in tourist-related businesses and at any given moment, one of them needs a bartender, waitress, dishwasher, or chambermaid. For those willing to roll up their sleeves, agriculture is another industry that runs on an immigrant labor pool.

Name Withheld By Request
Florence, Italy
It is a breeze to work illegally in Italy if you are willing to work for cheap. You can nanny, wait tables, work in outdoor markets, be a model for art schools, clean houses, tutor English or whatever anyone will pay cash for. I did that for years.

Part II
For Your Consideration:
The Rest of the World

Is It Any Better There?
Choosing the Country That's Right For You

Asking "what's the best country?" is a lot like asking whom you should marry. It all depends on what you like…and can live with. There are many variables that will influence your decision, beyond the ease (or difficulty) of entry and immigration requirements already discussed. Employment could be at the top of your list of considerations and lack of same could be a dealbreaker regardless of how much you love the place. Quality of life can mean different things to different people. Some prefer sandy beaches; others, gritty cities. Many consider a certain standard of roads, schools, and Internet connectivity to be crucial. Others might place a high value on the availability of familiar foods and products. Or you may be seeking to get as far away from all that as possible. Obviously, in many areas, from climate to culture, you might not necessarily be choosing a country so much as choosing a specific place—or type of place, anyway.

While few people would even go somewhere on vacation without getting an idea of what kind of climate to expect (if only to know what to pack), there are many who would move abroad without taking into consideration a constellation of other aspects that might impact their quality of life to an equal if not greater extent. You're probably going to have to make some kind of prioritization and no doubt have to make sacrifices, as well. So while there are many nuances that make it impossible to completely "know before you go," these are some things you might want to look into, certainly before you commit.

The following pages can offer only the slightest taste of the nearly infinite quantity and variety of information and data out there. Visiting the sites mentioned here will supply you with more expanded and detailed information. And if those don't fully satisfy your insatiable hunger for knowledge, you'll find a veritable buffet in the Resources section at the back of the book.

Does Anyone Speak English?
For Those Who'll Never Learn

If you don't or can't make the effort to learn the local language, you limit your zone of comfort to large urban centers, tourist traps, and expat enclaves. You

ENGLISH SPOKEN HERE

risk alienation because you're constantly surrounded by conversation that you can't understand. You may need to run the letter from your gas company through Google Translate or constantly get friends, neighbors and often strangers to explain even the most mundane communication.

That is, of course, unless you happen to find yourself in one of these English-speaking nations:

Antigua	Gambia	Papua New Guinea
Australia	Ghana	Philippines
The Bahamas	Gibraltar	Seychelles
Bangladesh	India	Sierra Leone
Barbados	Ireland	South Africa
Belize	Jamaica	Sri Lanka
Bermuda	Kenya	Swaziland
Botswana	Lesotho	Tanzania
Brunei	Liberia	Trinidad and Tobago
Cameroon	Malawi	Uganda
Canada	Malta	United Kingdom
Cayman Islands	Mauritius	Zambia
Dominica	New Zealand	Zimbabwe
Fiji	Nigeria	

English is also so widely spoken in Holland, Belgium, Germany, Switzerland, Austria, Scandinavia (and to a lesser extent, Japan and South Korea), that you could probably survive well enough without language skills. Though pop culture, mass tourism (and the need to sell something to them) and the Internet all contribute to greater English penetration around the world (and the younger the person you encounter is, the more likely it would be that he or she speaks English), your degree of comfort deteriorates, especially as you move further from the developed world. Even if you've landed in an exotic corner of the linguisticstan, there's little excuse not to make an effort to learn the language of your adopted home. From local tutors, language meetups, to schools and multimedia home courses—not to mention McLanguage schools like Berlitz —you should find something that can suit your learning time and schedule. If you can, of course, start your education before you leave.

Edna Vuong
Beijing, China

You should probably know some Mandarin to live here. You don't have to know much to get by. I grew up speaking Cantonese and I took some Mandarin courses in university so I can get by pretty easily. I also know expats who just know numbers and street names and have no trouble. Chinese classes are also widely available and inexpensive.

Marlane O'Neill
Narbonne, France

I speak French, not perfectly and with an accent. My husband is learning to speak, he really doesn't speak yet. People are very nice to him about his English; they really seem to want to learn English! However not many people speak English in Narbonne as compared to, say, Paris.

So you really need to have some French. Most of the Americans and English people we know do speak at least some French, and many are fluent.

Gary Lukatch
Budapest, Hungary

Americans stay mostly within their small groups and rarely attempt to learn more than a few words of Hungarian. There is a large expat community here, from all over the world, who use English as a common language, plus a good-size British contingent. And, of course, Hungarians who speak English and want to keep improving their skills. Generally, it's pretty easy these days to get by, as more people here speak at least some English than did 10 years ago.

Vina Rathbone
Buenos Aires, Argentina

It would be fairly difficult to get by speaking only English, but indubitably manageable to a patient and creative communicator. There are many affordable Spanish classes. In general the population is patient and friendly with a non-native speaker, but many of them have difficulty with accents.

I speak the corrupted Castilian Rioplatense Spanish, which is unique only to Buenos Aires. It is essentially Spanish spoken with an Italian rhythm with a German accent and with the haughtiness of French.

Buenos Aires is a city of immigrants, mostly Europeans from the second World War, and this is very much inflected in the local language. I think it is much more fun and dynamic to speak than general Spanish. Many people here also speak Italian. The local slang is called *lunfardo*, which is somewhat derived from Italian, and worth picking up.

Paul Schuble
Hyogo Prefecture, Japan
While it definitely makes life a lot easier to be able to speak and read the local language, I've known people who have come here with zero knowledge of Japanese, made little or no effort to learn, and gotten by just fine. Fortunately for them, most Japanese do understand some degree of English and many people here are very accommodating.

Tyler Watts
Ho Chi Minh City (Saigon), Vietnam
If you live in Saigon or Hanoi then you can get by quite easily without Vietnamese (particularly in certain downtown areas). Even in areas with large tourist flow there is sufficient English ability among local Vietnamese (Hue, Nha Trang, Dalat, Can Tho). As English is the required foreign language among students, even as low as first grade in the cities.

Scott
Riyadh, Saudi Arabia
It is easy to get by on just English. Most here know very basic greetings or common shopping words. With the huge mix of nationalities in KSA, most people you will encounter will speak English. It is greatly appreciated, however, when a Westerner speaks (or makes the attempt to speak) Arabic.

Paul Tenney
Singapore
Singapore is a former British colony and everyone here speaks English. The majority of the population is Chinese by descent and speaks Mandarin as their first language, but everyone is required to speak English in school growing up. The accents might seem a little funny to you at first and your accent might seem a little funny to everyone else, but there are no real language issues here.

Art F.
Sihanoukville, Cambodia

Many people that deal with expats and tourists speak at least some English. Many others speak French, a holdover from colonial days. My girlfriend speaks Khmer and this helps a lot.

Tinuola
Prague, Czech Republic

There are expats who have lived here for almost a decade and longer who speak very little Czech and they've survived. Of course, this is the case in Prague, not the rest of the country. In fact, the best way to quickly pick up the Czech language is to live outside of Prague. Without being fluent in Czech, making friends with the locals is a challenge. Many of my friends are other English-speaking expats, and some Czechs who are fluent in English.

Bryn Martin
Lausanne, Switzerland

Life for an American in Lausanne can be quite alienating. The language and social barrier is very difficult. Most Francophones definitely don't react like a Spanish-speaking person when you butcher their language. The Swiss Romande are also not renowned for their openness. I hear there is a saying about Switzerland that goes something along the lines of "The first time you enter a friend's house is when you carry their casket out." However, there are a lot of expats that you can get chummy with while they are around! Social life with expats can be great. If you learn French, social life can be really super.

The Shock Doctrine: A Word About Culture

If you want to leave America but would rather everything else besides the government look and act pretty much the same, you'd head for:

Canada, Australia and New Zealand

Being fully anglicized former British colonies (whose early settlers have to a greater or less extent, er, displaced the native population), you'll find the most similarities here—and as a result, they tend to be popular choices. Though you couldn't call it a carbon copy, Canada offers proximity along with familiarity—same architecture, same products, even the same electrical outlets, and only the barest hint of an accent/dialect in the conversation around you. You could almost forget you're in another country—unless you want to visit a doctor or buy a handgun, that is. European society, particularly Western Europe and more so U.K. and Ireland (obviously), would still be comprehensible to most Americans. After that, things generally feel more alien (depending on your own background, of course). There's probably no way to avoid culture shock completely, nor are there many quick and easy cures. Culture pervades everything, from the way people greet each other to how they do business to how they find lifemates or bedmates. Patience, flexibility and a sincere effort to get to know and understand your neighbors, however, certainly couldn't hurt. As for how the local culture might mesh with your overall tastes and preferences, you're encouraged to read as much as you can about the places you are considering and ideally schedule an initial exploratory visit so you can feel it out for yourself.

How Much Does It Cost? Bargain vs. Boutique

The young and single often fan out to where the rent is still cheap, but life is not quite so slow. However, urban areas are generally pricier than anywhere else. Conversely, fixed-income pensioners might want a place in the sun without paying resort prices. But be aware: the almighty dollar ain't buying what it used to buy. Its plummeting value is probably the biggest hurdle and hassle that anyone will face when contemplating a move abroad (that, and the ever-expanding no-fly list, that is). That's not to say that you can't finance a lifestyle on a fraction of what it would cost in the U.S., but the differences aren't what they used to be. Cheap, that is to say, has become a lot more relative. And unless you have some magic strategy to knock some fiscal sense into the Fed and Federal Reserve, you're going to have to resign yourself to that particular aspect being out of your control.

That said, if it's bargains you're after, your search would tend to be south, toward the countries of Latin America. Southeast Asia also beckons along with India. The eastern part of Europe (old Soviet Bloc countries) are generally cheaper than the Western European ones, offering affordable opportunities for sophisticated or bohemian urban living. China's cheap unless you want to live in a major city (i.e., any of the ones you've actually heard of) in which case you'd probably have saved money staying home. Ditto, Russia. Tourist resorts are also more expensive than a plot in the middle of nowhere and often more than in a major city. Thanks to the high-paid labor attracted by their oil boom, the disparity between the cost of living in Luanda, Angola's capital, vs. the rest of the country is mind-boggling.

The prices one might pay for food, rent and transportation don't necessarily align with the relative price of consumer electronics and brand-name clothing so a lot depends on your lifestyle as well. Organizations such as Mercer keep track of costs of living, generally aimed at the transfer and per diem set and provide a lot of helpful data free on their website **www.mercer.com**. Numbeo (**www.numbeo.com**) operates a wiki-style cost-of-living database—everything from the rent cost of a three-bedroom flat in Chiang Mai to a loaf of bread in Prague—and compiles averages and rankings of consumer price, rent price and grocery price by city and country and even lets you compare a variety of costs between two cities/areas. Generally, you can look at a population's average income (how "rich" they are) and get an idea of whether the country is cheap or expensive to live in. These stats are as close as your local wikipedia (**www.wikipedia.org**) or to see the numbers crunched and weighted every which way, have a look at the IMF's (**www.imf.org**) World Economic Outlook database.

Income Per Capita: Richest Countries

Country	Income	Country	Income
Luxembourg	$108,831.70	Austria	$44,986.58
Norway	$84,443.63	Finland	$44,488.64
Qatar	$76,167.85	Singapore	$43,116.69
Switzerland	$67,246.00	Japan	$42,820.39
United Arab Emirates	$59,716.85	Belgium	$42,630.11
Denmark	$56,147.14	France	$41,018.60
Australia	$55,589.55	Germany	$40,631.24
Sweden	$48,874.61	Iceland	$39,025.70
United States	$47,283.63	Kuwait	$36,412.00
Netherlands	$47,172.14	United Kingdom	$36,119.85
Canada	$46,214.91	Italy	$34,058.72
Ireland	$45,688.76	New Zealand	$32,145.23

Source: International Monetary Fund: World Economic Outlook Database, April 2011 www.imf.org

Income Per Capita: Poorest Countries

Haiti	$672.92	Mozambique	$458.33
Bangladesh	$637.91	Guinea	$448.49
Gambia	$616.56	Central African Republic	$435.98
Burkina Faso	$597.53	Eritrea	$397.72
Zimbabwe	$594.33	Madagascar	$391.82
Timor-Leste	$588.43	Niger	$381.16
Rwanda	$562.31	Ethiopia	$350.46
Nepal	$561.87	Sierra Leone	$325.76
Tanzania	$548.28	Malawi	$321.94
Afghanistan	$517.18	Liberia	$226.05
Guinea-Bissau	$508.66	Dem. Republic of Congo	$186.28
Uganda	$500.65	Burundi	$180.07
Togo	$458.79		

Source: International Monetary Fund: World Economic Outlook Database, April 2011 www.imf.org

Most Expensive Cities

1 Luanda, Angola
2 Tokyo, Japan
3 Ndjamena, Chad
4 Moscow, Russia
5 Geneva, Switzerland
6 Osaka, Japan
7 Libreville, Gabon
8 Zurich, Switzerland
8 Hong Kong
10 Copenhagen, Denmark
11 Singapore, Singapore
11 Oslo, Norway
13 Victoria, Seychelles
14 Seoul, South Korea
15 Milan, Italy
16 Beijing, China
17 London, U.K.
17 Paris, France
19 Tel Aviv, Israel

Least Expensive Cities

1 Karachi, Pakistan
2 Harare, Zimbabwe
3 Islamabad, Pakistan
4 La Paz, Bolivia
5 Ashkhabad, Turkmenistan
6 Bishkek, Kyrgyzstan
7 Addis Ababa, Ethiopia
8 Calcutta, India
9 Tegucigalpa, Honduras
10 Windhoek, Namibia
11 Asunción, Paraguay
12 Gaborone, Botswana
13 Tashkent, Uzbekistan
14 San Salvador, El Salvador
15 Tirana, Albania
16 Tunis, Tunisia
17 Skopje, Macedonia
18 Sarajevo, Bosnia-Herzegovina
19 Chennai, India

Source: Mercer

Bryn Martin
Lausanne, Switzerland

When we first moved to Switzerland I thought we were not going to make it. There were so many unexpected expenses, such as the three-month rent deposit required to get an apartment and high costs for getting living permits etc.! I would not recommend moving to Switzerland as a small family without at least $15,000 in the bank and a job secured that will start paying immediately after you arrive. After being in Switzerland for six months things will get better if you cook at home and are frugal. Of course, this picture can look much different if you are a two-income household or have a higher-tier income.

David Morrill
Cuenca, Ecuador

In general, where I live, expats live on 25% to 30% what they did in the U.S. An average couple can live well on $1,200 to $1,500 a month. I know some expats who get by on $500 to $700 but it's a spartan existence.

Liberty and Justice For All?
Freedom, Democracy And Good Governance

There are some truly badass regimes out there. Sure, their power may be puny compared to the United States, but they more than compensate by inflicting a level of oppression on their citizens that may leave you feeling fondly nostalgic for your home country's Department of Homeland Security. That said, in many countries where citizens live under unenlightened rule, particularly in the Third World, it's still possible to live out your days and barely be aware that the government even exists. Of course you will need to keep a low profile and avoid getting involved in politics, labor unions, and things like that.

The mainstream window into the dark heart of state oppression is the watchdog organization Freedom House (**www.freedomhouse.org.**) They issue a comprehensive report each year that determines whether the country ranks as "free," "partly free" and "not free" in more or less the sense that a person who grew up in a Western-style democracy would conceive of the word. The organization and the related "democracy-promoting" efforts of the National Endowment for Democracy are hardly above suspicion that they aren't busy rigging the political arenas they purport to monitor. Amnesty International (www.amnesty.org) does more case history and raw number tracking of human rights abuses across the globe. If you really want to know how badly a given government could turn on its people, you're best investigating reports by human rights groups that are most involved in the country you have in mind. Human Rights Watch (www.hrw.org) publishes an annual report covering human rights conditions in 90 countries worldwide. Searching human rights + INSERT COUNTRY on Twitter will provide you with up to-the-minute tweets.

A related issue is whether you are moving to a nation of laws or a hotbed of criminals in politicians' clothing. Do you bribe your way out of legal trouble or hire a lawyer? Ineffectual governments tend to preside over countries with frequent power outages, strikes, food and fuel shortages, currency crises, social unrest, and any number of unwelcome disruptions.

One omnibus monitoring group of state corruption is Transparency International (www.transparency.org). Your friends at the World Bank also monitor the quality of government in countries around the world as part of what they straight-facedly call their "poverty alleviation mission," and generously share their findings on their website www.worldbank.org. As for who monitors the World Bank, well, nobody's really sure.

Least Corrupt Countries

1	Denmark	9.3		11	Iceland	8.5
1	New Zealand	9.3		11	Luxembourg	8.5
1	Singapore	9.3		13	Hong Kong	8.4
4	Finland	9.2		14	Ireland	8.0
4	Sweden	9.2		15	Austria	7.9
6	Canada	8.9		15	Germany	7.9
7	Netherlands	8.8		17	Barbados	7.8
8	Australia	8.7		17	Japan	7.8
8	Switzerland	8.7		19	Qatar	7.7
10	Norway	8.6		20	U.K.	7.6

Most Corrupt Countries

178	Somalia	1.1	168	Angola	1.9
176	Afghanistan	1.4	164	Venezuela	2.0
176	Myanmar	1.4	164	Kyrgyzstan	2.0
175	Iraq	1.5	164	Guinea	2.0
172	Sudan	1.6	164	Dem. Republic of Congo	2.0
172	Turkmenistan	1.6	154	Tajikistan	2.1
172	Uzbekistan	1.6	154	Russia	2.1
171	Chad	1.7	154	Papua New Guinea	2.1
170	Burundi	1.8	154	Laos	2.1
168	Equatorial Guinea	1.9	154	Kenya	2.1

Note: 10 = "Very Clean," 0 ="Highly Corrupt"
Source: Transparency International, Corruptions Perception Index 2010.

J. M.
Pushkin, Russia

The laws in Russia can seem at some times much stricter than in the USA. The difference, of course, is that in the U.S. you are expected to actually follow them. In Russia, with the exception of major things like robbery or murder or political crimes, there's not much that you can't arrange to be able to do, or get okayed post-facto.

The legal system is different, and has some significantly different foundational assumptions from U.S. law. Some examples:

There is no such thing as having both names (that is, yours and your wife's) on a property title. This is not because you can't both own a house—it is because you cannot both be owners. If you are married, there is automatic dual-ownership of everything. Having two names on a title isn't dual-ownership-in-whole; it is each party having some separate percentage of ownership. It takes some getting used to.

In court, the arresting (or ticketing) officer is considered one of the parties to the case, and as such his testimony carries very little weight (at least, it carries the exact same weight as does your testimony, saying "no, I didn't"). Presumption of innocence and burden of proof are taken very seriously.

Driving a car is considered "operating a piece of dangerous equipment"—exactly the same thing as, for example, handling a loaded rifle. If you hurt a person with your car, and they weren't themselves in a car at the time, it is your fault. Period. You were the one who brought the dangerous equipment to the game, you failed to protect everything and everyone around you from it. I had a pedestrian walk out in front of my car, and lightly clipped her. Expect to have to pay a decent chunk of change in either fines and medical costs or in bribes or in just smoothing-it-over money if you do something like that. It means drive carefully.

Do the Trains Run on Time?
Infrastructure/Availability of Goods + Services

 Do you demand to see potable running water every time you turn on the tap? Can you live without DSL, pizza delivery or a faithful supply of electricity? Do you expect a hardware store to be open at 3 a.m.? If these are important concerns, you'll have to sort the developing world from the already developed (and mega-developed) world. You will often find that many expat communities in Third World countries establish themselves in particular areas because a higher standard of service is available there. Check local forums and websites for such localized information. Because infrastructure development is of great interest to corporate elites, it's no surprise that their supporting institutions have given this dimension a fair bit of coverage. The World Bank webpage (**econ.worldbank.org**) provides downloadable reports and information on development in specific countries. Similar types of reports are also put out by the World Economic Forum (**www.weforum.com**). The always-helpful CIA World Factbook is another good source (**www.cia.gov**). Because your Internet connectivity is probably your lifeline, it's good to check out what the hi-speed situation will be in your new home. You can find tons of Internet usage stats for any country (including the number of Facebook subscribers!) at **www.internetworldstats.com**. To get an idea of who's getting how much download (and upload) speed, check out the stats at **www.speedtest.net**.

Smooth and Efficient: Top-Ranked Infrastructure

7 = best and 1 = worst

1	Switzerland	6.8		11	UAE	6.2
2	Hong Kong	6.7		12	South Korea	6.0
3	Singapore	6.6		13	Canada	6.0
4	France	6.6		14	Portugal	6.0
5	Iceland	6.6		15	Japan	6.0
6	Austria	6.4		16	Luxembourg	6.0
7	Sweden	6.4		17	Netherlands	5.9
8	Finland	6.4		18	Barbados	5.9
9	Germany	6.3		19	Taiwan	5.9
10	Denmark	6.3		20	Belgium	5.8

Delay and Decay: Least-Developed Infrastructure

139	Bosnia & Herzegovina	2.0		129	Timor-Leste	2.7
138	Angola	2.2		128	Burkina Faso	2.8
137	Mongolia	2.3		127	Mauritania	2.8
136	Romania	2.4		126	Burundi	2.8
135	Paraguay	2.4		125	Benin	2.9
134	Nigeria	2.4		124	Tanzania	3.0
133	Nepal	2.4		123	Vietnam	3.0
132	Lebanon	2.5		122	Serbia	3.0
131	Chad	2.5		121	Cameroon	3.1
130	Bangladesh	2.7		120	Bulgaria	3.1

Source: World Economic Forum: The Global Competitiveness Report 2010–2011

Internet Penetration (%): Top Countries

Greenland	**90.3**	Falkland Islands	**76.7**
Iceland	**90.0**	South Korea	**76.1**
Norway	**86.0**	Switzerland	**76.0**
Finland	**83.0**	Luxembourg	**74.9**
The Netherlands	**82.9**	Israel	**74.0**
Sweden	**80.7**	Japan	**73.8**
Australia	**80.6**	U.S.	**73.2**
New Zealand	**80.5**	Canada	**72.3**
Denmark	**80.4**	U.K.	**71.8**
Faroe Islands	**77.1**	Andorra	**71.3**

Source: www.internetworldstats.com

Internet Speed: World's Fastest Downloads

1	South Korea	34.48 Mbps	**6**	Netherlands	23.58 Mbps
2	Sweden	27.07 Mbps	**7**	Moldova	21.37 Mbps
3	Lithuania	26.34 Mbps	**8**	Switzerland	18.77 Mbps
4	Romania	24.05 Mbps	**9**	Germany	18.50 Mbps
5	Latvia	23.74 Mbps	**10**	Belgium	18.22 Mbps

Source: Speedtest.net

Cara Smiley

Oaxaca, Mexico

I continue to miss good infrastructure (roads, garbage, schools, telephones, government office efficiency, etc.). In general, Mexican government offices are understaffed and underequipped and are not as efficient as their counterparts in the USA.

Marshall Creamer

Hong Kong

Hong Kong has the best public transit system I have ever seen....Chicago might be the worst I've ever seen. I think most Americans have a hard time dealing with the fact that other countries/cities are better than our country/cities...Internet, goods, and services are easily accessible anywhere.

Is it Safe? Crime and Terror

The many travel warnings issued by the U.S. State Department notwithstanding (and few experienced travelers regard them as anything but overly shrill and paranoid pronouncements), there aren't many places on planet Earth, unless they are engulfed by war or massive civil unrest, as dangerous as your typical U.S. metropolis or meth-addled exurbia. And while the odds of getting mugged, raped or assaulted might decrease when you leave this country, the likelihood of being swindled, pickpocketed or burgled tends to the fill the crime vacuum. Obviously, like in the States, crime risk varies dramatically between different regions, between cities and towns, and even within neighborhoods, so overall country lowdowns have only limited value. Still, you could check out the UN's Office on Drugs and Crime (**www.unodc.org**) for reports and stats though their latest ranking surveys are getting pretty old. The Legatum Institute publishes a prosperity index (**www.prosperity.org**) that looks at crime and public safety, among the many factors affecting and affected by human happiness and prosperity. And in the developed world, check out what the Organization for Economic Co-operation and Development (**www.oecd.org**) has to say as well as the UN-affiliated European Institute for Crime Prevention and Control (**www.heuni.fi**). Also, you have to factor in how various jurisdictions define certain crimes, how willing the population is to report any crimes to the police, and how willing a particular government is willing to share those stats (particularly when it doesn't make them look good). Any decent travel guide can give you the crime picture in any given area. Asking the locals, of course, is even better.

For a truly comprehensive quantification addressing all manner of anxieties, Maplecroft (**www.maplecroft.com**), a global risk management company, assesses your relative safety, from terrorism and political upheaval to natural disasters and climate change, and publishes an annual Global Risk atlas and other ratings and ranking indexes.

Ten Safest Countries in the World

1	Iceland	**6**	Denmark
2	Norway	**7**	New Zealand
3	Finland	**8**	Sweden
4	Ireland	**9**	Slovenia
5	Singapore	**10**	Taiwan

Source: Legatum Institute: "Ten Safest Countries in the World"

Nations in Terror:
Top 10 Terrorist Hotspots (November, 2010)

1 Somalia

2 Pakistan

3 Iraq

4 Afghanistan

5 Palestinian Occupied Territory

6 Colombia

7 Thailand

8 Philippines

9 Yemen

10 Russia

Source: Maplecroft

Getting Away From Murder: Countries with a Lower Murder Rate Than the U.S. (Per 100,000 Ppl)

United States of America	**6.0**	Saudi Arabia	3.2
Dominica	5.9	Turkey	3.0
Chile	5.8	Libyan Arab Jamahiriya	2.9
Cuba	5.5	Mauritius	2.7
India	5.5	Syrian Arab Republic	2.6
São Tomé and Principe	5.3	Iran (Islamic Republic of)	2.5
Lao People's Democratic Rep.	5.2	Lebanon	2.5
Argentina	5.0	Yemen	2.5
Grenada	4.9	Romania	2.5
Uruguay	4.7	Republic of Korea	2.2
Israel	4.7	Finland	2.2
Bhutan	4.3	China	2.1
Albania	4.2	Armenia	2.0
Vietnam	3.8	Oman	2.0
Bolivia (Plurinational State of)	3.7	Serbia	2.0
Georgia	3.7	Tajikistan	1.9
Seychelles	3.6	Azerbaijan	1.9
Uzbekistan	3.5	Bulgaria	1.9
Djibouti	3.4	Hungary	1.9
Afghanistan	3.4	Bosnia and Herzegovina	1.9
Pakistan	3.4	Croatia	1.8
Peru	3.3	Portugal	1.8
Mongolia	3.3	Marshall Islands	1.8

Former Yugoslav Rep. of Macedonia	3.3	Tunisia	1.7
Somalia	3.2	Norway	1.0
Maldives	1.7	Slovenia	1.0
Slovakia	1.7	Tonga	1.0
Belgium	1.7	Ireland	0.9
Canada	1.6	Sweden	0.9
Luxembourg	1.5	Italy	0.9
Solomon Islands	1.5	Spain	0.9
Kuwait	1.4	Netherlands	0.9
Poland	1.4	Vanuatu	0.9
New Zealand	1.4	Micronesia (Federated States of)	0.9
Singapore	1.3	Denmark	0.7
Cyprus	1.3	Malta	0.7
Andorra	1.3	France	0.7
Australia	1.3	Fiji	0.7
Egypt	1.2	Iceland	0.6
Greece	1.2	Austria	0.6
Morocco	1.1	Germany	0.6
Brunei Darussalam	1.1	Switzerland	0.6
Bahrain	1.1	Japan	0.5
Czech Republic	1.1	United Arab Emirates	0.5
Samoa	1.1	Monaco	0.0
Qatar	1.0	Palau	0.0

Source: United Nations Office on Drugs and Crime (UNODC),
Homicide Statistics, 2003–2008 www.unodc.org

You're Less Likely To Be Assaulted In...

Reported Cases per 100,000

U.S.	281.6	Finland	39.1
Germany	183.1	Poland	38.9
Canada	173.8	England and Wales	32.2
Mexico	160.4	Japan	26.7
New Zealand	150.4	Denmark	26.7
Scotland	127.5	Spain	25.2
Italy	100.3	Iceland	20.2
Ireland	93.9	Czech Republic	8.3
Luxembourg	91.8	Slovakia	8.0
Hungary	80.7	Portugal	6.5
Northern Ireland	70.3	Australia	3.1
Norway	69.1	Switzerland	2.9
Sweden	52.8	Slovenia	1.0
Chile	49.4	France	0.3

Source: European Institute for Crime Prevention and Control,
Latest International Comparison of Crime in OECD Countries

Burglaries: An International Sampling

Reported Cases per 100,000

Australia	1530.2	Belgium	586.6
New Zealand	1476.3	Ireland	567.9
Denmark	1317.9	Czech Republic	523.3
Austria	1203.3	Finland	467.2
England and Wales	1157.7	Poland	455.3
Sweden	1094.2	Hungary	442.2
Iceland	950.4	Portugal	429.1
Slovenia	902.9	Holland	427.5
Spain	878.9	Greece	292.3
Switzerland	758.1	Japan	234.0
U.S.	714.4	Turkey	216.9
Canada	680.9	Italy	190.2
Northern Ireland	663.9	Slovakia	186.8
Luxembourg	659.1	Chile	134.0
Germany	631.6	Norway	75.0
France	622.4	Mexico	20.6
Scotland	597.6	Korea	4.4

Source: Institute for the Study of Civil Society (Civitas):
Latest International Comparison of Crime in OECD Countries (www.civitas.org)

Paul Schuble

Hyogo Prefecture, Japan

Japan happens to be one of the safest countries in the world. Of course there is crime, like anywhere else, but to a lesser degree. It's not uncommon for lost wallets to be returned with all the cash still inside, and articles lost on buses and trains are often turned in to station attendants surprisingly quickly.

Cara Smiley

Oaxaca, Mexico

Mexico has been in the news a lot lately because of narco-trafficking. While there are many areas of Mexico where even innocent citizens are affected by the violence of the drug trade and other related businesses, this is not the case in Oaxaca City. That said, there has been and continues to be a great deal of social unrest in Oaxaca which has on occasion led to violence, but most often leads to marches and blockades of the principal streets in the city and which make it difficult/impossible to drive in the city.

Ande Wanderer

Buenos Aires, Argentina

The crime here is definitely increasing—I've been held up twice at gunpoint on my own block, but got away both times.

Healthcare: How Free and How Good?

The availability (or lack thereof) of decent affordable healthcare ranks toward the top of the reasons people leave the United States. All of the developed world and much of the developing world offer a comprehensive national health plan to citizens and residents. The U.S. spent the highest portion of its Gross Domestic Product (GDP) on health services (and near the top, per capita) and gets less to show for it than much of the developed and even some of the underdeveloped world. So there is little doubt that you can "trade up" when it comes to healthcare.

The UN's World Health Organization (**www.who.int**) will give you the bird's-eye view of the health situation in any country. You'll get the basic stats, plus bulletins or reports on health and disease triumphs and outbreaks around the world.

The Organization of Economic Co-operation and Development (**www.oecd.org**) compiles up-to-date reports on various aspects of the health, healthcare and health insurance of its 30+ (and growing) member countries. Comprehensive statistics on health (among other topics) and healthcare can be found at **stats.oecd.org**.

Per Capita Healthcare Spending: Top Countries

Luxembourg	**7,439**	Australia	**3,986**
Norway	**7,354**	San Marino	**3,878**
Monaco	**7,338**	U.K.	**3,867**
U.S.	**7,285**	Finland	**3,809**
Switzerland	**6,108**	Italy	**3,136**
Iceland	**5,971**	Andorra	**2,948**
Denmark	**5,551**	New Zealand	**2,790**
France	**4,627**	Japan	**2,751**
Ireland	**4,556**	Spain	**2,712**
Austria	**4,523**	Greece	**2,679**
Sweden	**4,495**	Qatar	**2,403**
Canada	**4,409**	Portugal	**2,108**
Netherlands	**4,243**	Israel	**1,893**
Germany	**4,209**	Slovenia	**1,836**
Belgium	**4,056**	Cyprus	**1,778**

Note: Amounts measured in dollars and reflect per capita total of public and private healthcare expense.
Source: World Bank: World Development Indicators, "Health expenditure per capita (current US$)."

Infant Mortality: Top Countries

Deaths/1,000 live births		Deaths/1,000 live births	
Monaco	1.78	Norway	3.55
Singapore	2.32	Guernsey	3.58
Bermuda	2.46	Malta	3.72
Sweden	2.74	Czech Republic	3.76
Japan	2.79	Andorra	3.84
Hong Kong	2.91	Ireland	3.89
Macau	3.20	Germany	3.95
Iceland	3.21	Jersey	4.02
France	3.31	Switzerland	4.12
Spain	3.42	Israel	4.17
Finland	3.45	Liechtenstein	4.20
Anguilla	3.49	Slovenia	4.21

Note: Figures indicate total number of deaths of infants under one year old in a given year per 1,000 live births. Source: The World Factbook 2010. Washington, DC: Central Intelligence Agency, 2010.

Life Expectancy at Birth: Top Countries

Monaco	89.78	Sweden	80.97
Macau	84.38	Switzerland	80.97
San Marino	82.95	Israel	80.86
Andorra	82.36	Iceland	80.79
Japan	82.17	Anguilla	80.77
Guernsey	82.08	Bermuda	80.60
Singapore	82.06	Cayman Islands	80.57
Hong Kong	81.96	Isle of Man	80.53
Australia	81.72	New Zealand	80.48
Canada	81.29	Italy	80.33
Jersey	81.28	Liechtenstein	80.19
France	81.09	Norway	80.08
Spain	81.07		

Source: The World Factbook 2010. Washington, DC: Central Intelligence Agency, 2010.

Jude Angione

Toronto, Canada

Since there is so much talk and so much controversy surrounding proposed changes to the healthcare system in the U.S., I'll try to lay out what the medical system is like in Canada so you can understand how it functions. Universal healthcare is mandated by the Federal government and carried out by the provinces. Each province sets rates, methods of payment and the services provided, although a medical card from any-where in Canada is recognized in all provinces.

I spent a week in Victoria, BC, and developed a terrible cough. I went to a clinic, showed my Ontario Health Card and got to see a doctor free of charge. All visits to MDs are covered—general practitioners and specialists. Most drug tests are covered. All hospitalization costs are covered. Alternative services such as chiropractic and massage therapy are funded partially by some provinces. And the cost for all of this? In British Columbia the rate for a single person is approximately $60 per month and for a family of three or up, it's $120. That's it. And, if you are low-income, there are subsidies. In Ontario, it's even more amazing, thanks to an agreement brokered when the NDP (New Democratic Party—equivalent to the British Labour Party) was part of a coalition with Liberals, no one in Ontario pays for healthcare directly. The entire system is paid for by a universal employer tax.

The downside to all of this? Basically, you have to wait longer for non-urgent care in Canada than you do in the U.S. Elective surgeries can take years to schedule, but urgent care is right up there with the care you get in the U.S. and all the day-to-day stuff is covered. No one loses their home in Canada because they need heart surgery. They might have to wait if it isn't critical but they won't have to pay once their place in line comes up.

Turner Wright

Bugu, South Korea

I've had a hiccup in getting healthcare, as teachers in small private schools like mine don't qualify for healthcare until they've been in the country for three months. We'll see if this becomes an issue. In general, though, based on my experience in Japan, the healthcare system is solid. Everyone is required to get coverage with the national or employee system (though smaller companies provide additional service). I broke my wrist in Japan, forcing me to deal with medical Japanese terminology and testing my insurance policy for the first time; the treatment I received was excellent, and the cost was pretty low, considering I needed minor surgery. As a whole, I believe the systems in place in Korea and Japan are superior to that of the U.S.; all their citizens receive healthcare, and pre-existing conditions do not apply.

Libby Hansen
Copenhagen, Denmark

Medical services are free, including doctor visits and hospitalization. A recent experience in my family shows how well the system works: A year ago my husband had a heart attack. An ambulance arrived after a very short wait; he was given medicine and a few tests including EKG before the ambulance even left the driveway. This was apparently to determine whether he should go directly to the hospital that is the center for heart problems or to the local hospital that is also equipped with a Cardiology Department but not able to do heart surgery. In five days he was back home after having had an angioplasty and the insertion of three stents, hopefully as good as new. Had he needed bypass surgery, that would have been also done as soon as possible. There was never a discussion of what a procedure would cost. That is something that isn't part of the equation unless one chooses to go to a private hospital instead of a public one.

Noemi S.
North Shore City, New Zealand

The first time I had to go the the doctor here, I thought I was going to have to pay at least a few hundred dollars, but the NZ$15 for the visit and the $1 prescription were welcomed surprises. Everything for anyone is subsidized by the government. I have read that the conservative political party wants to implement a private system like the U.S., and if that ever goes into play, then I'm out of here. I do, however, have extra insurance for specialist visits and hospitalisations which only costs me NZ$48/month. Most of my Kiwi friends don't have that supplemental coverage but I guess I'm used to this coming from America.

Gary Lukatch
Budapest, Hungary

Dental care in Hungary is incredible and cutting-edge, while remaining extremely inexpensive. The U.K. and Ireland actually offer Dental Tours to come here—stay for a week or two and have dental work done, as the total cost is still less than in the U.K. and Ireland. I recently had three implants done, accompanied by three teeth pulled, temporary bridges and permanent bridges, and total cost was around $4,500—probably would have been closer to $20,000 in the states. All other dental care is comparable: a cleaning is around $30, X-rays $25.

Medical care, on the other hand, varies widely depending on what you need. I had to have an angioplasty a few years ago, and the hospital staff, ICU staff and my doctor, whom I'd never seen before, were fantastic; from arrival at the hospital to being wheeled back to the recovery room, it was around two to three hours. Stayed in ICU for two days and in regular wards (not nice places) for two more days. Total cost for everything was around $12,000. Still a positive experience. There are other alternatives here, like an American-style health service, but the cost is probably the same as in the U.S., i.e., quite high.

Re: insurance, it is available, both from the state and privately. Medicare/Medicaid does not apply here, but anyone can buy any other insurance. Legal residence requires either proof of personal health insurance or purchasing it from the state—very expensive.

Frank
Orosi, Costa Rica
My daughter was born here in 2005 and we had no health insurance and we went to the second best hospital in the country. It cost us $1500 with a year of aftercare. My son was a C-section and it was $3000. I've had the best dental care since I've been here.

Gabrielle Van Leuven
Beijing, China
There is a hospital in my neighborhood, the China-Japan Friendship Hospital. In the Chinese branch of the hospital, a consultation with a doctor costs between $1 and $3. In the foreigner's branch, the same visits cost between $15 and $30—but I have reason to believe the doctors are only bringing home a few dollars a day. This means that they tend to go out of their way to get you to come back to the hospital as many times as possible—a prescription must be renewed with a doctor visit and pills are handed out in five-day supplies. While I'm not eager to get back to the world of insurance companies, I do miss having a doctor who isn't scrimping for pennies.

Tinuola
Prague, Czech Republic
If Americans really understood how the "socialist" healthcare in Europe worked and they experienced it for themselves, they'd be outraged at their politicians. Let's just say, an ambulance ride would not cost you a week's salary.

Name Withheld by Request
San Miguel de Allende, Mexico

I can (and have) gone to the doctor for an average of 28 USD per visit. I got food poisoning from some bad shrimp from a Chinese restaurant recently...this could happen anywhere...felt so bad that I decided to see if the doctor would come over. He did. He brought antibiotics and several other medications, cost of the visit including the meds was about 50 USD. A HOUSE CALL, you ask? Yes. The doctor I go to is German. Trained in Germany, U.S. and Mexico. There is nothing wrong with the healthcare here!

J.M.
Pushkin, Russia

Healthcare in Russia is two-tiered. The free healthcare (once you're a grownup—for kids, primary care is done through the school doctors, and is just an automatic part of being in school) is purely at a level of 'keep you from dying'—and they do a good job of that. Outside that, you can pay for pretty much any level of healthcare you want. As with so many other things in Russia, the cost of healthcare and the quality of what you can get are far superior to the U.S. system.

As an example, our third son was born in Pushkin. For prenatal visits, we saw no need to go fancy, and just used a doctor at the local maternity center. They saw us regularly, did much the same types of checkups, ultrasounds, etc. that the U.S. docs did on our first two kids. Appointments were always kept, and we spent much less time waiting in Russia (which is sort of unexpected) than we did in the U.S. Then when it came time to have the baby, we arranged with the local maternity hospital to have their highest-end deluxe private room and the whole works (the other end of the scale—free care—has four mothers sharing a room that is spartan in the extreme). Our son resisted coming out but the doctors and nurses remained calm and professional throughout. Then when he finally arrived, he wasn't breathing and didn't react at all. They whisked him immediately out to their intensive care section, leaving my wife and I with a doctor and nurse. Ten minutes or so later (it felt a lot longer, but you've got to respect the fact that the kid was the docs' only priority) our doc came up to fill us in. They got our boy up and breathing and everything quick as a wink, but had put him on a feeding tube and incubator-type thing. He was moved to a bigger hospital in St. Petersburg to be observed, so they could figure out what had happened and, more importantly, make sure it wasn't going to happen again. I rented a room for my wife in the children's hospital, where our son was in the Neonatal ICU. He stayed in the NICU for five days, then with her in her room for another week—regular EKGs and whatnot to make sure he was getting along as he should.

The other side of medicine in Russia is home-visits. Since we lived out of the city, it was often more convenient to call a doctor out to us (in particular for the regular checkups they insisted our youngest son have for his first two years). We were able to have a neurologist come out to our house evenings or on Saturdays (it was cheaper to do it during regular hours, but I preferred to be home for it) for at most 2500 rubles ($90), all-inclusive.

There's simply no comparison between healthcare in Russia and the pitiful thing they call healthcare in the States.

Ted Hung
Melbourne, Australia

The healthcare system in Australia is pretty good. My wife and I have never held any private healthcare insurance in Australia, but we are automatically covered by the government Medicare system as a result of our permanent residency...whether we work or not. Depending on the clinic, Medicare will pay all or most of the bill for a doctor's visit. On the other hand, while looking for a GP in the city, we have had a very hard time finding a doctor who is readily available on the Medicare system. Most of them are quite crowded and require you to book an appointment far in advance.

Thus, our main encounters with the healthcare system here have been when we needed immediate help and went to the emergency room of a hospital. I went once when I got an infection of my finger, and my wife has gone several times when she has had an eye infection. Some hospitals here are private and some are public, and it was a bit of a challenge to find an appropriate public hospital near us. Upon arrival, the emergency room put us through a triage process to determine what order the doctors would see us based on the severity of the problem. We have found that the wait times to see a doctor vary, but sometimes it can be quite long (up to four or five hours). Overall, the quality of doctors and care have been quite high...and it is clear that the doctors really do care about their patients.

James Lindzey
Medellín, Colombia

Healthcare is excellent. Get a premium policy. I'm 43, I pay about $120 a month, had three surgeries with no deductible. Emergency room costs $10, if you don't want to wait to see a doctor. Plastic surgery is popular here. I had a hernia operation and ulnar nerve decompression. The surgeries went well. Overall, you get much better treatment here than with doctors in the USA.

Gimme Shelter: Taxes Abroad

Nobody likes paying taxes and once the deficit-spending express comes to a crashing halt, you may find that whatever wealth you've managed to cling to will prove irresistible to a broke and desperate Fed. For those searching for a more laissez-faire host to park yourself and your assets, there are still countries that levy little or no income and capital gains taxes, particularly if it's earned outside the country. In most cases, if you have to ask which ones they are, you can't afford them. Even if you're cool with paying your share, you won't be able to make any kind of costs vs. income calculations regarding moving abroad, unless you first find out what kind of cut the government is going to take. You can find an overview of a given country's taxation scheme, plus plenty of general articles about business and taxation worldwide at **www.worldwide-tax. com** and at the Tax Articles International Articles Directory (**www.taxarticles. info**). The Organization for Economic Co-operation and Development also keeps tax stats and reports on its member nations at **www.oecd.org**.

	Income Tax Rate %	Capital Gains Tax Rate %
Andorra	0	**Real Estate (0–15)**
Anguilla	0	0
Bahamas	0	0
Bahrain	0	0
Bermuda	0	0
British Virgin Islands	0	0
Brunei	0	0
Cayman Islands	0	0
Kuwait	0	15
Maldives	0	0
Monaco	0	0
Montenegro	9	0
Oman	0	0
St. Kitts & Nevis	0	20*
United Arab Emirates	0	0
Vanuatu	0	0

*Does not apply to trusts or limited partnerships. Source: www.taxrates.cc

Nanny States: Tax Revenue as Share of GDP

	% of GDP		% of GDP
Denmark	**48.2**	Hungary	**39.1**
Sweden	**46.4**	Slovenia	**37.9**
Italy	**43.5**	Luxembourg	**37.5**
Belgium	**43.2**	Germany	**37.0**
Finland	**43.1**	Czech Republic	**34.8**
Austria	**42.8**	U.K.	**34.3**
France	**41.9**	Ireland	**34.1**
Norway	**41.0**		

Source: OECD Tax Database (2009–10)

Bob Hand
Rio Grande do Sul, Brazil

Brazil is one of the most heavily taxed countries in the world. It's one of the main reasons certain items are more expensive here than in the USA, especially if they are imported. Sales taxes are hidden from the consumer. When you buy something sales tax is not added on. It is included in the price so the consumer never sees it. But tax can amount to as much as 65% of the price.

Paul Tenney
Singapore

Singapore has unspeakably low taxes relative to the U.S., and even though the Feds still have a claim on you abroad (and are the only country in the world that does so), the net result is still more take-home pay and more savings. Better still, Singapore does NOT have withholding tax, which makes an absolutely stunning difference in your feelings and your attitude about how much money you have, and in actual (not emotional) terms it allows you to do things with that money until it is owed, so you in fact can achieve a return on that money and improve your overall wealth.

The Singapore tax system is very friendly and transparent—they have a relatively low income tax of 10–20% that you pay based on a graduated basis (i.e., your first x dollars are taxed at 10%, your next y dollars are taxed at 12%, etc.). They have no capital gains taxes in Singapore, so if you are able to invest locally you may do so. I will pay tax in the United States as I'm legally obligated to do so, despite the fact that I'm paid by a foreign entity entirely into a foreign bank account. I will receive the Foreign Earned

Income Tax Exclusion on the first $90k+ for which I need not pay any federal tax, but after that I will owe taxes on the rest. I can, of course, deduct what I pay in Singapore taxes on the remaining income over the excluded amount from what I'll ultimately owe to Uncle Sam.

J.M.
Pushkin, Russia

In Russia, foreigners are taxed at 30% of income—but, it is reported income. And no one in Russia will cooperate with the taxing authorities to get them a good number for income. I've seen statistics claiming that the average pay in Russia is on the order of a couple hundred dollars a month. That's completely laughable. A couple hundred bucks a month is just the average that people are willing to report. My mechanics make 10 times that in a not-remarkable month. The cleaning lady gets more than twice the reported statistic for average wage. So we pay tax in Russia, but it isn't much.

Adam Lederer
Berlin, Germany

Yes, I pay a lot in taxes, but in return there is a functional healthcare system. I've never heard of anybody who has gone into debt because they got sick. There is also an amazing public transportation network, fast intercity trains, and well-maintained roads. I might note that on all these counts, the United States generally fails.

Going for Broke:
Business Climate and Economic Health

What's your bottom line? Earn less in exchange for a slower pace, friendly locals, and scenic surroundings…or do you see yourself landing a high-paying overseas gig or launching a new business abroad? In some nations, state-run bureaucracies seem almost designed to stifle businesses and employment. If you're looking for where the hiring has gone wild and building and business permits are more plentiful than zoning restrictions, you've got a friend in the World Bank (**www.worldbank.org**). Their Doing Business Index (**www.doing-business.org**) provides up-to-date information about the business climate in over 180 different countries. The rankings cover everything from tax policies to, yes, building permits. The Manpower Group (**www.manpowergroup.com**) keeps watch on the world labor market and offers many free reports on their site. The World Bank, the World Economic Forum (**www.weforum.org**), the CIA (**www.cia.gov**) and many other less scary institutions will provide you with all the economic health data you can handle.

Where The Jobs Are... And Aren't:

Employment Increase 2010–11		Employment Increase 2010–11	
China	**+14**	Greece	**−10**
India	**+13**	Peru	**−9**
Romania	**+12**	Costa Rica	**−7**
Taiwan	**+11**	Guatemala	**−5**
Belgium	**+9**	Switzerland	**−2**
Czech Republic	**+9**	Sweden	**−2**
Italy	**+9**	South Africa	**−2**
Japan	**+8**	Austria	**−2**
Panama	**+7**	Poland	**−1**
Germany	**+6**	Australia	**−1**
Hungary	**+6**	Norway	**0**
Mexico	**+6**		

Source: Manpower Group: Employment Outlook Survey (2nd Quarter 2011)

Getting Your Foot in The Door: Best Countries To Start a Business

World Bank Ranking

New Zealand	**1**	Ireland	**11**	France	**21**
Australia	**2**	Mauritius	**12**	Armenia	**22**
Canada	**3**	Saudi Arabia	**13**	Panama	**23**
Singapore	**4**	Kyrgyzstan	**14**	Taiwan	**24**
Macedonia	**5**	Azerbaijan	**15**	Afghanistan	**25**
Hong Kong	**6**	Puerto Rico	**16**	Cyprus	**26**
Belarus	**7**	U.K.	**17**	Denmark	**27**
Georgia	**8**	Jamaica	**18**	Slovenia	**28**
USA	**9**	Egypt	**18**	Iceland	**29**
Rwanda	**9**	Samoa	**20**	Tonga	**30**

Source: World Bank Doing Business Project, Ease of Doing Business Index (2011)
See: www.doingbusiness.org/rankings

Where Your Money Is Safe:
The World's Soundest Banking Systems
(7 = financially sound)

Canada	6.7	Finland	6.3	Sweden	6.0
New Zealand	6.6	Barbados	6.3	Cyprus	6.0
Australia	6.6	Malta	6.3	Trinidad and Tobago	6.0
Chile	6.5	Luxembourg	6.2	Spain	6.0
Hong Kong	6.4	Slovakia	6.2	India	5.9
South Africa	6.4	Mauritius	6.2	Peru	5.9
Namibia	6.3	Qatar	6.2	Austria	5.9
Singapore	6.3	Bahrain	6.1	Senegal	5.9
Panama	6.3	Israel	6.1	Czech Republic	5.9
Brazil	6.3	Norway	6.1	Costa Rica	5.8

Source: World Economic Forum, Executive Opinion Survey (2008, 2009)

Sovereign vs. Debt: Public Debt as Percentage of GDP (2010)

1	Japan	225.80	19	Germany	78.80
2	St. Kitts & Nevis	185.00	20	Dominica	78.00
3	Lebanon	150.70	21	Nicaragua	78.00
4	Zimbabwe	149.00	22	Israel	77.30
5	Greece	144.00	23	United Kingdom	76.50
6	Iceland	123.80	24	Malta	72.60
7	Jamaica	123.20	25	Austria	70.40
8	Italy	118.10	26	Netherlands	64.60
9	Singapore	102.40	27	Spain	63.40
10	Belgium	98.60	28	Cote d'Ivoire	63.30
11	Ireland	94.20	29	Jordan	61.40
12	Sudan	94.20	30	Cyprus	61.10
13	Sri Lanka	86.70	31	Brazil	60.80
14	France	83.50	32	Mauritius	60.50
15	Portugal	83.20	33	Ghana	59.90
16	Egypt	80.50	34	World	59.30
17	Belize	80.00	35	Albania	59.30
18	Hungary	79.60	36	Bahrain	59.20
37	United States	58.90 (net debt)	70	Malawi	40.40
38	Seychelles	58.80	71	Czech Republic	40.00
39	Morocco	58.20	72	Panama	40.00
40	Bhutan	57.80	73	Bolivia	39.70
41	Guyana	57.00	74	Bangladesh	39.30
42	Vietnam	56.70	75	Ethiopia	39.30
43	Philippines	56.50	76	Yemen	39.10
44	Uruguay	56.00	77	Bosnia & Herzegovina	39.00
45	India	55.90	78	Ukraine	38.40
46	Croatia	55.00	79	Switzerland	38.20
47	El Salvador	55.00	80	Montenegro	38.00
48	Poland	53.60	81	Lithuania	36.70
49	Malaysia	53.10	82	Slovenia	35.50
50	Kenya	50.90	83	Romania	34.80
51	Argentina	50.30	84	Cuba	34.40

52 Pakistan	49.90	**85** Macedonia	34.20
53 Tunisia	49.50	**86** Canada	34.00
54 Turkey	48.10	**87** Taiwan	33.90
55 Norway	47.70	**88** South Africa	33.20
56 Denmark	46.60	**89** Senegal	32.10
57 Aruba	46.30	**90** Syria	29.80
58 Latvia	46.20	**91** Guatemala	29.60
59 Finland	45.40	**92** Papua New Guinea	27.80
60 Colombia	44.80	**93** Indonesia	26.40
61 UAE	44.60	**94** Trinidad & Tobago	26.40
62 Costa Rica	42.40	**95** Honduras	26.10
63 Thailand	42.30	**96** Gabon	25.80
64 Dominican Rep.	41.70	**97** Algeria	25.70
65 Mexico	41.50	**98** New Zealand	25.50
66 Serbia	41.50	**99** Venezuela	25.50
67 Slovakia	41.00	**100** Moldova	25.00
68 Mozambique	40.80	**101** Zambia	24.10
69 Sweden	40.80	**102** South Korea	23.70
103 Peru	23.60	**118** Kazakhstan	16.20
104 Tanzania	23.30	**119** Nigeria	13.40
105 Ecuador	23.20	**120** Kuwait	12.60
106 Paraguay	22.80	**121** Qatar	10.30
107 Botswana	22.60	**122** Cameroon	9.60
108 Australia	22.40	**123** Russia	9.50
109 Uganda	20.40	**124** Uzbekistan	9.00
110 Angola	20.30	**125** Estonia	7.70
111 Namibia	20.00	**126** Gibraltar	7.50
112 Hong Kong	18.20	**127** Chile	6.20
113 China	17.50	**128** Wallis & Futuna	5.60
114 Saudi Arabia	16.70	**129** Azerbaijan	4.60
115 Bulgaria	16.20	**130** Oman	4.40
116 Iran	16.20	**131** Equatorial Guinea	4.10
117 Luxembourg	16.20	**132** Libya	3.30

Source: CIA factbook

Kathleen O'Donnell
Central Mexico

The red tape involved in starting a business and doing business here is terrible. Go as high up the ladder as you can for answers and advice. I got sent here because two men had previously failed at getting permissions to start the business. The President of our company had promised our largest customer he would open a local support facility and our customer wasn't happy that the company had been unable to do that. He asked me to look through the files and see if I could find out why it hadn't happened. It didn't take long to see that Mexican lawyers were sending everyone in circles asking for duplicate and triplicate documents, telling them how difficult it was, etc.—and the only thing actually getting done was they were sending large invoices! No one was really keeping track of the paper trail, and I so advised him. Shortly after that he asked me to go to Mexico and open a branch.

Once I arrived here, local attorneys tried the same thing; estimates to do the startup paperwork were astronomical and they all emphasized they needed unlimited, irrevocable power of attorney, something the owner of the company was not willing to give any attorney. One insisted the only way we could open a branch was if he was made manager.

But my assistant and I were able to determine that the decision on all foreign companies coming to Mexico was made in Mexico City at SECOFI (Ministry of the Economy). So one evening my assistant called up SECOFI and said in her most important tone of voice (and she could fake importance very well): "Very important business lady from the United States requires some assistance from the Secretary of Economy." I was put in touch with the Secretary of Economy. He didn't waste much time with me but he did refer me to two new grads who had just started to work for the government and instructed them to do whatever it took to help me and get this new business established. They jumped through hoops, and it ended up costing less than U.S. $50.

I am quite careful to watch the paperwork details, or to make sure an employee is watching that. The Mexican government employs people who do nothing but go through paperwork to see that every minute detail is completed; if not, there's a fine. Also, do not succumb to the local tradition of paying bribes to expedite things. It does speed things up when you're trying to meet a deadline, but trust me, they'll be back again and again expecting larger and larger payoffs.

Frank

Orosi, Costa Rica

It's kind of like a Communist country here because the government runs everything. There is no free enterprise. Most of the people who have a job here work for the government one way or another. Phone, power, water, everything like that is all government-run.

Tyler Watts

Ho Chi Minh City (Saigon), Vietnam

Living in a Socialist Republic or a Communist country people assume that there are myriad difficulties and regulations and problems but I somehow find it more free than America in many ways. That is not to say that there is not censorship, unjust imprisonments, land issues and the like, but what country is completely free from such things? I believe the laws here allow for more entrepreneurship and it is evidenced by the sheer amount of businesses and commercial activity within the country. It's alive and humming in trade and selling in a way I've never seen in the States. And I've certainly never felt hindered by the laws here.

Paul Tenney

Singapore

I think the key thing in terms of managing your money is your outlook on the value of the U.S. Dollar, and making a decision about how to manage those risks. Without performing an overly detailed analysis, I think it's pretty safe to assume that most anyone considering expatriation probably has serious concerns about the U.S. Dollar—if you don't, you should. I would say that getting yourself out of the U.S. Dollar entirely is probably the single best reason to consider expatriation sooner rather than later.

Greener Pastures: Ecology and Sustainability

In recent years, a steady stream of environmentally-minded Americans have packed up and left the States in search of pristine surroundings, sustainable living options, and a more life-friendly relationship to the environment. Whether you're seeking a land of wind farms and solar panels or where natural habitat is cherished and allowed to flourish, the Yale University Environmental Performance Index might be a good place to start. The Index (see below) ranks over 160 countries on over two dozen performance indicators relating to everything from public health to pollution to conservation efforts. The website also provides detailed reports for each individual country (**www.epi.yale.edu**). The New Economics Foundation (**www.neweconomics.org**), which is dedicated to "Economics as if people and the planet mattered," publishes a ranked list of countries by their ecological footprint as well as oodles of supporting data in their Happy Planet Index (**www.happyplanetindex.org**).

Environmental Performance Index: Top Countries

1	Iceland	93.5		14	U.K.	74.2
2	Switzerland	89.1		15	New Zealand	73.4
3	Costa Rica	86.4		16	Chile	73.3
4	Sweden	86.0		17	Germany	73.2
5	Norway	81.1		18	Italy	73.1
6	Mauritius	80.6		19	Portugal	73.0
7	France	78.2		20	Japan	72.5
8	Austria	78.1		21	Latvia	72.5
9	Cuba	78.1		22	Czech Republic	71.6
10	Colombia	76.8		23	Albania	71.4
11	Malta	76.3		24	Panama	71.4
12	Finland	74.7		25	Spain	70.6
13	Slovakia	74.5				

Source: Yale Center for Environmental Law & Policy (Yale University):
Environmental Performance Index 2010. See: epi.yale.edu

Ecological Footprint: A World Map

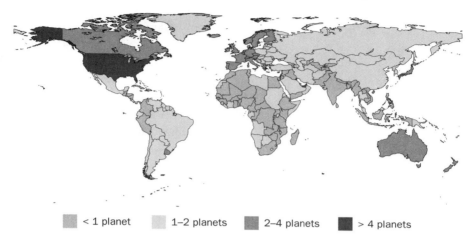

| < 1 planet | 1–2 planets | 2–4 planets | > 4 planets |

Source: New Economic Foundation, Happy Planet Index

Top 10 Solar-Powered Countries
Capacity (in Megawatts)

Germany	**9,785**	Czech Republic	**465**
Spain	**3,386**	Belgium	**363**
Japan	**2,633**	China	**305**
U.S.	**1,160**	France	**272**
Italy	**1,167**	India	**120**

Source: European Photovoltaic Industry Association (www.epia.org)

Wind Power: Top Countries
Capacity (in Megawatts)

China	**42,287**	Italy	**5,660**
U.S.	**40,180**	France	**5,660**
Germany	**27,214**	U.K.	**5,204**
Spain	**20,676**	Canada	**4,009**
India	**13,065**	Denmark	**3,752**

Source: Wikipedia

Yes, Nukes

Operable Reactors

Argentina	2	Mexico	2
Armenia	1	Netherlands	1
Belgium	7	Pakistan	3
Brazil	2	Romania	2
Bulgaria	2	Russia	32
Canada	18	Slovakia	4
China	13	Slovenia	1
Czech Republic	6	South Africa	2
Finland	4	Spain	8
France	58	Sweden	10
Germany	17	Switzerland	5
Hungary	4	Ukraine	15
India	20	United Kingdom	19
Japan	51	USA	104
Korea RO (South)	21		

Source: World Nuclear Association: www.world-nuclear.org

What's To Eat? Food and Agriculture

 There isn't much to say about food except that it's incredibly important since you're probably going to be eating locally, oh, about three or so times a day. Most of the developed world has a similar variety of restaurants and dishes—sushi, pizza, pasta, chow mein, etc.—found in most U.S. cities and towns. Unless you're actively trying to avoid civilization in general, you're not likely to be that far from the megachains (McDonalds, Starbucks, Subway, etc.), and their websites (not to mention a variety of smartphone technologies) will gladly show you where the closest outlets are to your particular GPS coordinates. Still, food—from the quality and availability of ingredients to appealingness of the cuisine—can vary not just from country to country but from region to

region and from town to city. Many expatriates find their deepest joy out of the simple buying of fresh-squeezed juices for less than a dollar on the streets of Mexico or being able to sip fantastic espresso at practically any café in Italy and Portugal. You can get a general lowdown from travel guides and foodie magazines, but unfortunately, you won't really know what it tastes like until you get there. Even simple things like milk, butter, cheese and bread often have a different flavor than what you might be used to. Speaking of milk, Canada, Australia and Scotland (but not England) restrict or prohibit sales of raw milk or cheese. The E.U. has outlawed or restricted (prescription only) a number of healing herbs. And some things you like to eat just might not grow in your new location.

If your destination is so exotic that you want to know if the food is even safe to eat, the Bites webpage (**bites.ksu.edu**) tracks everything from salmonella to indigestion all across the globe.

Best Countries for Vegetarians

India	U.K.	Hong Kong
Malaysia	Taiwan	Israel
Vietnam	Thailand	Canada

Source: expatify.com

Frankenfood: Where the GMO Crops Grow

Hectares under Cultivation

U.S.	**66.8 million**	South Africa	**2.2 million**
Brazil	**25.4 million**	Uruguay	**1.1 million**
Argentina	**22.9 million**	Bolivia	**0.9 million**
India	**9.4 million**	Australia	**0.7 million**
Canada	**8.8 million**	Philippines	**0.5 million**
China	**3.5 million**	Burkina Faso	**0.3 million**
Paraguay	**2.6 million**	Mexico	**0.1 million**
Pakistan	**2.4 million**	Spain	**0.1 million**

Source: The Economist Online

Noemi S.

Auckland, NZ

Being that the U.S. is THE land of convenience there are things I miss but the pangs for Mexican food usually pass once I get a good Indian curry.

God and Country: Religion and You

Do you prefer to mingle with people who call their deity by some specific name, or are you someone who wishes if people must resort to belief in such entities, that they should please just keep it to themselves—and for God's (or whomever's) sake, don't mix it with government? Depending on how you count, there are maybe 20 major religions in the world, although most expatriates who aren't on some kind of anthropology or missionary kick need only concern themselves with fewer than a dozen that could conceivably have any influence on a society (much less government) in which you'd likely find yourself.

Then there is the matter of the level of religiosity of the society. It's important to remember that many Islamic countries, such as Turkey, Morocco and Egypt, even if they are not theocracies, per se, often have Islamic values embedded in their cultural norms if not the legal system. Northern European countries tend to be nominally Protestant, but in practice, religion is not taken seriously beyond the usual holidays and homilies. You'd probably find the influence of Catholicism is more palpable in Ireland and Central and South America than it is in France, Spain or the former Soviet Bloc countries, with the exception of perhaps Poland and Romania.

The CIA factbook (**www.cia.gov/library**) will give you the basic breakdown, by religion, of any country. For more in-depth and detailed information, **Adherents.com** has gathered a pretty comprehensive database of all things religious.

A (Wo)Man's World? Gender Issues

If you are concerned about a possible reversal of the *Roe v. Wade* precedent, the issue of women's rights, particularly reproductive rights, might be high on your list of concerns. Currently, more than 61% of the world's people live in countries where induced abortion is permitted either for a wide range of or reasons or without restriction as to reason. The

Center for Reproductive Rights (**www.reproductiverights.org**) keeps tabs on reproductive rights around the globe.

While abortion is a good litmus test for a nation's attitude toward the rights of women, it hardly tells the whole story. There are parts of Eastern Europe and Russia where domestic violence is considered simply the way things are, although much of the former Soviet world still enjoys liberal abortion laws, a holdover from the Communist days when church and imam had little influence in the legislation of morality. In Latin American countries, domestic violence continues to receive scant attention from the legal system. There is variation in the Islamic world, too. Some countries—Saudi Arabia, most notoriously—treat women essentially as legal minors under the eternal guardianship of their male family members. Other more secular countries still have cultural restrictions governing how women may dress, act or where she can even go. A general breakdown of how each country treats their women (and children) can be viewed at **www.savethechildren.org**. For more income- and employment-related measures, check out the World Economic Forum's (**www.weforum.org**) Global Gender Gap report.

Gender Gap Index:
Top Countries for Women Workers and Entrepreneurs

1	Iceland	16	Sri Lanka
2	Norway	17	Netherlands
3	Finland	18	Latvia
4	Sweden	19	U.S.
5	New Zealand	20	Canada
6	Ireland	21	Trinidad & Tobago
7	Denmark	22	Mozambique
8	Lesotho	23	Australia
9	Philippines	24	Cuba
10	Switzerland	25	Namibia
11	Spain	26	Luxembourg
12	South Africa	27	Mongolia
13	Germany	28	Costa Rica
14	Belgium	29	Argentina
15	U.K.	30	Nicaragua

Source: World Economic Forum: The Global Gender Gap Report, 2010 (www.weforum.org)

World Abortion Laws

Severely Restricted or Prohibited Altogether
(countries in bold allow procedure to save the woman's life)

Afghanistan	Gabon	**Mali**	Sao Tome & Principe
Andorra	**Guatemala**	Malta	Senegal
Angola	Guinea-Bissau	Marshall Islands	**Solomon Islands**
Antigua & Barbuda	Haiti	Mauritania	Somalia
Bangladesh	Honduras	Mauritius	**Sri Lanka**
Bhutan	**Indonesia**	**Mexico**	**Sudan**
Brazil	**Iran**	Micronesia	Suriname
Brunei	Iraq	**Myanmar**	**Syria**
Central African Rep.	**Ireland**	Nicaragua	**Tanzania**
Chile	Kenya	**Nigeria**	**Timor-Leste**
Congo (Brazzaville)	**Kiribati**	Oman	Tonga
Côte d'Ivoire	Laos	Palau	**Tuvalu**
Dem. Rep. of Congo	**Lebanon**	**Panama**	**Uganda**
Dominica	Lesotho	**Papua New Guinea**	**United Arab Emirates**
Dominican Republic	**Libya**	**Paraguay**	**Venezuela**
Egypt	Madagascar	Philippines	**West Bank & Gaza Strip**
El Salvador	**Malawi**	San Marino	**Yemen**

Very Restricted (Generally to Preserve Physical Health)

Argentina	Equatorial Guinea	Niger
Bahamas	Eritrea	Pakistan
Benin	Ethiopia	Peru
Bolivia	Grenada	Poland
Burkina Faso	Guinea	Qatar
Burundi	Jordan	South Korea
Cameroon	Kuwait	Rwanda
Chad	Liechtenstein	Saudi Arabia
Comoros	Maldives	Togo
Costa Rica	Monaco	Uruguay
Djibouti	Morocco	Vanuatu
Ecuador	Mozambique	Zimbabwe

Restricted (Allowance Also to Preserve Mental Health)

Algeria	Liberia	Samoa
Botswana	Malaysia	Seychelles
Colombia	Namibia	Sierra Leone
Gambia	Nauru	Spain
Ghana	New Zealand	Swaziland
Hong Kong	Northern Ireland	Thailand
Israel	St. Kitts & Nevis	Trinidad & Tobago
Jamaica	Saint Lucia	

Somewhat Restricted (Allowed Also on Socioeconomic Grounds)

Australia	Finland	Luxembourg
Barbados	U.K.	Saint Vincent & Grenadines
Belize	Iceland	Taiwan
Cyprus	India	Zambia
Fiji	Japan	

Little or No Restriction

Albania	Cuba	Kazakhstan	Serbia
Armenia	Czech Rep.	Kyrgyzstan	Singapore
Austria	North Korea	Latvia	Slovakia
Azerbaijan	Denmark	Lithuania	South Africa
Bahrain	Estonia	Moldova	Sweden
Belarus	France	Mongolia	Switzerland
Belgium	Fmr. Yugoslav Rep.	Montenegro	Tajikistan
Bosnia-Herzegovina	Macedonia	Nepal	Tunisia
Bulgaria	Georgia	Netherlands	Turkey
Cambodia	Germany	Norway	Turkmenistan
Canada	Greece	Portugal	Ukraine
Cape Verde	Guyana	Puerto Rico	United States
China	Hungary	Romania	Uzbekistan
Croatia	Italy	Russia	Vietnam

Source: Center for Reproductive Rights: "The World's Abortion Laws: Fact Sheet," (2009)
www.reproductiverights.org

Ande Wanderer
Buenos Aires, Argentina

Abortion is a big issue now in Argentina and may soon be legalized. Also, oral contraception is not difficult to get hold of now but it may not be the kind that women from the developing world are accustomed to—what is available are generally the old-school variety that have high hormone levels. Condoms are easily obtained and a new law in Buenos Aires even requires them to be available in all late-night establishments, such as bars and restaurants, but there's no way to put it delicately—the national brand condoms suck. They are not the fancy 'for her pleasure' kind that those from developed countries may be used to.

Jennifer Ashley
Beijing, China

As a "Caucasian" woman in China, I've found it much more difficult to meet potential romantic partners than I did in the U.S. I think this is due to many Chinese men's perception that Western women are, for a variety of reasons, unsuitable for a long-term, take-home-to-meet-your-parents type of relationship. Chinese women, on the other hand, seem much more open to dating foreign men, which makes the pool of potential dating candidates that much smaller to foreign women. I've known plenty of foreign women in China who are perpetually single or seem to have only short-lived relationships, and not for lack of trying to find a romantic partner, or because they just wanted to stay single. That said, I've been in a relationship with another expat for the past two years, and I've got foreign female friends in long-term relationships with other foreigners or locals, so it's not entirely impossible. Just, perhaps, more difficult than we're used to.

Kathleen O'Donnell
Central Mexico

I am pale-skinned and blonde so my appearance is quite different from most locals. As for being a single, over-60 female managing a business in a foreign country...I have found my experience in Mexico much better than in the U.S. If someone doesn't like doing business with me because I'm a woman, at least Mexican people are polite. I haven't found that to always be true in the U.S. But in my 15 years here, I have only had one experience where someone expressed a disinterest in doing business with me...and he was not Mexican!

LGBT: Who Do You Love?

Most progressive countries have struck down laws against homosexual behavior and many have replaced them with laws against discrimination based on sexual preference. Sodomy Laws (**www.sodomylaws.org**), the International Gay and Lesbian Human Rights Commission (**www.iglhrc.org**) and your faithful Wikipedia (search "LGBT_rights_by_country_or_territory") provides an excellent overview of gay rights by country.

However, cultural acceptance is another matter. Laws in your favor don't guarantee you won't be harassed or worse. By and large, the news is good. According to a recent opinion study by National Opinion Research Center at the University of Chicago, most countries are becoming more tolerant toward gays and lesbians, but the trend is not universal (approval is dropping in Cyprus, the Czech Republic, Latvia and Russia) and obviously varies between urban and cosmopolitan areas and the hinterland. Try the Gay Times (**www.gaytimes. co.uk/gt/listings.asp**) or the International Gay and Lesbian Travel Association (**www.iglta.org**) for a more detailed lowdown on how necessary it is to keep it on the down-low.

Five Most Tolerant Countries Toward Homosexual Behavior

Netherlands
Denmark
Norway
Switzerland
Belgium

Source: University of Chicago,
National Opinion Research Center study, 2011

The Following Countries Have Enforceable Laws Against Sex Between Consenting Adults of the Same Sex:

Afghanistan
Algeria
Angola
Bahrain
Bangladesh
Barbados
Bhutan
Botswana
Brunei
Burundi
Cameroon
Djibouti
Eritrea
Ethiopia
Gambia
Ghana
Grenada
Guinea

Guyana
Iran
Jamaica
Kenya
Kosovar Auto. Rep.
Kuwait
Lebanon
Liberia
Libya
Malawi
Malaysia
Maldives
Marshall Islands
Mauritania
Mauritius
Morocco
Mozambique
Myanmar

Namibia
Nepal
Nicaragua
Nigeria
Oman
Pakistan
Palestine Territory
Papua New Guinea
Qatar
Russia: Chechnya
Saint Lucia
Saudi Arabia
Senegal
Seychelles
Sierra Leone
Singapore
Solomon Islands
Somalia

Sri Lanka
Sudan
Swaziland
Syria
Tanzania
Togo
Tonga
Trinidad & Tobago
Tunisia
Turkmenistan
Uganda
UAE
Uzbekistan
Western Samoa
Yemen
Zambia
Zimbabwe

Rights Conferred on Same-Sex Partners Worldwide:
(Formal legal recognitions of same-sex partnerships at the national, state, and provincial levels)

Andorra
Argentina
Australia
Austria
Belgium
Brazil
Canada
Colombia
Croatia
Czech Republic
Denmark
Ecuador

Falkland Islands
Finland
France
French Guyana
Germany
Greenland
Hungary
Iceland
Ireland
Israel
Luxembourg
Mexico

Netherlands
New Zealand
Norway
Portugal
Slovenia
South Africa
Spain
Sweden
Switzerland
United Kingdom
Uruguay

Sources: International Gay and Lesbian Human Rights Commission (www.iglhrc.org)
Wikipedia (www.wikipedia.org)

The Following Countries Offer Immigration Benefits To Same-Sex Couples:

Argentina	Israel
Australia	Luxembourg
Belgium	Netherlands
Brazil	New Zealand
Canada	Norway
Czech Republic	Portugal
Denmark	Romania
Finland	South Africa
France	Spain
Germany	Sweden
Greenland	Switzerland
Hungary	U.K.
Iceland	

Source: en.wikipedia.org/wiki/Immigration_equality

Jude Angione
Toronto, Canada

If you're a gay or lesbian, Canada is a terrific place to live. I can now marry a same-sex partner if I find someone to settle down with. Toronto is very cosmopolitan. Different races and ethnic groups mix more easily than in the States and that's really nice. Interracial couples raise absolutely no eyebrows here either.

Bill Agee
Copenhagen, Denmark

Scandinavia is the most equality-focused region of the world that I know of, whether it concerns gender, race, age or sexual orientation. Gay marriage has been on the law books here for many years. The politicians fight amongst themselves over who gets the biggest billing in the Pride parade every year, and virtually all parties are working for the LGBT vote. This has led to full integration into Danish society, which means that there are not the gay ghettos and huge number of LGBT clubs/bars that you find in large U.S. cities, which is a bit of a surprise to some LGBT people who move here. Nevertheless, Copenhagen and the other big Scandinavian cities all have a full array of bars and clubs for LGBT people. In Denmark, there is even a group for expats, called Pangea (www.lbl.dk/2538/) that offers LGBT newcomers an introduction and a startup social network. I met my partner, who is Danish, while I was living in Sweden.

Leslie Reed
Incheon, South Korea

Unfortunately, it is still legal to fire someone from a job for their sexual preference and gays have no legal protections in Korea.

While many lesbians go to the hill ("Homo Hill" in Seoul), the dedicated lesbian bars are very hidden, and strictly women only.

Expat High: Drugs and the Law

One person's pastime is another country's felony. Thanks in large measure to the War on Drugs, Americans represent 5% of the global population but U.S. prisons hold a quarter of the world's inmates. Not every government thinks this is the optimal way to run a society and many have passed laws to that effect. Other countries, such as India, Morocco, Egypt and Thailand, have harsh drug penalties but lax enforcement, and cannabis, hashish and sometimes even opium are widely smoked.

But of course, squalid jail time and usurious fines are not unheard of. If you want to get a good overview of global drug laws and prefer the wonky stuff, the International Hard Reduction Association (**www.ihra.net**) keeps pretty good tabs on who's doing what. For the view from the street, the stoners/reporters at **webehigh.com** give the ganja lowdown in cities and countries around the world. The vaults of Erowid (**www.erowid.org**) also can provide valuable information, particularly as it relates to the more mind-expanding end of the pharmacology spectrum.

The Right to Self-Medicate: Where Tolerance Reigns

Argentina
On August 25, 2009, the Argentine Supreme Court ruled that imposing criminal penalties on citizens for the personal possession of drugs is unconstitutional. Word on the street is that decriminalization for personal use is not far away.

Brazil

Two separate legislative measures, enacted in 2002 and 2006, have led to the partial decriminalization of drug possession for personal use. Instead of prison sentences, defendants are now given the option of treatment and community service.

Czech Republic

Check out what's considered a legal stash (worst case scenario, a fine):
Amphetamine: 2 grams or less
Hashish: 5 grams or less
Cannabis: 15 grams or less
Heroin: 1.5 grams or less
Cocaine: 1 gram or less
LSD: 5 tabs or less
Ecstasy: 4 tablets or less
Methamphetamine: 2 grams or less
Hallucinogenic Mushrooms: 40 pieces or less

Mexico

In 2009, Mexico nixed all criminal penalties for personal possession/ use. (e.g. up to five grams of cannabis, half a gram of cocaine, and one-tenth of a gram of heroin). Those found in possession will now be offered treatment instead of jail.

The Netherlands

While Holland still pursues a laid-back, harm reduction model against minor drug offenses, lately there has been some pushback against the proliferation of coffee shops and the government is seeking to limit the number of pot clubs in operation, and non-residents will be increasingly restricted from buying Dutch cannabis over the counter.

Portugal

No criminal penalties for purchase, possession and use of any drug. Period. Marijuana, methamphetamine, cocaine, heroin—doesn't matter. As long as it's for personal use (defined as a 10-day supply).

Uruguay

Uruguay never really ever outlawed drugs for personal use to begin with. Judges have latitude, but ordinary users are not given penalties.

Cannabis Countries:
Where pot smokers are seldom, if ever, prosecuted
(countries in bold have no criminal penalties for personal use):

Argentina	**Mexico**
Australia*	**Netherlands**
Belgium	**Portugal**
Canada	**Spain**
Colombia	United Kingdom
Czech Republic	**Uruguay**
Germany	**Venezuela**
Luxembourg	

*cannabis laws vary by state

The Don't-Even-Think-About-It Countries

Good luck getting the U.S. State Department to care if you're busted in...

China: China has a zero-tolerance policy for drug possession/use and a flexible approach to capital offenses. An estimated 68 different crimes can result in execution, including drug offenses. Possession of even small amounts will land you in a police-run rehabilitation center that is hardly distinguishable from a forced labor camp.

Iran: As the nation tries to squelch a growing addiction problem, hanging of drug offenders is becoming the regime's deterrent of choice. Between May–June 2010 another 30 narcotics offenders were put to death for trafficking in marijuana, cocaine, opium, and methamphetamine.

Malaysia: Malaysia's drug laws are merciless. Over 100 people, roughly a third of them foreigners, have been hanged in Malaysia for drug offenses since the nation's mandatory death sentence for trafficking was introduced over two decades ago.

Saudi Arabia: Should you be convicted of the import, manufacture, possession, or consumption of illegal drugs, or much else that most of the Western world considers fun, you will face an array of harsh penalties that may include a lengthy prison stay, an exorbitant fine, deportation, and possibly a public flogging. If you are convicted of drug trafficking, the penalty is death and there are no exceptions.

Singapore: Newly arriving visitors to the Republic are given forms by immigration authorities that say "Warning. Death for Drug Traffickers under Singapore Law." Anyone found in possession of more than 15 grams of cannabis or three grams of cocaine is presumed to be a trafficker which merits a mandatory death sentence. Casual users are jailed. The fortunate ones get off with a mere caning.

United Arab Emirates: Despite its liberal Gulf State reputation, the UAE tolerates not the slightest iota of drugs. Most notoriously, a British tourist was given a four-year prison sentence after high-tech scanning equipment detected a mite-sized speck of marijuana (0.03g) on the bottom of his shoe as he passed through customs. Even over-the-counter medications and doctor-prescribed pills can get you arrested.

Jennifer St. Martin
Lisbon, Portugal

One thing that has reduced the crime rate is that Portugal decriminalized drugs, and when someone is caught with them, they help them get to a free rehab program instead of throwing them in jail. I have read articles stating that this country has the highest success rate in eliminating drug problems.

Paul Tenney
Singapore

I think most people in the U.S. have a skewed view of Singapore. The laws don't affect me at all. There are two things going on here: while Singapore IS very strict on punishment for certain things like drug trafficking and violent crime, you will find that in day-to-day life you will feel a sense of freedom that you can't imagine in the U.S. The first thing going on is that Singapore is not a police state like the U.S. is—you will hardly ever even see a police officer, and yet crime rates are almost non-existent here (no crime doesn't mean no crime though, as they like to remind you). Second, I perceive something of a double standard for expats vs. the local population—an expat is not going to get arrested for spitting on the street or smoking in the wrong place or jaywalking. Most people will just look away, or at the worst a security guard (not a cop) might ask you to modify your behavior. Also, if you were to get into some kind of trouble, the most likely first step is that they would simply deport you (very promptly) but this seems much better than being thrown in jail.

Hailey McPherson

Hong Kong

It's VERY illegal to bring drugs into here, but that doesn't affect me at all. If you're American and coming to Hong Kong, keep the weed at home.

On Dry Land: Where Liquor Is Illegal
The following countries either prohibit liquor or severely limit any and all consumption:

Afghanistan	Libya
Bangladesh*	Pakistan
Brunei*	Saudi Arabia
Iran	Sudan
Kuwait	United Arab Emirates*

*legal availability for non-Muslims

Scott

Riyadh, Saudi Arabia

Alcohol is generally "not allowed" but at the same time "generally permitted." That is only on the (expat) compound. Take stuff off compound and risk is all yours. Sell it off compound and the risk has just been amplified. Provide it or give it to the locals and there will be far more than hell to pay. Normally, companies will consider you a kite— when something like that happens, they cut your string and let the authorities handle you. If one is lucky, the company will get you deported without jail time.

Drinking and driving is dangerous anywhere, but here it is especially so, even if you don't have an accident. Frequently there are random checkpoints set up throughout the city (including the Ring Road and main streets and sub main streets). It wouldn't be a pretty thing to get caught at a checkpoint blitzed!

The Right to Bear Arms: Gun Control

Over 120 countries have stricter gun control measures than the strictest gun control states in the U.S. and less than a handful have more liberal policies than your average Red State. Regardless of whether you believe that guns kill people or people kill people, knowing the facts about who's allowed to pack heat and how much there is of it around is critical info. The Free Existence Index of Worldwide Gun Rights (**www.freeexistence.org**) has an impressive online database of gun laws from around the world, in case you're thinking about spraying some lead abroad…or trying to avoid other people who do. Also, the Small Arms Survey (**www.smallarmssurvey.org**) keeps track of where the guns are…and aren't.

Countries With More Gun Freedom Than Any U.S. State

Bolivia
Czech Republic
Lithuania

Source: freeexistence.org

Strictest Gun Control Laws

China	Vietnam
Luxembourg	Korea (South)
Solomon Islands	Taiwan
Timor	Venezuela
Uganda	Hong Kong
Uzbekistan	Singapore
Kuwait	United Kingdom
Iran	

From My Cold, Dead Hands:
Top Gun-Owning Countries

Guns per 100 residents

U.S.	**88.8**	Sweden	**31.6**
Yemen	**54.8**	Norway	**31.3**
Switzerland	**45.7**	France	**31.2**
Finland	**45.3**	Canada	**30.8**
Serbia	**37.8**	Iceland	**30.3**
Cyprus	**36.4**	Germany	**30.3**
Saudi Arabia	**35.0**	Oman	**25.4**
Iraq	**34.2**	Bahrain	**24.8**
Uruguay	**31.8**	Kuwait	**24.8**
Sweden	**31.6**	Macedonia	**24.1**

Source: www.smallarmssurvey.org

Is Everybody Happy?
Happiness and Life Satisfaction

Happiness. Isn't that what it's really all about in the end? So all right, your line of thinking might go, 'to find the best country to live in, why not just see where the people are happiest?' Sure, but concepts such as happiness and life satisfaction are a bit more elusive than Gross Domestic Product when it comes to both defining and quantifying them. Not that that's stopped numerous well-funded efforts from trying to do just that. The Organization of Economic Co-operation and Development (**www.oecd.org**) keeps its survey feelers out to gauge happiness among its member states and they, no surprise, conclude that it pretty well correlates with, er, Gross Domestic Product (well, national affluence, anyway). The Happy Planet Index (**www.happyplanetindex.org**) looks at human well-being in relation to their connection to environment and ecological footprint. Their ranking metrics put the Latin American countries, Costa Rica in particular, on top, while much of the so-called "developed" world vacillates between glum and miserable, once you factor in how much pollution and resource exploitation they're generating just to keep their spirits up. The World Database of Happiness at Erasmus University, Rotterdam (**worlddatabaseofhappiness.eur.nl**) offers a "continuous register of scientific research on subjective appreciation of life" and ranks around 150 countries on various measures of their per capita joie de vivre.

The Happiest Places on Earth: Countries With Higher "Happiness Index" Than the U.S.

Brazil	**7.5**	Canada	**7.8**
New Zealand	**7.5**	Panama	**7.8**
Venezuela	**7.5**	Sweden	**7.8**
Austria	**7.6**	Finland	**7.9**
Dominican Republic	**7.6**	Mexico	**7.9**
Ireland	**7.6**	Norway	**7.9**
Netherlands	**7.6**	Switzerland	**8.0**
Australia	**7.7**	Iceland	**8.2**
Colombia	**7.7**	Denmark	**8.3**
Luxembourg	**7.7**	Costa Rica	**8.5**

Source: Veenhoven, R., World Database of Happiness, Erasmus University Rotterdam

May We Suggest?
The Getting Out 61 +1

May We Suggest? The Getting Out 61+1

So...Where To Go?

While you're bound to find Americans living in almost any country you'd care to name, certain nations (and areas within) attract far more than others (Canada, Mexico, U.K., many; Iran, Sudan and North Korea, not so many). There are some, like the Scandinavian countries, who make residency too difficult for the average mortal. Others are downright inhospitable. More than a fair share of undeveloped nations—particularly in Africa and Central Asia—suffer from too much crushing poverty, lawlessness, corruption and lack of even basic services to offer anything approaching a tolerable quality of life.

If your net worth has mulitple commas, you'd be welcome almost anywhere and can hire the right people to make the proper introductions. On the chance that you've fallen in love with a native of some country (particularly if marriage is involved), have family there or land a job offer or a transfer, then the decision about where to go has already been made for you—and many of the most daunting "Getting In" hurdles will have been removed from your path.

For the rest of you out there who are casting about for a place to live that isn't the USA, the following countries offer the most logical balance of desirability, cost, ease of entry and availability of work. As you'll see, some may favor one at the expense of another, so that's where your personal preferences and attributes enter into it. And while it's highly unlikely that you'd be forced to rub elbows with other Americans if you don't want to, these represent the places where you're most likely to find them, for the very reason that they offer some package of features that makes these countries both attractive and possible. But you'll also find among these a few relatively undiscovered gems.

In short, you'll find samples of every type of nation. There are brutal regimes with good working conditions, paradises on earth if they let you in and/or you can afford it, cheap and funky living if you can deal with the hassles, and everything in between. Each profile represents a synthesis of everything that's been covered in the previous chapters, plus a whole lot more. Once you get the hang of sizing up a potential new home country, you'll be able to do it for yourself for anywhere in the world you'd like to go (should you care to do so).

Again, much of the information contained in the following pages is greatly condensed. It is intended to give you a general idea of what kind of life you might expect there and who it might appeal to, and what possible avenues of residency and employment are most likely available. In the case of visas and residency, in particular, what is presented here are the most relevant categories for an American seeking to move there and, rather than an exhaustive list of all possible conditions, options and requirements, the focus is on giving you a feel for whether such an avenue would be possible for you.

Ultimately, moving anywhere will necessitate contact with government bureaus—particularly the Consular Affairs department of that country's embassy in the U.S. (usually, the first stop) and/or their Ministry of Foreign Affairs/Immigration Bureau—and it is they who will provide you with all the current procedural details and make the ultimate decision about whether you'll be allowed to stay. These and hundreds of other additional resources and contacts can be found in the last section of the book, covering almost every country in the world, connecting you to whatever else you might need to put your particular Getting Out plan into action.

But first, planet Earth. Even if you're not one of those Americans who can't find their hometown on Google Maps, a little geographical orientation couldn't hurt. Herewith, we circle the globe with Getting Out in mind.

Ready for a short trip around the world?

Good Neighbors: Canada and the Caribbean:

Some people who want to flee don't feel the need to flee very far (makes frequent family, business and shopping trips back "home" much easier). Head north to **Canada (9)**, and your cultural transition is minimal, though your immigration hurdles can be significant. And the weather, well, in some places it's not too bad. Off America's Eastern Seaboard, on the other hand, lies a speckled sun-kissed world of tin drums and tax shelters—not to mention some alarming crime, poverty and human rights abuses, depending on where you land. Even in the best of that world, opportunities are scarcer than snowflakes, and generally only the affluently self-sufficient (if not the idle rich) could even cast their sails in that direction. Of these, passport-hunters choose **St. Kitts and Nevis (45)**, where citizenship comes to those who pay, though they'll likely actually live elsewhere. Those who park themselves in-country (often aboard a yacht) gravitate toward the **Bahamas (4)**, which offers an agreeable blend of proximity and banking discretion. But if you're of more modest means, the

Dominican Republic (17) offers the best combination of Caribbean perks at a reasonable price-point.

The Gringo Trail: Mexico, Central and South America

Cross the Rio Grande and you're in a very different world. Immigration issues are easier and the dollar's buying power surges, but goods and services are harder to come by, roads are rougher and nepotism and bribery are facts of life. Here begins "the Gringo trail," where for centuries, disgruntled Americans have traveled in search of exotic tropical living, young brides and cheap booze. While **Mexico's (34)** borderlands (particularly in Baja California) used to be pretty popular with the quick escape crowd, narco violence has pushed the action further south where there's not so much lead whizzing through the air. In recent years, there has also been a steady migration of "green" expats seeking a post-carbon existence living in sustainable "eco-villages" and hoping to forge a deeper connection with nature. You'll find them in **Belize (5)**, **Costa Rica (13)** and **Panama (39)**, which offer the most political stability in the region, though look for **Nicaragua (38)**, the low-priced upstart, to make some headway in this regard. In South America, **Venezuela (60)** puts you at the center of the new populist political alignment, though it's really its neighbor, **Colombia (12)**, now putting its narco nightmare behind it, that is earning a reputation as a new expatriate frontier. With the giant blade of Andes running down its Western flank, it, along with **Ecuador (18)** and **Peru (40)**, offers every kind of climate and ecosystem in very compact areas, providing simple living and spectacular natural diversity at rock-bottom prices. South America's largest nation, the former Portuguese colony of **Brazil (6)**, is shaping up to be the next powerhouse economy of the Americas, offering great beaches and a great (though shrinking) Amazon rainforest in your backyard. Not-so-tropical **Argentina (2)** attracts bargain-hunting sophisticates with its Euro-centric vibe, while stretched out along the coast on the opposite side (in many ways besides geography), **Chile (10)** offers the best infrastructure on the continent, its highest mountains, most open markets and the least sunshine. And for easy Mediterranean-style living without too much immigration competition, you could do worse than sturdy little **Uruguay (58)**.

Which Europe? One Continent, Many Unions

So you want to move to Europe? Which one? Europe is a continent in the Western Hemisphere comprising as many as 51 countries, depending on whether you include certain autonomous regions. The European Union, on the other hand, is a political union, comprising only 27 countries with an additional handful of applications pending. Citizenship in one member state gives you residency and employment privileges in all of them, though residency and work permits for non-E.U. citizens generally apply only to the country issuing them. Confusing matters even more is that the Eurozone—i.e., the countries using the Euro as their monetary unit—comprises 23 countries, while other European nations, such as the U.K., are part of the E.U. but not the Eurozone, and Switzerland, right in the center of Europe, is a member of neither. And finally, you should be aware that the Schengen Area, the 26 countries signatory to a common border treaty that treats all members as a single entity in terms of entry and passport control, does not precisely match any of the other groups exactly either.

Countries of Europe

Albania	Denmark	Liechtenstein	Russia
Andorra	Estonia	Lithuania	San Marino
Armenia	Finland	Luxembourg	Serbia
Austria	France	Macedonia	Slovakia
Azerbaijan	Georgia	Malta	Slovenia
Belarus	Germany	Moldova	Spain
Belarus	Greece	Monaco	Sweden
Belgium	Hungary	Montenegro	Switzerland
Bosnia & Herzegovina	Iceland	The Netherlands	Turkey
Bulgaria	Ireland	Norway	Ukraine
Croatia	Italy	Poland	United Kingdom
Cyprus	Kosovo	Portugal	Vatican City (Holy See)
Czech Republic	Latvia	Romania	

Member States of the European Union

Austria	Germany	The Netherlands
Belgium	Greece	Poland
Bulgaria	Hungary	Portugal
Cyprus	Ireland	Romania
Czech Republic	Italy	Slovakia
Denmark	Latvia	Slovenia
Estonia	Lithuania	Spain
Finland	Luxembourg	Sweden
France	Malta	United Kingdom

Candidate Countries:

Croatia (Accession to be completed in latter half of 2011, full ratification by member states expected in 2013)

Former Yugoslav Republic of Macedonia (still in Accession process)

Iceland (Application began in July, 2009. Disputes over fisheries have delayed accession).

Montenegro: Officially granted candidate status in December, 2010.
Turkey: Expected to be recognized as member state in approx. 2015.

Countries of the Eurozone

Andorra	France	Luxembourg	San Marino
Austria	Germany	Malta	Slovakia
Belgium	Greece	Monaco	Slovenia
Cyprus	Ireland	Montenegro	Spain
Estonia	Italy	Netherlands	Vatican City
Finland	Kosovo	Portugal	

Candidate Countries:
As of 2011, Denmark, Latvia, and Lithuania currently in process of applying.

Schengen Countries

Austria	Germany	Liechtenstein*	Portugal
Belgium	Greece	Lithuania	Slovakia
Czech Republic	Hungary	Luxembourg	Slovenia
Denmark	Iceland	Malta	Spain
Finland	Italy	Netherlands	Sweden
Estonia	Latvia	Norway Poland	Switzerland
France			

*Signatory but awaiting full membership. Scheduled for late 2011.

Once upon a time, Europe was also divided into Western and Eastern halves, divided by an "Iron Curtain." Though differences between the two erode further over time, these distinctions still persist and prove useful when contemplating a move here.

Western (or "Old") Europe: A large (albeit shrinking) portion of the American melting pot traces its origins on the Continent. In the case of **Ireland (28)** and **Italy (30)**, ancestral roots will make some headway with immigration. The hurdles you have to jump to get into the **U.K. (57)** and **France (21)** are daunting, both in terms of entry requirements and cost of living, but their large American/international populations are a testament to their achievability. Likewise, **Spain (51)**, **The Netherlands (a.k.a. Holland; 36)**, **Greece (23)**, **Portugal (43)** and especially **Germany (22)** are far more do-able. The northern half seems to keep the trains running on time better than the south, though this seems to work in inverse ratio to the quality of the native cuisine. In Scandinavia, populations tend to be more homogeneous and visa and immigration issues are daunting, though people still attempt to make a go of it in progressive, though downright pricey, paradises such as **Sweden (52)** and **Denmark (16)**. Social democracy is the rule here, and there's not much here for the tax-aversive who aren't also captains of the Fortune 500. **Switzerland (53)**, for instance, offers a superior quality of life compared to just about any country in the world, and partly as a result, residency is only for the most tenacious (or lucky). Shelter-seekers of merely affluent status would probably have to settle for **Andorra (1)**...unless of course, proximity to the sea is an issue, in which case, mid-priced **Malta (33)** might be an option.

Eastern ("New") Europe: The old Soviet Bloc countries on the continent's eastern half offer Eurovibe at a fraction of the cost, though popular and rapidly developing economies like the **Czech Republic (15)** are reaching parity with depressed Western bargain countries. Barriers to immigration are more negotiable and while infrastructure might not be tip-top, it's hardly bottom of the barrel and definitely on an upward trend. Most of the international crowd congregates in the cities. Besides Prague, there's cheap urban sophistication to be had in **Budapest, Hungary (25)**, **Ljubljana, Slovenia (48)**, **Riga, Latvia (32)** and **Talinn, Estonia (20)**, the latter choices offering better values with a lot of the same semi-exotic charm. Budget resort-seekers will find what they're after in **Croatia (14)** and **Bulgaria (7)**. **Poland (42)** and **Russia (44)**, on the other hand, offer little in the way of comfortable weather but far more of that most valuable of Getting Out commodities—jobs.

Bright Spots: Turkey, the Middle East and Africa

As a secular Islamic state with one foot in the E.U., **Turkey (55)** offers Mediterranean living and a gateway to the more exotic Middle East. Across the sea, North Africa seems to have erupted in turmoil though it's not yet arrived as far west as **Morocco (35)**, while in **Egypt (19)**, the heady days of revolution are now receding and expatriate life there appears to be going on (for better and worse) as before. Full of cheap shabby charm and ancient splendor, these nations offer decadent and exotic slumming within earshot of the call of the muezzin. **Israel (29)** is still welcoming world Jewry, and an overwhelming number who take up the offer are American-born. **Saudi Arabia (46)** and the **United Arab Emirates (UAE) (56)**, though hardly the roaring economies of yesteryear, haven't stopped offering fat contracts to anyone with the right skills willing to pull a year or more of air-conditioned expatriatism out in the Arabian dunes. Sitting at Africa's southern tip like a low-hanging fruit, and less victimized by political and economic chaos relative to much of the rest of the continent, **South Africa (49)** is pulling itself back out of crime-swamped doldrums, offering superior infrastructure, spectacular coastline and plenty of wild terrain to anyone with the means or the know-how to make a go of it.

Re-Orient Yourself: Asia

Although Asia is the world's largest continent, much of the interior is a mess of brutal and primitive dictatorships, and the action pretty much congregates along its Indian and Pacific coasts. Its two behemoths, **China (11)** and **India (26)**, which together account for around 37% of the population of Planet Earth, are now attracting job-seekers fleeing the moribund U.S. employment scene. Banking and finance types weaned on first-world culture and infrastructure keep tiny sort-of-autonomous **Hong Kong (24)** buzzing. Still reeling from the 2011 earthquake/tsunami/meltdown disaster, the magnitude of which will take decades to fully assess, **Japan (31)** is still welcoming English teachers to come over on teach-and-live deals. Across the Sea of Japan, what **South Korea (50)** might lack in cultural verve it makes up for with very attractive overseas work packages. Then there is that other, steamier Asia, offering surf, sex and sunshine on the cheap, while offering greater sacrifices of modern comforts and conveniences in return. Despite hiccups of unrest, **Thailand (54)** still reigns supreme among them, though cutting-edge bargain-hunters are staking out their turf next door in even less-developed **Cambodia (8)**. **Vietnam (61)**, the **Philippines (41)** and **Indonesia (27)**, also offer attractive rates on slices of paradise while still maintaining some pulse of economic activity—and opportunity. On the tiny island nation of **Singapore (47)**, that pulse—stimulated by one of the most laissez-faire business climates in the world—has become a roar that pretty much drowns out everything else and some of the world's most generous expat salaries, best infrastructure, lowest taxes and highest cost of living can be found here.

South Pacific: Australia, New Zealand and Polynesia

This watery region in the far corner of the globe offers lifestyles both modern and primitive. You've got **Australia (3)**, far far away from the U.S. by land, but familiar enough in culture and lifestyle, and they've got lots of space and a need for people. Even further down under, but equally familiar in terms of culture and lifestyle, **New Zealand (37)** is pretty predisposed to rolling out the welcome mat should you decide pack up and move to the other side of the world. Most of Polynesia, however, is made up of tiny enchanting atolls, often pristine and undeveloped, spread out in a vast coral blue sea, many of them divvied up between the U.S., France and the U.K.. For an almost affordable taste of sun-kissed tiki wonderland thousands of nautical miles away from the closest maddening crowd, you can try and put down roots on the tiny island nation of **Vanuatu (59)**.

Can't decide? Why not try them all (61+)!

1. Andorra

Climate: Temperate; snowy, cold winters and warm, dry summers
Government: Parliamentary democracy that retains as its heads of state two co-princes
Population: 83,888
Currency: Euro (EUR): 1 EUR = 1.36 USD
Language: Catalan (official), French, Castilian, Portuguese
Religious Groups: Roman Catholic (predominant)
Ethnic Groups: Spanish (43%), Andorran (33%), Portuguese (11%), French (7%), other (6%)
Cost of Living compared to the U.S.: Not too outrageous but don't expect any bargains, particularly if the Euro is strong

Perched high in Pyrenees, overlooking France and Spain (on either side), the tiny nation of Andorra doesn't have a whole lot of excitement to offer besides a shelter for your hard-earned cash and fairly straightforward entry requirements (as long as you don't intend to work there).

Living There

Governance: Free and fair elections, although more than half of Andorra's residents are non-citizens and cannot vote. The country has a French-style legal and judicial system that guarantees basic rights. A 2009 court decision gave legal recognition to unions.
Infrastructure: Good
Internet: Approximately one in four residents
Healthcare: New residents need to sign up for a private medical scheme. There is an excellent new hospital.
GDP: $3.3 billion
GDP (per capita): $46,700
Sovereign Debt: N/A
Working There: Europeans get first crack at available jobs. It's not unheard of to find gigs as bartenders, service personnel, and ski instructors during ski season but that's about it.
Regulatory Environment: Generally less stringent than the rest of Europe.
Taxes: Andorra is Europe's least-known tax haven. There is no income tax—although the new deposit system for passive residents effectively loses you the interest on €24,000. There is a new property purchase tax of 1.25% and a 4% tax levied on all

real estate transactions. 0–15% capital gains tax on real estate transactions based on number of years real estate has been owned by taxpayer. Otherwise, there is no inheritance tax, no wealth tax, no profits tax, and no VAT.

Cannabis: Illegal

Homosexuality: Civil unions recognized. Discrimination against sexual orientation illegal.

Abortion: Prohibited

Women's Issues: Women enjoy the same across-the-board rights that men do, although they are underrepresented in government. Violence/harassment against women is a problem and no laws exist to address it. The government has no departments dealing with women's issues nor do they run any shelters for battered women.

Guns: Guns, pistols, shotguns legal but require licensing and there are storage requirements.

Crime: Low, and mostly of the petty variety.

Real Estate: The government encourages foreign investment, including real estate. Mortgages are available. Minimum loan of €30,000 but cannot exceed 70% of purchase price. Five to 30 years, rates from approximately 5%.

Life Expectancy: 82.51 years

Moving There:

Residence permits are a matter of show-them-the-money, in this case, three times the Andorran minimum wage, or around $1350 a month, plus the equivalent of the annual minimum wage for every dependent. As long as you're of independent means or have a reasonably remunerative home- or Internet-based business, life here is within your reach.

Schengen Visa: 90-day stay allowed within six-month period.

Residence permits, called *residencias*, are available to applicants, retired or otherwise, who have an address in the Principality and who genuinely wish to reside in Andorra for an extended period and take part in community life. Applicants must show proof of a sufficient private income and the permit is renewable each year. The bad news? The application process is conducted entirely in the Catalan language. Permits are one year, renewable.

Work Permit: A temporary work permit can be issued for seasonal (ski resort) work, should you be lucky enough to get hired somewhere, but they are only valid from October–May, after which you get shown the door. Permanent work permits are said to exist, though no one has actually seen one.

Student visas: Available per the usual requirements.

Eligible to apply for citizenship after 25 years.

2. Argentina

Climate: Mostly temperate; arid in southeast; subantarctic in southwest
Government: Republic
Population: 40,913,584
Currency: Argentine Peso (ARS): 1 ARS = 0.24 USD
Language: Spanish (official), English, Italian, German, French
Religious Groups: Roman Catholic (92%), Protestant (2%), Jewish (2%), other (4%)
Ethnic Groups: white (97%), mestizo (3%)
Cost of Living compared to the U.S.: Cheap...for now

The land of the tango boasts the sophistication and modernity of Europe with a more Latin American sticker price. Having the survived the one-two punch of fascism and IMF-engineered financial collapse, the resource-rich country, its social-progressive government, and its generally tolerant people look to a brighter future. The capital, Buenos Aires, has been rated as one of the lowest-cost major cities in the world and there is even cheaper land to be had out on the pampas. Not only that, but from the renewability of a tourist visa to the requirements for citizenship, the barriers to long-term stay are reasonably surmountable. Little wonder it's become a mecca attracting 60,000 or so disaffected Americans and other interlopers. Vegetarians, however, might find the overemphasis on meat-eating difficult to, you know, swallow.

Living There

Governance: Free and fair elections with corruption still a factor but in decline. Healthy freedom of the press, academic freedom and freedom to organize and strike. People can generally practice their religion freely. The government has been taking steps to create a more independent judiciary though problems still exist.

Infrastructure: Good. Extensive highways as well as rail and subway. Argentina also has one of the best developed telecommunications systems in Latin America.

Internet: Very good. Argentina's Internet penetration is twice the world average and the broadband market is one of the most developed in Latin America. Hi-speed Internet widely available.

Healthcare: Argentina provides free emergency and non-emergency services to anyone, regardless of their immigration status. Private hospitals in Buenos Aires are generally good, but facilities outside the capital might leave a bit to be desired. Private physicians, clinics, and hospitals often expect immediate cash upon service.

GDP: $596 billion

GDP (Per Capita): $14,700

Sovereign Debt: 50.3% of GDP

Working There: Seasoned expats warn that you'll struggle if your Spanish skills aren't up to par—you'll be limited to teaching English or working in a tourism-related industry. If you're bilingual, you may find something in IT, nursing, telecommunications, accounting, customer service or finance. Unemployment, once as high as 21% is now down to single digits so hopefully you won't face the highly competitive job environment that previous expats encountered.

Regulatory Environment: Somewhat burdensome and lacks transparency.

Taxes: Argentina uses a progressive system for personal income tax that ranges between 9% and 35%. Businesses must pay a flat tax of 35% on income. VAT of 21%.

Cannabis: Decriminalized

Homosexuality: On July 15, 2010, Argentina legalized same sex marriage. Gay couples are also allowed to adopt children. In Buenos Aires, there is a ban on discrimination based on sexual preference, and a national anti-discrimination law is pending. Argentines are culturally tolerant and there is a large gay scene, particularly in Buenos Aires.

Abortion: Only to preserve physical health or in case of rape.

Women's Issues: Women are well-represented in business and government, though sexual harassment and violence are hardly unheard of.

Guns: Private gun ownership legal for target shooting, hunting, and self-defense. Government authorization required.

Crime: Not too bad, though you might not agree if you lived in Buenos Aires or in the sketchier districts of other major cities, where robbery can be a fact of life and violent crime is a growing concern. Mostly petty crime elsewhere.

Real Estate: Foreigners can buy land in Argentina—vineyards, ranches and homestead plots are plentiful. Prices are very reasonable compared to the U.S. but they're rising. Financing is seldom available, however, so property must be paid for in cash. There's a limit of $10,000 that can legally be brought into the country, and money wired from U.S. banks will be hit with a 4% fee. Be sure to calculate accordingly.

Life Expectancy: 76.76 years

Moving There

Some expats take advantage of the rather loosey-goosey approach to visa enforcement and never graduate from tourist status, though the government is slowly tightening up oversight. For those without a job offer—either from an Argentine company or a U.S. company operating in Argentina—the financier visa is the typical way to earn legal long-term status. Most Argentine visas are issued for one year and renewable. When you have resided in Argentina for three years as a temporary resident, you can apply for permanent legal residency, which allows you to seek and hold employment, as well. If you stay in the country for two more years as a legal resident, you can then apply for citizenship.

Tourist Visa: No visa required for stays of less than 90 days. You can apply for one additional 90-day extension before you have to leave the country. Argentina recently raised the fine for overstaying your visa from $12 to $76.

Temporary Residence Visas:

Labor Contract: This visa is available to employees outside the country who are offered a job inside Argentina and requires a valid job offer/contract of at least six–12 months. It is NOT available to foreigners already residing in Argentina who are looking for local employment.

Secondment: This visa is issued to foreigners coming to work in Argentina on behalf of a non-Argentine company with operations in Argentina. No contract is required but the government does have to approve the assignment.

Financier Visa: Applicants must show proof of a guaranteed monthly income of 2,600 pesos (approximately $900) that can be transferred to an Argentine bank. Income can come from a trust, business dividends, an annuity, or a business and other sources. You just have to show proof that you will continue receiving the minimum income after you've settled in Argentina.

Private Income/Pensioner Visa: Applicants must provide a letter from Social Security Administration or pension fund showing a monthly income that is at least the equivalent of 2,100 Argentine Pesos (approximately $700). Monthly income must be transferred to an Argentine bank. Argentina also has a rentista program which requires a guaranteed monthly income of approximately $2,000/month.

Immigrant with Capital: To qualify, you must invest a minimum of 102,000 Argentine pesos (approximately $40,000) in a government-approved "productive activity" like agriculture, cattle ranching, and a few other select economic sectors. Buying a home or apartment in Argentina usually does not count toward this visa. If certain conditions are met, the Immigrant with Capital visa can be issued on a permanent basis and does not require renewal.

Students (coming to Argentina on a valid study program at Argentine University), **Businesspeople/Entrepreneurs** (who can convince the Argentine consulate of their experience and expertise) and **Owners of Foreign Companies** (with approval of the Argentine Chamber of Commerce and Argentine Consulate) can also receive Temporary Residence Permits. Parents, children and spouses of Argentine Nationals can apply for either **Temporary** or **Permanent Residency.**

Permanent Residency: Three years of legal temporary residency makes you eligible to reside in Argentina permanently. Two more years, and you can apply for citizenship.

Vina Rathbone
Buenos Aires, Argentina

I have been living in Buenos Aires for one year and four months. One thing that differs greatly is the pace of life. My average time spent in a restaurant here is no less than three hours. I relish those long relaxing meals. But then my average time waiting in the checkout line at the supermarket is a miserable 15 minutes. My rent and cost of living are less expensive, but I don't have luxuries like a self-igniting oven or central heating and air conditioning. I'm from a smaller city, so sometimes big-city life is overwhelming, but just last week I went out to the countryside to ride horses and watch a polo game.

A lot of expats can't hack it in Buenos Aires. Everything here is extreme. When things are good, they are the best—the wine, the architecture, the friendships, the romantic men. But the lows are the lowest—the poverty, the corruption, the pollution, the traffic. I wouldn't recommend this city to anyone who isn't extremely patient, open-minded and flexible. Life certainly isn't very easy here, but when things are good, it's the best.

I came here from Seattle where people are very friendly but do not easily welcome others into their social circles. It's a phenomenon known to non-Seattle natives as "the Seattle freeze," and it was very frustrating. In Buenos Aires I loved how easy it was to make friendships with Argentines and especially with other expats, who tend to stick together. People aren't necessarily friendlier here, but in my experience, Argentine friendships are very caring. Personal relationships mean everything here, and when I was ever in a time of need, I was blown away by the willingness of my Argentine friends and acquaintances to help and support me, even with sometimes personal issues like homesickness or medical problems.

As an American woman, it has been very easy to meet Argentine men. However, to my major disappointment I've had much more difficultly forming solid friendships with Argentine women. I think patriarchy plays a big part in having no solid 'sisterhood' like that I was used to in the U.S.

Inflation is another really big problem here. Prices are much higher now than when I came and they change on a daily basis. This is difficult when coming from a country with a very stable economy, and you have to worry about making enough money to support yourself even with inflated prices. Counterfeit money is also a problem here. These seem like huge crises, but in Argentina, it's just another normal day.

Bud Smith (and Sumana Harrison)

San Salvador de Jujuy, Argentina

Throughout the broad and greatly varied lands of Argentina there is a higher appreciation for the finer things in life: wine, food, music and good times! Argentines are also exceptionally polite and caring people and are more accepting of foreigners than elsewhere: indeed, a large proportion of the population is a late-generation mix of European immigrants who arrived in the 18th century. I am currently in San Salvador de Jujuy (or just "hoo-HOOEY") in far northwestern Argentina at the eastern face of the Andes. In this city of 300,000 residents my girlfriend and I appear to be the only "gringos" around!! Nearby Salta, where we have also lived, is a metro area of about 500,000 and is slowly becoming discovered as a tourist and retirement "mecca," so the word is gradually getting out about the many wonders of this part of Argentina.

3. Australia

Climate: Relatively dry, ranging from temperate in the south to tropical in the north. The overwhelming majority of the population lives near the coast and surfers and snorkelers often confuse this place with heaven.

Government: Democratic, federal-state system recognizing British monarch as sovereign

Population: 21,515,754

Currency: Australian Dollar (AUD): 1 AUD = 1.04 USD

Language: English

Religious Groups: Catholic (25.8%), Anglican (18.7%), Uniting Church (5.7%), Presbyterian and Reformed (3%), Eastern Orthodox (2.7%), other Christian (7.9%), Buddhist (2.1%), Muslim (1.7%), other (2.4%), unspecified (11.3%), none (18.7%)

Ethnic Groups: white (92%), Asian (7%), aboriginal and other (1%)

Cost of Living compared to the U.S: Reasonable

Like Canada, Australia has too much land and not enough people. Unemployment is generally lower than most Western countries and there's a critical shortage of skilled workers. Their lifestyle is like ours, their culture (almost) comprehensible, crime is low and the weather couldn't be better—Mediterranean on the coast (where most people live) and spectacular desert inland. The greatest coral reef is right off the coast and now that the hole in the ozone layer is shrinking, you can enjoy the beach more. The government is encouraging migration to the outback (or lesser populated centers), so if you love nature, or are willing to stick it out among the kangaroos for a couple of years until you get established, this could be your new home. Students, mid-career-level workers and retirees can all find ways to reside legally. English teachers, however, aren't too much in demand.

Living There

Governance: Australia is a stable, vibrant democracy that holds regular, free and fair elections and has an independent judiciary. The human rights of Australia's citizens are generally respected by government authorities.

Infrastructure: Developed

Internet: There are a number of Internet Service Providers (ISPs), national and local, with a large number of plans to choose from. Broadband penetration is approximately 50% but the government hopes to expand this number to 69% by 2013.

Healthcare: Australia's health system offers a comprehensive range of public and privately funded health services. You can choose whether to have Medicare (www.medicare.gov.au) or a combination of Medicare and private health insurance. Medicare, the Australian government health scheme, provides help with basic medical expenses like free treatment in public hospitals and free or subsidized treatment by general practitioners and some specialists. All permanent residents are eligible to join Medicare, with restricted access granted to citizens of certain countries which have a reciprocal healthcare agreement with Australia.

GDP: $889.6 billion

GDP (Per Capita): $41,300

Sovereign Debt: 22.4% of GDP

Working There: Opportunities in temp labor, tourism and hospitality industries, ski jobs, temporary construction, sales, healthcare, retail, production jobs, farming and au pairs.

Regulatory Environment: Highly efficient, transparent, and conducive to business and innovation.

Taxes: Corporate: 30%, Individual: 0–45%, GST: 10% (no tax on essential items). Residents taxed on worldwide income but there are some offsets and exemptions.

Cannabis: Illegal, but penalties and enforcement vary in each state or territory. Most jurisdictions require those found in possession of a small amount to pay a fine (akin to a parking ticket) or attend a court-ordered diversion program. Penalties against cultivation have become more stringent in recent years, resulting in reduction of potsmokers and an uptick in meth-heads.

Homosexuality: Legal. Some state recognition of same-sex unions. Laws against discrimination.

Abortion: Abortion laws determined at state level. The majority of jurisdictions allow abortion on socioeconomic grounds, to save a woman's life, physical health, or mental health.

Women's Issues: Equal status under Australian law and this includes equity in pay. Australian women play a significant role in business, government, and politics. Laws against discrimination and sexual harassment. Domestic violence a problem in Aboriginal communities.

Guns: To purchase a firearm, a "Permit to Acquire" is required and a "genuine reason" must be given. Hunting or collecting might pass, but if you say "self-defense," you'll simply be told to get a dog.

Crime: Low violent crime. Petty theft exists in cities.

Real Estate: Americans who are not permanent residents of Australia must first get government permission before purchasing real estate. Generally, the government will only approve such investments if it increases the supply of available housing. Otherwise 25–30-year mortgages are usually available with 10–20% down payment. Titles must be checked to determine whether property is freehold or leasehold.

Life Expectancy: 81.72 years

Moving There

The Australian Department of Immigration and Citizenship (**www.immi.gov.au**) has an inviting, easy-to-use website with a "visa wizard" that lets you plug in your current status (age, citizenship, length of stay, reason, etc.) and spits out the visa programs you would be eligible for. There are many. You need a reason to stay—and work, study, business, creating art and enjoying your golden years are all good reasons. Uniting with your family is good, too. But if it's only a boyfriend or girlfriend, you'll be expected to get married in nine months, by which time you might of course be the parent of an Australian citizen. Generally, though, expatriates follow a migration path, involving work or business, with attainable citizenship in less than five years. Despite being such a laid-back place, surprisingly, unless you're of retirement age, there's no visa that just lets you go there and slack off.

Tourist Visa (subclass 676): Issued to visitors for stays of three, six, or 12 months and with single or multiple entries. Sufficient funds to finance stay and health insurance are required. Applicants can apply both inside and outside Australia.

Student Visa: There are many varieties. Basically, if you're enrolled in a course of study at an Australian university, you'll get one.

Work Visa: Australia issues several different types of visas for foreigners seeking to work and settle in Australia. The government maintains a General Skilled Occupation list (GSO) that lists the types of professions and skills that are needed. You may be required to have a license or fulfill registration requirements to qualify. If you are accepted into the General Skilled Migration program, you can qualify for permanent residency. The government also maintains a skills-matching database that can link you up with prospective employers. You also have the option of being sponsored for a worker visa by an Australian firm. The Australian Department of Immigration and Citizenship page provides a good overview of what kinds of work visas foreigners can apply for.

Business Visa: Like the work visa, Australia offers several different types of business visas for a number of commercial activities ranging from investing a substantial sum in Australia to owning and operating a business that employs local labor. Most require that the applicant be under 45 years of age, possess sufficient assets, and some entail investment in the Australian economy. Many offer permanent residency and the opportunity to apply for Australia's Medicare health insurance program. Extensive business experience and proof of good character are usually required.

Retirement Visa: Australia's retirement visa program has very specific requirements and limitations. First-time applicants can only apply for the Investor Retirement Visa (subclass 405). Assets of approximately $740,000 are required ($493,000 for regional Australia). You must also be sponsored by an agency of a specific state or territory and make a designated long-term investment in that jurisdiction of approximately $750,000 ($493,000 for regional Australia). Depending on where you settle, an annual income of between $49,000 and $64,000 is also required (the lower amount for designated "low growth" areas). The visa is issued for four years with multiple entries but you must continue to maintain your investment. Additionally, applicants must be in good health, at least 55 years of age, and show proof of health insurance as the program does not allow retirees to apply for Australia's Medicare scheme. Retirement visa holders are not eligible for Australian citizenship.

Citizenship: Applicants must reside at least four years in Australia with valid visa and at least 12 months as permanent resident. You cannot have been absent from Australia for more than one year during the four-year period, including no more than 90 days before applying.

Ted Hung
Melbourne, Australia

The culture is really laid-back and it permeates into all aspects of life and work here. Melbourne was and still is one of the most livable cities I have ever been in. Australians are friendly, the culture is diverse, and there are so many beautiful natural wonders here. Also, Melbourne has one of the best transport systems that I have seen in any city. The biggest minus about living here is that because the culture is so laid-back, it seems like people are less ambitious here. They are less willing to start up a company, push the limits of a field, or take major risks in general.

The job market in Australia is generally quite good. On average, the unemployment in Australia tends to hover around the 5% mark. On-the-job training and other sorts of career advancement opportunities are not as readily available in companies in Australia, and expenditures on employee retention are scarce. On the other hand, the workplace and work is significantly less stressful here.

4. The Bahamas

Climate: Tropical marine; moderated by warm waters of Gulf Stream. Sea temperatures range between 74°F in February and 82°F in August.

Government: Constitutional parliamentary democracy and a Commonwealth realm

Population: 309,156

Currency: Bahamian Dollar (BSD): 1 BSD = 1.01 USD

Language: English (official), Creole (spoken by Haitian immigrants)

Religious Groups: Baptist (35.4%), Anglican (15.1%), Roman Catholic (13.5%), Pentecostal (8.1%), Church of God (4.8%), Methodist (4.2%), other Christian (15.2%), none or unspecified (2.9%), other (0.8%)

Ethnic Groups: black (85%), white (12%), Asian and Hispanic (3%)

Cost of Living (compared to U.S.): Pricey

Got half a million lying around? Then you can live out your life watching the tranquil blue waters of a Bahamian beach, while you listen to Calypso music and your accumulated wealth sits in a nearby bank, out of reach of the IRS.

Living There

Governance: Bahamians can change their government democratically. Healthy, independent and privately-owned media can and do criticize the government, although allegations exist that the state-run broadcaster tilts toward the ruling party. There is unfettered access to the Internet. Religious and academic freedom are respected. Labor, business, and professional organizations are generally free from governmental interference. Unions have the right to strike, and collective bargaining is prevalent. There is a Western-style judicial system in place.

Infrastructure/Internet: The two main islands have first-world infrastructure with hi-speed Internet widely available.

Healthcare: High-quality medical care and facilities, though expensive.

GDP: $8.878 billion

GDP (Per Capita): $28,600

Sovereign Debt: 64% of GDP

Working There: Not very receptive to employment of foreigners. You're expected to bring your own money with you.

Regulatory Environment: Overall, a good environment for business development, but the licensing process can be arbitrary.

Taxes: No income tax but the government does place duties on various imports that can sometimes be quite high for certain items.

Cannabis: Illegal

Homosexuality: Legal. No recognition of same-sex unions. No laws against discrimination. Gay scene is invisible; some homophobia, though the government openly condemns prejudice.

Women's Issues: Violence against women an ongoing concern.

Guns: License required for shotguns and rifles. Handguns require special license. License must be renewed each year.

Crime: Compared to neighboring countries, the Bahamas has a high crime rate, particularly New Providence Island. According to a 2007 U.N. report, the Bahamas has the highest number of reported rapes in the Caribbean. Overall, most tourist and business areas are relatively safe.

Real Estate: Non-Bahamians who are buying less than five acres for single family use need only to register their investment with the government. If a land purchase is for other than single family use or is over five acres in size, then a government permit is required. A graduated tax is applied as follows:
Up to $20,000: 4%
$20,000—$50,000: 6%
$50,001—$100,000: 8%
$100,001—$250,000: 10%
$250,001 and up: 12%

Bahamians and permanent residents who have the right to work are exempted from government Stamp Duty provided they are first-time homeowners and the home is a dwelling valued at below $500,000. Mortgages are available.

Life Expectancy: 70.84 years

Moving There

Visa not required for U.S. citizens for stays up to eight months. Given its proximity to the U.S. (particularly Florida), you may not need much more.

Annual Residency: Applicants for annual residency status most show evidence of financial support (or some real estate holdings) and pay $1000 fee. Minimum support amount is unspecified.

Permanent Residency: The Bahamian government promises "speedy consideration of your permanent residency application if you make a local investment of $1,500,000 (e.g. buying property). Permanent residency is available to spouses of Bahamian nationals after five years of marriage. Certain professionals, as well as charitable and religious institution workers, can be eligible after 10 years. Other annual residents who can hang in for that long can be bumped up to permanent resident after 20 years. Cost of Permanent Residence is, ouch, $10,000, plus $100 per dependent.

Work Permits: The Bahamian government can be quite inflexible when it comes to expat labor. Permits will only be issued when it can be demonstrated that no

Bahamian is suitable for the job. Valid one year. Each work permit is for specified person and job. Depending on the job category the fee for a Work Permit can range from $350 to $20,000 per year. In practice, this really isn't much of an option.

Student Visas are available, per the usual documentation.

Citizenship: Applicants must reside in Bahamas between six to nine years as legal resident before applying. Knowledge of Bahamian language and customs also required.

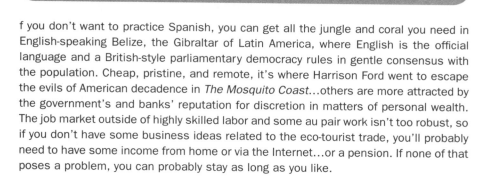

5. Belize

Climate: Tropical; very hot and humid; rainy season (May to November); dry season (February to May)
Government: Parliamentary Democracy
Population: 307,899
Currency: Belizean Dollar (BZD): 1 BZD = 0.51 USD
Language: English (official), Spanish, Garifuna (Carib), Creole
Religious Groups: Roman Catholic (49.6%), Protestant (27%), other (14%), none (9.4%)
Ethnic Groups: Mestizo (48.7%), Creole (29.4%), Maya (10.6%), Garifuna (6.1%), other (9.7%)
Cost of Living compared to the U.S.: Cheap

f you don't want to practice Spanish, you can get all the jungle and coral you need in English-speaking Belize, the Gibraltar of Latin America, where English is the official language and a British-style parliamentary democracy rules in gentle consensus with the population. Cheap, pristine, and remote, it's where Harrison Ford went to escape the evils of American decadence in *The Mosquito Coast*...others are more attracted by the government's and banks' reputation for discretion in matters of personal wealth. The job market outside of highly skilled labor and some au pair work isn't too robust, so if you don't have some business ideas related to the eco-tourist trade, you'll probably need to have some income from home or via the Internet...or a pension. If none of that poses a problem, you can probably stay as long as you like.

Living There

Governance: Free and fair elections, independent judiciary, free press, and a government that guarantees basic rights. Corruption, however, is rampant—from high officials to street cops—and bribery and payoffs are a way of life.

Infrastructure: Basic utility service is good, but costs, especially electricity, are the highest in the region. Because of poorly maintained roads and unlicensed taxis, traffic accidents and fatalities are common.

Internet: Small broadband penetration. Hi-speed connections are usually satellite-based.

Healthcare: Government-operated. Basic medical care in urban areas. Little advanced care is available.

GDP: $2.652 billion

GDP (Per Capita): $8,400

Sovereign Debt: 80% of GDP

Working There: Eco-tourism, au pairs. Some demand for skilled labor and technical personnel.

Regulatory Environment: Inefficient, costly, and lacking transparency. The judiciary is such in name only.

Taxes: Corporate: 25%, Individual: 25% (flat tax), VAT 10%. Tax is applied to non-resident corporations and individuals on a variety of business transactions.

Cannabis: Illegal, but widely available

Homosexuality: Legal (for women). No recognition of same-sex unions. No laws against discrimination. Culturally, homosexuality is stigmatized and gay life is invisible.

Abortion: Allowed for socioeconomic as well as physical or mental health.

Women's Issues: Violence against women a problem.

Guns: Shotguns along with some small arms are legal to purchase but a costly special license is required.

Crime: Crime is a concern, especially in Belize City and in outlying rural sections. Natives are poor; Americans are perceived as rich. Cops and courts are useless. Not a good formula for security, unless it's of the private variety.

Real Estate: Belizean government allows non-citizens to own property. No capital gains taxes and low property taxes. 5% transfer tax on all land purchases.

Life Expectancy: 68.23 years

Moving There

It isn't all that difficult to reside legally in Belize. Most Americans come over with some business idea or on the retirement program. If you intend to getting any kind of residency, you'll have to come over first on a tourist visa and keep extending it while you push through your paperwork. Nothing can be accomplished from the U.S.

Tourist Visa: A 30-day visa will be issued on arrival, and extensions (up to six months, $12.50 per extension) may be obtained from any Immigration Office. After that, you can leave the country, return, and start the process over.

Work Permit: Must be a legal resident for at least six months. Employer must demonstrate to the Labor officer that an exhaustive search for a qualified local candidate came up empty. Permit is valid for one year.

Temporary Self-Employment: Freelance writers to scuba camp operators all fall under this rubric. Proof of sufficient funds for the proposed venture and a reference from the relevant ministry or local organization is required. Special consideration is given to those who show the potential to hire Belizeans.

Qualified Retired Person: Available to anyone over 45 with a monthly income of not less than U.S. $2,000 through a pension or annuity generated outside of Belize. (Note: QPR status bars you from working and you will not be legally considered a resident.)

Permanent Residency: You may apply for Permanent Residency after having resided legally in the country for one continuous year. You are eligible to apply for citizenship after five years.

Citizenship: Foreigners are eligible to apply for citizenship after five years of legal residency.

Sharon Hiebing
San Ignacio Town, Belize

Life in Belize is much simpler and slower. It's hard to remember how busy and stressed out I was back in the States. Here, I only do what I want to. There's no pressure put upon you by anyone to rush, which is so refreshing! Getting together and grilling and sharing a bottle of rum is a common pasttime. Plus there's plenty of bars where expats and locals congregate. Some areas you will find more expats, and others less—it's really up to you how much you want to interact with the locals or not. I now have a Belizean boyfriend, so I have really found myself immersed in the culture.

The climate is one of the biggest changes—my normal attire is a tank top and shorts. And the cost of living is amazing. I pay $250 USD for a two-bedroom/one-bath home in a quiet Belizean neighborhood. The river is a mere seven-minute drive away. Palm trees and other lovely vegetation await me outside my door.

Food costs about $400 USD a month for two people. Gasoline is higher than the States, at about $5.50 USD a gallon, but I don't drive nearly as much here as I did in the States, since the area is more compact. (Belize only has a population of a little over 300,000 people, 180 miles long and 68 miles wide!)

In terms of day-to-day life, just be prepared for long lines everywhere. Also, Belize doesn't have any networked computer systems, so sometimes things take a little longer to "process." I've never been hassled by anyone in law enforcement or otherwise. I don't feel like I gave up any of my civil liberties or freedoms by moving here. Belize is actually quite an ethnically diverse country.

My biggest advice is to please come and visit a couple of times first, just to make sure it is right for you. If it is, live here for at least six months, preferably a year, before buying property. Lastly, remember that you will always be the minority here (this would be true in any foreign country). Please don't come to Belize and try to reshape it into your home country. That will never happen, no one wants it to happen, and if you like where you came from so much, then why aren't you still there? Instead, embrace all the change a new country has to offer—your experience will be amazing if you do!

6. Brazil

Climate: Mostly tropical or semitropical; temperate in the south
Government: Federal Republic
Population: 198,739,269
Currency: Real (BRL): 1 BRL = 0.61 USD
Language: Portuguese
Religious Groups: Roman Catholic (73.6%), Protestant (15.4%), Spiritualist (1.3%), Bantu/voodoo (0.3%), other (1.8%), unspecified (0.2%), none (7.4%)
Ethnic Groups: white (53.7%), mixed (38.5%), black (6.2%), other (1.6%)
Cost of Living compared to the U.S.: Reasonable

The fifth largest nation in the world, and one of the BRIC countries (Brazil, Russia, India, China—the emerging economies of the 21st century), Brazil's got plenty of optimism to match its landmass (half of South America). Aligned with the populist post-colonial and post-neo-colonial political movement of South America, it's also resource-rich and a good choice for anyone looking for a buffer against the upcoming era of increasing austerity and scarcity. For the rest, it offers miles of tropical beaches, the great shrinking Amazon rain forest, and a live-to-party sensibility that is the envy of any Spring Breaker. Crime and pollution are the major problems in the cities, as is poverty, but economic inequality is dropping at a faster rate here than almost anywhere else in the world (unlike the U.S. which is trending in the opposite direction). The biggest expat community is in São Paulo around the Zona Sul, though many Americans forced off their land by U.S. agribusiness have been lured here with government incentives for agricultural development. Crop-ready land in Brazil can be had for as little as $400 to $500 an acre compared to the $2,400 and up in the U.S. Brazil's climate supports two harvests a year.

Living There

Governance: Free and fair elections, though many government institutions marred by corruption. Freedom of the press hampered by violence and intimidation of journalists. Freedom to organize and strike respected as is academic freedom and freedom of religion.

Infrastructure: Developed in cities and many outlying areas. Low landline density in favor of mobile phones.

Internet: For sheer numbers, Brazil dominates the South American Internet market. In terms of broadband penetration, however, Brazil ranks third behind Chile and Uruguay. The transition to hi-speed is underway and DSL is becoming much more common.

Healthcare: Facilities range from state-of-the art to only the most basic care.

GDP: $2.194 trillion

GDP (Per Capita): $10,900

Sovereign Debt: 60.8% of GDP

Working There: Brazil now has the eighth largest economy in the world. Employment opportunities are becoming available for expats in fields like finance, IT and telecommunications. Teaching English and tourism may offer other possibilities.

Regulatory Environment: Bureaucratic, expensive, and often time-consuming. Some improvements have been made in recent years.

Taxes: Compared to other nations in the region, Brazil's tax rates are considered moderate. Personal income ranges from 15%–27.5%. Corporate taxes are 15% but a 10% surtax and mandatory social contribution levy on net profits of most industries amount to approximately 35%.

Cannabis: Smoked openly. If found in possession of small amounts police will issue a warning and offenders will be given community service and in some cases mandatory rehab.

Homosexuality: Legal. Same-sex unions recognized. A recent Supreme Court decision (May 2011) grants most (but not all) of the same legal privileges that heterosexual married couples enjoy to same-sex unions. A 2009 Presidential decree, which has the power of law, recognizes same-sex unions, allows for same-sex adoption, and legally prohibits homophobia. Overall, generally tolerant of homosexuality. Brazil boasts a large and flamboyant gay scene. São Paulo is home to the world's largest Gay Pride Parade with an estimated four million people in attendance for the event in 2009.

Abortion: Prohibited except to save the woman's life, or in case of rape.

Women's Issues: In 2001, the Brazilian government passed its version of an Equal Rights Amendment. Although women are outpacing men in both literacy and university attendance, they are still underrepresented in management and higher political office. Violence against women and sexual harassment remain problematic.

Guns: All guns must be licensed and minimum age to own a firearm is 25.

Crime: Dangerously high violent crime in São Paulo and Rio de Janeiro. Armed robbery of pedestrians common. Urban crime exceeds most major U.S. cities.

Real Estate: By law Brazilians and foreigners are on almost equal footing when it comes to property ownership and tenant rights. The Brazilian government actively encourages agricultural investment by Americans. More than 200 American farmers, including a Mennonite colony, own farms in Brazil, often selling their farms back home to pay for it or by setting up investment pools.

Life Expectancy: 72.26 years

Moving There

Marry a Brazilian or have Brazilian family (or come over as a student), and you won't have much trouble, but if you're under 50, you're pretty much going to have to buy your way into Brazil as an investor or be offered a job. Scientists, professors or researchers; director or administrator of a social assistance and/or religious institution are particularly invited to move to Brazil. If you have skills, then work permits are possible. There are also some special permits that are granted to English teachers. The magic 50 is retirement age and you're invited to settle here permanently if you qualify.

NOTE: Brazil's visa system is a bit more complicated than other nations in the region. For more information about living and working in Brazil consult **www.brazilian-consulate.org**, though a clearer breakdown can be found at the website of one of the consulates in the U.S. – i.e. **www.brazilsf.org** The government has been charging exorbitant fees for visas ($140 for a single-entry tourist visa) in retaliation for similar changes made by the U.S.

Tourist Visa: The Brazilian tourist visa allows for a stay of up to 90 days in Brazil over a one-year period. You can also apply to the Brazilian Federal Police Department (Delegacia de Estrangeiros) for a one-time 90-day extension.

Work Permits: A Work Visa is required if you plan on doing research in Brazil, providing services to the government, working for a Brazilian company, engaging in any kind of volunteer or charitable work, working at a branch office of an American firm, teaching foreign languages to professors and/or instructors and other possible occupations. If you plan on working for a Brazilian company, you must show a letter of invitation. All applicants must show proof of health insurance valid in Brazil and documentation showing that the organization or business employing you will provide sufficient funds to pay your expenses, and proof that the business or organization is currently in Brazil and in operation. Most applicants for work permits must also receive authorization from the Brazilian Ministry of Labor. Your length of stay will be decided by consular authorities but this can be renewed multiple times.

Permanent Retirement Visa: If you are 50 years of age or older and can provide proof that you are receiving an "official monthly pension" (Social Security or similar) of at least $2,000 individually or for a family of up to three persons, you're living in Brazil for as long as you like.

Permanent Investor/Senior Executive Visa: If you're willing to pony up 150,000 Reals ($100,000) in a new business or expansion of an existing one, and you can commit to hiring Brazilian employees, you can get this "permanent" visa, which is actually a three-year visa but indefinitely renewable as long as your investor/employer status holds. This is also granted to big-time executives who have a résumé/portfolio worthy of a captain of industry.

Citizenship: Four years of legal residency required, applicants cannot leave the country during period of residency for any extended period of time. Must be in good health, gainfully employed, and speak and write fluently in Portuguese.

Bob Hand
Rio Grande do Sul, Brasil

Brazil is a very bureaucratic country. Because of this, it is technically difficult to accomplish things, if you obey the laws. Of course, the Brazilians know how to circumvent the laws. But big companies have a harder time avoiding the bureaucracy, and therefore it takes much time to get anything accomplished with them. For example, when trying to make a change with the telephone company, it takes weeks, with almost daily conversations with six or more employees, none of whom have the authority to make a decision.

And items imported can get delayed in the customs department for several weeks, while someone decides whether or not to impose a duty.

In almost all of Brazil, there is more crime than in the USA. This is especially true in the big cities (São Paulo, Rio de Janeiro, Belo Horizonte, Salvador, Porto Alegre, etc.) Rio de Janeiro is known as one of the most violent cities in the world. In most cities, large or small, the people secure their houses with bars on the windows, bars on the doors, a wall around the house with a locked gate and coiled barbed or razor wire on top.

One of the attractive features of Nova Petropolis as a place to live is that the crime level is very low. Most houses are not jails; there is no constant violence; one can walk the streets at night without fear. It's a tranquil place to live. That's why we chose it. The city where Cidinha lived in Minas Gerais, also a small town, had a much higher rate of crime and all houses were private forts. If Americans come here to live, they probably go to highly populated coastal areas or to the big cities. There they will find expats with whom to associate. The two Americans I know here are both widowers and currently live alone. Both are retired with adequate pensions. Both own houses.

People in general are friendly in Brazil and not antagonistic toward Americans. In fact, they seem to like things about the USA and want to emulate some of them. The Brazilian government has often been hostile to the U.S. government, but that's politics.

The Brazilian people often say they are about 20 years behind the USA. But I don't find that to be true. They are high users of the Internet and cellular phones. Supermarkets use bar code checkout equipment. There are huge modern shopping malls in most major cities. Credit cards and debit cards are useful everywhere.

Air transportation to major cities is good, although often overcrowded. Bus transportation is much more convenient than in the USA. You can go anywhere in Brazil by bus, and the buses are modern and comfortable. In fact, the world's largest manufacturer of buses, Marcopolo, is located about 35 km from where I live. There is almost no passenger train service, and very little freight train service. Cars are generally small size and economical...all new cars can burn either alcohol or gasoline, and alcohol is cheaper.

I knew nothing about Rio Grande do Sul until we moved here. What I found was a spirit of liberty that has deep roots in the culture of the Gaúcho. There is even a separatist movement in Rio Grande do Sul, albeit not very strong at the moment.

7. Bulgaria

Climate: The climate in Bulgaria is temperate but with four distinct seasons. Summers are hot and dry, but comfortable due to low humidity, while winter weather is cold but not bitter. Conditions are even milder in the towns along the Black Sea coast.

Government: Parliamentary Democracy

Population: 7,204,687

Currency: Lev (BGN): 1 BGN = 0.75 USD

Language: Bulgarian, other languages closely correspond to the nation's ethnic makeup (Turkish, Romany, Armenian, Hebrew, etc.)

Religious Groups: Bulgarian Orthodox (82.6%), Muslim (12.2%), other Christian (1.2%), other (4%)

Ethnic Groups: Bulgarian (83.9%), Turk (9.4%), Roma (4.7%), other (2%) [including Macedonian, Armenian, Tatar, Circassian]

Cost of Living compared to the U.S.: Very cheap

This tiny country sandwiched between Serbia, Greece, Romania and Turkey is chock full of ancient ruins and modern real estate speculation, as foreigners, particularly the British, have been buying up cheap houses and condos. Despite the bargain-basement prices and none-too-difficult residency hurdles, Americans have yet to really discover the place in any great numbers, daunted perhaps by the Cyrillic alphabet and the fact that English-speaking is not as pervasive as some might like. The action takes place in the capital, Sofia, in the central mountains, and in the resort towns of Bulgaria's fabled Black Sea Coast like Varna and Nesebar. Their corporate and income taxes rank among the lowest in the E.U., since the government is trying to encourage investment, which also means a reduction in a lot of bureaucratic hassles. The diverse geography (mountainous to semi-Mediterranean coast) offers many different climates for such a small area.

Living There

Governance: Generally an open democracy, with free and fair elections, academic and religious freedom and an independent judiciary, Bulgaria's biggest drawback is corruption. While the law guarantees press freedom, the government has often been accused of strong-arming journalists. There have also been unsettling allegations of ongoing torture and police brutality.

Infrastructure: Reasonably well-developed but has suffered from low spending and maintenance in recent years. The country's admission to the E.U. in 2007 has accelerated infrastructure development.

Internet: Fast connections and good service in larger cities. For most of the country, however, dial-up remains the norm; Bulgaria has the lowest broadband penetration rate in the E.U. (13%). Improvements are expected over the next few years.

Healthcare: The National Health Insurance Fund has a direct contract with medical institutions to provide care to patients who pay contributions to the fund. Medical staff in Bulgaria are highly trained, though hospitals and clinics in general may not have all the equipment we expect in the U.S.

GDP: $92.21 billion

GDP (Per Capita): $12,800

Sovereign Debt: 16.2% of GDP

Working There: Opportunities in seasonal skiing, teach English, volunteer construction or conservation; not much else as the recent economic crisis has plunged the country into deep recession and unemployment remains high.

Regulatory Environment: Although once burdensome, recent reforms have eased licensing requirements and cut back on bureaucratic red tape. Some corruption.

Taxes: Corporate: 10%, Individual: 10%, VAT: 20%.

Cannabis: Illegal. Bulgarian drug policy makes no distinction between "hard" and "soft" drugs; possession of any amount can result in a one- to six-year prison sentence and a hefty fine. Still, stories have surfaced that there are "cannabis villages" near the Greek and Macedonian borders where the herb is cultivated as a cash crop.

Homosexuality: Legal. No recognition of same-sex unions. However, the Bulgarian Supreme Court ruled unanimously to allow a gay man to inherit half the estate of his deceased longtime partner. Laws against discrimination. Cultural taboos are eroding, but slowly. Gay-oriented establishments and institutions are allowed a certain degree of visibility.

Abortion: Legal without restriction as to reason.

Women's Issues: Women have equal rights and are well-represented in government. However, research cited by Bulgarian National Television (BNT) in 2010, indicates that one-in-four Bulgarian women have suffered some form of domestic violence. Convictions rarely occur as prosecutors tend to view spousal abuse as a family problem and not a criminal offense.

Guns: Civilian ownership of some firearms is allowed but owners must be licensed and registration is required. Owner must also show a demonstrated need.

Crime: Higher rate of crime than other E.U. countries. Pickpocketing and purse-snatching commonly occur in larger cities. Violent crime on the rise, particularly contract killings by organized crime groups. Perpetrators often escape prosecution due to an ineffective and sometimes corrupt judiciary.

Real Estate: Foreigners can legally buy only buildings but not land. So while that suffices for condo purchases, to buy land or to own the plot where a house is situated, it is necessary to form a company which is easy to do in Bulgaria. It is not necessary for any Bulgarians to have interest in the property. Although prices surged during the property boom of 2006–2008, today apartments in the resort town of Varna with an ocean view can be had for under $70,000. Seaside homes in the same area can be had for as low as $100,000.

Life Expectancy: 73.09 years

Moving There

Generally, if you look like you can support yourself and you're not a troublemaker, chances are they'll let you stick around.

Tourist Visa: U.S. citizens do not need a visa to stay in Bulgaria for up to 90 days. You may be asked to show proof of medical insurance valid for Bulgaria. (Note: Bulgaria is expected to become a Schengen country in October 2011.)

Long-Term Visa: For stays longer than 90 days, U.S. citizens are required to apply for long-term (D type) visa at Bulgarian consulate in the U.S. These are issued routinely and are valid for 90 days. A foreigner must enter Bulgaria with a long-stay visa to apply for a long-term residence permit from the Ministry of Internal Affairs.

Residence Permit: Applicants must possess type D visa (see above) to apply for resident status. Generally three categories of permit: employee, freelance professional, and pensioner. There is also a select category of permit for individuals who invest at least $500,000 in Bulgaria. Pensioner permit requires proof of retirement income. The permit is valid for one year and renewable.

Student visas available per the usual requirements.

Permanent Residency: Five years residency required for permanent resident permit.

Citizenship: Five years of permanent residency, fluency in Bulgarian, and gainful employment or regular income required.

Extended stays in Bulgaria usually require that you open a local bank account.

8. Cambodia

Climate: Tropical; rainy, monsoon season (May to November); dry season (December to April); little seasonal temperature variation
Government: Multiparty democracy under a constitutional monarchy established in September 1993
Population: 14,453,680
Currency: Riel (KHR): 1 KHR = 0.00024 USD
Language: Khmer [official] (95%), French, English
Religious Groups: Theravada Buddhist (95%), other (5%)
Ethnic Groups: Khmer (90%), Vietnamese (5%), Chinese (1%), other (4%)
Cost of Living compared to the U.S: Dirt cheap

For a heavy dose of the raw, cheap, and exotic, cutting-edge expats have been choosing Cambodia. Its worst days seem to be fading into the past and instead of Killing Fields, there is lush jungle, ancient temples, and pristine beaches—just so long as you don't mind giving up many of the conveniences you took for granted and you're OK with poor hygiene, poor sanitation and poor people. The appeal here is for those seeking rock-bottom prices on a tropical Asian lifestyle and few of the trappings of Western consumerism. Laws are anticipated that will make it easier for foreigners to buy property, and it might be a good idea to scout out the choice locations early.

Living There

Governance: Cambodia is making small steps toward building a viable democracy but charges of election fraud and voter intimidation are not uncommon. The country lacks an independent judiciary, and intimidation, harassment, and other measures are frequently used to silence criticism of the government. Human rights abuses are a continuing concern.
Infrastructure: Primitive and underdeveloped due to years of conflict and civil war.
Internet: Poor. Less than 1% of all Cambodians have access to the Internet.
Healthcare: Adequate in Phnom Penh, poor to non-existent elsewhere.
GDP: $30.13 billion
GDP (Per Capita): $2,000
Sovereign Debt: Unavailable
Working There: Teach English. There's not much in the way of work. Most of the expatriate community works with aid agencies.
Regulatory Environment: Stifling and often arbitrary but recent reforms are slowly improving conditions for new businesses.

Taxes: Corporate: 20%, Individual: 0–20%, VAT: 10%. Tax on worldwide income.

Cannabis: Illegal but widely available

Homosexuality: Legal. No legal protections for same-sex unions. No laws against discrimination.

Abortion: Legal within 14-week gestational limit. No restrictions as to reason.

Women's Issues: Laws prohibiting discrimination. Domestic violence a problem.

Guns: Stringent laws limiting private ownership.

Crime: Not insubstantial. Armed robberies are not unheard of but mostly you have to deal with street crime and petty theft, which are common in the cities.

Real Estate: Property laws are set to change to allow foreigners to purchase property. Until the prospective reforms are initiated, foreigners can buy 70–year leases for the land, buy only the building, or set up a company where a Cambodian owns 51% and signs a proxy giving his voting rights to you. Mortgages are rare, as interest rates are high and most purchases are made in cash.

Life Expectancy: 62.28 years

Moving There

If you plan to stay (and not marry), you'll need a business visa (technically, a "non-immigrant visa, business type," but whatever), and while you could theoretically conduct business, in practice, these visas are pretty much issued as revenue-generators (cost: $295). Show up with money and you needn't expect to answer a lot of questions.

Tourist Visa: One-month tourist visa can be extended for one month, but one time only. Cambodia now has "E-Visa" program that allows visitors to apply for a Tourist Visa online: **www.mfaic.gov.kh/evisa**

Business Visa: Valid for up to one year, can be renewed indefinitely.

Work Permit: The Ministry of the Interior does issue work permits, issued on presentation of a work contract and other documentation, though few of the expat workforce in the country has seen one. These are valid as long as your business visa is valid.

Investor Visa: Investors in a variety of government-authorized investments can receive one- or two-year visas, renewable indefinitely.

Student Visas also available, per the usual requirements. Visas for **journalists, skilled workers** and **dependents** and spouses of Cambodian nationals also available.

Permanent residency is available under certain limited conditions, however, few take this route.

Art F.

Sihanoukville, Cambodia

One thing people have to remember is that this is a third-world country. The infrastructure can be challenging. The power grid is under capacity, and there are daily outages, lasting from five minutes to 13 hours. Driving is a challenge, as the idea of driving on any particular side of the road is optional. Passing is done whenever the driver pleases. There are frequent accidents on the main roads, mostly because the bus drivers are all insane, and bully their way around. They pass any time they like, oftentimes forcing oncoming traffic onto the shoulder. Watch out for the morons in Lexus SUVs—they are all arrogant bullies, and do not give anyone else any respect.

Medical care here is OK at best. A person who needs constant medical support should look elsewhere. Clinics are all over, and very inexpensive.

What makes it attractive living here is that the cost of living is very low. I rent a three-bedroom, four-bath house, on a well-paved road, for $300 a month. My rent will go down each year—next year it's $270, the year after that $250. My electric bill is around $40 a month. Cable TV is $8 a month. Internet is $53. Gasoline is about $4 a gallon (about $1 per liter)

Outside of Phnom Penh, it's pretty much the jungle. If you like a sterile house, this is not a place for you. My house has many open vents to the outside. This lets in a nice breeze, but also mosquitos, and many other bugs. There are geckos all over. I have at least four in the house, they take care of many of the insects. I have not seen any snakes around the house, but there are many toxic vipers, cobras, kraits, Russell Vipers, Burmese Pythons, etc. The rats here are HUGE—look like brown squirrels and they are not afraid of you.

9. Canada

Climate: Varies from temperate in south to subarctic to arctic in north
Government: Constitutional Monarchy/ Parliamentary Democracy/ Federation
Population: 33.4 million
Currency: Canadian Dollar (CAD): 1 CAD = 1.01 USD
Language: English (official), French (official)
Religious Groups: Roman Catholic (43%), Protestant (23%), other Christian (4%), Muslim (2%), other and unspecified (12%), none (16%)
Ethnic Groups: British Isles origin (28%), French origin (23%), other European (15%), Amerindian (2%), other, mostly Asian, African, Arab (6%), mixed background (26%).
Cost of Living (compared to U.S.): About the same

"That's it! I'm moving to Canada" has been the cry of disaffected and draft-dodging Americans since the time of slavery. The country's recent lurch to the right and its absorption into NORTHCOM (United States Northern Command) over the past decade have tempered this some, but universal health coverage, gay marriage, near-legal pot and a generous social safety net still prevail. An estimated one million Americans (that is, people from the USA) live there. The availability of goods and services is comparable to the U.S., the conveniences of civilization equally available, but guns and violent crime are nearly non-existent by U.S. standards. They're basically like us, only nicer. And with the exception of Quebec, they look and speak almost like us, so nobody even has to know you're a Stateside transplant.

Best of all, the country has a lot more room than it has people, so there's not much immigrant animus. Close to a fifth of Canucks are foreign-born (just 11.5% of the U.S. population can say the same). They maintain one of the world's only permanent immigration programs as well as an easy-to-navigate immigrant website that invites you to come move here. Scenery-wise, you can pick from the lush green islands and temperate rainforests of British Columbia, the Rocky Mountains of Alberta and the salty fishing towns in Nova Scotia and Newfoundland. There are also incentives that make immigration easier if you move to the boonies.

Living There

Governance: Canada is a Western-style liberal democracy with free and fair elections. Most rights are protected under the 1982 Federal Charter of Rights and Freedoms but there is a clause that allows each province to opt out of the agreement. The country has an outspoken free press, notoriously independent judiciary, and the government is one of the least corrupt in the world.

Infrastructure: First World

Internet: Hi-speed widely available. As of 2010, Canada's broadband penetration per capita was higher than the U.S. In a ranking of 30 OECD countries, Canada was ranked 10th and the U.S. was ranked 15th. The government of Canada has committed to making high-capacity Internet access available to all Canadians.

Cannabis: Decriminalized and widely used

Homosexuality: Legal; same-sex marriage is allowed, nationwide laws against discrimination. Canada has a liberal and active gay scene.

Women's Issues: Women's rights are protected in law and in practice. Women have strong representation in government and most professions. Problems with violence against women exist in some aboriginal communities.

Abortion: Legal

Guns: All firearm owners must be licensed, all guns must be registered. Licensing requires background check and safety instruction. Weapons must be kept locked and unloaded.

Crime: Violent crimes far less common than in the U.S. Strict gun control. Petty crime levels on par with U.S. although Canada is higher in some types of property crimes like vehicle theft. Overall, crime in Canada has been in decline since 1991.

Healthcare: Socialized medicine. High standard of care and facilities.

GDP: $1.334 trillion

GDP (Per Capita): $39,600

Sovereign Debt: 34% of GDP

Working There: Labor market conditions vary by region. Employment opportunities include high-tech industries, construction, truck driving, engineering, food services, and tourism.

Regulatory Environment: Efficient, transparent, and designed to encourage entrepreneurs.

Taxes: Moderate income tax. Individual: 0–29%; Corporate 11–18%, 32–42%. Provincial tax: Individual: 0–24%, Corporate: 2–16% (depending on location). Non-residents may be subject to tax on Canadian-source income such as employment, business and capital gains. Residents taxed on worldwide income.

Real Estate: Mortgages usually given with a 35% down payment amortized over 25 years with a five-year term. Mortgage interest is not deductible in Canada but there is no capital gains tax on or requirement to reinvest in real estate if you sell your property at a profit.

Life Expectancy: 81.29 years

Moving There

There are myriad of ways to live permanently or at least long-term in Canada.Prospective immigrants, however, must declare their intentions upon arrival at the port of entry, so get your ducks in a row before fleeing to the Great White North. Residency visas must be obtained before arriving. Application can be done online at the government's very user-friendly immigration website: **www.cic.gc.ca** The relevant categories for Americans are as follows:

Work Permits: Issued for the duration of a sponsored employment contract which is usually up to three years.

Working Holiday Visa: U.S. citizens can enroll in the SWAP Canada program, which allows American college and university students (18–30 years of age) to travel and work in Canada for up to six months. Program is managed through **www.swap.ca** and **www.bunac.com**

Skilled Worker: Skilled workers can enjoy permanent residency in Canada providing they can prove they will be economically self-sufficient. Before your application will even be processed you must show proficiency in English and/or French (there is a test), have a valid offer for employment, or show proof of at least one year of continuous employment in a select occupation (the list is available on Canada's immigration web page).

If you meet the basic requirements, your application will be processed according to six selection factors: age, education, work experience, ability to speak English and/or French, whether or not you have arranged for employment in Canada (or current employment on a work permit), and adaptability to life in Canada. You will also need to show proof that you have enough money to support yourself and your family once you have arrived in Canada.

Family: To immigrate to Canada as a family class member, you must be sponsored by a Canadian citizen or permanent resident who is at least 18 years of age: fiancé, spouse (including same-sex), common-law or conjugal partner; dependent child, parent or grandparent; an orphaned sister, brother, niece, nephew or grandchild (under 18); and any relative if you are that sponsor's closest living relative. The most common type of family class application is for those who are married to or engaged to a Canadian citizen or permanent resident.

Business/Self-Employed: Limited to farmers and those who can demonstrate the potential to make a cultural, artistic, or sporting contribution to Canada.

Business/Entrepreneur Class: Must possess a total net worth of at least CAD 300,000 (approx. $307,000), establish or purchase a business upon arrival in Canada, and within three years must hold at least one-third equity in the company and establish at least one new full-time job for a Canadian.

Business/Investor Class: Must possess a total net worth of CAD 1,600,000 (approx. $1.6 million) and provide proof of business experience. Applicants must invest CAD 800,000 (approx. $800,000) of this amount for five years. Although not a requirement, it is recommended that this transaction be carried out by a government-approved facilitator which is a financial institution that enjoys the protection of the Canadian Deposit Insurance Corporation (CDIC). Investor class holders don't have to actively own and operate a business, and you are issued permanent residence immediately upon arrival. Limited number of visas issued per year.

Provincial Nominee Program: Alberta, Manitoba, Newfoundland and Labrador, Ontario, Saskatchewan, British Columbia, New Brunswick, Nova Scotia, Prince Edward Island, Yukon, and Northwest Territories allow their own yearly quotas based on labor and social needs. Upon acceptance, immigrants receive a permanent residence visa. To retain their status as permanent residents, individuals must physically reside in Canada for two years (730 days) out of every five-year period.

Student visas available per the usual requirements.

Applications approved under any of the Canadian immigration schemes can apply for a Permanent Resident Card, and are then eligible to apply for Canadian citizenship after living there three of the previous four years.

Jude Angione

Toronto, Canada

The city of Toronto is now part of the "GTA": Greater Toronto Area. The amalgamation was forced on the city and surrounding suburbs by the province a few years ago. It was not a welcome amalgamation but people have gotten used to it. Although the TTC (Toronto Transit Commission) is starting to fall behind and is in need of a multi-billion-dollar update, Toronto is still one of the best cities in North America for public transit and walking. You absolutely do not need to own a vehicle if you live in Toronto. Twenty-four-hour service even to far-flung areas of the city, a choice of subway, bus or streetcar, all laid out in a highly sensible and easy-to-understand grid system.

There is less crime in general, but Vancouver and Toronto are getting up there. It's much safer to walk the streets here. I walk everywhere 24 hours a day and have never felt in danger. You generally feel safer on the streets than in most American cities.

As for the cost of living, salaries are lower and taxes are higher. Semi-socialized healthcare is a big help. Let's just say that if you're going to be poor, you're better off in Canada than the U.S. No one loses their home in Canada because they need heart surgery. They might have to wait if it isn't critical but they won't have to pay once their place in line comes up.

There is a lot of anti-Americanism in Canada, some of it quite cruel and gratuitous. I still have dual citizenship and I love both my countries but on a day-to-day basis I think it's less crazy-making to be living in Canada rather than the U.S.

10. Chile

Climate: Temperate; dry, arid desert in the north; moderate, Mediterranean-style weather in central regions; cool and damp in the south
Government: Republic
Population: 16,601,707
Currency: Chilean Peso (CLP): 1 CLP = 0.002 USD
Language: Spanish (official), Mapudungun, German, English.
Religious Groups: Roman Catholic (70%), Evangelical (15.1%), Jehovah's Witness (1.1%), other Christian (1%), other (4.6%), none (8.3%)
Ethnic Groups: White and Amerindian (94.5%), Mapuche (4%), other indigenous groups (0.06%)
Cost of Living compared to the U.S: Somewhat cheaper than the U.S.

A little sliver of land between the craggy Andean peaks and the Pacific Ocean, Chile, like its neighbor Argentina, with whom it shares most of its border, offers some of the most modern living in Latin America, though it's far from the bargain that most of the rest of the region is. Somewhat conservative in terms of drugs, gays and abortion, Chile is still far from the autocratic horror show of the Pinochet era. Free marketeers will enjoy the open business environment and the only privatized social security system on the planet.

Living There

Governance: Free and fair elections, an overall respect for human rights, and a judiciary largely untainted by political corruption. Chile is considered the least corrupt country in Latin America, where, admittedly, the bar has not been set very high.

Infrastructure: Semi-developed. Chile has shown remarkable resilience following an 8.8 earthquake in February, 2010. Experts point to the country's adherence to Western-style building standards and earthquake-proofing measures as a major reason why. As Chile rebuilds, many are predicting that modernization efforts will gather momentum. Telecommunications infrastructure is one of the best in Latin America but the Chilean rail system has long suffered from neglect.

Internet: Widely available; Chile has an advanced telecommunications infrastructure and boasts the highest Internet usage and broadband penetration rates in Latin America.

Healthcare: Residents who are employed and paying local taxes can apply to receive healthcare through FONASA, Chile's public healthcare plan. Private insurance is also available at an affordable price. Overall, Chile's healthcare system is efficiently run and provides some of the best quality care in Latin America.

GPD: $260 billion

GDP (Per Capita): $15,500

Sovereign Debt: 6.2% of GDP

Working There: Some IT, start a business, teach English, tourism, NGO work. Under-the-table employment is also a possibility.

Regulatory Environment: Simple, efficient and not burdensome to new businesses.

Taxes: Individual: 0–40%, Corporate: 17%, VAT: 19%. Non-residents (staying less than six months in the country for two consecutive years) taxed only on Chilean-source income. Chilean tax authorities do not tax worldwide income for first three years of residency. Term may be extended for an additional three years.

Cannabis: Illegal, widely used. Private use tolerated.

Homosexuality: Legal, no recognition of same-sex unions, no laws against discrimination.

Abortion: Illegal

Women's Issues: Despite laws against rape and domestic abuse, violence against women remains a problem within Chilean society. Although women enjoy the same legal rights as men, there are still sizable wage disparities between men and women.

Guns: Some types of guns are legal to own but a permit is required. Chilean law restricts the number of firearms and ammunition that can be owned.

Crime: Moderate; some street crime in major cities and near tourist attractions. Generally property crimes like pickpocketing, purse snatching, theft from vehicles, etc.

Real Estate: Foreigners can buy property in most parts of Chile (some border areas are off-limits). Private property rights are strongly protected in Chile and the dispute process is known for being both efficient and transparent. Prices vary considerably. Condos and apartments can be had for under $100,000 while some of the larger homes can run into the millions. Attorney and agent fees will generally run to between 5% and 8% of purchase price.

Life Expectancy: 77.34 years

Moving There

If you're here to do business or retire, you'll have little difficulty. If you're lucky enough to land a job contract, it's not a problem either. Hurdles are a little steeper for the self-employed freelancer.

Tourist Visa: U.S. citizens do not need a visa to stay up to 90 days in Chile. Tourists have the option of applying for a longer-term visa while in the country. Letter of invitation required but hotel reservation will suffice.

Temporary Resident Visa: Available for stays of up to one year in Chile. Self-sufficiency and something the authorities would consider a valid reason for wanting to live in Chile is required. The visa is valid for one year and renewable. Temporary residents can apply for permanent residency after one year.

Business and Investment Visa: Applicant must submit detailed business plan showing that prospective venture will contribute to Chilean economy. While this visa is generally easy to obtain, each year business operations are closely examined by Chilean immigration authorities and the visa will not be renewed if the enterprise is considered questionable or illegitimate. Business visa is valid for one year, renewable as long is business is considered viable.

Work Permit: Applicants must possess job offer or work contract from Chilean employer. Visa is valid for duration of employment.

Rentista/Retirement Visa: Chile is a bit more flexible than other countries in awarding rentista/retirement visas. Applicant need only show proof of adequate income for stay in Chile. Income can be derived from Social Security, interest income, rent payments or annuities, property ownership, stock portfolios, or sufficient savings. Visa applicants can also apply for work permit or business visa.

Permanent Residency Visa: Available to applicants who have lived in Chile for at least 180 days as temporary resident over a one-year period. Proof of sufficient income required. Valid for five years and can be renewed indefinitely.

Student visa available per the usual requirements. Priority visas also issued for spouses and dependents of Chilean nationals.

Citizenship: Available to permanent residents who have lived in Chile for at least five years. Proof of sufficient income required. Applicants have the option of applying for dual citizenship should they choose to retain U.S. citizenship.

11. China, People's Republic of (excluding Hong Kong)

Climate: China has a variety of temperature and rainfall zones, including continental monsoon areas. The northeast, which includes Beijing, usually experiences a long, cold winter, and a short but hot and sunny summer. Southern provinces are warmer and more humid while desert conditions prevail in the west.

Government: Communist party-led state

Population: 1,338,612,968

Currency: Yuan (CNY): 1 CNY = 0.14 USD

Language: Standard Chinese or Mandarin (Putonghua, based on the Beijing dialect), Yue (Cantonese), Wu (Shanghainese), Minbei (Fuzhou), Minnan (Hokkien-Taiwanese), Xiang, Gan, Hakka dialects, minority languages

Religious Groups: Daoist (Taoist), Buddhist, Muslim (1–2%), Christian, other [note: China is officially atheist]

Ethnic Groups: Han Chinese (92%), other [including Tibetan, Mongol, Korean, Manchu, and Uighur] (8%)

Cost of Living compared to the U.S.: Comparable in the main cities, cheap in the boonies

If you want to see what it's like when the most populous nation on earth runs hell-bent on free-market capitalism (behind a thin veneer of Communism) and rapid industrialization, head to the People's Republic. One-hundred-story skyscrapers are thrown up seasonally in Shanghai, while in the special economic zones in the South, cities of millions have been springing up like mushrooms around Guangzhou. Just about every object we touch or use is made there but at quite a cost. Environmentally, it's a catastrophe—Dickens-era London but on a far more massive scale. Factory waste runs wherever it can, smog can be blinding, pesticides are sprayed with abandon and the Three Gorges Dam, completed in 2006, flooded 1,300 priceless cultural and archaeological sites and displaced over a million people. Much of the tap water is not fit to drink without boiling. But opportunities abound, and in 2011, over 70,000 were making their home, at least temporarily, on the mainland. Teaching packages are as comprehensive as they are in Japan, at a fraction of the cost of living. Also high is the demand for architects and engineers, computer specialists and anyone else with the know-how to help with the instant infrastructure that's going up. Those who come to wheel and deal will find the government friendly and the labor laws favorable (to employers, that is). Should you ever get lonely for home, you can visit one of China's estimated 1,000 McDonald's franchises for a taste of good old American-style processed food. Some familiarity with Mandarin and proxy servers can go a long way.

Living There

Governance: All power rests with the Chinese Communist Party (CCP) and woe to those who mess with them. Popular elections for executive positions do not exist. Media are heavily censored and Internet sites are routinely and often capriciously blocked. Corruption and bribery run through all strata of business and government, and the country's human rights record is abysmal.

Infrastructure: Adequate in the Special Economic Zones, pathetic elsewhere.

Internet: Subject to government censorship. Hi-speed available in developed areas.

Healthcare: Although the Chinese government once provided medical care to all residents at little to no cost, China's new entrepreneurial outlook has led to a system favoring private insurance and cash-for-services style medical treatment.

GDP: 9.872 trillion

GDP (Per Capita): $7,400

Sovereign Debt: 17.5% of GDP

Working There: Teachers, architects, IT, construction, engineering, business and marketing

Regulatory Environment: Inconsistent, complicated, and lacking in transparency. Some corruption. Businesses face byzantine licensing procedures, and respect for intellectual property is nonexistent. The overall outlook, despite all this, is bullish.

Taxes: Corporate: 25%, (though foreign businesses involved in state-approved industries like high technology are taxed at a preferential rate as low as 15%), Individual: 5–35%, VAT: 17% (reduced rate of 3% and 13% on certain items), Consumption: 3–45% on alcohol, fuel, jewelry, and cars.

Cannabis: Possession cases usually receive no less than seven years imprisonment, and if you are caught smuggling, possibly execution.

Homosexuality: Legislation prohibiting homosexual contact repealed in 1997. Chinese authorities removed homosexuality from the country's list of mental illnesses in 2001. Still, there is no recognition of same-sex unions, no laws against discrimination, and strong cultural biases still exist. Nevertheless there are signs of reform. Gay bars and organizations are appearing, particularly in the southern city of Shenzen.

Abortion: Legal without restriction as to reason

Women's Issues: Gender discrimination occurs at almost all levels of Chinese society.

Guns: Strictly illegal. Unauthorized possession of a firearm can be a capital offense.

Crime: Very low

Real Estate: China has recently placed limits on foreign investment. Current regulations limit foreigners to one residential unit per person and the property must be for self-use. Foreign firms can only buy property that will be specifically used for company operations. It's somewhat daunting negotiating all the

paperwork and requirements, but financing can be obtained by foreigners through institutions like Bank of China and China Constructions Bank. There are also overseas lenders available that provide mortgages for properties in China.
Life Expectancy: 73.47 years

Moving There

The expatriate scene is as massive as one might expect from the world's most populous nation and expanding economy. If you're truly doing business or are engaged in (or have been offered) gainful employ, a little patience and a lot of documentation should get you in.

NOTE: Additional permits are required to visit many remote areas, including Tibet. Visa requirements for Hong Kong are not the same as those for the People's Republic of China.

Tourist Visa ("L" Visa): U.S. Citizens are eligible to apply for single entry (three to six months), double entry (six months), or multiple entry visa (six to 12 months). Extensions are limited. The preferred method for longer-term stay (if you can't secure an F, Z or other visa) is to make a border run to Hong Kong and reapply.

Business/Official Visit Visa ("F" Visa): U.S citizens eligible to apply for single entry, double entry, or multiple entry visas valid for six months or 12 months "as needed." Americans can also apply for "F" Visa valid for 24 months if documents are provided showing applicant has made an investment in China or "established a collaboration" with a Chinese company (business license, contract, notarized letter, etc.) If you have been issued an "F" visa at least twice within 24 months, you can also apply for the 24-month visa (copies must be submitted with application).

Employment Visa ("Z" Visa): Required for aliens entering China with the intention of employment, self-employment, or as part of an academic exchange. Applicant must submit work permit issued by Ministry of Human Resources and Social Security and for freelance work, Foreign Expert's License issued by Chinese Foreign Expert Bureau. Generally valid for three months with no duration of stay; holders of Z visa must apply within 30 days of arrival in China for Residence permit at local public security authority.

Residence Visa ("D" Visa): China is not that interested in letting people stay permanently. Those with Chinese ties—spouse, family, etc.—are the only ones who should even bother.

Student Visas (X) and **Journalist Visas (J-1, J-2)** are also available with appropriate documentation. Practicing journalism in China without the proper approval and paperwork is a good way to get arrested, jailed and/or deported.

Jennifer Ashley

Chengdu, Sichuan Province, China

I think the pluses of living in China include the lower cost of living than in the U.S. and the resulting personal opportunities (travel, leisure time, pursuit of other professional areas of interest, etc.) that it affords. To me another big plus is the fact that the average citizen here does not own a car, making bicycle or public transportation the standard means of commuting. The minuses (viewed through, of course, an American-centric lens) are the dangerously high levels of pollution (air mostly, but also water and even noise), general dirtiness, lack of privacy/personal space due to the large population, and an immature capitalist economy (oftentimes meaning poor customer service, quality of goods, etc.).

It's fairly easy in terms of visas. Employers usually take care of work visas; at times I've been a student and then was able to apply for a student visa. As long as you're gainfully employed or gainfully enrolled in school, or any number of other reasons the Chinese government will grant you a visa. The regulations are constantly changing and it's a bit of a hassle, but I don't think that it's as difficult as, say, a Chinese national trying to get a visa to live in the U.S. There's no requirement to know even a word of the Chinese language, for instance.

The city I live in now, Chengdu, seems to attract expatriates who are long(ish)-term ESL teachers and/or performing musicians, Peace Corps volunteers, or Christian missionaries. Most have chosen or been required to learn a substantial amount of Chinese (in the case of the latter two groups, they receive language training). The city I lived in last year, Suzhou, is in the wealthier East Coast area, and attracts a significant amount of foreign investment. They have many expatriates who have been sent there by their companies and are unable or unwilling to speak/learn Chinese. Likewise, the English teachers in Suzhou often seem to be travelers or people taking a year off from their lives at home, many of whom don't invest much time in studying Chinese. So there is much more catering to that fact, in terms of restaurants, bars, etc. that require their staff to speak English—as well as even shops along the tourist streets where the shopkeepers have picked up enough English from daily contact with English speakers. I can't say there are really any English-speaking enclaves. There are the bar districts where you might hear plenty of English, but Chinese still dominates, and there are residential districts that attract a relatively high number of expatriates, but there are still far more Chinese people living in them.

For Americans specifically, I think it's important to be sensitive to the fact that being American carries with it many connotations and that whether or not you want to be, when you're outside of America, you're serving as a representative of your country. And because many American companies (KFC, McDonald's, Coca-Cola, Pepsi, Nike, Proctor & Gamble, Microsoft, Nestle, Johnson & Johnson, Nabisco, Starbucks, etc.) have a very visible presence in China, I've heard that there is some related resentment but I have never encountered any outright hostility in this regard. (In my experience,

Chinese more frequently disparage local products/services and hold American products/services as a model to which Chinese companies should aspire.)

There's a lot of talk among Americans about China's internal policies, but I'd say on the whole they don't affect me very much—or, at least, I can't think of anything that I would ordinarily do in the U.S. that I'm restricted by law from doing here, and, in fact, restrictions that affect daily life might be fewer here. To briefly illustrate: in China it is acceptable to walk down the street drinking a beer, purchase alcohol or tobacco at any age and at any time of the day or night, disobey traffic lights, and so forth. There is evidently a law that makes it illegal for university students to have boyfriends or girlfriends, but it is entirely ignored. On the other hand, police turn the other cheek when passing by the thinly disguised brothels that can be found all over. I have voiced opinions, both orally, via emails, blogs, discussion forums, and U.S.-based press, on China, from China, and have never had a problem. I take the word of the local English-language newspapers with a grain of salt, but I can say the same when I read any newspaper. (The grain of salt in China might just be a bit bigger.) I'm able to use proxies to circumvent the governmental firewall, which blocks a number of websites I view or have wanted to view. But I should acknowledge that while the laws regarding freedom of the press do not affect my life directly, I do teach over 200 university students, so it does affect me in that I must be careful with what I say in class at times, and I also have to silently listen to what I view as misinformation from students frequently.

In terms of personal safety, I definitely feel safer walking around at any hour of the day or night here than I did in Los Angeles. There is much more petty crime, like pickpocketing and bicycle theft, so I'm careful with my money and valuables when outside, but violent crimes are far less common here, and even guards tend to be unarmed, or armed, at most, with a club.

I do sometimes miss the standard of cleanliness in restaurants and particularly public toilets in the U.S. I think public transportation is actually better here than it is in L.A. since the majority of the population here relies on it whereas in L.A. public transportation users are a small minority. To be sure, the buses here are more crowded, less comfortable etc., but they perform their main function (transporting people) better. Access to the Internet can be frustrating at times here as it can be slow, and the government blocks various websites (sometimes at random it seems). But even this usually can be circumvented. But I'd have to say, all things aside, life here is actually more "convenient." I do miss pizza delivery—believe it nor not, home delivery is not very common in China. I guess I also miss, to a lesser extent, the comfort in knowing I would be able to access quality medical care in the event of an emergency. The construction here isn't of the highest quality, and there are many building features that would be considered unsafe (and the stuff lawsuits are made of) in the U.S. (no fire exits, even in 25-story buildings, uneven ledges that can easily be tripped over, slippery walking surfaces such as granite, drops with no railings, etc.). The insulation is also extremely poor as the buildings tend to be steel and concrete so it feels particularly cold (and difficult to heat) during the cold season since the indoors is nearly as cold as the outdoors. Lastly, I've never encountered a Chinese water heater that functions as well as its American counterpart.

Edna Vuong
Beijing, China

Living in Beijing is not that difficult. The expat community in Beijing is pretty big. I work long hours. Much longer than if I were working in the U.S. My pay is much lower than what I would make in the States, but I think that that varies. People who work in larger foreign offices are able to secure wages comparable to the U.S. Local offices pay MUCH less and work you much much harder.

Cost of living is so low that I manage to save a significant portion of my salary while living very comfortably. Everything is so cheap that expats tend to live extravagantly. A taxi costs $1.50 USD for the first 3 km; a maid costs roughly $3.50 USD an hour; a massage is about $15 USD an hour.

The difficult thing about living in China is the government. Everything is censored. You can't trust the news. Foreign news tends to be blocked. Most blogs are blocked. No Facebook, YouTube, Blogspot, Wordpress, Twitter, HuffingtonPost, etc. You get used to hearing about ridiculous government antics. They control the weather. When it rains we discuss if it is real rain or government rain. Before every major public holiday the government seeds the clouds to ensure that the weather is perfect for the holidays. Local women are not allowed to know the sex of their children in case they abort because it is not a boy, because they are only allowed to have one. They have no problems telling whole neighborhoods they are not allowed to leave their homes or look out their windows so that the government can rehearse for parade. The general public does not even know about the Tiananmen Square Protests in 1989. If you even google Tiananmen riots your Internet will stop working for about five minutes. The censorship leaves you a bit ignorant, which I guess is the point. There are ways around the censorship, but it is a daily hassle you have to learn to live with.

I pay for a VPN (Virtual Private Network). I'm not sure how it works, but it somehow routes your signal so it seems like you are not in China. So I have access to blocked websites. It's slower than normal Internet, but it is better than nothing.

Pollution is also something you have to learn to deal with. It is not rare for weeks to go by before you get a blue sky. So if you have respiratory problems, Beijing is probably not the place for you. You also have to be careful what you eat. There was the whole melamine in the milk powder thing. Then there was news that street vendors were shredding cardboard and adding it to dumpling filling so that they didn't have to pay for as much meat. Restaurants tend to throw their fryer oil into the gutters and the news reported that vendors were siphoning the oil from the gutters to reuse in their restaurants. I don't know if this is all true, but it was in the local newspapers.

There are large expat communities all around Beijing. There is a Russian district near Ritan Park. Younger expats go to the Sanlitun area where there are lots of expat bars and foreign restaurants. GuoMao is the central business district. Shunyi is expat suburbs with identical rows of tract homes and fenced in backyards. Wudaokou is the university area. There is a large Korean community out there.

Every expat community has its own strip of foreign groceries and restaurants. If you miss something, it is not difficult to get your hands on it if you are willing to pay. Online expat forums like thebeijinger.com and cityweekend.com.cn are also helpful. You can also find apartment listings on these websites.

The population is beyond imagination. There are people everywhere and they tend to be pushy and disregard personal space. People spit, kids pee and shit on the streets, and have a general disregard for simple rules like standing in line. Despite the large expat community, locals still blatantly stare and point at foreigners. Some will actually stare and point as they walk by and then turn around to do a second pass. It's important to realize that it's just in their culture. China was, until very recently, a very closed society with very little outside exposure. It's easy to get angry or look down on the locals, and it's something that most expats fall into, but we moved here and are living in their country by choice. Things are just the way they are and you just have to deal with it.

In my opinion, the best thing about living in China is how easy it is to travel. It is significantly cheaper to fly to Europe from China than it is from the U.S. Korea and Japan are only a few hours away. You can fly to Southeast Asia for a couple hundred dollars. China is also huge and diverse so it's worth taking long weekends all over the country.

I think living in China can be difficult at times so expats tend to be very welcoming and it's not too difficult to make friends. I find it is more difficult making friends with locals. They are friendly, but tend to be a little distant. You also have to watch what you say. They tend to be extremely proud of their country and disparaging remarks about their government are not appreciated especially since they have only heard what their government has told them. This is not always the case, but many locals feel that the government does what is best for them and don't believe that their civil rights are being violated.

Gabriella Van Leuven
Beijing, China

While China has come a long way in recent years, and I consider myself fairly open-minded, there are some things which I don't believe I'll ever get used to.

Everywhere you go there are huge crowds. Everywhere. There is constant noise and traffic. Grocery stores, buses, trains, sidewalks...all filled with people at all times of the day. You will get shoved, elbowed and ogled. People will cut in front of you in line, kids will point and strangers will stare unabashedly—both at you and into your shopping basket.

The number of cars on the roads in China has increased tenfold in as many years. Also, to get a driver's license here you need only have money, not actual knowledge of traffic rules or driving skills. Cars drive in the bike lane, on the sidewalk, against red lights, against the direction of traffic and against all logic in general. Horns are used liberally.

People do spit, often and noisily. There is a long-held belief, based in traditional Chinese medicine, that spitting is healthy and rids the body of toxins. Actually, I don't mind it, but it seems to bother a lot of my fellow foreigners. For some reason, Western men especially seem to have a problem with the idea of attractive women spitting loudly. I think it's funny.

Whereas in the U.S. we do like to offer our bus seats and spots in line to the elderly, in China the elderly don't wait for the chance to be offered. It's disconcerting at first to have old ladies elbow past you to get on the bus or openly cut to the front of the line—but I guess it does make sense, after all.

People will ask you "how much did you pay for that?" Having lived in both Northern California and the Midwest, I've experienced a range of attitudes toward asking people "personal" questions. I tend to fall on the Northern California side of the line here, but still feel uncomfortable answering this question. I usually quote my Chinese co-workers about half of what I actually paid, knowing that I probably paid the "foreigner tax" anyway.

When I first arrived, I ate in a restaurant every night. I could not believe that I could get a meal and a beer for two or three dollars. While the novelty hasn't worn off, the liberal use of MSG, soybean oil and salt wore me out. Also, that beer, even though it's cheaper than water, is a lot like water, but worse-tasting.

I love going to the gym and was delighted to find a brand-new Western-style gym right down the street from my apartment. Gyms are a new phenomenon here, though the tradition of daily exercise amongst Chinese is strong. The gym I belong to also has its own fashion line, but most people just wear their work clothes. I often see people running on the treadmill in jeans and dress shoes—whilst talking on their cell phones, no less. I like to take the aerobics classes here, and have found that, yes, the stuff the teacher is saying must be useless because I get by without it just fine. Most classes end with a little bit of Tai Chi to cool down.

Taxis are another luxury I've taken on while I'm here. Not only do taxi drivers not expect tips, they often won't accept tips. Taxi flag in Beijing is 10 rmb: about $1.50. From there it's 2 rmb/kilometer. Strangely, gas here is about $4 a gallon. My father, a taxi driver in San Francisco, was baffled by these numbers. I've heard that taxi drivers often live in the basements of abandoned buildings or camp in construction sites. My average taxi ride costs about $3—10 times the cost of the subway and 20 times the cost of the bus.

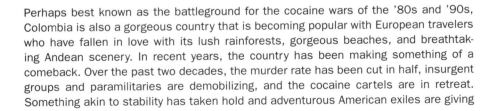

12. Colombia

Climate: Tropical along coast and eastern plains; cooler in highlands
Government: Republic
Population: 44,725,543
Currency: Colombian Peso (COP): 1 COP = 0.0005 USD
Language: Spanish (official)
Religious Groups: Catholic (90%), other (10%)
Ethnic Groups: mestizo (85%), white (20%), mulatto (14%), black (4%), mixed black-Amerindian (3%), Amerindian (1%)
Cost of Living Compared to U.S.: Cheap

Perhaps best known as the battleground for the cocaine wars of the '80s and '90s, Colombia is also a gorgeous country that is becoming popular with European travelers who have fallen in love with its lush rainforests, gorgeous beaches, and breathtaking Andean scenery. In recent years, the country has been making something of a comeback. Over the past two decades, the murder rate has been cut in half, insurgent groups and paramilitaries are demobilizing, and the cocaine cartels are in retreat. Something akin to stability has taken hold and adventurous American exiles are giving

Colombia a second look. If you're looking for an unpopulated surf haven, a low-cost setting to launch your business, or simply a beautiful place with friendly locals to spend your retirement years, Colombia might be the perfect destination. Expats have been flocking to Cartagena, a port city on the Caribbean Coast and Medellín, which has shed its once-notorious image and is becoming a popular destination for Americans who have fallen in love with the "City of Eternal Spring."

Living There

Governance: Colombia is an electoral democracy but elections in the past have been marred by allegations of vote-rigging and intimidation by paramilitary groups. Conditions have improved for recent elections. The justice system is overburdened and has been plagued with corruption. Although the Colombian government guarantees basic human rights and political freedoms, the military, insurgents, and paramilitary groups often target political enemies. Although progress has been made, crime and political violence remain a problem.

Infrastructure: Semi-developed. The rail system is outdated and many roads are unpaved. Electrical capacity lags behind other countries in the region. The telecommunications infrastructure is fully modern and there are a number of mobile phone providers.

Internet: Internet penetration is average for the region; less than half of Colombia's residents enjoy Internet access. Major cities have hi-speed Internet and broadband access is available.

Healthcare: Private insurance is available for those who can afford it. There is also a public healthcare system but the program is struggling due to lack of funding. The hospitals and medical facilities in the larger cities are considered comparable to what any western country might offer. The quality of care is significantly lower in rural areas.

GPD: $431.9 billion

GDP (Per Capita): $9,800

Sovereign Debt: 44.8% of GDP

Working There: Teach English, translate

Regulatory Environment: Simple and efficient

Taxes: Individual: 0–33%, Corporate: 33%, VAT: 16%. Residents taxed on worldwide income.

Cannabis: Decriminalized for small amounts (up to 20 grams)

Homosexuality: Legal, same-sex unions enjoy legal protections akin to common law marriage. No laws against discrimination. Although there are openly gay neighborhoods in Bogotá, there is a past history of intolerance and violence directed at homosexuals.

Abortion: Allowed to save woman's life, preserve physical and mental health, and in cases of rape, incest, or fetal impairment.

Women's Issues: Although women enjoy the same legal rights as men, sexual harassment, workplace discrimination, and pay disparities remain a concern.

Guns: Limited ownership allowed. Permits required. Military oversees and regulates civilian firearm ownership.

Crime: Although terrorism has decreased significantly, robbery and other violent crimes are common in larger cities. Scams, petty theft, and other property crimes are also common in urban areas. Your personal security plummets if you get involved in labor organizing or political reform.

Real Estate: Foreigners are allowed to buy property in Colombia but financing is generally not available through local banking institutions. Notary fee of 0.5% of purchase price, registration fee and local tax come to 1.5% of purchase price. Homes and apartments in a popular location like Cartagena on the Caribbean coast range from $40,000 up into the millions (depending on size and location). Prices are significantly less in more remote areas.

Life Expectancy: 74.55 years

Moving There

While you probably shouldn't count on a work permit, few livable countries offer as many cheap and easy legal residency paths.

Tourist Visa: Visa not required for U.S. citizens to stay in Colombia for up to 90 days.

Student Visa: Eligible to anyone enrolled in an approved course of study in Colombia. Taking as few as 10 hours of Spanish language classes per week can qualify.

Temporary Resident Visa: Depending on reason for stay (there are several visas of this type available) period of validity generally ranges from six months to a year.

Qualified Resident Visa: Five years with valid temporary visa required. Equivalent to a Permanent Resident Visa. No renewals required.

Monthly Income Visa: Akin to a pensioner visa, applicant must show proof of minimum monthly income. Valid one year, renewable.

Pensioner Visa: Applicant must show proof of pension or source of monthly income (approx. $1,400/month). Valid one year, renewable.

Resident Investor Visa: Home purchase or investment of at least $200,000 entitles applicant to immediate permanent resident status. Funds must remain in Colombia a minimum of three years. Visa is considered permanent, renewal is not required.

Work Permit: Applicant must show proof of offer of employment by Colombian company, copy of work contract, and certificate of goodwill issued by sponsoring company, and proof of qualifications. Valid for duration of employment.

Citizenship: Five years legal residency required.

Josh Plotkin

Medellín, Colombia

Medellín is just starting to be discovered by gringos and they are mostly contained to the upper class Parque Lleras district. There is where you can find a three-bedroom luxury apartment for $1000 a month, McDonald's, high-end clubs and the most expensive restaurants in town. Some places have menus in English, but English is still not very widely spoken. Colombian Spanish is clear and easy to understand. The currency is the Colombian Peso, which at the time of writing trades for about 1,800 to 1. A typical Colombian lunch or dinner of rice, beans, meat, salad, french fries and a fried banana costs 7,000 COP at most places. A beer costs about 2,000 in restaurants, or 6,000 if you are at a club in Parque Lleras. Food prices are slightly lower than the U.S. but not as cheap as you'd expect from South America. Rent is significantly cheaper if you go out-side of Parque Lleras and search in Spanish online classified sites.

Colombians are very warm and friendly people, and many will be excited to talk to a gringo. I met quite a few people who said I was the only gringo they've ever talked to. Colombians are quite fond of Western-style clothing and if you put earplugs in you might think you're somewhere in the U.S. But then you will see a group of guys walk by with mullet haircuts and bright-colored braces, and you'll know you're in Medellín.

James Lindzey
Medellín, Colombia

Average Medellín temp any time of the year is about 74 degrees! Although it's about the same altitude as Denver, Colorado, the mile-high city, there's no snow here. The rebels have been pushed out of these areas since 2005 and small cities and villages around Medellín are now safe to live.

Colombian neighborhoods are divided into social economic zones which range from 1 to 6, with 1 being the poorest and 6 the richest. I do not recommend foreigners live in anything less than a 3 or 4 zone. I live in a 6, as a necessity for working with tourists and being near our most desirable vacation rentals. I pay $1000 bucks a month for a brand new three-bedroom apartment. However you can get apartments from 500 bucks a month, if you're out of the heart (i.e. expensive) part of town. Again I'm here for business reasons really.

Rent, utilities, and groceries vary greatly depending on the neighborhood you live in. I can afford to eat out four or five times as much as in the States, with the exception of sushi. Decent steak dinners run about $12 in an international restaurant. Typical food you can spend about five bucks for a plate of beans, rice, meat, and a soft drink.

Tips on shopping: pay your maid to buy meat (save 50%) on the way to work in a cheap neighborhood. 2) Drive just outside the more expensive zone/neighborhood to shop and save 30% on groceries. 3) Eat lots of fruit and veggies, the fruits are awesome in Colombia, and cheap.

The farmers' markets are the best place to buy stuff to get around national chain restaurant prices which actually are pretty close to USA prices, with the exception of fruits. Fruits are high in variety and cheap here.

Dating in Colombia, well, that depends on the class of woman you wish to go out with. There are many on dating sites and around town that just want to go out and have a good time, but they need someone to pay the bill. Don't think that one-nighters are normal here. If that happens, then the girl could actually be playing you, looking for a papi (sugar daddy). On the odd chance that she's a college kid and you're a college boy and you're just partying, well, that does happen.

13. Costa Rica

Climate: Tropical and subtropical; dry season (December to April); rainy season (May to November); cooler in highlands
Government: Democratic Republic
Population: 4,253,877
Currency: Costa Rican Colon (CRC): 1 CRC = 0.002 USD
Language: Spanish (official), English
Religious Groups: Roman Catholics (76.3%), Evangelical (13.7%), Jehovah's Witnesses (1.3%), other Protestant (0.7%), other (4.8%), none (3.2%)
Ethnic Groups: white and mestizo (94%), black (3%), Amerindian (1%), Chinese (1%), other (1%)
Cost of Living compared to the U.S.: Cheap-ish

Pura vida, as the local *ticos* call it: "pure life." They must be onto something because many international surveys find Costa Rica to be the happiest country on earth. A model of political stability, this Central American mecca offers all the palm trees and sandy beaches, but without the typical turmoil of your more rickety banana republics. And if you have a Green streak, over 25% of the Costa Rica's land is protected reserve and a large majority of the nation's electricity is generated with renewable resources. Although still inexpensive, its popularity has led to rising costs and beachfront homes—topping the $1 million mark—though bargains are still to be had by moving further afield from the main communities around La Fortuna, in the mountains around Arenal, and along the Pacific coast in Puntarenas. The Caribbean side now also feels the impact of the expanding Gringolandia.

Living There
Governance: The Costa Rican state is known for its enlightened environmental policies. Civil and political liberties are respected, the country has a well-regarded judiciary, but the court system suffers from inefficiency. Corruption can be a problem and as the country is becoming a way station in the global cocaine trade, security concerns are growing.

Infrastructure: Excellent by Latin American standards, but roads, telecommunications and power grid are in need of additional investment. Telephone service is run by a government monopoly so landlines are difficult to get if your home doesn't already have one, though cell phones are everywhere.

Internet: Broadband Internet service is available in many areas through cable modems; also DSL and ISDN lines are commonly available.

Healthcare: Costa Rica has universal healthcare, considered one of the best health systems in Latin America. Even Rush Limbaugh considered using it.

GDP: $51.55 billion

GDP (Per Capita): $11,400

Sovereign Debt: 42.4% of GDP

Working There: Some English teaching, but mostly retirees and volunteers

Regulatory Environment: Regulations can be onerous and time-consuming for new businesses.

Taxes: Corporate: 10–30%. Individual: 10–25%. VAT: 13%. There is no wealth or inheritance tax in Costa Rica.

Cannabis: Illegal, but widely available

Homosexuality: Legal; same-sex unions are not legally recognized but efforts to extend legal rights to same-sex couples are gaining momentum. Laws against discrimination. Generally tolerant attitudes toward homosexuality, particularly by Latin American standards. There are gay communities in San Jose and in resort towns along the Pacific coast where there are even gay hotels and a gay beach.

Abortion: To preserve physical health

Women's Issues: Though not condoned by the government, violence against women and sexual harassment are problematic. Women are discriminated against in the workplace.

Guns: Legal, registration required. Concealed carry allowed.

Crime: Daytime robberies by armed criminal gangs have been known to occur but petty theft and burglary are more prevalent. Kidnapping for cash does occur.

Real Estate: Ownership of land available to non-citizens. Mortgage financing available. Typically short-term (less than 10 years) and up to 70% of appraised value.

Life Expectancy: 77.54 years

Moving There

Not for nothing has Costa Rica been the first choice for Americans fleeing to Latin America. It's fairly do-able for the fleeing middle class or retirees, having spawned an expansive industry for facilitating their relevant legal paperwork. The young and short of means will find that while the overhead is low, they'll have to deal with a tricky schedule of border runs every 90 days. Telecommuters and others who get their income from outside Costa Rica can do so under any legal residency option. Costa Rica does not even issue special visas for students.

Tourist Visa: U.S. citizens can stay in Costa Rica for up to 90 days without a visa. Prepaid airline ticket home or to other country required. In 2010, the government stiffened penalties for overstaying your visa—$100 for every month or a prohibition from reentering the country for triple the time of your unauthorized stay.

Pensionado/Rentista Visa: To qualify for the *Pensionado*, you must show proof of a minimum of $1,000 per month income from a pension plan, retirement account, or Social Security. This amount must be converted every month into the local currency and you must live in Costa Rica at least four months each year. A *Rentista* must prove a monthly income of $2,500 from a guaranteed bank or make a deposit of at least $150,000 in a Costa Rican bank. This visa also requires that you change at least $2,500 per month into the local currency each month and you must live in Costa Rica at least four months out of the year. You are not allowed to work but can own a company and receive income. Generally issued for five years but you can apply for permanent residency in three.

Residency for Investors (*Inversionista*): If you invest at least $50,000 in a business or industry approved by the Center for the Promotion of Exports and Investments (PROCOMER) you can qualify for permanent residence as an investor. Non-PROCOMER investments need to be at least $200,000. A minimum investment of $100,000 is required for rainforest reforestation projects. You must live in Costa Rica for six months per year. Generally issued for five years but you can apply for permanent residency in three.

Company Representative (*Representante*): If you hold some executive, managerial or technical position in a company that meets certain financial requirements, particularly one that hires local employees, you can qualify for this visa that will also allow you to draw a salary from that position.

Permanent Resident: Available to "first degree" relatives of Costa Rica citizens, e.g. a spouse or the father or mother of a Costa Rican child. You can also apply after three years of legal residency. Permanent residents are allowed to work in Costa Rica.

Citizenship: Seven years legal residency is required; along with proficiency in Spanish and Costa Rican history, two Costa Rican citizens must attest to your character.

Kelly Kittel

Tamarindo, Costa Rica

My life? No shopping except for groceries. Spend the day swimming, walking, biking, boogie boarding, surfing, all outdoors, lots of Vitamin D. No plans, take life as it comes. None of the mad dashing around from sporting events to parties like in U.S. A big trip might be a walk down the beach to town for a smoothie. Plenty of time to read and write and chat with friends. IN PERSON. Phones are frustrating anyway so don't use them much. Do rely on the computer though. I have a helper and a gardener six days a week which I do not have in the U.S.

I pay $1200 for a great three-bedroom, three-bath house right on the beach, which is less than usual as it is a friend's house. Normal long-term rent would be more like $1800 or more for it. Fabulous location. Rustic house but comfortable. Crabs like to come in during rainy season and scuttle across the tiled floor but, hey, it's a beach house! No tarantulas, scorpions, or snakes here on the beach unlike elsewhere. Very few roaches. Super secure (owners are German) so theft not an issue. Usually good to have a dog here but we have been fine w/o one so far. Lovely gardens with grapefruit, lime, coconut and mango trees. Howler monkeys come thru often and eat the mangos. Upper balcony overlooks the beach which is only steps away.

It's not as affordable as it used to be. In general, local produce in season is inexpensive and anything else is not. Bananas are super cheap and potatoes are expensive. Some examples:

15 eggs: $2; 1 kg carrots: $1; 700g strawberries: $5.40; 12 imported apples: $5.50; 6 local apples: $2; cantaloupe melon: .50/kg; 3 passionfruit: .60; 3 zucchini: $3.50 (what?!).

½ gal of OJ: $5; ½ gal (1.8 liters) milk: $1.80; 1 gal: $4; 1 lb butter: $5.60; Single serving yogurt: $1.20; A small block of cheese, maybe 8 oz, is $10

1 whole chicken: $8; small package chicken breast strips: $6; burger (10% fat) $7.40/kg

Ranch dressing $4; Regular-sized box of cereal: $5.20; frozen waffles: $5.40; 1 sleeve local Ritz-like crackers: .60; 2 kg sugar: $2.30

Internet: $25 to $27/month for excellent strength reliable wireless service, came with the house. I had a VERY difficult time getting it installed in the last house so it is important if you are renting to make sure it is already in place and working well. Does go out with power outages but not often and no problem resetting. Yes, it is a HUGE hassle to get any utilities turned on in my experience. We also had cable trouble with our last house and phone as well and it took MONTHS to resolve. It's common wisdom here that you give the workers a cold drink in order to get service!

Electricity: also expensive, ranges from $175 to $300 for both houses. I never use a/c as there is always a breeze so far and it cools down nicely at night. My other house was not on the beach so I have to conclude things are "cooler" on the beach.

Ticos are lovely, laid-back, Pura Vida people. No road rage. Plenty of expats depending where you live. Americans and plenty of Europeans, also. Here in Tamarindo, as well as San José, Arenal, Jaco, Dominical, to name a few. They choose this area for the surfing/beach lifestyle, although many live on golf/tennis resorts. Many have spouses working in the States who visit occasionally.

Frank
Orosi, Costa Rica

There's a lot of people who come here and love it and some that just can't stand it. They are people that like the modern conveniences and they like to go shopping and they like the fabricated stuff that they're used to, they're not going to find much here. If you're looking to eat good fresh food, breathing fresh air and being around healthy and happy people, Costa Rica is the place.

We planned originally on Jacos, Manuel Antonio or someplace where the tourists go. The cost of living out there is a lot more, but it's the heat and the bugs that make it just unbearable. Orosi is up in the mountains. It averages around 75 degrees all year round. It never gets really hot or really cold. There's a rainy season, five or six months out of the year, but the sun still shines. But it's not what you'd expect from a rainforest. Orosi is near the rainforest and my farm is actually right on the border of it.

A banana will cost you a couple of cents. You can go out for a meal for $6-$10. If it's imported, it's expensive. If you want Jiffy peanut butter, you're going to pay twice what you pay in the States. For DSL, I pay $15 a month.

Not just your cost of living goes down here, but your stress level. You hear mañana all the time, which literally means tomorrow but really they mean not now. It is hard to get things done quickly here, but there is just not a whole lot of stress. You don't have the stress of trying to pay crazy bills and the stress of always trying to get someplace. You show up 20 minutes late and people think you're 45 minutes early.

It's kind of like a Communist country here because the government runs everything. There is no free enterprise. Most of the people who have a job here work for the government one way or another. Phone, power, water, everything like that is all government-run.

Anywhere you spend money, there's always somebody there who can speak English. People who've lived here for years never bothered learning the language because you really don't need to. You can't go to a bank and not find somebody who speaks English.

14. Croatia

Climate: Mediterranean and continental; continental climate predominant with hot summers and cold winters; mild winters, dry summers along coast
Government: Parliamentary Democracy
Population: 4,489,409
Currency: Kuna (HRK): 1 HRK = 0.19 USD
Language: Croatian (South Slavic language, using the Roman script)
Religious Groups: Roman Catholic (87.8%), Orthodox (4.4%), other Christian (0.4%), Muslim (1.3%), other and unspecified (0.9%), none (5.2%)
Ethnic Groups: Croat (89.6%), Serb (4.5%), other [including Bosniak, Hungarian, Slovene, Czech, and Roma] (5.9%)
Cost of Living compared to the U.S.: Cheap

Sun-worshippers and bargain-chasers have been making Croatia, in the former Republic of Yugoslavia, the hottest new expat mecca in Eastern Europe. Having woken up from its civil war/ethnic cleansing nightmare, life is good and they are making entry easy for Western immigrants. You can squeeze by on a few hundred dollars a month if you avoid the tourist zones or buy a house on the Dalmatian coast for under $100,000.

Living There

Governance: Croatians enjoy free and fair elections, freedom of assembly and expression, as well as religious freedom. Government still controls a substantial portion of the media, though its overall record on human rights is good. Most of its judicial shortfalls concern its dealing with issues from the ethnic wars with Serbia in the 1990s. Internet is uncensored.
Infrastructure: There is ample transport capacity with few exceptions, although much infrastructure is in fair or poor condition because maintenance was deferred.
Internet: Hi-speed widely available. Broadband service rapidly spreading throughout the country.
Healthcare: The standard of healthcare in Croatia is generally on par with that in many European countries, but not considered expensive overall. What state-run facilities lack in aesthetic appeal, they more than make up for in quality of care. All visiting foreigners are entitled to free basic emergency treatment at state hospitals.
GDP: $78.52 billion
GDP (Per Capita): $17,500
Sovereign Debt: 55% of GDP

Working There: Opportunities in tourist industry, teach English in private schools or volunteering.

Regulatory Environment: Heavy bureaucracy and some corruption

Taxes: Corporate: 20%, Individual: 15–45%, VAT: 23%. Surtax is charged in certain municipalities (e.g. in Zagreb—18%). Non-residents are taxed on their Croatian income. Residents (defined as someone residing 183 days or more in Croatia over a given tax year) are taxed on worldwide income.

Cannabis: Illegal and under new "Zero Tolerance" drug laws, the government will prosecute for even small amounts, though you'll still find that it's readily available and widely consumed. Veterans suffering from PTSD allowed to light up following a 2009 Supreme Court decision.

Homosexuality: Legal. Limited recognition of same-sex couples. Laws against discrimination. A small number of hate crimes have occurred in reaction to the new visibility of gays and lesbians.

Abortion: No restrictions as to reason; however, parental authorization/notification is required.

Women's Issues: Gender equality is a matter of law, although domestic violence is considered to be a large underreported problem. Women are well-represented in business and politics.

Guns: Most firearms require a permit.

Crime: Croatia has a relatively low crime rate, and violent crime is rare.

Real Estate: To purchase property, foreigners must either apply for permission from the Croatian Ministry of Justice or form a holding company. Mortgages are not readily available in Croatia and most deals are paid in cash.

Life Expectancy: 75.35 years

Moving There

Outside of the usual fast-track paths (study, marry, reunite with family), Croatia would be most accessible to people intent on starting or investing in the country's tourism industry.

Tourist Visa: U.S. Citizens can stay up to 90 days without a visa.

First Temporary Residence Visa: If you wish to work, attend school, or reside in Croatia for more than 90 days, you must apply for a First Temporary Residence Visa. Applicants are required to provide evidence of sufficient income, lodging accommodations in Croatia, and proof of health insurance. Croatian authorities also require documents verifying reason for stay. If you plan on studying, an acceptance letter from a Croatian university is required. If you are seeking to work, an employment contract and work permit are required. If you plan on operating a business, you must show proof that your company or firm is officially registered in the Republic of Croatia.

Permanent Residence: Applicants must show they have renewed temporary visa for five years or be married to a Croat for three years, or be a minor with a parent who has a permanent residency permit.

Work Permits: The Republic of Croatia is strictly bound by legislation limiting the number of foreign workers. Still, there is a quota system that allows a certain number of expat professionals who possess needed skills to fill certain occupations so it might be worth your while to apply for a work permit. A work permit is required even if you are just looking for employment but if you've located a job, your employer can apply on your behalf.

Student Visa: also available, per the usual requirements.

Jessica Ujevic

Split, Croatia

I came here from South Carolina in 2005 with my husband, who is originally from this area.

I am asked routinely why I would choose to move here, and the phrase that I use most often is "quality versus quantity." At home, I was working around 55–60 hours a week. I did have buying power. I just didn't have time to enjoy it. Living in Croatia, I may not have the same resources for consumption, but the things that I do have are much more worthwhile.

The town of Split itself is over 1700 years old. The city has grown up around the original walls of Diocletian's palace. Stone, stone, and more stone. Walking through the streets takes you back in time. There is a real feeling of security when you are traveling on walkways people have been using for so long. The stone under your feet is as smooth as glass, polished by countless footsteps. There are nooks and crannies around every corner with beautiful balustrades and balconies, flowering vines and fig trees, church spires and pillars. The frontal area of Split is known as the Riva. It is outside one of four main gates, which are the entrance to the palace. On one side you have a gorgeous view of the sea with islands dotting the horizon, and behind you the looming palace walls. Here, the whole street is lined with shops and cafés. People are very active and every afternoon is perfect for people-watching.

15. Czech Republic

Climate: Temperate
Government: Parliamentary Republic
Population: 10,211,904
Currency: Czech Koruna or "Crown"
  (CZK): 1 CZK = 0.05 USD
Language: Czech
Religious Groups: Atheist (39.8%), Catholic (39.2%), Protestant (4.6%),
  other (17.4%)
Ethnic Groups: Czech (81.2%), Moravian (13.2%), Slovak (3.1%), other (3.5%)
Cost of Living compared to the U.S.: Not as low as it used to be, but still
  appreciably cheaper

Prague was once known as the Paris of the '90s when the slacker generation flocked to the Czech Republic (formerly Czechoslovakia) for low-budget living and great beer. Its increased affluence has eroded some of that appeal, but the country still offers a great balance of sophistication, convenience, price and affordability, while the food, at least in Prague, is no longer the most dismal in Europe. As the headquarters of Radio Free Europe, and a vibrant literary expat scene, it hosts more English-language media than other foreign capitals many times its size. The burgeoning Hollywood of Eastern Europe, it provides plenty of opportunities for people in the entertainment industry. Outside the capital, prices plummet.

Living There
Governance: Since the velvet revolution of 1989, then-Czechoslovakia (now the Czech Republic) has embraced Western-style liberal democracy, with free and fair elections, independent judiciary, respect for religious freedom, freedom of expression, etc.
Infrastructure: Developed
Internet: Nearly seven in 10 Czech households have Internet access and broadband is now widely available.
Healthcare: The quality of medical care across the Czech Republic varies, but there are several excellent facilities available in Prague. Generally, medical care and facilities on par with the West.
GDP: $262.8 billion
GDP (Per Capita): $25,600
Sovereign Debt: 40% of GDP
Working There: Highly skilled workers have a shot and English teachers and translators do eke out a living. A gig at Radio Free Europe would be golden, but otherwise opportunities are hard to come by.

Regulatory Environment: The licensing process can be lengthy, but reforms have cut down on red tape.

Taxes: Corporate: 20%, Individual: 15%, VAT: 20% (10% on certain goods). Generally, foreigners considered tax residents are subject to income tax on their worldwide income and nonresident foreigners are subject to income tax only on their Czech-source income.

Cannabis: Since 2010, up to 15 grams (or five plants) are allowed for personal use.

Homosexuality: Legal. Since 2006, registered same-sex couples legally recognized. Laws against discrimination. Czech culture is fairly progressive and tolerant, and open gay communities are commonplace, particularly in Prague.

Abortion: No restrictions as to reason; however, parental authorization/notification is required.

Women's Issues: Gender equality is a matter of law, but discrimination and harassment, particularly in the workplace, is still a fact of life. Nevertheless, women's representation in business and politics is high.

Guns: Firearms allowed but subject to strict licensing and owners must pass exams to own certain types of weapons depending on reason for use.

Crime: The Czech Republic generally has a low rate of crime. There are occasional incidents of pickpocketing (especially on public transportation) and occasional muggings. Although there has been a slight increase in violent crime, this hardly registers by U.S. urban standards.

Real Estate: The Czech Republic recently relaxed restrictions on foreigners owning property. U.S. citizens should possess a residency permit or form a limited corporation (known as SROs) to be considered for a mortgage. Prices are still low compared to much of Europe but rising.

Life Expectancy: 76.81 years

Moving There

If you're lucky enough to land a job in the CR, your legalities can usually be worked out. If you've come to study or do research at one of the country's fine universities or institutes, no problem either. Otherwise, you're best having a good freelancing gig going or a nest egg unless you like living off the radar.

NOTE: If you apply for a visa at a Czech consulate, you will receive your visa in the U.S. and not in the Czech Republic. The process can often take a great deal of time and Czech immigration authorities urge applicants to add at least four months to their prospective departure date to allow for processing time. The Catch-22 is that you have to provide proof of accommodation for the duration of your visa (usually one year). Universities and employers may help provide this, but DIYers will have to either rent remotely (risky) or find someone to "offer" you space in an apartment or house. You don't have to actually live there once you arrive.

Schengen Visa: 90-day stay allowed within 180-day period.

Long Stay Visa: Applicants must provide proof of sufficient financial means (approx. $3,000/month), proof of travel medical insurance, and documents confirming accommodation in Czech Republic (notarized statement of accommodation, notarized copy of lease agreement, etc.) . You will also need a purpose of stay, which is evaluated by the Foreign Police on a case-by-case basis. If marriage and family ties don't bind you, then these are your options:

For study: Proof of enrollment, self-sufficiency, medical insurance, accommodation, etc.

For business: Either form your own company (capitalized at approx. $10,000) or get a trade license to practice your trade in Czech Republic.

For Employment + Work Permit: Employer must apply with Czech Employment Administration Office (EAO) for work permit before visa is granted. Applicants must also provide documents confirming accommodation in Czech Republic, medical travel insurance, etc.

Family reunion cases and certain academics and scholars can also apply to longer-term (five-year) Residence Permits.

Permanent Residency: Applicant must be legal resident for at least five years, have sufficient income, and show that continued residence is "in the interest of the Czech Republic."

Student Visa: also available, per the usual requirements.

Citizenship: Five years permanent residency (most of that time spent in Czech Republic), proficiency in Czech language, renunciation of U.S. citizenship, and no arrest record in previous five years.

Tinuola
Prague, Czech Republic

I live in Prague 7, Holesovice. It's a largely Czech area, but with two of the city's largest parks (Stromovka and Letna), great tram connections and affordable rent prices it's gradually picking up on the real-estate radar for expats. What it currently lacks is the vibrant restaurant scene of Vinohrady, Prague 2. There's also a fair bit of traffic that runs through the neighborhood, which makes it a bit noisy during the daytime. I enjoy that the neighborhood is very local, and some days I feel quite protective of its "Czechness" knowing that anytime soon many others will discover what a prime location it is.

My quality of life has improved dramatically since moving to the Czech Republic. The particulars—concerts, movies, exhibitions, exercise, dining out—aren't that different from when I was in the States, only that I'm doing them more often and with a relaxed approach. Back in the States, I heard and read tons about work-life balance; I didn't experience it or get it till I moved to Europe. Consumerism is still at moderate levels here, I think—people aren't just working to acquire "stuff" or to keep up with the Joneses. There's a strong emphasis on having shared/interpersonal experiences and the culture accommodates this need.

It also helps that social activities in Prague don't cost as much as in New York, for example (or even in other popular European cities). I admit that it would be nice to have more upscale lounges and less smoky pubs/bars in which to socialize and meet friends for drinks. In NYC, you don't have just three good after-work or late-night lounges, you have dozens to choose from—and many of them excellent. The same goes for restaurants and shops. After years in Prague, I have had to reframe my expectations. I don't get bent out of shape about the lack of variety or creativity as much. Where before I may have complained that too many restaurants have the same pizza-pasta menu, now I just focus on which one makes risotto nearly right.

16. Denmark

Climate: Temperate, generally overcast; mild winters and cool summers
Government: Constitutional Monarchy
Population: 5,515,575
Currency: Danish Krone (DKK):
    1 DKK = 0.18 USD
Language: Danish, Faroese, Greenlandic, German (English is common second language)
Religious Groups: Lutheran (95%), other Christian (3%), Muslim (2%)
Ethnic Groups: Scandinavian, Inuit, Faroese, German, Turkish, Iranian, Somali
Cost of Living compared to the U.S: Painful. Slightly more affordable outside of major cities

Affluent, civil and socially progressive, Denmark ranks high on the list of preferred countries, though like the rest of Scandinavia, they act like an exclusive club and proving you're good enough to be allowed entry is far from easy. Even spouses of Danish citizens have a hard time. Skilled workers, academics and those with Danish parentage have a shot. Still, if you qualify for one of their schemes, you can live in one of the finest societies European social democracy has to offer, as long as you don't place too much of a premium on warm sunshine. In any case, those who aren't paid in local currency will soon find the prices here a bit on the brutal side.

Living There
Governance: Denmark is practically the standard by which all free and fair governments are judged. Political rights and civil liberties are well-respected. Elections are squeaky-clean, the judiciary's behavior seems strikingly in concert

with the laws of the land. Government operations are generally efficient, and corruption among public officials is notoriously low.

Infrastructure: Well-developed. Everything works.

Internet: Cutting-edge; 86% of the Danish population has Internet access and Denmark's broadband penetration rates are some of the highest in the world.

Healthcare: The Danes are quite happy with their healthcare. Most medical services are free and health authorities have adopted a decentralized approach that allows residents to conveniently connect with providers in their region or district. Quality is comparable to most European countries.

GDP: $201.4 billion

GDP (Per Capita): $36,700

Sovereign Debt: 46.6% of GDP

Working There: Teaching English, IT, some sales and marketing, some healthcare. If you land a job, consider yourself extremely fortunate.

Regulatory Environment: Highly efficient and friendly to new businesses.

Taxes: Corporate: 26%, Individual: 36.57%–60%, VAT: 25%. All residents taxed on worldwide income.

Cannabis: Illegal, widely used. With a few interruptions, the Copenhagen "Freetown" borough of Christiania has been an open-air pot and hash market since the early 1970s, though its future is uncertain.

Homosexuality: Legal. Denmark was the first country in the world to legally recognize same-sex unions and has a long history of tolerance toward homosexuals. Laws against discrimination.

Abortion: No restrictions, parental authorization required.

Women's Issues: Strict laws against domestic violence and sexual harassment. Women enjoy the same legal status as men and the law requires equal pay for equal work. However, there are still some wage disparities between men and women.

Guns: Some firearms legal for civilian ownership but licensing required.

Crime: Generally low. We could nitpick, but you're not likely to find anyplace else in the free world where the crime rate is lower.

Real Estate: Foreign buyers can purchase property but must first be granted residency status from the Danish Ministry of Justice. There is a deed tax of 1,400 kroner (approx. $250) plus 0.06% of the purchase price on all real estate transactions. Mortgages are available but buyers must pay an additional 1.5% tax plus 1,400 kroner. Home prices in Denmark have declined significantly since the housing bubble collapsed.

Life Expectancy: 78.47 years

Moving There

Get someone to hire you or marry you. Neither is going to be all that easy.

Schengen Visa: 90-day stay allowed within six-month period.

Residence/Work Permit: Denmark currently has 11 different "schemes" that allow foreigners to reside in Denmark and/or obtain a work permit. If you are a skilled professional, the country maintains a "Positive List" of occupations that are in demand. American expats may want to apply for the "Green Card" scheme which allows immigrants to move to Denmark to seek work. The Green Card scheme is based on four criteria: education, language skills, work experience, and age. Applicants are given "bonus points" if they practice a profession or possess a skill that is in great demand. Self-employed applicants must also obtain a work permit to be granted residency and must show proof that Danish businesses will be connected to the enterprise, that the applicant has sufficient financial means, and is required for the day-to-day operations of his or her business. First time Residency/Work Permit is valid for up to three years and is renewable.

Student Visa: Applicant must show proof of enrollment in higher education, sufficient funds to finance stay and tuition, and proficiency in the language in which courses will be taught. Visa is valid until completion of studies.

Permanent Residency: A minimum of four years of legal residency required. Applicants must also accumulate 100 points. Points are awarded based on length of legal residence, absence of any arrests or public debts, duration of employment, language proficiency (a test is required), and applicants cannot have applied for any kind of public assistance.

Citizenship: Applicant must be a legal resident of Denmark for at least nine years, show proficiency in Danish language and knowledge of culture (test must be passed), show proof of viable income and clean criminal record, and must renounce U.S. citizenship.

Bill Agee

Copenhagen, Denmark

Life here in Copenhagen is just so much more livable than any place I've experienced in the U.S. I take a train and a boat to work. I ride my bike to buy groceries and go to the cinema. I have a balcony where I can sit and watch the rides at Tivoli Gardens, the amusement park in the center of Copenhagen that inspired Walt Disney. And when Copenhagen is not enough, I take a one-hour flight to London, Paris, Amsterdam or Prague for the weekend. This is what I left the U.S. for—to experience a way of life that just doesn't exist in the United States.

Copenhagen is a little big city. It has all the attractions of a big, capital city, such as innumerable bars, restaurants, cafés, clubs, theaters, museums and variety, without the travel difficulty of a huge city, like London or Rome. It is intimate enough that you can easily run into friends and neighbors walking in other parts of town, but yet still keep a low profile, if that's what you need. I have lived in Manhattan, Philadelphia and Miami, and find Copenhagen to be the most user-friendly of the cities in which I have lived. The public transit system runs like a dream and can get you to even the most remote corner of the city or even the country quite easily. But I rarely take the metro or busses within the city, since everything is walkable or an easy bike-ride away. Since it is the capital of Denmark, there is opera, ballet, theater, the parliament, the royal pageants, and even the supposedly best restaurant in the world, NOMA.

The downside is that because Denmark has one of the highest living standards in the world, prices here can sometimes seem outrageous. Especially for things like dinner for two or a beer at a bar. With the minimum wage about $25 an hour, you know that your bar tab has to be rather high to cover overhead. On the other hand, CEOs are not making $100 million a year, so you don't see the conspicuous consumption and thus don't feel so poor here. Apartment rents for a one-bedroom/one-bath bath in the center of Copenhagen run about $1100/month, which is much lower than NYC but higher than most other U.S. cities. Movie tickets cost about $18, which is higher than the U.S., and opera tickets about $45, which is much lower than many U.S. cities. National taxes are high here, but when you compare the total tax charge we pay in the U.S., including state, local and real estate taxes, there is not really a big difference. And when you see what you get for the taxes paid, particularly healthcare, education including university, and the safety net, it is actually quite reasonable. Being a wealthy country with a high safety net, it has the problem of many western European countries of not being able to figure out how to integrate new people from abroad into their system. There are periodic outbursts of the right wing which can be pretty brutal at times. This too shall pass, and quickly I hope.

Copenhagen is one of those cities of major contrasts. It did not get bombed during WWII and was not particularly wealthy during the grey-box 1960s, so there is a huge amount of old, lovely architecture around. However, with designers like Jørn Utzon (Sydney Opera House) and companies like Bang & Olufsen, Denmark has been extremely progressive for the past 60 years. Things are efficient, fast and smooth. I just show my "yellow card" at the doctor. I purchase train tickets with my mobile. Not a lot of traffic, except in the bike lanes, which can be pretty dangerous since I am neither fast nor very observant on a bike.

Libby Hansen
Tikoeb, Denmark

Denmark is not an inexpensive country to live in. Cars are much more expensive than in the U.S. For example, a Ford Grand C-Max, or VW Touran averages about 400,000 Danish crowns (80,000 USD). Gasoline has been around $8/gal for a long time now.

Income tax is never lower than 40% and often as high as 75% (marginal tax) on the top dollar if you have a good salary. The VAT (value added tax) is 25%, one of the highest in Europe. That alone makes most goods more expensive than in the U.S.

A television license (which many people ignore) is required if you own a TV, radio and/or a computer. That costs about $600/yr. Most young people ignore it because there really is no way to enforce the law.

On the positive side, education is free. Both my children have received postgraduate educations, receiving a "salary" from the state while they studied! Medical services are free, including doctor visits and hospitalization. To see a specialist, one needs to be referred from the General Practitioner. Depending on the specialty, there could be a few months waiting time. I feel that the health system here could do a lot more in the way of prevention. That is, screening for diseases before a patient presents with full-blown symptoms. People here don't get routine "health checks" like we do in the U.S. But the cost of doing so is probably prohibitive since there is never a co-payment on the part of the patient. I have not had a negative experience with healthcare here.

I don't work any longer but in general the work week here is shorter than in the U.S. 37 hrs/week is the norm. Vacation time is five or six weeks for most people!

Maternity leave is six months with the possibility to extend to a whole year with 80% pay for the mother and a couple of months 80% paid leave for the father.

17. Dominican Republic

Climate: tropical maritime; little seasonal temperature variation; rainfall varies by season
Government: Democratic Republic
Population: 9,956,648
Currency: Dominican Peso (DOP):
  1 DOP = 0.02 USD
Language: Spanish (official)
Religious Groups: Roman Catholic (95%), other (5%)
Ethnic Groups: mixed (73%), white (16%), black (11%)
Cost of Living compared to the U.S.: Cheap

This janky tropical paradise is an economic dynamo compared to its neighbor, Haiti, with whom it shares the Caribbean island of Hispaniola. Citizenship-seekers flock here, attracted by the easy terms (a bona fide second passport after about two years of residency and $20,000 worth of fees) and a taxman that pays scant attention to the asset repositories of the affluent class (i.e., real estate and bank accounts). Residency is there for the asking (or not asking, since many people simply overstay their visitor visa and pay the negligibly small fees when they leave the country) and nobody needs no stinkin' work permit (though the place is hardly brimming with job opportunities). Rent and basics are cheap and as plentiful as the sunshine. Self-sufficient types who don't mind things like adding a home generator to make up for gaps in an unreliable power supply can best reap the benefits of balmy days of liberty under laissez-faire governance, to the extent of creating economic incentive zones to attract business and capital. Tourism is on the upswing, too, offering tantalizing investment opportunities in related businesses and real estate. Poverty is still pervasive as is the associated crime, though as Caribbean nations go, it's hardly bottom-of-the-barrel.

Living There

Governance: Free and fair elections. The government guarantees basic human rights and the Dominican Republic has a thriving free press. However, corruption in the judiciary and among public officials is not uncommon. Human rights groups are also concerned by extrajudicial killings by police.

Infrastructure: Somewhat developed due to growth of tourism industry. Roads are well paved near city centers but lacking in rural areas. Airports have been built or expanded. The country has had problems meeting energy demands and electrical service can be unreliable. Telecommunications infrastructure is in somewhat better shape.

Internet: Approximately 30% of residents enjoy regular Internet access. Hi-speed Internet available in major cities and tourist areas.

Healthcare: Public health system is underfunded and the quality of care is not optimal. There are many private pay clinics that provide excellent treatment at an affordable price—the typical choice for expats. There are also a number of private insurers offering coverage that are aligned with some of the better hospitals and clinics.

GDP: $87.25 billion

GDP (Per Capita): $8,900

Sovereign Debt: 41.7% of GDP

Working There: Tourism, teach English, some construction, admin, IT, and sales.

Regulatory Environment: Licensing and regulations governing businesses have been streamlined in recent years but reforms have taken a long time to implement and minor corruption has hampered progress. The country does offer a number of "Free Zones" throughout the country where businesses can operate tax-free for up to 20 years.

Taxes: Individual: 0–25%, Corporate: 25%, VAT: 16%. Residents taxed on worldwide income as of third taxable year after obtaining residency.

Cannabis: Strictly illegal

Homosexuality: Although legal, public intolerance toward gays is a fact of life in the Dominican Republic. Same-sex unions are not legally recognized, and the country's new constitution, unveiled in 2010, includes restrictions against gay marriage. There are no anti-discrimination laws.

Abortion: Strictly prohibited

Women's Issues: Rape and domestic violence remain a serious problem. Laws against workplace sexual harassment. Although women enjoy the same legal status as men under the law, they are underrepresented in business and politics and there are significant wage disparities.

Guns: License required. Applicant must submit to psychological evaluation. If there is viable reason to fear for one's safety, authorities will allow a civilian with license to carry a firearm.

Crime: Crime is a serious problem. Muggings, petty theft, and pickpocketing are common in large cities and tourist areas. Narco crime has also been increasing.

Real Estate: Foreigners are allowed to purchase property in the Dominican Republic. Depending on the property that is purchased and how it is financed, there may be a small transfer and real estate tax. Financing is available from local banks for up to 75% of purchase price. The U.S. State Department has issued a warning urging prospective buyers to exercise a "high degree of caution" as property rights are often not strictly enforced in the Dominican Republic. There have been problems with squatters (some backed by the government and/or political groups) taking possession of absentee properties owned by Americans. It can often take years to evict and threats of violence have occurred over disputed properties. The State Department advises would-be American expats to retain a reputable local attorney who will practice due diligence and ensure you have clear title before buying any property. Home prices vary according to location. In Lucerna and Cancino, two- and three-bedroom homes can be had for as little as $60,000. In Santo Domingo and other large cities, prices are higher but you can still find homes for under $100,000.

Life Expectancy: 77.31 years

Moving There

Though remaining in the Dominican Republic for as long as you like is not a problem, should you want to engage in typical resident activities like banking, contracting with utilities, buying or selling your car, etc., you will probably want to get a Dominican Republic ID card, known as a *cedula*. Cedulas are issued to any legal resident or citizen. Some expats do manage to get by using just their passports as ID but if you're planning on making your home here, it's worth going the official route, since the residency requirements are not all that great, anyway.

NOTE: The Dominican Republic does not issue work permits. All legal residents of the country are allowed to be employed by anyone who will hire them. And, for what it's worth, Student visas are available, per the usual rigmarole, though not many Americans find it worthwhile to pursue this option.

Tourist Card: Visitors must purchase tourist card upon arrival to the country. Cost is $10 and allows visitor to legally stay in the country for up to 60 days. Extensions are available at the Migration Department in Santo Domingo.

Residence Visa: If you plan on staying longer than 60 days, you must first apply for a residence visa at the Ministry of Foreign Affairs. Applicants must provide proof of financial self-sufficiency and a certification of good behavior from the police department of original place of residency. A letter of guarantee from a Dominican or legal resident must also be submitted and, if you have obtained employment, a copy of work contract.

Provisional Residency: Once you have received the residence visa, you have 60 days to apply for provisional residency. The requirements are similar to the residence visa. Valid for one year and you can apply for permanent residency after this period.

Permanent Residency: One year provisional residency is required before you can apply for permanent residency. Applicant must provide sworn statement by two legal residents or citizens of Dominican Republic attesting to good conduct; notarized letter of guarantee from Dominican citizen or resident assuming responsibility for applicant; bank letter certifying account in Dominican bank; and copy of job contract if applicant is employed. Valid for one year, renewable.

Citizenship: Two years permanent residency required. Applicants are interviewed and must show knowledge of Dominican Republic history, culture, government, and traditions.

18. Ecuador

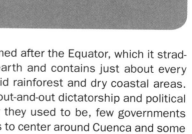

Climate: Tropical in coastal region, cooler inland and at higher elevations; tropical in jungle lowlands

Government: Republic

Population: 14,573.101

Currency: U.S. Dollar (USD)

Language: Spanish (official), Amerindian languages (primarily Quechua)

Religious Groups: Roman Catholic (95%), other (5%)

Ethnic Groups: mestizo [Amerindian and white] (65%), Amerindian (25%), Spanish and others (7%), black (3%)

Cost of Living compared to the U.S: Cheap

Thanks to its varied topography, tiny Ecuador—named after the Equator, which it straddles—is one of the most biodiverse nations on earth and contains just about every kind of climate—from frigid Andean peaks to humid rainforest and dry coastal areas. Politics has been an ever-shifting circus and while out-and-out dictatorship and political assassination aren't the order of the day the way they used to be, few governments hang on to power here for very long. Expat life tends to center around Cuenca and some of the beach towns, with a generous representation of folks of retirement age. While their lives for the most part remain unaffected by the turmoil in government, the level of crime is a different matter.

Living There

Governance: Ecuador does not have the most stable political system (eight presidents since 1996), but recent elections were deemed free and fair by international observers. The constitution recognizes the right to free speech and other basic freedoms but there are still instances of police and military misconduct. Corruption and inefficiency are a recurring problem in the judiciary and other state institutions.

Infrastructure: Somewhat developed: Ecuadorians enjoy an efficient transport and a gradually improving highway system that makes much of the country accessible. Electrical and telecommunications services are state-owned and performance is less than optimal.

Internet: Available in major cities. Ecuador lags behind other South American nations (less than 20% of consumers have Internet access) but recent modernization efforts have phased out most dial-up services and the majority of subscribers have broadband.

Healthcare: In most major cities the overall quality of care is quite good. The majority of healthcare professionals are European- or American-trained and medical care is very affordable. If you choose to live in an outlying region, the quality and availability of care plummets.

GDP: $115.3 billion

GDP (Per Capita): $8,000

Sovereign Debt: 23.2% of GDP

Working There: Some IT, energy (oil) and mining, teach English, translator, tourism.

Regulatory Environment: Can be costly and difficult to start a business.

Taxes: Individual: 0–35%, Corporate: 25%, VAT: 12%. Residents taxed on income from all sources. Domestic corporations taxed on worldwide income with credits for income tax paid abroad.

Cannabis: Illegal, strictly enforced

Homosexuality: Legal, government recognizes same-sex unions. Laws against discrimination. Quito has a growing gay scene but there is still some lingering cultural intolerance.

Abortion: Allowed to preserve physical health or save a woman's life. Also permitted in cases where a woman with a mental disability is raped.

Women's Issues: Ecuador's new constitution grants women greater rights, but discrimination is still common and women remain underrepresented in business and politics. Rape and domestic violence are still a problem.

Guns: Some firearms legal, registration required. Open carry of guns is common in Ecuador.

Crime: Crime is a recurring problem in Ecuador and because of underfunded police and court system, many perpetrators are not apprehended or prosecuted. Violent crime occurs, but mostly in the sketchy urban areas. Thievery in all its manifestations is the top concern. Conditions in Cuenca are slightly better than in most towns.

Real Estate: Foreigners are allowed to buy land in Ecuador but some properties near the coast and the borders are off limits. Prices are affordable. Apartments and condos are under $100,000 and four-bedroom homes can be had for under $200,000. Closing costs, fees and taxes usually run to about 1.5% of the purchase price.

Life Expectancy: 75.3 years

Moving There

The easy pensioner visa ($900 a month minimum income) explains the preponderance of retirees. Investors (business or real estate) don't have much trouble. In addition to a visa, visitors who stay more than 90 days (though single-extension tourists don't usually bother with this) must also apply for a national identity card or *censo*. Needless to say, you need a valid visa (plus the usual photos, paperwork, etc.) to get one. Even the student visas don't have too many requirements.

Non-Immigrant Visas: The following visas are issued to applicants who do not intend to reside permanently in Ecuador:

Tourist Visa: U.S. citizens do not need a visa to stay up to 90 days in Ecuador. After that, you can apply for one extension for a total of 180 days per calendar year. Ecuador will no longer "convert" your tourist status to resident. If you intend to remain in Ecuador, you must apply for the proper visa before you get here.

Work Visa (Non-Immigrant: 12-IX): Available to students, scientists, professional athletes, artists and businesspeople. Applicant must provide letter from banking institution showing "economic good standing," completed *Certificado de Visación* form, and copy of round-trip ticket to Ecuador. Not particularly useful if you plan on staying a while since they are valid a maximum of six months and can only be granted once per year.

Work Visa (Non-Immigrant: 12-VI): Available to professionals in specialized fields (particularly IT). Visa application must be filed at consulate in U.S. Applicant must submit copy of degree or certification, letter from sponsoring company detailing why specific skills are needed and how prospective position will contribute to company operations, copy of work contract certified by Ecuador Court of Labor, and copy of Labor authorization granted by Ministry of Labor. Visa is valid for duration of work contract.

Immigrant Visas: The following visas are valid for an unlimited period (equivalent to a Permanent Resident visa). During the first two years after the visa is issued, applicant must not leave Ecuador for more than 90 days in any given year. After two years, applicant can leave for up to 18 consecutive months.

Pensioner Visa: Retirees of any age can score a pensioner visa by submitting notarized certificate of income (minimum $800/month, plus an additional $100 per dependent) issued by Social Security Administration or other private institution. Annuity recipients and trustees who deposit a minimum amount in the Central Bank of Ecuador can also qualify for this type of visa.

Real Estate and Securities Investor or Fiduciary Documents Investor Visa: Available to individuals who invest in the Ecuadorean economy. Proof of investment (real estate, CD, stocks, government bonds, etc.) deemed sufficient for the applicant and any dependents to "live adequately" (minimum is generally around $25,000).

Investor in Agricultural, Livestock, Commerce and other Industries: Available to individuals who invest in or establish a partnership or sole ownership of a company in Ecuador. Visa is also extended to those who invest a minimum of $30,000 in livestock, agriculture, or mining concerns.

Professional: Available to foreign professionals. Applicant must submit copy of university degree or technical certification. Diplomas or certificates must be translated into Spanish and notarized by Ecuadorean consulate. Certification or degree must have a recognized equivalent at an Ecuadorean institute of higher education.

Economical Dependence Visa: Issued to dependents of Ecuadoran nationals as well as non-nationals who receive an Immigrant (prefix 10) Visa.

Other long-term visas include **Student Visas, Religious/Volunteer Visas** and **Cultural Exchange Visas.**

Citizenship: Legal residents of Ecuador who have lived in the country for three years are eligible to apply for citizenship. Applicant must be at least 18 years of age, speak and write Spanish, have a basic knowledge of Ecuadorian history, geography and constitution, and possess sufficient financial means to live independently (job, business, investment etc.).

David Morrill
Cuenca, Ecuador

Day-to-day life is simple in Ecuador. The pace of life is slower and family values are stronger than in North America or Europe. This is changing, of course, as the country modernizes. There is minimal government interference and most of us living here have little contact with it except for situations such as getting a driver's license or renewing visa documents.

The cost of living in Ecuador is very low compared not just to the U.S. but to the rest of Latin America, as well. I own a condo in Cuenca's historic district. It's convenient to everything (restaurants, mercados, supermarkets and a couple small malls) and, like most expats here, I get by without a car (taxis are cheap and buses are 25 cents). Rents are cheap too, $200 to $400 for a nice place. My utilities run about $40 to $50 a month. Natural gas is subsidized by the govt. at about 15% of market rate so we run as many appliances as possible on it. Because of the elevation and being near the equator (8200 ft.), we don't need heat or AC.

Where I live, in Cuenca, social life for expats is fairly active. There are a handful of expat-owned bars and restaurants. There are a couple of "gringo night" happy hours each week that draw good crowds. There are groups involved in charity and volunteer work. There are a couple of writers' workshops. There are religious groups. There's a good network for information sharing. I run an email service for 2,500 subscribers called GringoTree that reports events such as concerts, art exhibits, festivals, etc.

The infrastructure is good in Cuenca. Public transportation is cheap and plentiful and roads are generally in good repair. We have modern supermarkets and shopping malls, good restaurants and an active cultural agenda. Healthcare is excellent and costs a fraction of what it does in the States.

There are huge challenges and plenty of frustrations, starting with the language and culture generally. This is not an efficient country. The government bureaucracy is slow and cumbersome. The same can be said for businesses. Life here requires a lot of patience and the ability to adapt. I don't recommend it for people with type-A personalities.

19. Egypt

Climate: Hot and dry
Government: Republic
Population: 78,866,635
Currency: Egyptian Pound (EGP);
    1 EGP = 0.16 USD
Language: Arabic (official), English and French
    widely understood by educated classes
Religious Groups: Muslim [mostly Sunni] (90%),
    Coptic (9%), other Christian (1%)
Ethnic Groups: Egyptian (99.6%), other (0.4%)
Cost of Living compared to the U.S.: Cheap

Egypt has appeal for those seeking something cheap and exotic. Life in Cairo offers $200-a-month apartments and a view of the Pyramids from the freeway. In the Sinai, where a more laid-back governance holds sway, Euro-trancers, yoga gurus and scuba divers have all set up shop in the coastal villages of the Red Sea. In early 2011, Egyptian protesters had overthrown the 20-year-long Mubarak dictatorship in a nonviolent revolution and the country was placed in the hands of an interim military government. Parliamentary elections were held in late 2011, but the nation's future is still uncertain.

Living There
Governance: Egypt's autocratic days (indefinite detentions, torture, political assassination, etc.) may be a thing of the past. Then again, it may simply be

undergoing a "meet the new boss/same as the old boss" transition. This one is too early to call.

Infrastructure: Adequate in the cities, poor in rural areas.

Internet: Egypt has one of the largest Internet markets in Africa but access is mainly concentrated in tourist areas and major cities. Approximately one in five Egyptians has regular Internet access. The government was trying to increase broadband penetration fourfold in the next few years but of course that government is now gone.

Healthcare: Medical facilities are adequate for non-emergency matters, particularly in tourist areas. Emergency and intensive care facilities are limited. Outside Cairo, Alexandria, and Sharm El Sheikh, facilities fall short of U.S. standards.

GDP: $500.9 billion

GDP (Per Capita): $6,200

Sovereign Debt: 80.5% of GDP

Working There: Opportunities in English teaching, business and technology and tourism.

Regulatory Environment: Egypt has become friendlier to entrepreneurs in recent years but obtaining the required licensees is still a lengthy process and the corruption can be exasperating.

Taxes: Corporate: 20%, Individual: 10–20%, VAT: 10%. Residents taxed on worldwide income. No capital gains tax except for some real estate transactions.

Cannabis: Widely available but the penalties are harsh

Homosexuality: Technically legal, though the government often prosecutes homosexual behavior under murky vice laws and the culture isn't all that friendly to the lifestyle. No recognition of same-sex unions. No laws against discrimination.

Abortion: Prohibited altogether

Women's Issues: Gender equality is a matter of law, but in practice, it's quite different, though many institutions are religious in nature and don't apply to non-Muslims. Women's literacy is half that of men. Domestic violence is common and unescorted women (particularly Western women) are likely to be hassled or harassed. Again, should society liberalize as a result of the revolution, this too may change.

Guns: Some types of guns are legal but require a permit.

Crime: Low. Some petty property crimes in tourist areas. Occasional terrorist attacks directed against Westerners.

Real Estate: Foreigners can buy and own property in Egypt except for agricultural land. More than two properties or properties that are historical sites require permission of the Prime Minister's office. Most of the other restrictions apply to large-scale developers and not individuals. Taxes and other costs associated with real estate purchases come to approximately 6.1% of the overall property value.

Life Expectancy: 72.12 years

Moving There

It helps to have an articulable reason for why you want to remain in Egypt (study, research, husband, wife, etc.) but generally if you have the will, there is a way. Investors can sink a modest investment into the banking system.

Foreigners are first required to obtain a $15 **Entry Visa** from an Egyptian consulate or at a port of entry.

Tourist Visa: Tourist visas (Temporary Tourist Residence Permit) are available for up to one year, renewable.

Temporary Non-Tourist Residence Permit: Granted to students with proof of enrollment, workers with job offer from an Egyptian firm, volunteers, or foreigners willing to deposit a minimum of $50,000 in an Egyptian bank and owners of Egyptian real estate. Permit is valid for a maximum of five years. Dependents and family members can also be issued visas, usually for one to five years, renewable.

Longer residence permits are generally only granted to applicants with family connections in Egypt.

Citizenship: Non-Muslims with no family connections to Egypt can apply for citizenship after 10 years legal residency. Must be sane(!), of good conduct, financially self-sufficient and proficient in Arabic.

20. Estonia

Climate: For most of the year, the Estonian climate is temperate. The summers are often warm and humid; the winters are often extremely cold and dry

Government: Parliamentary Democracy

Population: 1,299,371

Currency: Euro (EUR): 1 EUR = 1.36 USD

Language: Estonian [official] (67.3%), Russian (29.7%), other (2.3%), unknown (0.7%)

Religious Groups: Evangelical Lutheran (13.6%), Orthodox (12.8%), other Christian (1.4%), unaffiliated (34.1%), other an unspecified (32%), none (6.1%)

Ethnic Groups: Estonian (68.7%), Russian (25.6%), Ukrainian (2.1%), Belarusian (1.2%), Finn (0.8%), other (1.6%)

Cost of Living compared to the U.S.: Cheap

Bohemians priced out of Prague have been slumming in art nouveau splendor in Tallinn. Having been ravaged by the global neoliberal hustle, their economies don't offer much in the way of work, or in the way of anything, really. The winters can be quite brutal, but life here is as cheap as anywhere on the continent and the people are generally pro-

American. Best to establish yourself here now before everyone else discovers these little gems. Even work is legally possible without too much hassle.

Living There

Governance: Estonia is a liberal Western-style democracy with free elections, independent media and judiciary, and general respect for human rights. Corruption is a minor problem.

Infrastructure: In Estonia, public transport is well integrated in urban areas. The telecommunications sector in Estonia is one of the most liberalized in Eastern Europe. There are well-maintained modern phone lines and three mobile phone service providers.

Internet: Estonia enjoys high Internet penetration rates (approximately 75%). Hi-speed Internet widely available.

Healthcare: Improving but short of Western standards.

GDP: $24.65 billion

GDP (Per Capita): $19,000

Sovereign Debt: 7.7% of GDP

Working There: Teach English. Work for Skype. They have their biggest office in Tallinn. Temporary employment is available without a work permit.

Regulatory Environment: Far more efficient than many countries in the region. Estonia is ranked 17th in the World Bank Doing Business Index.

Taxes: Corporate: 21%, individual: 21%, VAT: 20% (9% on certain goods and services). Estonian residents are taxed on income whether it's derived inside or outside the country. Foreign nationals who have a permanent home in Estonia, or who stay more than 183 days per year, are considered residents for the purpose of taxation. Anyone employed by an Estonian company may be liable for income tax even if they stay less than the amount of days required for tax residency.

Cannabis: Illegal but widely available

Homosexuality: Legal. No legal recognition of same-sex unions. Laws against discrimination. There is a general tolerance toward homosexuality in Estonia, particularly in Tallinn.

Abortion: No restriction as to reason

Women's Issues: Gender equality is a matter of law, although women still have some catching up to do before they achieve parity with men with respect to wages and representation in upper levels of business and government.

Guns: Firearm ownership allowed, permit required for each weapon along with safety and first-aid course. Concealed carry allowed with permit.

Crime: Very low crime rates.

Real Estate: One-room detached house near the coast in Parnu can go for as little as $35,000. Price of a new 500-square-foot flat in medieval Tallinn, the capital, is around $125,000. Land tax of 0.5–2.5% depending on value of property. When the global property bubble was at its apex, Estonia shot to the top of the European house price growth table in 2005 after property values surged 28%. Things have cooled off since the bubble burst. Mortgages are available.

Life Expectancy: 72.82 years

Moving There

Permits to reside in Estonia are not all that hard to get by European standards. Assuming you have no local job offer, no university enrollment and no family or spouse, you should still be able to swing a residence permit if you can demonstrate that you have or make enough money to live there without having to engage in illegal employment or crime. Annual immigration quotas do not apply to U.S. citizens. Part-time work is usually allowed.

Schengen Visa: 90-day stay allowed within six-month period.

Temporary Residence Permit: Available to applicants with spouse or close relative permanently residing in Estonia. Foreigners who believe their presence in Estonia will provide "substantial" benefit to the public interest may also apply. As a matter of fact, anyone who can prove sufficient income to live and has a "valid reason" for wanting to live in Estonia can get one of these. This also covers students, volunteers, freelancers and many other cases. Allows up to six months per year employment after registration with Citizenship and Migration Board. Proof of lodgings, medical insurance, sufficient income, and documents justifying stay are required. Valid for two years. Can be renewed but is often more difficult the second time around.

Long-Term Residence Permit: Granted to individuals who have legally resided in Estonia on the basis of temporary residence permit for at least five years. Includes the right to employment. Registered residence, permanent legal income, and health insurance required. The final hurdle is what is called the "Integration Requirement" which entails a certain amount of proficiency in the Estonian language.

Residence Permit for Employment: Residence permit with allowance for full employment is granted if a particular position cannot be filled by Estonian national, E.U. citizen, or alien with permanent residency status in Estonia. Some professions like journalist, teacher, researcher, may be exempt from this requirement.

Citizenship: Five years legal residence in Estonia required along with proficiency in Estonian language and knowledge of Estonian constitution. Applicants must also show proof of financial means and swear an oath of allegiance to the Estonian state.

Chris Jacobs

Tartu, Estonia

I chose Estonia for a number of reasons. First, I became fascinated with the Baltics about four years ago, along with the Scandinavian countries. Estonia caught my attention because of its history, unique language, unheard-of existence, and its story of survival. Compared to life in the U.S., it is very similar because so much has changed there in the last 20 years after becoming independent from the Soviet Union. Every young person now speaks English, and it maintains one of the top 10 highest literacy rates in the world. Because the country is so small, it is very diverse and international compared to the United States. Of course life is quite similar with McDonald's, cars, the countryside, but it has a distinct culture which separates it from a number of other places I have been.

Estonia is a great place to live. I lucked out with a nice studio apartment for about 200 euros a month ($280), which represents 15% of my salary. About 20% of my salary goes to living expenses. I live in Tartu's old town, in the heart of the city, with access to shops and walking distance to any and every store. I live well enough to have bought a car, although I really do not need a car. I rate my quality of life as pretty good. Although I make A LOT less here than I would make in the U.S., I surely spend a lot less than I would need to in the U.S.. The public transportation here is EXCELLENT, the people mind their own business, and over 70% of the people I come across speak English. And those who are educated, 95% of them speak English. However, when taking care of official business, for example, dealing with utility companies, or registering your newly purchased car, knowing some Estonian, or having an Estonian friend may be necessary in order to carry out activities of the sort.

I enjoy living here for several reasons, including those mentioned above. The old atmosphere here is very lush, the country isn't bastardized by a large number of foreigners, which I kind of like. The weather sucks, but if you can deal with the cold temperatures most of the year, you are going to do well here. There is not a huge U.S. citizen support network, but ample opportunities to mingle with expats from other countries. Of course, there are several events taking place with the U.S. embassy, U.S. Chamber of Commerce, and other foundations that have something to do with the U.S. So if you get lonely, it's not that difficult to find something to do.

Working in Estonia can be difficult, as the job market is very limited. You must have an employer willing to cover the state fee for hiring an alien and it is required by law that they pay you a livable wage as noted by the Estonian Board of Labor. Temporary workers (employed under three months) must obtain permission to work from the migration office where the employer and yourself go to document paperwork filled out by the employer and the employee. Of course there is paperwork for employment in Estonia, but less for temporary (three months or less) employment. For temporary employment, you do not pay taxes, but your information is reported to the United States IRS because of the Estonian Tax Treaty with the U.S. This helps make things less complicated when being subject to double taxation. You will be taxed under U.S. law for this type of employment so therefore, your paycheck in Estonia will be for the full amount as noted in your salary. For long-term employment, you are eligible to work if you hold a temporary residence permit, but then you are subject to Estonian taxes, but will soon be covered under national healthcare there.

The housing situation in the capital, Tallinn, where I used to live, is very abundant. The more expensive housing is closer to downtown. The majority of apartments (flats) that are available usually exist in re-modeled Soviet complexes. Rent is generally very cheap in these locations ($150–$250/mo), but when you consider that the wages are still 40% lower than in the U.S., it is still cheap relative to what Americans pay in the U.S.

21. France

Climate: Temperate, similar to that of the eastern U.S.
Government: Republic
Population: 64,057,792
Currency: Euro (EUR): 1 EUR = 1.36 USD
Language: French
Religious Groups: Roman Catholic (83%–88%), Protestant (2%), Jewish (1%), Muslim (5%–10%), unaffiliated (4%)
Ethnic Groups: Celtic and Latin with Teutonic, Slavic, North African, Indochinese, Basque minorities
Cost of Living compared to the U.S.: Pricey

Moving to France is not easy. They are fussy about whom they let in and everyone will insist you speak French. But the motivation to live there is great, the food and wine incomparable, and more than 100,000 Americans have found a way to live there according to 2010 State Department figures, and that number is increasing. Work permits are hard to come by, unless you offer some skill that most French people can't do—translating, providing cultural orientation to French people who are moving to America, giving guided tours in English or whatever other language you know, etc. While there's a famously international scene in Paris, Francophiles all have their own ideas of where the "true heart of France" lies, and you'll find them fanned out from the Normandy coast, in country villages and along the Côte D'Azur. Should your ultimate goal be to live in the densest population of rich people on the planet—i.e. Monaco—and enjoy the longest life expectancy and no income tax, your entry will still be through the French government.

Living There

Governance: France operates as a Western-style democracy with free and fair elections, independent judiciary, and the freedom to organize, dissent, and, especially, strike is usually on display on a weekly and often daily basis. Some criticize laws forbidding "ostentatious" displays of religious symbols in the schools, generally regarded as a measure against wearing the Muslim hijab.

Infrastructure: Developed

Internet: Hi-speed Internet widely available.

Healthcare: Standards are high. Universal healthcare is available.

GDP: $2.16 trillion

GDP (Per Capita): $33,300

Sovereign Debt: 83.5% of GDP

Working There: A serious challenge. Many professions and job categories barred to non-E.U. citizens. Unemployment high (especially among immigrants). Your best bet is anything requiring English-speaking skills...or try your luck at a EuroDisney audition.

Regulatory Environment: France has modernized its regulatory system and made it easier and less cumbersome for entrepreneurs, though anyone weaned on American can-do will find the culture maddening, all the same.

Taxes: Corporate: 33.3%, Individual: 0–40%, VAT: 19.6%. Residents taxed on worldwide income.

Cannabis: Hashish is smoked openly, though possession and use are still illegal.

Homosexuality: Legal recognition of civil unions (for both same- and opposite-sex couples), laws against discrimination. France is tolerant of homosexuals and gay lifestyle is openly practiced all over the country.

Abortion: No restrictions up to 14 weeks

Women's Issues: Equal rights guaranteed for women. They are well-represented in business and politics, though de facto wage discrimination still exists.

Guns: Some hunting rifles can be purchased without license. Most handguns and other weapons require a license. Some calibers require additional licensing.

Crime: Low rate of violent crime. Car theft a problem, particularly in the south.

Real Estate: There are no restrictions on foreigners owning property. Mortgages are available and do not depend on a structural survey. Small apartments in Paris start at around $400,000.

Life Expectancy: 80.98 years

Moving There

Your frustration will begin well before you hit the continent, which is where your application process should begin. Unless you're loaded (or are in one of the easy-visa categories—student, spouse, etc.), the successful strategy is to convince the French that you will be adding to their fantastic culture. Artists and others with credits and credentials, however, will often find their welcome far less than frosty. As with any French system, the visa situation is a bit on the baroque side, so it's a good idea to review the options at the French consulate's website: www.consulfrance-washington.org. Those who dream of retiring in Monaco also begin their journey here.

Schengen Visa: 90-day stay allowed within six-month period.

Long-Stay Visa: This visa is required for any stay in France longer than 90 days and must be applied for at the French embassy or consulate in your country. As you will likely be barred from working, you must provide ample proof that you have sufficient funds to pay all your expenses while in France. The long-stay visa is good for a maximum of one year, but if you plan on staying longer, you can contact the Prefecture of your place of residence within 90 days of expiry and request a Residence Permit (Carte de Séjour).

Long-Stay Visa for Monaco: Similar to the Long-Stay visa for the rest of France, just more stringent. Among other things, they'll need to see notarized letter stating you've never declared bankruptcy, in addition to proof of your self-sufficiency. Depending on your stated reasons for going, you may also be required to present an employment contract signed by the Labor Department in Monaco or an authorization to set up or manage a company in Monaco. Monaco is however an independent monarchy and citizenship rules and approval for citizenship are separate from the French system.

Residence Permit (Carte de Séjour): For stays longer than one year, a Residence Permit (Carte de Séjour) is required. No Carte de Séjour can be issued without first obtaining a long-stay visa in your home country, even if you are married to a French citizen. Cartes de Séjour are issued at your local prefecture. Many documents and forms will be filled out. And based on the caprice of the functionaries involved and a few loose rules, a decision will be made on whether the Carte will be issued and for how long (up to five years). Upon renewal, you can apply to upgrade to the Holy Grail of expat Francophiles: **the 10-year Carte de Residence.**

Skills and Talents Visa (Carte Compétences & Talents): If you're the creative type and have a project or endeavor in mind that you believe will assist France's economic development or make a lasting intellectual, scientific, cultural, humanitarian, or athletic contribution to the French nation (and the U.S.), you may qualify for this unique visa. The visa is good for three years (with one renewal allowed). If you're leaning toward an economic project, applicants are required to invest at least €300,000 or your plan must entail the creation of at least two sustainable jobs in France. Academic applicants must have a Ph.D. If you only have a bachelor's degree you must possess at least five years of professional experience in your field of expertise. The visa is also open to independent professionals such as businessmen, artists, authors, athletes, etc. Applicants are required to provide proof of income as well as professional and/or academic standing. French consular officials have the final say whether a given project meets the criteria for this visa.

Work Permits: As a non-E.U. citizen, finding employment in France won't be easy and work permits are considered one of the toughest visas to get in France. Even if you are planning on working for only a few months, you will need to provide immigration authorities with a signed contract from your employer and various other forms and documents before you will be given the green light to begin work. Still, there are various types of work permits offered by the French government and you may find a loophole somewhere, or simple persistence may pay off.

Student Visas: Foreigners wishing to study in France must first enroll with "Campus France" (www.campusfrance.org) before applying for a visa. Americans can apply at www.usa.campusfrance.org. After one year of study at a French institution, some part-time work is allowed.

Citizenship: Five years legal residence in France required for naturalization. Primary source of income must be in France during period of residency. Applicant must show knowledge of French language, history and institutions. (Period of required residency reduced to two years if applicant has studied at least two years at a French university.) Citizenship is awarded to spouses of French nationals only after the fourth years of marriage, among other requirements.

Serena Page
Paris, France

There is a very large American expatriate community in France. You find them in cities all over the country. Many come as students, either to study French or get a degree at a French university, and others are transferred by their jobs in the States on expatriate contracts for either a definite or indefinite period of time. And many come on their own, with or without work papers and find jobs once they are here. You can find Americans who work as English teachers in language schools, as nannies/au pairs, in pubs, restaurants and shops, as personal assistants and secretaries and other types of jobs.

Still others with financial or technical backgrounds find that their experience and skills, coupled with being an English mother tongue speaker, makes them in demand with companies that have regular contact with Anglophone countries; for example: companies with headquarters based in the U.K., or whose supplier is based in a non-French speaking country and they need employees who can communicate with them in English, etc. And many more Americans come to France because they have fallen in love with a French person and have decided to make their lives here with that person.

I would certainly recommend Paris to other expats. One of the things I like about it is the fact that there is a large American community here, which can be incredibly helpful during the transition process, since you have access to people who have already gone through it and can guide you. It's quite easy to find American food projects and American-style places when you are homesick. Paris is a very cosmopolitan city and you will find expatriates of every nationality. And the rest of Europe is very accessible by train or plane.

The drawbacks are the winter weather, which is very damp and gray, and the red tape in this country, which is unbelievable. It can seem never-ending and getting papers in order can be a frustrating, hair-pulling experience.

French people can appear to be standoffish at first, but they are very warm people once you get to know them. Americans don't often realize how difficult it is at first to make French friends. French people take friendship very seriously and do not open their arms wide at first. They take their time cultivating true friendships, so at first, life in Paris can be quite lonely.

Bruce Epstein
Orsay, France

Overall, we find that France is more aligned with our personal values, especially work-life balance. We enjoy the French lifestyle that emphasizes personal relationships and social activities; we are delighted to live in a cosmopolitan area where on a daily basis we encounter people from a wide variety of national and cultural backgrounds. Having unfortunately suffered from a number of serious health issues, we have also benefited from what the WHO (World Health Organization) considers the finest healthcare system in the world, never once encountering the slightest insurance hassle or extra cost. In addition, having seven weeks of paid vacation per year is a wonderful perk!

Marlane O'Neill
Narbonne, France

Compared to the U.S., I find the cost of living here in Narbonne cheaper by around 30% for food and about 50% cheaper for wine (this is wine country). Gas is more expensive but our car is more efficient (Citroen C-4). Utilities are about the same but electricity is more expensive (around 30% more) so we use lots of high-efficiency appliances and light bulbs. An average bill for two for a nice three-course meal with wine is usually under 65 euros compared to about 100 dollars in the U.S. Having a group get together in the café usually comes to about 15 euros a head with lots of plates of appetizers and carafes of wine. In the USA we would spend about double that or more. We have the bonus in Narbonne of being in a town with a major train station so we enjoy traveling around locally by train. Train travel in the USA has become rather rare.

22. Germany

Climate: Temperate; cooler and rainier than much of the United States; winters in the north can be particularly brutal
Government: Federal Republic
Population: 82,329,758
Currency: Euro (EUR): 1 EUR = 1.36 USD
Language: German
Religious Groups: Protestant (34%), Roman Catholic (34%), Muslim (3.7%), unaffiliated or other (28.3%)
Ethnic Groups: German (91.5%), Turkish (2.4%), other (6.1%)—made up largely of Greek, Italian, Polish, Russian, Serbo-Croatian, Spanish
Cost of Living compared to the U.S.: About the same in the West; cheaper in the East

Europe's periphery may be ailing, but here in the center of the Eurozone, the economy's pulse beats strong. The standard of living is high, universal healthcare system has been the norm since the rule of Otto von Bismarck, and there's still no speed limit on the Autobahn. Best of all, for a major European nation, Germany is surprisingly easy in terms of legal residency, and even work permits (and actual jobs) are available. Besides the growing shortage of skilled labor which has resulted in moves to ease restrictions on the import of foreign labor (particularly vis à vis foreign credentials), the large American military presence offers the possibility of easy employment as cashiers, military hospital clerks and even janitors. Most of the opportunities tend to be in the blander cities of the former West Germany, while most of the expat action (and the fun, in general) revolves around "poor but sexy" Berlin, home to a growing wave of partiers, slackers and more than a few actual artists. Almost considered a separate country, you'll find little of the stereotypical uptightness, scant evidence of an economic miracle, and no support for the German reputation for efficiency in the nation's reunited capital—and that's how everyone there likes it. Jobs completely disappear and prices plummet anywhere else in the old Soviet half.

Living There
Governance: Germany grants all the freedoms and rights expected of a Western-style democracy, though for reasons pertaining to its history, current laws do not allow extreme political parties or denial of the Holocaust.
Infrastructure: First-rate, though the now-privatized rail network has been criticized for its high user-cost and low reliability.
Internet: Nearly eight in 10 Germans have Internet access. Second highest number of broadband subscribers in Europe. Hi-speed Internet widely available. 5Mbps DSL and 35 Mbps cable modem speeds are common.

Healthcare: The majority of German nationals (92%) are insured under the national health insurance program, which is subsidized by the government. The program is compulsory for individuals whose earnings do not exceed a preset government income ceiling. Those who exceed the income limits have the option of opting out of the program and paying for private insurance. Medical facilities are very good in Germany, but they are very expensive.

GDP: $2.96 trillion

GDP (Per Capita): $35,900

Sovereign Debt: 78.8% of GDP

Working There: Difficult for non-E.U. citizens to get positions. Some opportunities teaching English, working on or near U.S. military bases, and there is some demand for IT professionals particularly in the telecom sector. New laws, however, have relaxed restrictions since Germany is facing a shortage of skilled workers and Germany's Federal Employment Agency does sponsor online job fairs that allow American job-seekers to post résumés (or CVs as they are called in Europe) and establish contacts with prospective German employers. If you work in a field that is much in demand, your chances have never been better to land a position in Germany.

Regulatory Environment: Germany's center-right government has streamlined its regulatory system to encourage new businesses and innovation—though an American may still find the rules a bit stifling.

Taxes: Corporate: 29.8 % (average), Individual: 0–45%, VAT: 19% (on certain goods is 7%). Residents taxed on worldwide income.

Cannabis: Illegal, but possession of small amounts tolerated by government, though northern German states tend to be more lenient (plenty of public smoking in Berlin and Hamburg) than southern states like Bavaria where users tend to be more discreet.

Homosexuality: Recognition of same-sex unions, laws against discrimination. Generally tolerant, though some cultural biases still survive in the old Eastern half.

Abortion: No restriction as to reason up to 14 weeks

Women's Issues: Women's rights actively guaranteed. Germany is one of the most women-friendly countries on earth.

Guns: Firearms ownership license required prior to purchasing weapon. In public, weapons must be unloaded, secured, and in locked container. Owners must purchase insurance.

Crime: Generally low. Some skinhead violence in major cities, especially in the East.

Real Estate: There are no restrictions on Americans buying property in Germany. The high price of houses and the difficulties in securing financing (down payments are typically half the purchase price) means that few do. Prices for a detached one-family home range from $200,000 in rural areas to around $700,000 or more in Munich.

Life Expectancy: 79.26 years

Moving There

Get there on a tourist visa. Tell the immigration bureau you want to stay. Show them you have health insurance and an income in excess of $11k/year and you should be fine. An artist need prove even less. If you're here to study or have an offer of work then *Herzlich Wilkommen*.

Schengen Visa: 90-day stay allowed within six-month period.

Residence Permit: Citizens of the United States can apply for a residence permit after entering Germany. There are various categories (including student; enrollment in language courses counts, as well) and special processes for artists, journos and other creative types. Others must demonstrate sufficient income to live in Germany (poverty level is around €7500/$10,500 per year). Applicants must provide information detailing how they will sustain themselves during their stay in Germany and proof of health insurance. Usually valid for one to three years and renewable.

Work Permits: While permits for freelancers are not that difficult to come by (particularly if they're issued for activities requiring native English speakers), you cannot apply for a work permit without a documented job offer from a German employer. Because Americans are considered third-country nationals (non-German, non-E.U.) the government has usually discouraged the hiring of workers from the U.S. though a shortage of skilled labor in Germany has resulted in a slight relaxation of these restrictions. Students are allowed limited employment (equivalent to 90 full employment days per year). Upon graduation from a German university, there is the possibility of obtaining a work permit for a job consistent with your field of study.

Permanent Residency: Eligibility after five years of legal residency (longer for students and others receiving some form of government support). Basic knowledge of the German language and legal system and culture required.

Citizenship: Eight years of permanent residency required. Applicants must show proficiency in German language and must show proof of viable means of support. Generally, dual citizenship is not allowed, but exemptions are routinely made in cases where doing so involves economic or other hardships.

Adam Lederer

Berlin, Germany

Housing in Germany is, generally speaking, smaller. Actually I've come to wonder why people in the United States need so much space. I currently live in a 50 square meter (538 square feet) apartment in the middle of Berlin. It's cozy and fine, for me. I think if I had a spouse we could live together quite comfortably. When I am in the U.S., I sometimes watch "House Hunters" and I hear people talk about needing 2 or 3,000 square feet for their family of two or three and I am flabbergasted. That's a lot of space!

One of the greatest challenges as a non-local is understanding how local housing markets work. For example, in Germany a lot of apartments do not include kitchens.

There is a room that can be used as a kitchen, complete with pipes for a sink and per-haps a random back-splash, or two, but it is the responsibility of the renter to buy and install a kitchen. One time I looked at 15 apartments; only one had a kitchen built in (the one I ultimately took). Often there is a side agreement where the previous tenant sells the next tenant the kitchen for €5–600.

Another challenge in Germany is the difference between "cold" and "warm" rents. You search by cold rents, but you pay warm rents. Cold rent is the profit of the build-ing's owner. Then you add on some other costs (typically water, heating, common-space maintenance, to name three—but this can vary), and get the warm rent. You actually pay the warm rent. But that's not all—if the costs for these other items are not covered by what you've already paid, you will get a bill at the end of the year for the extra costs. Sometimes you'll even get a credit back if you've overpaid, but it rarely works out that you've overpaid.

Easton West
Berlin, Germany

I have met a crazy amount of people in Berlin that I never thought I would talk to again in my entire life. Berlin has a weird energy about it that seems to bring people from your past back to you again. It's great. I have made friends with people from all over the world. Never have I ever had such a diverse group of friends. However, a lot of people who "move" here will mostly stay for about six months at most. And then... POOF!...you have an entirely new group of friends to become acquainted with. This gives Berlin expats a notoriously snobby attitude. I think people move to Berlin in the hopes of being immersed in art, design, music, clubs, etc. But they quickly either party too much or run out of money. It's not always as easy as it looks to live in Berlin even if all you see are pictures of people partying, making art and grilling Nackensteak next to the canals.

The biggest piece of advice that I can give to people who want to move to Berlin is to come here with an idea of the things you want to do. This is a city that supports the weirdest and most outlandish ideas to the most simple and hegemonic ideas. You will not find much support if you just want to find a job and pay the bills. Perhaps if you are headhunted to move here but that's it. *EIN TIPP!* Be wary of "internships"...most of the time this means a business is going to have you work for minuscule to no pay for six months and then get rid of you.

23. Greece

Climate: Mediterranean; mild, wet winter and hot, dry summer
Government: Parliamentary Republic
Population: 10,737,428
Currency: Euro (EUR): 1 EUR = 1.36 USD
Language: Greek (99%) [official], other (1%) includes English and French
Religious Groups: Greek Orthodox (98%), Muslim (1.3%), other (0.7%)
Ethnic Groups: Greek (93%), other (7%)
Cost of Living compared to the U.S.: Reasonable

Land of Plato, Aristotle, sunshine and *souvlaki*. Those with visible means of support will find the country fairly welcoming, at least greater than elsewhere in Western Europe, and many expats live here under various schemes and differing levels of legitimacy. Athens remains the cultural hub (though scenesters and contemporary culture vultures should consider the port town of Thessaloniki). As a result of its debt crisis, Greece, particularly the capital, Athens, has been enveloped in civil unrest which can be violently suppressed. Its future under austerity and privatization is uncertain. Then again, for the well-to-do, there are a multitude of Mediterranean islands (likely going up for a sovereign distress sale) where even the problems of Greece, not to mention America and the rest of the world, can seem far, far away.

Living There

Governance: The Greek state holds free and fair elections and respects basic political and civil liberties. There are some limitations on free speech due to prohibitions on speech that may incite fear, hatred, or national disharmony. There is some corruption and bureaucratic inefficiency.

Infrastructure: Good—considerably upgraded after 2004 Athens Olympics.

Internet: Dial-up connections and ISDN are widely available. ADSL and/broadband available in the bigger towns and suburbs, but not yet available in most parts of the country. Lower broadband usage than most of the rest of Europe.

Healthcare: The Greek National Health Service covers all Greek citizens' healthcare. If you are legally working in Greece and paying into the National Health scheme, you are entitled to free healthcare when you have paid up to 50 "stamps" or days of work.

GDP: $321.7 billion
GDP (Per Capita): $30,200
Sovereign Debt: 144% of GDP

Working There: Au pairs, harvesting work, teaching English—resort jobs available during tourist season (May and September). Women obtain jobs more easily in bars and clubs.

Regulatory Environment: The regulatory bureaucracy can hamper business development. The World Bank Doing Business Index ranks Greece 149th out of 183 countries for ease of starting a business.

Taxes: Corporate: 24%, Individual: 0–40%, VAT: 19% (11% on specific goods). Nonresidents are taxed only on income from Greek sources. Residents taxed on worldwide income. There is a form of "wealth tax" on property, land, cars, etc. and the value of these is required to be declared as income.

Cannabis: Illegal to grow or possess but for small amounts (less than one gram) sometimes overlooked depending on the region

Homosexuality: Legal; no recognition of same-sex unions or marriage, law against employment discrimination. While open gay communities exist in Athens and on some resort islands, Greeks have strong cultural biases against homosexuals, and gays and lesbians can expect to put up with all kinds of discrimination and harassment.

Abortion: No restriction as to reason, but parental authorization/notification is required.

Women's Issues: Women are making significant inroads in business and politics but there are still lingering disparities in pay. Laws against workplace sexual harassment. Greece lacks specific legislation to deal with domestic violence.

Guns: Some firearms legal to own. Registration and permit required.

Crime: Generally low. Occasional pickpocketing and purse-snatching.

Real Estate: Purchase of real estate by foreigners allowed except in a few designated border areas. Transfer tax of 11% of the "published value" is assessed by the tax office (which is usually a good deal lower than the actual cost), plus various other fees. Annual taxes are payable in Greece on properties owned over the value of approximately $328,251.

Life Expectancy: 79.66 years

Moving There

If you can afford to live in Greece and can prove it, you have a pretty good chance of getting your permit approved. Otherwise, study or get married. Work permits, however, might be too much to ask for, particularly in the new age of austerity.

Schengen Visa: 90-day stay allowed within six-month period. Greece also issues a Temporary Residence Permit valid for up to six months (though this visa is not Schengen-wide).

Residency Permit: Anyone planning on staying in Greece for longer than three months must apply for a residency permit. Due to recent changes to Greek immigration codes, there are now over 10 different categories of residency permits. These include the predictable categories of Student, Volunteer, Religious Groups, Researchers, Self-Employment (including entrepreneurs and investors) and Salaried Employment, and less predictable categories such as Tour Groups Leaders. Immigrants can apply to live in Greece for school, research, athletics, salaried employment, self-employment and others. Depending on the category, visas can be valid for one or two years, renewable. Proof of sufficient income is required if you don't plan on working in Greece.

Work Permits: As an E.U. country, work permits aren't granted to non-European citizens unless the applicant has located a position that cannot be filled by a Greek or E.U. citizen. If this is the case, your employer will usually assist with the required paperwork. Some seasonal and temporary positions do not have these kinds of strict requirements but you will still need to apply for a work permit to be employed in Greece and the permit will only be valid for the time you are employed.

Citizenship: Seven years continuous legal residency (Residency Permit), viable source of income, certification showing proficiency in Greek language and knowledge of Greek history and culture. Marriage to a Greek can shorten that requirement to three years. Greece recognizes descent back to the grandparent and also offer automatic citizenship to foreign monks admitted to one of the monasteries on Mount Athos.

Sarah Madole
Athens, Greece

I love living in Greece...and I hate it. Sure, the riots are cool but the sanitation, transit, and the odd pharmacy/hospital strikes are...less cool. As a graduate student at an American institution, I don't actually interact with the Greek community as much as I do the foreign archaeological one, which is—as one could imagine in the headquarters of the classical Greek world—massive. That's one of the things I love about living in Athens: my motley crew of friends. At times we'll have a single representative of say, 10 countries sitting around some Balkan bar like an archaeological U.N.

It's taken me nearly two years to figure out the opening—or more aptly, closing—hours of shops, which always seem to be shut in my neighborhood. I'm lucky this year to live near a grocery that's open until 8 on a Saturday; in my old neighborhood they closed at 6, reopening as always, Monday morning. As a New Yorker, I'm used to 24/7 access to many things, and this country's operating system has humbled me, although I do enjoy the late-night dining culture, which goes on well after midnight. Other challenges include walking down the sidewalk, which is invariably single-file in breadth, pitted with missing or loosened paving stones, overrun with trash from an overflowing bin, littered with scooters and the odd car that have parked on the sidewalk, or being used as a road by the owners of said scooters, and you're stuck walking behind the petrol fumes.

I live for the laïke, the weekly vegetable market. The one in my neighborhood (which is an immigrant "suburb" in the Athenian sprawl, only a few kilometers from the center) goes on forever. Seasonal fruits and vegetables so fresh the slugs and spiders are still alive when you wash the fruit, and one unfortunate dinner guest found a giant worm sticking out of a half-eaten artichoke. Fresh-cut flowers that last forever, fish mongers, surprisingly delicious fresh wine in 1.5 kilo plastic bottles—all cheap. In Athens I feed six people for the price of lunch for one in New York. Another wonderful thing about Athens: glimpses of the Parthenon walking through certain neighborhoods, if you know to look for it. Athens isn't like Rome, for example, where it seems like every street has beauty (and certainly lots of old stuff, which an ancient art historian like me really goes for). Athens is a gritty city but it makes beauty, when you find it, that much more striking.

When there are scheduled riots (and they're always scheduled, on the Internet, very explicitly and in a very organized manner, sometimes weeks in advance), I keep away from the center, where I technically live, but it's more of a suburb, and we don't see the crazy. I have friends who like to go and watch but I keep away. I find the "anarchist" trend unsettling, and I'm not entirely sure they really know what anarchy actually entails. In any case, I steer clear of these "peaceful" demonstrations, which often involve violence and tear gas (which the law enforcers/"peace keepers" ran out of a couple of years ago and Israel had to spot Greece some of their super-XXX stuff). That was when people were rioting about that unarmed boy the cops murdered, before the whole tax fraud thing led to the austerity measures and all those related riots. Athenians still commemorate that unarmed boy the cops murdered by annual demonstrations/ riots in early December, but they're nowhere near as violent as they were in 2008. People here are hard up, and the austerity measures are hitting the lower economic bracket that could barely get by before. As much as the demonstrations and strikes complicate life a bit, it's tough to say whether they're wrong or right. Sometimes, when I don't know that there's been a demonstration and I'm walking through Syntagma (Parliament square), it's eerily quiet, covered in red paint and various signs of the clash that just occurred.

Holland
(see Netherlands)

24. Hong Kong

Climate: Tropical monsoon. Cool and humid in winter, hot and rainy from spring through summer, warm and sunny in fall

Government: Special Administrative Region (SAR) of China, with its own constitution (Basic Law)

Population: 7,055,071

Currency: Hong Kong Dollar (HKD): 1 HKD = 0.12 USD

Language: Cantonese [official] (90.8%), English (2.8%), Mandarin (0.9%), other Chinese dialects (4.4%), other (1.1%)

Religious Groups: Eclectic mixture of local religions (90%), Christian (10%)

Ethnic Groups: Chinese (95%), Filipino (1.6%), Indonesian (1.3%), other (2.1%)

Cost of Living compared to the U.S.: Pricey

Though technically part of China since the British handed it over in 1999, Hong Kong is still allowed to operate under its own set of rules. While it still holds its own as a world-class hub of business and finance (and movies), they're feeling the heat from the mainland's mushrooming megalopolises.

Living There

Governance: Although technically a part of China, Hong Kong enjoys a high degree of autonomy and its own constitution (Basic Law). Compared to the mainland, the government of Hong Kong shows a greater respect for human rights and overall the country is a more free and open society. Although electoral reforms have been slow (the Chief Executive is elected by an 800-person election committee), legislators are elected by popular vote and elections are considered free and fair. The country has an independent judiciary and respect for the rule of law but concerns about police brutality linger and freedom of assembly is restricted.

Infrastructure: Highly developed

Internet: Nearly 70% of the population enjoys Internet access and broadband is cheap and can be easily installed. Broadband penetration is expected to reach 90% in the next few years.

Healthcare: Good medical facilities are available, and there are many Western-trained physicians in Hong Kong.

GDP: $327 billion

GDP (Per Capita): $45,600

Sovereign Debt: 18.2% of GDP

Working There: Banking and finance

Regulatory Climate: Highly efficient and friendly to new businesses. The World Bank Ease of Doing Business Index ranks Hong Kong the second best location in the world to do business.

Taxes: Corporate: 16.5% (Unincorporated businesses pay 15%), Individual: 2–17%. No VAT.

Cannabis: Illegal in Hong Kong. Note: since cannabis is quite a big industry in China (cloth, rope, etc.), cannabis cultivation is legal.

Homosexuality: Legal. No recognition of same-sex unions. The Hong Kong Bill of Rights Ordinance of 1991 has been interpreted by the courts to prohibit discrimination based on sexual orientation but these protections have not been extended to the private sector.

Abortion: Legal to preserve mental health, save a woman's life, or physical health. Also allowed in cases of rape, incest, or fetal impairment.

Women's Issues: Sexual discrimination in the workplace prohibited by law. Domestic violence and cultural biases against women still a problem.

Guns: Some firearms legal with license but weapon must be stored at shooting range or similar location.

Crime: Very low

Real Estate: Legal for foreigners to buy property but few can afford it. Tiny one-bedroom apartments in giant Hong Kong apartment blocks usually run between $600,000 and $1.2 million. Mortgage financing is usually available to foreigners. Broker's fees generally range from 0.5–1% of the purchase price: lawyer's fees generally run around $750. Stamp duty is 0.75–3.75% of the price.

Life Expectancy: 81.86 years

Moving There:

You don't move to Hong Kong just to hang out, find yourself, write your novel or retire. You're brought over to work, train or (to a very limited extent) study.

Tourist Visa: No visa is required for U.S. citizens who wish to stay up to 90 days. Proof of adequate funds during stay and return ticket required.

Work Visa: All non-residents of Hong Kong require a work visa and ID card. Work visa requires proof of a job offer and applicant must possess a graduate degree or extensive experience in his or her given field. Employer must also attest that position cannot be filled by a Hong Kong resident or there is a labor shortage in that particular economic sector. Independent contractors cannot apply. The visa is issued for one year, renewable.

Training Visa: A detailed training program must accompany an application for a Training Visa, which is usually valid for a period of up to 12 months.

Investor Visa: Requires investment of approximately $1.2 million (10 million HKD). Entrants admitted under this scheme may bring in their spouses and unmarried dependent children under the age of 18.

Permanent Residence: Legal residents can apply for Permanent Residence **(Permanent Hong Kong Identification Card)** after seven years.

Citizenship: Since Hong Kong has never been an independent nation, there is no provision for citizenship.

Hailey McPherson
Hong Kong

Our apartment is a one-bedroom with a tiny kitchenfor HKD 9,000—that's about $1,200. I could easily get a much bigger one-bedroom with a real kitchen in a quiet building with grass and trees outside for $700 in Minneapolis.

Hong Kong food is dirt cheap. You can get a giant bowl of soup with rice or noodles and all kinds of vegetables for HKD 25 ($3.25). The same meal at a typical Chinese restaurant in Minneapolis would also be "25," but that's more like HKD 200—and the Hong Kong version is so much better. The downside is that real "Western" food is hard to find, but who moves halfway around the world to eat the food they can get back home?

The transportation here is great—even better than at home. Hong Kong's Octopus Card gets you on any bus and MTR for HKD 100/month. The Minneapolis Metropass is $76/month.

Getting the Internet hooked up was hard, but now that we have it, everything's easy. All of the groceries are different, but you can find pretty much anything.

Marshall Creamer
Hong Kong

Since Hong Kong is the most expensive place to live in regards to housing prices, I found a roommate to share a flat with. I just want a place to sleep at night and to be somewhat comfortable...it doesn't have to be amazing. So we agreed to finding a very cheap apartment so we could use the savings on trips around Asia, or enjoying ourselves here in Hong Kong.

I'm located in a high-rise apartment complex on the 35th floor. It's an approximately 500—550 sq. ft. unfurnished two-bedroom apartment. (Compared to what I'm used to in the U.S., it's tiny, but by HK standards it's a very decent-sized place.) Our apartment came unfurnished when we signed the lease. It has A/C in both bedrooms and the living room, a small kitchen with a washer/dryer, a gas stove but no oven or microwave. Our complex has two club houses with basketball, squash, rock-climbing walls, study rooms, Internet, gym, outdoor swimming pool and a lot of other things I haven't had the time to explore. We have a shopping mall, restaurants, and a grocery store all in the lower levels of our complex as well, so this place is beyond convenient for us. My roommate's company helped us with finding a few agents to speak with.

There are not that many expats where I live. My roommate and I were seeking a cheap place with some of the facilities mentioned above and a nice view, this place just happened to be a steal.

Our total rent is 11,000 HKD/month ($1400), split between two people. Utilities are very cheap compared to Chicago. Our first power bill came after two months and was under 100 HKD ($13) for two months, though we weren't using the a/c. Our Internet is 110 HKD/month. Our gas was less than 100 HKD for two months.

I was able to meet a lot of expats on www.meetup.com (it's a website that has activities like hiking, photography, eating, and so on). I joined that before coming here and joined the hiking group. I met a lot of people through that and we have created our own Facebook group so that all of us can plan smaller events.

We hike all over Hong Kong—this only costs the transit amount and however much you want to spend on water/snacks...I haven't seen any parks/trails where we are required to pay.

We plan dinners all over Hong Kong as well. We got the idea of going to different types of restaurants each week. We typically spend around 100-150 HKD ($13—20) for our culinary dinners.

For bars, we go to Lan Kwai Fong in Central because that's where most expats go for beer. Beer will cost about 50—60 HKD ($6.50—$7.00) and a shot will run around 70—80 HKD (~$10), so it's a little expensive. However, drinking on the streets is legal, so if you go outside, it's easy to pick up a 10-20 HKD (~$1.50) beer from 7-Eleven to drink while making your way to the next bar.

I've found that everything else—food, transportation, entertainment—are all cheaper than living in Chicago.

25. Hungary

Climate: Hungary's climate is temperate and continental, with four distinct seasons. Summers are usually hot and winters very cold.
Government: Republic
Population: 9,905,596
Currency: Forint (HUF):
1 HUF = 0.04 USD
Language: Hungarian (93.6%), other or unspecified (6.4%)
Religious Groups: Catholic (51.9%), Calvinist (15.9%), Lutheran (3%), Greek Catholic (2.6%), other Christian (1%), other or unspecified (11.1%), unaffiliated (14.5%)
Ethnic Groups: Hungarian (92.3%), Roma (1.9%), other or unknown (5.8%)
Cost of Living compared to the U.S.: Affordable

The language is weird, the wine is good, and the range of goods and services available is above par for Eastern Europe thanks to a market economy that was allowed to flourish even during the Soviet period. Most of the 40,000 expats hole up in Budapest, where there are two English-speaking weeklies (The *Budapest Sun* and *Budapest Business Journal*). Resort life revolves around Lake Balaton and the winemaking region around Tokaj. Cheap air travel on the continent has resulted in a recent real estate boom, and many outsiders, particularly from Western Europe, are buying second or retirement homes here. However, the recent financial crisis has cooled the market a bit and prices are beginning to come down. The political climate has taken a lurch toward right-wing nationalism.

Living There

Governance: Generally, Hungary functions as a liberal democracy, although elections have been marred by campaign improprieties, with state media giving preferential treatment to the ruling party. There are independent media outlets and freedom of speech is respected, there is a separation of church and state, the judiciary is independent and the Internet is free of censorship.
Infrastructure: Good
Internet: There are a number of Internet service providers in Hungary and access is good and reasonably priced; majority of connections are broadband.
Healthcare: Universal healthcare provided to Hungarians and employees of Hungarian companies. Costs are relatively low, treatment is adequate but facilities are not comparable to those found in the U.S.
GDP: $190 billion
GDP (Per Capita): $19,000

Sovereign Debt: 79.6% of GDP

Working There: It is difficult for foreign nationals to find jobs in Hungary, unless they are employed by a foreign-owned company, at one of the embassies, or as an English-language teacher. If employed by a domestic company you will normally be required to speak Hungarian, and should not expect to earn much, as the recent economic crisis has weakened the nation's currency, and salaries in Hungary are low.

Regulatory Environment: Recent reforms have lent more transparency and greater flexibility to Hungary's regulatory climate.

Taxes: Corporate: 10% and 19%, Individual: 17% and 32%. VAT: 25%. Residents taxed on worldwide income.

Cannabis: Zero tolerance

Homosexuality: Legal. Some recognition of same-sex unions. Laws against discrimination. Despite being a staunchly Catholic country, Hungary is tolerant of gays and lesbians. Budapest has a large and visible gay community.

Abortion: No restriction as to reason

Women's Issues: There is gender equality under the law, but in practice women face discrimination in hiring and pay and are underrepresented in upper-level business and government posts.

Guns: Legal to own guns for hunting, sporting, and self-defense. Permit required. Storage requirements very strict.

Crime: In terms of crime, Hungary is somewhere in the middle compared to the rest of Europe. Although larger cities like Budapest are experiencing a small rise in violent crime, the majority of criminal offenses are petty theft and residential burglaries.

Real Estate: Foreign nationals are entitled to buy property in Hungary but must obtain a permit from the local administrative office. Individual buyers are limited to the purchase of one property, unless they form a limited company. Companies also receive favorable tax treatment. Twenty-five-year mortgages are available with a minimum 30% down payment. Budapest apartments start at around $80,000 but prices are dropping.

Life Expectancy: 73.44 years

Moving There

Prospective residents who do not fall into the usual categories (student, volunteer, approved contracted employee) will need to present a valid reason for wanting to remain in Hungary.

Schengen Visa: 90-day stay allowed within six-month period.

Residence Permit: If you plan on a long-term stay, you must apply for a residence permit at a Hungarian consulate in the U.S. If your application is successful, you will receive a permit allowing you to enter Hungary that is valid for 30 days. During this period, you must go to a Hungarian Immigration Office to register your address and make an application for a long-stay residence permit. These can be issued for employment, study, family reunification, long-term visit to friends/

relatives, medical treatment, for research, volunteering or other reasons. Permits are valid up to two years, renewable.

If you are planning on working in Hungary, you must apply for a work permit and include this with your application. Applicants must also provide proof of valid lodgings in Hungary and evidence of sufficient income.

Permanent Residency/Settlement Permit: Applicants must show proof of at least three years continuous residency in Hungary, sufficient income, and lodgings.

Work Permit/Visa: Required for non-E.U. nationals to work in Hungary. Applicants must provide valid labor agreement with Hungarian employer and proof of accommodations during stay in Hungary. As long as you remain employed, work permit and visa are renewable each year.

Citizenship: Eight years continuous legal residency, proof of economic self-sufficiency and knowledge of Hungarian constitution (must pass examination). Spouses of Hungarian citizens can apply after three years. Descendents who have some Hungarian ancestry can apply for citizenship even without residency.

Gary Lukatch
Budapest, Hungary

There is a large expat community here, from all over the world, who use English as a common language, plus a good-size British contingent. And, of course, Hungarians who speak English and want to keep improving their skills. Most Americans in Budapest are embassy employees, students, English teachers and a few other varied workers, retirees and tourists. Most expats work for foreign companies with branches in Budapest. Or, if they speak Hungarian, have their own businesses or work for Hungarian companies or foreign companies that need bilingual skills. Expats gather at select pubs and restaurants, often run by other expats. Americans stay mostly within their small groups and rarely attempt to learn more than a few words of Hungarian.

Public transportation is amazing in Budapest—I haven't driven, or needed, a car since I moved here. Internet access is freely available, goods and services for nearly everything are readily available now. Of course, a few minor things are not obtainable, but the substitute's often better. Laws are much less restrictive here, as police are very lenient in many areas—also, unfortunately, often open to bribes, if offered. Police presence is noted, but unobtrusive for foreigners.

No expat is happy with the recent shift in Hungarian politics, but the general consensus is wait and see. We all have roots here now, and would hate to leave, so unless the government makes it difficult for expats to remain, I suppose we will all stay as long as possible. And, I'm not overly concerned; I just keep a low profile and keep doing what I'm doing and hope for the best.

As far as someone moving here now, unless it is a retired person, I'm not sure I'd recommend it, if only for the economic situation, i.e., lack of job opportunities. There just isn't as much career potential here now, and even the English teaching has fallen off drastically. For retirees, however, it's still a good deal, as their retirement dollar will still go a lot further than in the U.S. Students also still dribble in to study at various universities here, as cost is also less than many other countries.

26. India

Climate: Varies from tropical monsoon in south to temperate in north
Government: Federal Republic
Population: 1,173,108,018
Currency: Indian Rupee (INR): 1 INR = 0.02 USD
Language: English enjoys associate status but is the most important language for national, political, and commercial communication; Hindi is the national language and primary tongue of 30% of the people although there are 14 other official languages.
Religious Groups: Hindu (81.3%), Muslim (12%), Christian (2.3%), other (4.4%)
Ethnic Groups: Indo-Aryan (72%), Dravidian (25%), other (3%)
Cost of Living compared to the U.S: Dirt cheap

Traditionally a mecca for satori-seekers (whether in ashrams or the trance-party beaches at Goa), this booming Asian economy is attracting job-hunters with more than just call center management gigs. The living is cheap and the scenery magnificent, marred only by poor sanitation and the fact that you'll share your views with a billion or so other humans. The movie industry here has been doing pretty well, also.

Living There
Governance: Free and fair multiparty elections, an activist judiciary, and an independent media. India's development remains hampered by widespread political corruption and the country's stifling bureaucracy is notorious for bungling and inefficiency. India's police have also gained an ugly reputation for human rights abuses. Religious tensions between Hindus and Muslims can often erupt in violence, terrorism and military intervention.
Infrastructure: Below Western standards.
Internet: Poor. Less than 10% of Indian residents enjoy Internet access and the country's broadband penetration is one of the lowest in the region.

Healthcare: Adequate to excellent medical care is available in the major population centers, but is usually very limited or unavailable in rural areas.

GDP: $4.46 trillion

GDP (Per Capita): $3,400

Sovereign Debt: 55.9% of GDP

Working There: Historically, skilled workers and entrepreneurs used to leave India for the U.S., but lately, an expanding white-collar sector has triggered a flow in the opposite direction. The majority of Americans work in IT, but increasing numbers are finding employment in healthcare, entertainment and hospitality industries, while retail and marketing promises to be a new growth sector.

Regulatory Environment: Stifling, time-consuming, and cumbersome; the World Bank ranks India 165th out of 183 for ease of starting a business.

Taxes: Corporate: 33.99%, Individual: 0–30%, VAT: 12.5%. Residents taxed on worldwide income.

Cannabis: Illegal, but available

Homosexuality: In July, 2009, the Delhi High Court decriminalized homosexual intercourse between consenting adults as the law prohibiting this behavior was deemed a violation of the fundamental rights guaranteed by the Indian constitution. No laws against discrimination. Same-sex marriages are allowed within Hindu culture although cultural acceptance varies.

Abortion: Permitted to save a woman's life, physical health, and mental health. Allowed in cases of rape or fetal impairment. Parental authorization required.

Women's Issues: Women are considered equal to men under India's constitution and enjoy a prominent role in politics, business, the arts, etc. Although there are laws against domestic violence, violence against women remains a problem.

Guns: Some classes of firearms legal. License is required.

Crime: Petty crime is common throughout the country. Low incidence of violence except near border with Pakistan where crime and terrorism continue to make headlines.

Real Estate: It is very difficult for non-citizens of India to purchase, trade, or finance property.

Life Expectancy: 66.46 years

Moving There

While Americans can stay up to 10 years on a tourist visa, you'd have to follow a six months in/two months out kind of schedule, which might be OK if you're making India a second home. Otherwise, you need to have work (more and more possible as the economy expands) or be brought over for the purposes of engaging in business. The latter type of visas must be arranged before entering the country.

Tourist Visa: Tourist visas are issued for six months but five- and even 10-year visas are possible (via special treaty) for Americans, though you have to leave for two months after any six-month stay. Once you have been admitted into the country, Indian immigration laws do not allow you to change the status of your visa, e.g. from tourist to work visa.

Business Visa: Letter of invitation from Indian company or individual residing in India explaining business arrangement with applicant as well as purpose and length of stay required. Business letter on company letterhead introducing applicant and declaring his or her status or business relationship with company, length and purpose of stay, and entity or individual who will be financially responsible for visa holder required. Business visas are generally granted for one year, but can be granted for five and 10 years at the discretion of Indian consular authorities.

Work Visa: Applicant must submit proof of employment contract or engagement by Indian company as well as evidence of experience and/or professional qualifications. Employment visas are generally limited to skilled professionals who work in a field that is in demand or suffering a labor shortage. Indian work visas are valid for up to one year regardless of duration stated in work contract. Extensions of up to five years are authorized by the Ministry of Home Affairs/ Foreigners Regional Registration Office (FRRO) in the state where you will be staying.

Residence Permit: Foreign citizens entering India for work purposes or wishing to stay beyond 180 days must register with the nearest FRRO office within 14 days of arrival. Once your registration has been certified, you will need to obtain a Personal Account Number or PAN card to work or live in India. You can apply for the card online at www.tin-nsdl.com. If you are registered and possess a PAN card, you can then apply for residence at the nearest FRRO/police station. Permit can be valid for anywhere from six months to 10 years.

Student Visas and Missionary Visas are also available per the usual documentation.
Citizenship: 12 years legal residency.

27. Indonesia

Climate: Tropical; hot, humid; more moderate in highlands
Government: Republic
Population: 242,968,342
Currency: Indonesian Rupiah (IDR): 1 IDR = 0.0001 USD
Language: Bahasa Indonesia (official, modified form of Malay), English, Dutch, local dialects (the most widely spoken of which is Javanese)
Religious Groups: Muslim (88%), Protestant (5%), Roman Catholic (3%), other (4%)
Ethnic Groups: Javanese (45%), Sudanese (14%), Madurese (7.5%), Malay (7.5%), other (26%)
Cost of Living compared to the U.S: Cheap

It's a giant tropical nation, spread out over thousands of islands covering an area greater than the United States, but most expats will only find themselves in one or two places: business types congregate in the teeming capital, Jakarta, while the rest head straight to Bali, the only Hindu region in this otherwise Muslim country. Those willing to blaze a trail of their own can find pristine tropical beauty for pennies a day.

Living There

Governance: The fall of President Suharto's brutal regime in the late 1990s has ushered in a period of moderate political reform. Indonesia now holds free multiparty elections (although critics complain that election fraud is common) and efforts are being made to curtail human rights abuses and guarantee greater freedoms to the Indonesian people. Unfortunately, as many of Suharto's protégés dominate the country's political life, human rights abuses and crackdowns on the political opposition aren't uncommon.

Infrastructure: Roads range from good to dangerously poor. Driving is generally risky but public transportation is said to be unsafe as well. Available but oftentimes very slow.

Internet: Although once a tiny market, Indonesia now has over 30 million Internet subscribers with broadband mainly available in larger cities like Jakarta and Surabaya.

Healthcare: The general level of sanitation and healthcare in Indonesia is far below U.S. standards. Some routine medical care is available in all major cities, although most expatriates leave the country for serious medical procedures.

GDP: $1.033 trillion

GDP (Per Capita): $4,300

Sovereign Debt: 26.4% of GDP

Working There: Government policy states that foreigners who work in Indonesia must be "experts" in their field. The government defines an expert as someone who has been working in their field professionally for five–10 years. English teachers are exempted.

Regulatory Environment: Inefficient, time-consuming, and often expensive.

Taxes: Corporate: 25%, Individual: 5–30%, VAT: 10%. Even on a retirement visa, you are liable for 30% personal income tax if your income is over approximately $20,000 a year. Residents taxed on worldwide income.

Cannabis: Strictly illegal

Homosexuality: Legal (although Muslims in Aceh province can be prosecuted). No legal recognition of same-sex unions. No laws against discrimination.

Abortion: Only to save a woman's life

Women's Issues: Laws against domestic violence and human trafficking. Gender equality bill proposed for 2011. Although women are making inroads into Indonesian political and commercial life, there are still many restrictions and cultural barriers. Domestic violence remains a concern.

Guns: Some weapons legal. License required.

Crime: Low

Real Estate: It is illegal for foreigners to own land in Indonesia although the government is discussing the possibility of easing current restrictions. Foreigners can only take out 25-year leases or designate an Indonesian as owner in name only. Costs come out to a one-time payment of 1% to the notary, a transfer tax (usually 1–1.5% of the purchase price), and a .5–1% annual fee to the nominal owner.

Life Expectancy: 71.05 years

Moving There

Length of stay, entry and exit are all meticulously and individually regulated in the byzantine Indonesian visa/permit system. Most easy-to-acquire visas don't allow you to stay very long. A one-year business visa, for instance, still requires you to leave the country every 60 days. If you're not planning on getting married, a work permit or a substantial investment is the ticket to long-term legal residency. There is also a straightforward retiree option. While some resort to regular visa runs to Singapore (not cheap), a social visit Visitation Visa, good for six months and renewable, is the option to shoot for. It requires that you have a sponsor in Indonesia (a company or an individual) but there are also services who can "arrange" one. There are three regions in Indonesia that are off limits without express government permission: Aceh, Maluku, and Irian Jaya/West Papua. Anywhere else is OK.

NOTE: The Indonesian government has begun cracking down on illegal workers and those caught working without proper documentation can face stiff penalties including jail time.

Visa on Arrival (VOA): Available to American citizens upon arrival at specific airports and seaports in Indonesia. Applicants must show proof of round-trip airplane ticket. Valid for 30 days (30-day extension is available but you must declare your intention to stay longer than 30 days when requesting the initial visa).

Visitation Visa: Issued to individuals visiting Indonesia for tourism, business, social visit, research, and journalism. Proof of adequate funds and round-trip ticket required. Visas can be single or multiple entry depending on reason for stay. Visa also requires a local sponsor—either an individual or company. Research and Journalism visas require additional permission from Indonesian government. Valid for a maximum of 60 days but extensions can be obtained from immigration authorities.

Limited Stay Visa (VITAS): Single-entry visa for visit related to work, investment, research, family unification, performance, sport, or social activities. Applicant must provide letter from Indonesian sponsor and proof of adequate funds. Valid for one year, can be used to apply for KITAS (temporary residency/work permit).

Work Permit/Temporary Residence (KITAS): Available to investors, "foreign experts," members of the clergy, researchers, spouse of Indonesian wife or foreign national legally residing in Indonesia. Sponsor required and you must apply directly to Immigration Office in Indonesia. Valid for one year and renewable for up to five years.

Special Visa for Retired/Senior Citizen Visa: Applicant must be at least 55 years of age and provide letter from institution or bank showing available funds or income. Additional requirements: proof of health insurance (either American or Indonesian), written statement attesting to willingness to reside at "available accommodation" in Indonesia, and visa holders must agree to employ a domestic worker during stay in Indonesia. Applicant cannot work in Indonesia. Valid for one year and renewable for up to five years (extensions are available with approval from immigration authorities).

Permanent Stay Visa (KITAP): Applicant must possess KITAS for at least five years prior to applying. Valid for five years, renewable.

Citizenship: Five years legal residency required (10 years non-continuous), good health, proficient in Indonesian language, regular source of income, and acknowledge Pancasila (official governing philosophy) as basis of government and constitution in Indonesia.

28. Ireland

Climate: Temperate maritime; modified by North Atlantic Current; mild winters, cool summers; consistently humid; overcast about half the time

Government: Parliamentary Democracy

Population: 4,203,200

Currency: Euro (EUR): 1 EUR = 1.36 USD

Language: English is the language generally used, Irish (Gaelic or Gaeilge) spoken mainly in areas located along the western seaboard

Religious Groups: Catholic (87.4%), Church of Ireland (2.9%), other Christian (1.9%), other (2.1%), unspecified (1.5%), none (4.2%)

Ethnic Groups: Celtic, English (92%), Asian (1.3%), black (1.1%), mixed or unspecified (2.7%)

Cost of Living compared to the U.S.: Similar to the U.S.

Unless you want to invest a substantial sum in the country, most immigrants to Ireland either marry into it or take advantage of the "grandfather" clause that allows anyone with an Irish grandparent to claim citizenship. Once in, you enjoy full government benefits, including free healthcare and education—though the impact of the post-bailout austerity measures on those benefits might not leave you all that much once the smoke clears. A strong Catholic streak makes this place slightly more culturally conservative than the rest of Western Europe but those who like their beer dense and their whisky straight up will feel right at home. Ireland, one of the PIIGS (Portugal, Italy, Ireland,

Greece and Spain) countries, has suffered a banking and economic collapse and the social upheaval as a result of subsequent austerity measures have only begun to manifest.

Living There

Governance: Ireland is a Western-style democracy with free and fair elections (though government corruption has been an issue), healthy independent media and respect for basic human rights and political liberties. Internet is uncensored.

Infrastructure: Developed

Internet: Widely available; 65% of the population have Internet but hi-speed is lacking compared to the rest of Western Europe.

Healthcare: Everyone is entitled to healthcare in Ireland, and this is partly funded by social security contributions. Modern medical facilities and highly skilled medical practitioners are available in Ireland.

GDP: $172.3 billion

GDP (Per Capita): $37,600

Sovereign Debt: 94.2% of GDP

Working There: Tourist-area work in pubs, bars, restaurants, and hotels. Au pair wages are often low but food and accommodation are usually included. The nation's economic difficulties after the housing bubble collapse may limit employment opportunities and it's harder for non-E.U. citizens to find work.

Regulatory Environment: A prime location for entrepreneurs: transparent, efficient, and easy to navigate. The World Bank Ease of Doing Business Index ranks Ireland as the 9th best location in the world to open up a business.

Taxes: Corporate: 12.5%, Individual: 0 to 41% depending on income. VAT: 13.5% for services and 21.5% for goods. Residents taxed on worldwide income and capital gains.

Cannabis: Illegal but widely available. Arrest for small amounts may result in fine and possible jail term if you are a repeat offender. Irish police allowed discretion whether or not to arrest or fine.

Homosexuality: Legal. Discrimination based on sexual orientation outlawed. The passage of the Civil Partnership and Certain Rights and Obligations of Cohabitations Act 2010 ensures that same-sex civil unions are legally recognized.

Abortion: Prohibited except to save a woman's life

Women's Issues: Pay inequality issues exist, though discrimination is against the law.

Guns: Some firearms legal. "Per-gun" certificate required for ownership and use.

Crime: Crime rate low. There is some petty theft in tourist areas.

Real Estate: There are no restrictions on foreigners who wish to buy property in Ireland. Buyers must pay stamp duty on all property transactions (first €125,000 is exempt). Legal cost can also range between 0.5 and 1%. Financing is difficult for foreigners to acquire and many buyers pay in cash. Since Ireland's economy hit the skids, home prices have dropped by over 40%. Average home prices are still in the neighborhood of $300,000.

Life Expectancy: 78.24 years

Moving There

Skills and heredity will get you in. Otherwise, it's a pretty hard slog.

Tourist Visa: Americans are not required to apply for a tourist visa but staying beyond 90 days is not allowed and there are no extensions.

Entrepreneur/Business Permission Visa: Ireland may soon revamp its entrepreneur visa scheme, easing some requirements. An investment of €300,000 is necessary and employment of at least two EEA (European Economic Area) nationals.

Work Permits: Because Ireland is an E.U. member, Americans who wish to work in Ireland are required to obtain a Work Permit from the Department of Enterprise, Trade and employment. The Permits are only issued with proof of a job offer from an Irish employer who has made every effort to recruit an Irish or a resident of the European Economic Area (EEA) for the position. You must work for your employer for at least 12 months before you are allowed to move to a different position or employer. The permits are issued for two years and can be renewed for an additional three years. After that period, the permit can be renewed indefinitely.

Green Card Permit: The Green Card Permit "scheme" allows prospective non-Irish employees to live and work in Ireland in specified occupations where there is a "strategic skills shortage." Job offer must be for a minimum of two years' duration, after which, you can apply for permanent residency

Permanent Resident: Five years legal residency, applicant must show proof of good character, and economic self-sufficiency (job, income, etc.)

Student Visas are available per the usual documentation and holders of student visas are allowed to seek and accept part-time employment. Applicants for Student Visas must demonstrate their intention to leave Ireland after their studies are completed. There are also visas for **Creative Artists** (e.g. writers, visual artists, musicians, etc.). Eligibility is judged on a case-by-case basis.

Citizenship by Descent: If you have Irish blood in you, there's a chance you may be able to qualify for Irish citizenship and all the benefits that entails. If your grandfather or grandmother was born in Ireland, so long as you register at the Foreign Births Register at an Irish Embassy or Consular Office or Department of Foreign Affairs, you can become a citizen of the emerald isles. If your Irish roots go further back and you have a great-grandfather or great-grandmother born in Ireland, you may have a chance at citizenship but your parents had to have registered your name in the Foreign Births Register at the time of your birth. Naturalization will require research and the appropriate documents to prove your legitimate right to claim citizenship, but for many Americans of Irish descent, it may be well worth it. Ireland allows dual citizenship so you won't need to renounce your American citizenship and you will also become a citizen of the E.U. which allows you to live and work almost anywhere on the continent.

Citizenship (naturalization): Citizenship petitions can be submitted to the Irish Minister of Justice after five years of legal residency (three, with an Irish spouse), plus proof of good character, and expressed intention to continue living in Ireland are required.

29. Israel

Climate: Temperate; hot and dry in southern and eastern desert areas
Government: Parliamentary Democracy
Population: 7,233,701
Currency: Israeli New Shekel (ILS): 1 ILS = 0.28 USD
Language: Hebrew (official), Arabic used officially for Arab minority, English most commonly used foreign language.
Religious Groups: Jewish (75.5%), Muslim (16.8%), Christian (2.1%), Druze (1.7%), other (3.9%)
Ethnic Groups: Jewish (76.4%), non-Jewish [mostly Arab] (26.4%)
Cost of Living compared to the U.S.: Reasonable

Clinging to its splinter of land along the Mediterranean Sea and its plurality of biblical holy sites, Israel offers the most Western-friendly accommodations and boasts the largest American expat community relative to its size of any other country. This is comprised almost completely of Jews, who are encouraged by family and other institutions to make *aliya* and enticed by Israel's Law of Return and various incentives. There's fast food, shopping malls, and centuries of history—and animosity. If you're even contemplating a move here, you probably either know where you stand on I-P (Israel-Palestine) issues or don't care about it enough to find out.

Living There
Governance: A Western-style democracy, independent judiciary, and opinionated free press. Some corruption. The Israeli state guarantees basic political and civil liberties. Of course Israel's Arab minority have an entirely different perspective on things.
Infrastructure: Up to Western standards in Israel proper, less so in the occupied territories.
Internet: Hi-speed widely available
Healthcare: A large percentage of Israel's medical care is provided by the Histadrut, the national labor union. Medical care is excellent in Israel proper; care and facilities are much worse in the occupied territories.
GDP: $217.1 billion
GDP (Per Capita): $29,500
Sovereign Debt: 77.3% of GDP

Working There: Kibbutz and agricultural, high-tech, tourism

Regulatory Environment: Recent reforms have eased the process of starting a business in Israel and streamlined existing regulations.

Taxes: Corporate: 25%, Individual: 10–45%, VAT: 16%. Taxes levied on worldwide income (some exemptions for senior citizens and new arrivals).

Cannabis: Criminal penalties for possession and use. Widely available. Some medicinal use allowed.

Homosexuality: Legal. Same-sex unions legally recognized. Laws against discrimination. Active gay and lesbian community. Considered the most gay-friendly country in the Middle East, as defenders of the State's other excesses never tire of pointing out.

Abortion: To preserve physical and mental health and in cases of rape, incest and fetal impairment

Women's Issues: Israeli women well-represented in business and government. Laws against domestic violence and sexual harassment. Some lingering wage disparities between men and women. "Modesty Patrols" have been known to harass women in Haredi communities.

Guns: A wide range of firearms are legal. License required and renewed every three years. Open carry of firearms is legal and not uncommon.

Crime: Not insignificant, though it's the terrorists that get all the attention.

Real Estate: Americans are allowed to purchase property in Israel. Mortgages are available for 60–80% of the appraised value. Since 2008, interest rates have been between 1.5–2.5%.

Life Expectancy: 80.73 years

Moving There

One question: are you Jewish?

Tourist Visa: Valid only 90 days

Student Visa: Valid for one year. Renewable in Israel.

Work Permit: Request must be made by potential employer. Issued for varying periods. Note: permits are usually issued for one specific profession or type of work. You cannot change occupations or perform work unrelated to existing permit.

Citizenship (Law of Return): Jewish immigrants, those with Jewish ancestors (grandparents), and converts to Judaism have the right to legally reside in Israel and can choose to become citizens within three months of arrival. Certificate of Oleh required.

Citizenship (naturalization): Non-Jewish immigrants can apply for citizenship if they have legally resided for three years (out of the last five) in Israel. Applications are submitted to the Ministry of the Interior. Interior Minister is given discretion to grant or deny applications.

Marni Levin

Jerusalem, Israel

In some ways, life here in Israel is similar to life in the U.S. We are busy with our families, homes, jobs and everyday events. I switched to a different shift at my job. My husband has been writing essays and exams for the counseling course he is taking. We bought some new living room furniture. We attended our nephew's wedding. Yet at the same time it is a different, meaningful and more significant life. It is impossible to separate the cultural and religious aspects as for me they are intertwined. For example, yesterday we celebrated Purim when we recall our salvation from a Persian tyrant, Haman, who tried to destroy the Jews. And here we are, thousands of years later, and look what is happening. Persia is now called Iran and their president Ahmadinejad hates us just as much as his ancestor did and would like nothing better than to wipe us off the map.

Viewed in that way, life here is not ordinary, not when we feel connected to and part of our ongoing, fascinating history. And there is pain, too. Our sons serve in the army. Friends of theirs have been killed. Hearing our oldest granddaughter Avigail, our first little sabra (native-born Israeli) in the family, chatter away in both fluent English and Hebrew fills us with joy. Israel is unique, it is special, it is ours. I would not want to live anywhere else.

30. Italy

Climate: Generally mild Mediterranean; cold northern winters
Government: Republic
Population: 58,126,212
Currency: Euro (EUR): 1 EUR = 1.36 USD
Language: Italian
Religious Groups: Roman Catholic (predominant)
Ethnic Groups: Italian, small minorities of German, French, Slovenian, and Albanian
Cost of Living compared to the U.S.: Steep

Fantastically beautiful, with more history, architectural beauty and art per square mile than any other country, Italy attracts throngs of Americans in spite of steep costs (higher than any other Mediterranean country) and difficult residency barriers. If you're of Italian descent, that counts for a lot, bureaucratically speaking. Rome, Florence and Venice are popular but priced at the high end. Bear in mind the state religion is Roman

Catholic, not Efficiency and Convenience, so bring patience, money, your most fashionable attire and an appetite for pasta and Chianti.

Living There

Governance: Though Italy generally adheres to Western-style democratic principles, it is famously corrupt and media freedom has been hampered by government control of most outlets. Police brutality has also been an issue in parts of the country.

Infrastructure: Developed

Internet: Over 50% of the population has access to the Internet but Italian broadband penetration is far behind many other European nations. Italy has no cable television, and therefore, cable modems for broadband don't exist. DSL is the only option. The Italian government is committed to increasing broadband access and developing the wireless network. Telephones are modern, well-developed, fast; fully automated telephone, telex, and data services.

Healthcare: Medical facilities are available, but may be limited outside urban areas. Public hospitals, though generally free of charge for emergency services, sometimes do not maintain the same standards as hospitals in the United States. The Italian national health system ("Servizio Sanitario Nazionale" or SSN) offers low-cost healthcare of a good standard, with well-trained and dedicated doctors, though waiting lists can be long.

GDP: $1.782 trillion

GDP (Per Capita): $30,700

Sovereign Debt: 118.1% of GDP

Working There: Opportunities in summer and winter tourism at resorts, camping, TEFL-qualified language schools, au pairs.

Regulatory Environment: Complex, costly, and burdensome. Corruption is a problem.

Taxes: Corporate: 31.4%, Individual: 23–43%, VAT: 20% (4% on some goods like books and food).

Cannabis: Illegal but small amounts can be considered an administrative offense. If caught selling, you can go to prison.

Homosexuality: Legal. No legal recognition of same-sex unions at this time. Laws against discrimination. Culturally, Italy, with its strong ties to the Vatican, has a strong bias against homosexuals, and gays and lesbians tend to act more low-key here than in other areas of Western Europe.

Abortion: No restrictions as to reason, but parental authorization required.

Women's Issues: Women's rights are protected by law, though domestic violence and harassment are still big problems.

Guns: Some firearms legal. License required.

Crime: By European standards, crime rates, including violent crimes, are high, but still well below the U.S.

Real Estate: Foreigners can buy real estate in Italy. Mortgages available with 20% deposit. Purchase tax of 3–4% is levied (10% if you don't occupy the home).

Real estate tax is 3% of purchase, plus stamp duty of 7%, a local tax of between 0.4–0.8%, plus various fees.

Life Expectancy: 80.20 years

Moving There

Americans who aren't students or of Italian descent are going to find the process beyond daunting. Luckily for those who don't get papers but still want to stay, the enforcement arm of the government, like every other branch, wins no awards for their efficiency.

NOTE: Regardless of what kind of visa you possess, you are required to report your presence at a local police station within eight business days of your arrival in Italy or face expulsion.

Schengen Visa: Maximum 90-day stay for 180-day period. No extensions.

Residence Permit/*Permesso di Soggiorno*: Anyone wishing to remain in Italy longer than 90 days must apply for the proper visa at their local consulate beforehand. Within eight days of arrival (and all subsequent times) you must apply for a Residence Permit (*Permesso di Soggiorno*) at designated post offices. Purposes for which this can be granted are for people with an Italian spouse (and their family), work (with valid employment), self-employment, tourist, study and other non-employment related reasons. The latter (*Visto per Residenza Selettiva o Dimora*) is mainly geared toward retirees, but anyone showing sufficient independent wealth or income can apply. Those who don't fall into the easily-defined categories will find this road difficult. Should you be granted a permit, the validity period can vary, but it will be renewable up to five years.

EC Long-Term Resident Visa (Permanent Residence): This visa is issued to individuals after five years of legal residency and can demonstrate a minimum income equivalent to Italian Social Security benefits.

Work Permit If you plan on being self-employed while you live in Italy, you will need to apply for an Independent Work Visa. This kind of work permit is often subject to quota restrictions. There are also Subordinate Work Visas which require documentation that you have been hired by an Italian company. As an E.U. country, the Italian job market is tilted toward citizens of Europe and it won't be easy to land employment but there are openings in seasonal work and a few select occupations where there are shortages in Italy. Unsurprisingly, a lot of Americans work at cash jobs, off the books.

Citizenship: Granted to spouses and children of Italian nationals. Grandchildren of Italian nationals can also receive expedited claims and reduced residency (three years). Otherwise, 10 years legal residency, proof of economic self-sufficiency, and absence of criminal record.

Laura
Rome, Italy

The joke amongst expats is that you have to really really love it in order to put up with all the sh-t. My life isn't particularly glamorous, but for me it is the best possible life—sorry to be a dork but—I can go to the world's best museums and archaeological sites in a hop, skip and jump. Seeing a building or a painting or an ancient mosaic at an archaeological site that I had heretofore only seen in books is always a cool experience. I have weepy moments often, and they are almost all in front of art works. One time i was gazing at Bernini's "Daphne and Apollo" and crying (and then my cell rang!)

The first apartment I got was from expatriates.com which I now realize was a site to fish for "rich Americans." A studio with a comfortable sofa bed was €950 a month. After five months, I was out of money. I got another apartment a bit further out of the center of town, paying €800, plus utilities, including a gas tank next to my stove that had to be filled every two months. For the past two years, I've been sharing a rented apartment with my boyfriend. It's bigger (one bedroom plus huge terrace) and for not that much more than the studio (€1000 + expenses), and a bit more central. But while all the expats are renting, and it is no big thing, the Italians are very averse to paying rent, so the beau is trying to encourage me/us to buy a place but the real estate is to-the-moon expensive, and I am not sure I want to move to the ugly sprawly suburbs since I came to Rome to be in the center of the action, and renting affords me that opportunity.

If you are considering moving here, there is also a terrific resource, a Yahoo group called VCN, which stands for Volunteers and Consultants Network. It was originally established for U.N. volunteers, English speakers, who come to a strange town. It's like a craigslist.org, but it also has announcements of social events. You get answers to questions like, "Where do you find an English movie theater? Who wants to buy my motor scooter?" Tons of apartments for rent. It's really active.

There are LOTS of social activities for expats here. I also used a dating site called Meetic. Met my current beau on there even though online dating is not part of the landscape here the way it is in the States. My boyfriend is very attached to his family (wants to see them nearly every day), and that is one of the biggest points of conflict—after all I only see my family once or twice a year!

Anyway, dating an Italian is a great way to learn Italian (even if you are stubborn like me and don't really want to!) and I have made many Italian friends and acculturated to the way real Italians live (not the way we fantasize they do, as foreigners).

If you are thinking of moving here, just be prepared to let go of a lot of what you consider to be essential in the U.S. You have to learn to go at a much slower pace, deal with unimaginable bureaucracy, and live with a lot less money and consumer "stuff." But it's worth it!

31. Japan

Climate: Varies from subtropical to temperate
Government: Constitutional monarchy with a
    parliamentary government
Population: 127,078,679
Currency: Yen (JPY): 1 JPY = 0.01 USD
Language: Japanese
Religious Groups: Shinto (83.9%), Buddhism
    (71.4%), Christianity (2%), other (7.8%) [note:
    many Japanese are both Shinto and Buddhist]
Ethnic Groups: Japanese (98.5%), Koreans (0.5%), Chinese (0.4%),
    other (0.6%)
Cost of Living compared to the U.S.: Ouch

Despite being the one of the most expensive places on the planet, Japan manages to attract plenty of Americans. Most head for Tokyo, to be stuffed into subway cars, sleep in tiny apartments and live with tomorrow's gadgets today. Getting in isn't the problem, provided you can afford being there. Luckily, teaching English is an industry here. Jobs pay in the mighty yen, and often include accommodations, so Americans can often afford to send money back home just like Third World immigrants in the United States do. With a large media industry that puts a premium on Western or American looks, many musicians, actors and models worn out from the casting couch back home, have found it easier and more lucrative to be big in Japan. The 2011 earthquake and particularly the nuclear catastrophe still unfolding at press time (and likely to continue to unfold centuries after this book is out of print) has painted a radioactive cloud over the country's future—both in terms of its livability and economic underpinnings. On the other hand, the expat exodus has opened up more opportunities for those willing to pick up the slack.

Living There
Governance: Japan operates as a Western-style democracy, with free and fair
    elections and all the rights, privileges and civil liberties safeguards that entails.
Infrastructure: Developed
Internet: Widely used; approximately 78% of the population have Internet access.
    Hi-speed widely available. Japan's fiber-based FTTH network is considered one
    of the fastest in the world. An initiative by the Japanese government seeks to
    provide broadband access to 100% of the population by 2011.

Healthcare: Excellent. National health insurance available.

GDP: $4.338 trillion

GDP (Per Capita): $34,200

Sovereign Debt: 225.8% of GDP

Working There: Teaching English, healthcare (nurses and caregivers are needed for Japan's large aging population), entertainment industry, and some skilled factory labor.

Regulatory Environment: Starting a business is relatively easy but there is still some red tape to surmount.

Taxes: Corporate: 40.87%, Individual: 5–40%, VAT: 5%. Note: when local taxes are included, Japan's individual income tax rate tops out at around 50%. Non-residents only pay taxes on income earned in Japan.

Cannabis: Illegal. Stiff penalties for even the tiniest amount.

Homosexuality: Legal. No legal recognition of same-sex unions. Some local laws banning discrimination. Homosexual behavior is accepted but the lifestyle is not.

Abortion: Legal on socioeconomic grounds, to save the woman's life, physical or mental health. However, Japan's laws require spousal permission.

Women's Issues: Women often face discrimination in the workplace. Sexual harassment is widespread. Violence against women is believed to be grossly underreported for cultural reasons. Over the past few years, the Tokyo transportation system has been running "Women Only" carriages on trains so that secretaries can enjoy their morning commute without being groped.

Guns: Handguns strictly illegal. Only rifles and shotguns can be legally owned and they must be strictly for hunting or sporting purposes. License required. Even touching a firearm without proper license is prohibited by law.

Crime: Violent crime rare. Occasional pickpocketing or petty theft in tourist areas.

Real Estate: While no restrictions exist, real estate is exorbitantly expensive, particularly in major cities, and mortgage financing is difficult to obtain, especially for non-residents.

Life Expectancy: 82.12 years

Moving There

If you can afford to stay and/or have a gig lined up, getting the proper paperwork is a fairly easy matter. Your garden-variety youthful expat usually arrives via an English-teaching program. Ex-GIs and aging bachelors often marry their way in. Otherwise, there are scads of visa types for any category you can come up with.

Tourist Visa: For U.S. citizens, visa is not required for stay up to 90 days. You can look for employment while on a tourist visa, but you must apply for a working visa before you start your employment.

General Visa: Issued for "academic or artistic activities" which provide no income or research related to Japanese culture (e.g. tea ceremony, Judo, Zen Buddhism etc.). Visa is issued for one- and three-year periods.

Working Visa: There are 16 categories of working visas that cover professors employed at Japanese universities, journalists, working artists, accountants, medical service professionals, teachers, business owners, entertainers, skilled laborers etc. Each designated working visa has specific background requirements like professional certification, experience, and/or university degree. Visa issued for one or three years.

Student Visas are also available per the usual requirements.

Long term Resident: Mainly issued to foreigners of Japanese descent. If you fit the bill, it's issued for one to three years.

Most visas are renewable/extendable provided the original criteria still apply.

Permanent Resident: Criteria for Permanent Residency are not fixed and stingily granted. Even spouses can wait years. Generally, those without Japanese family or other connections must have lived 10 consecutive years in Japan, five of them with a valid work permit and fulfill various other requirements (good conduct, self-sufficiency, etc.).

Citizenship: Applicant must be at least 20 years of age, possessing sufficient funds, income, and/or professional skills to live independently, clean criminal record, and at least five years continuous legal residency in Japan. Minister of Justice is given discretion to grant or deny all naturalization requests.

Paul Schuble

Hyogo Prefecture, Japan

Life in Japan isn't radically different from living in America in terms of comfort. There are, of course, degrees of comfort in either country. Some of the bigger differences:

Weather and insulation: The Japanese love to brag that Japan has four seasons, as if this is something unique. But for many expats, these seasons aren't the normal spring, summer, winter, and fall we're used to. They're hot, cold, wet, and mild, with the latter being the most transient of the bunch. Temperatures and weather conditions aren't so extreme in Japan, but despite the country's reputation for advanced technology, its infrastructure can be found largely wanting. While many houses are constructed to stand up to earthquakes, the majority are built with relatively little insulation, resulting in hot summers, cold winters, and high electricity bills all around.

Toilets: Yes, there are technological wonders with all kinds of sensors and sprays and heated seats, but you won't have one of those unless you're wealthy or staying at a hotel. Although in most cases you can find a normal Western toilet, woe to the poor foreigner who can't fight nature's call and is left no recourse but the Japanese-style hole in the ground. Hope you like squatting.

Banking and convenience stores: In Japan most banks seem to close at 2:00 or 3:00 in the afternoon and aren't open on weekends, so banking can be a challenge. Fortunately, convenience stores really live up to their name. Most bills can be paid at the register, and ATMs can be accessed for a minor service charge.

Stamp, don't sign: In Japan, individuals and organizations own special stamps called *hanko* or *inkan*. These are used in place of a signature on official documents of all kinds. In the case of foreigners, signatures are often permissible. If you do choose to get a stamp, don't lose it! I've heard replacing it can be a huge rigmarole.

Transportation: Trains and buses are a lot more efficient, punctual, and safe in Japan, and most people own bicycles. It's pretty easy to live without a car. Back in the States it's a lot harder.

In my experience, there are mainly three kinds of expats in Japan. There are those who are here for an experience, be it exploring a new culture and then returning home (or moving on to the next adventure), or delaying life in "the real world." These folks stay here for one or several years.

Japan is expensive compared to America, though there is variation by region. In particular, meat and produce are much more expensive here. It's not uncommon to see peaches for 400 or 500 yen apiece (roughly $5 or $6). I think my most "wtf" moment at a Japanese supermarket was seeing a single melon selling for 10,000 yen (about $120).

Clothes and brand names are also much more expensive in Japan, and Japanese tourists to America often go shopping and load up on clothes to bring back because of the price difference.

There are those who stay here because quite frankly they can just drift. It's possible to live here without really knowing the language. There are easy jobs to be found for those who speak English, and there are guys and girls who will go out with you (or more) just because you're foreign and exotic.

Then there are those in it for the long haul, who have fallen in love with Japan or with one of the natives and have decided to put down roots here. I think the tradeoffs in convenience balance out, especially over a long period of time. Most permanent or long-term foreign residents that I know don't really miss much, except maybe Mexican food.

My feeling is that people in Japan are perhaps not friendlier than your average American, but are more polite and willing to be helpful. That's a broad generalization, of course.

There are certain social norms that are pretty different from what you would expect in America. For example, while this may be changing with the younger generations, men and women generally don't mix as casually as they do in the States. While they often tend to be more open to the fact that the situation may differ with foreigners, it's my understanding that men and women usually don't socialize casually as friends, for example, unless at some work or organizational social function.

As far as making friends, I haven't known anyone who has had problems. Japanese are required to study English in school, but most people here rarely get to use their English. It's also a mostly homogeneous society. As a result, although there are a small number of Japanese who develop an aversion to English and are uncomfortable around foreigners, there are also many natives who are interested in trying to use English and in meeting people who are different from them.

Jonathan Lukacek
Osaka, Japan

I have a Japanese wife and have one child. The three of us live in a 64 sqm apartment near Umeda in Osaka. Together we often go shopping, relax in cafés, visit local sites, but we are always exploring. Occasionally we will take a weekend off and do nothing but hang around near our apartment but when we get long breaks we tend to travel by train to places we've never been. I really love the huge variety of locally made goods each place we visit has. Some places have specialties in eyeglasses, others in pottery, some in lacquer ware, and in textiles.

I have few expat friends. I speak Japanese fairly fluently, and encourage all other foreigners living in Japan to do so as well. The majority of my friends I see on a regular basis are Japanese. I think of life here optimistically and feel extremely comfortable here. I don't find discrimination a big problem here contrary to other people's perspectives.

Life is different here, and it consumes you if you aren't careful. The huge differences between West and East seem trivial at first but soon come to be a daunting obstacle in living the life you've grown accustomed to in your home country. You really have to adjust your lifestyle. Things that you once thought were cheap become expensive habits. People are definitely more curious and open than they seem once you learn more of the local language, which for me is one of the best ways to adjust to life in Japan.

Korea
(see South Korea)

32. Latvia

Climate: Maritime; wet, moderate winters
Government: Parliamentary Democracy
Population: 2,231,503
Currency: Latvian Lat (LVL): 1 LVL = 2.06 USD
Language: Latvian [official] (58.2%), Russian
   (37.5%), Lithuanian and other (4.3%)
Religious Groups: Lutheran (19.6%), Orthodox (15.3%), other Christian (1%),
   other (0.4%), unspecified (63.7%)
Ethnic Groups: Latvian (59.3%), Russian (27.8%), Belarusian (3.6%),
   Ukrainian (2.5%), Polish (2.4%), Lithuanian (1.3%), other (3.1%)
Cost of Living compared to the U.S.: Dirt cheap

Like its neighbor Estonia, little Latvia crashed and burned thanks to the benevolent gifts of neoliberal privatization schemes, but for expats looking for life on the cheap in Art Nouveau splendor, it shouldn't make too much difference.

Living There

Governance: Generally, Latvia functions as a liberal, Western-style democracy with free elections, independent media and respect for human rights. Some problems with corruption exist, particularly within the judiciary.

Infrastructure: Developing

Internet: Nearly 60% of Latvia's population enjoys Internet access. Broadband services account for the majority of Internet subscriptions. Hi-speed Internet widely available.

Healthcare: Medical care in Latvia is steadily improving but is far from state-of-the-art. There are a few private clinics with adequate medical supplies and services which are nearly equal to Western Europe or U.S. standards.

GPD: $32.2 billion

GDP (Per Capita): $14,300

Sovereign Debt: 46.2% of GDP

Working There: Teach English or get a company to sponsor you.

Regulatory Environment: Overall, relatively simple and efficient.

Taxes: Corporate: 15%, Individual: 26%, (15% if self-employed), VAT: 21% (certain goods and services at reduced rate of 10%). Residents taxed on worldwide income.

Cannabis: Illegal...and available

Homosexuality: Legal. No legal recognition of same-sex unions. Laws against discrimination. General cultural prejudices don't allow for much more than a nascent gay scene in the capital, Riga.

Abortion: No restriction as to reason. Parental authorization/notification required.

Women's Issues: Domestic violence a recurring problem. Gender equality is a matter of law, but women still face hiring and pay discrimination. Laws against rape but no explicit legislation addressing spousal rape—although offenders can be charged under provisions of existing laws.

Guns: 9mm or lower caliber firearms allowed. Licensing and registration required.

Crime: Relatively safe. Majority of crime is nonviolent. In tourist areas pickpocketing, purse-snatching, and muggings have been known to occur. Cases have been reported to the U.S. State Department of Americans being given drugged drinks in bars and then robbed.

Real Estate: There are no restrictions on foreigners owning real estate in Latvia. Mortgages are available to nonresidents. Sale price will usually include agent commissions which are seldom over 5%. Property taxes are 1.5% of the state-assigned value of the property (almost always lower than market value).

Life Expectancy: 72.15 years

Moving There

An easy go, particularly for the investor and not too difficult for those who have access to a modest monthly independent/freelance income.

Schengen Visa: Maximum 90-day stay for 180-day period. No extensions.

Temporary Residence Permit: Applicants must submit documents confirming adequate funds to live in Latvia (approx. $600/month), chest X-ray, and a document verifying place of residence and right to reside there (e.g. lease or rental agreement). If you plan on being self-employed, you will also need to submit: a) an audited business plan signed by sworn auditor; b) a bank statement showing you have adequate funds to carry out proposed enterprise; c) license or certificate (if required); and d) statement from State Revenue Service that you have registered as a taxpayer. If employed by a Latvian company you will need to submit a letter of invitation authorized by State Employment Service. Once you have received a residence permit, you are required to show proof of valid health insurance. Valid for one to five years depending on reason for stay.

Investor: New legislation allows foreigners who invest in Latvian real estate (approx. $200,000 for cities, $100,000 rural areas), banks or credit institutions (approx. $412,000), or business (approx. $100,000) to receive temporary residence permit valid for five years

Permanent Residence: Five years residency in Latvia required. Applicant must also provide certification of proficiency in Latvian language.

Work Visa/Permit: Applicant must submit employment contract with business registered in Latvia. Some professions, like certified teachers, IT professionals, and others do not need to apply for work permit.

Citizenship: Five years legal residence, sufficient funds/income, proficiency in Latvian language and knowledge of Latvian history, customs, national anthem, and constitution, clean criminal record. Applications are submitted to Naturalization Department.

33. Malta

Climate: Mediterranean; summers are dry and hot, spring and autumn are warm, winters are short and mild. Humidity is quite high, but rainfall is low, particularly outside of the rainy season (October to March).
Government: Republic
Population: 405,165
Currency: Euro (EUR): 1 EUR = 1.36 USD
Language: Maltese (official), English (official)
Religious Groups: Roman Catholic (98%)
Ethnic Groups: Maltese (descendants of ancient Carthaginians and Phoenicians, with strong elements of Italian and other Mediterranean stock).
Cost of Living compared to the U.S.: Reasonable

If you're looking for a Mediterranean island nation that hasn't mortgaged its soul to tourism, you could do a lot worse than Malta. Costs are more bearable than the typically precious Greek islands (but is more dusty and densely populated, as well), and anyone with a bit of money can easily while away the years here. Not a destination for the career-minded or job-hungry, though. And thanks to the rather resilient patriarchal Catholic streak, it's not exactly the ideal environment for women, gays, hedonists and libertines.

Living There
Governance: Malta operates as a Western-style democracy with free and fair elections, independent media and judiciary, freedom of expression, the right to organize etc.
Infrastructure: Developed
Internet: Hi-speed widely available
Healthcare: Quality of facilities and care is high. All legal residents are entitled to free healthcare. Even tourists receive free emergency care.
GDP: $11.76 billion
GDP (Per Capita): $28,900
Sovereign Debt: 69.1% of GDP
Working There: Non-E.U. citizens have few working opportunities.
Regulatory Environment: Straightforward and not difficult to negotiate
Taxes: Corporate: 35%, Individual: 0–35%, VAT: 18%. There is no property tax in Malta. Residents taxed on worldwide income but some exemptions are available.
Cannabis: Illegal but available. Not a big law enforcement priority.

Homosexuality: Legal. No recognition of same-sex unions. Laws against discrimination. Generally tolerant, though most gay activity is kept low-key in this predominantly Catholic country.

Abortion: Illegal under any circumstances

Women's Issues: Divorce is not part of the Maltese legal system. Women are very under-represented in business. Domestic violence continues to be a problem.

Guns: Shotguns and antique weapons allowed. Strict storage requirements.

Crime: Moderate. Compared to other European nations, Malta has a high number of robberies but otherwise, a very low number of violent crimes.

Real Estate: Americans were once allowed only to purchase property in government-designated expatriate communities. Today, Malta's ascension to E.U. member status has lifted most restrictions for foreigners seeking to buy residential property. There are some preconditions for acquiring a second property. Local banks do offer mortgages to non-Maltese citizens. Typical rate is 4.5% and term is up to 40 years.

Life Expectancy: 79.44 years

Moving There

Pretty much geared toward the retiree and sit-on-your money crowd. There's talk of a whole range of new immigration schemes targeting "high net-worth" individuals.

Schengen Visa: Maximum of 90-day stay every 180 days, no exceptions.

Temporary Residence: Permit requires evidence of an annual income of approximately $15,000 plus $2,500 for every dependent. One year, renewable.

Permanent Resident: Requires evidence of an annual income of approximately $25,000 or capital of at least $425,000. Permanent residents are required to buy at least $125,000 worth of property or pay at least $4,500 a year in documented rent.

Work Permit: Must have offer of employment.

Student Visas available per the usual rigmarole.

Citizenship: Five years legal residency and renounce U.S. citizenship. However, naturalization is as at the discretion of Minister for Justice and Home Affairs, and requests are often turned down. Favored treatment is given to those of Maltese descent, residents who have lived in Malta for 18 years or more, and individuals who were born in Malta.

34. Mexico

Climate: Cooler in the mountains, varies from tropical to desert
Government: Federal Republic
Population: 111,211,789
Currency: Mexican Peso (MXN):
   1 MXN = 0.08 USD
Language: Over 90% Spanish but a small minority still speak indigenous languages (Mayan, Nahuatl etc.)
Religious Groups: Roman Catholic (76.5%), Protestant (6.3%), Other (0.3%), unspecified (13.8%), none (3.1%)
Ethnic Groups: mestizo (Amerindian-Spanish) (60%), Amerindian or predominantly Amerindian (30%), white (9%), other 1%
Cost of Living compared to the U.S.: Cheap

South of the Border has been a destination for Americans fleeing the law, the rat race or winter gloom since the dawn of our republic. Our NAFTA partner offers business and residency requirements that are a simple matter for anyone of modest means. Houses can be found for as little as $30,000 (although in well-heeled expat communities, prices for deluxe residences can reach half a million dollars or more). Many expats used to purchase second homes here, usually on the Baja coast around Ensenada, but border violence has moved the action further south. Urban *sophisticados* make their home in Mexico City, while artists, wiccans and other bohemians flock to the Mexican Sedona, San Miguel de Allende. Altogether an estimated one million Americans living there, and the most popular locales such as Cancún and Los Cabos are still quite safe. Keeping your distance from the border is the general rule of thumb. Low-crime (and scenic) locales like Cozumel, Querétero, Campeche, and Puebla count among Mexico's safest areas.

Living There
Governance: Government can be changed democratically, though elections are often tainted by corruption. Many cases of media intimidation have been reported. In regions where drug-related violence is high, journalists have been threatened, beaten, and even killed by members of drug cartels who are so intertwined with government as to be nearly indistinguishable. Religious freedom by and large respected but religious groups must register with the government. Dissent is often stifled. Labor and peasant leaders have been murdered, particularly in the southern states. Judicial system is often corrupt. Despite a massive military crackdown in border areas, cartel-related violence has not only continued unabated but has actually intensified into periodic low-intensity warfare.

Infrastructure: Low telephone density, non-toll roads are often inadequate. A general sense of shoddiness prevails.

Internet: Hi-speed available in the cities and the more developed areas. Mexico Internet usage is the second-highest in South America with over 23 million users (Brazil is first).

Healthcare: Healthcare in Mexico is inexpensive (as much as 70% lower) and private insurance is unheard of, and bargain-seeking Americans often make trips here solely for medical or dental procedures. You can expect to pay anywhere from $3 to $5 for a quick consultation, to $10–$25 for a more extensive evaluation. This pertains to private doctors as well as a visit to a hospital for a routine or even some emergency visits. The level of care, especially in remote areas, is uneven and may be well below what Americans are used to. Mexico allows anyone regardless of their immigrant status to enroll in the national healthcare program (IMSS). Cost: $100–$300 per year.

GDP: $1.56 trillion

GDP (Per Capita): $13,800

Sovereign Debt: 41.5% of GDP

Working There: Teach English, work at resorts, not much else, aside from American corporations.

Regulatory Environment: Recent reforms have made it easier to launch new businesses (just over two weeks) but efficiency will often vary from state to state, as will the extent of corruption.

Taxes: Individual: 0–30%, Corporate: 30%, VAT: 16%. Non-residents—both individuals and corporations—are taxed on their Mexican income only. Residents taxed on income earned abroad.

Cannabis: Adults can possess small amounts of marijuana without fear of arrest. You're apt to smell it in areas where young people gather.

Homosexuality: Legal. Federal constitution was amended in 2001 to prohibit discrimination based on sexual orientation. Legislation permitting same-sex marriage in Mexico City ruled constitutional by Mexico's highest court. Large gay communities in Mexico City, Guadalajara, Tijuana, Cancún, and Puerto Vallarta. In recent years Mexican society has been showing new signs of tolerance toward homosexuals, however in many places cultural taboos remain.

Abortion: Prohibited except to save a woman's life or in case of rape

Women's Issues: Women underrepresented in government and professional positions. Domestic violence and sexual harassment an ongoing problem.

Guns: Certain classes of firearms can be owned for hunting or self-defense with approval from the military. Background check required.

Crime: The border areas are devolving into no-go areas. Armed street crime a problem in all major cities. Kidnapping also occurs. Elsewhere, crime is more of the petty nuisance variety. Cops and criminals are often indistinguishable.

Real Estate: Foreigners cannot buy property within 30 miles of the coastline or within 60 miles of any Mexican border. There are numerous ways around this and much of Mexico's coastal land does in fact belong to foreigners. Otherwise, Americans can buy most other property without restriction. No title insurance in Mexico. Real estate agents are not licensed or regulated by the government. Transaction fees vary by state but are usually between 1–2% of purchase price. The average home price is just over $140,000. Significantly cheaper homes can be found outside the resort areas and expat enclaves. In the more upscale districts homes begin at $250,000 or so and run all the way into seven figures.

Life Expectancy: 76.26 years

Moving There

There are all sorts of ways to legally reside in Mexico. The Mexican economy is still propped up by dollars flowing down from *El Norte*, and as long as you can be counted upon to bring a few with you and spend them here, you shouldn't encounter too much resistance.

Tourist Visa/FMM: Tourists who intend to travel farther than the "free zone" of more than 20 miles from the U.S. border need to get a tourist visa (FMT). Visa is generally valid for 180 days.

Non-Immigrant Visa/FM3: An FM3 is a one-year permit to reside in Mexico and comes in a variety of categories: business, student, retiree, technician, journalism, etc. This document makes the holder a No Inmigrante (Non-Immigrant) like the tourist visa but, unlike the tourist visa, you are allowed to live in the country for an extended period of time. The document must be renewed each year as long as you continue to reside in Mexico. After your fifth year you can either upgrade to an FM2 or simply request a new FM3. Applicant must prove monthly income of approximately $1,000/per month, plus half this amount per month for each family member 15 years of age or older; or have your Mexican employer present a letter to immigration authorities requesting a specialized service and the job duties to be performed; or a letter from an American company, along with proof the company exists, stating the specific responsibilities/purpose to be conducted while in Mexico and length of stay. For a couple of thousand dollars, expats can create a Mexican company and hire themselves without having to actually engage in much business and receive their visa that way. Years of residency on an FM3 visa do not accrue toward permanent residency or citizenship.

    Visitor: is the foreigner that enters Mexico for a specific profitable or non profitable activity and is granted for up to one year.

    Religious (for ministers and such): one year, renewable.

    Student: valid while the student is studying.

    Distinguished Visitor: a scientist or humanist of international prestige. This is probably not you. Six months, renewable.

    Journalist: Can be issued upon proper documentation but freelancers are probably better off.

Immigrant Visa/FM2: An FM2 is a one-year permit to reside in Mexico as an immigrant. The document must be renewed each year as long as you continue to reside in Mexico. The main distinction between FM2 and FM3 is with the FM2, you can apply to become a permanent resident or citizen after five years. Relevant categories include:

Independent Income: Can include interest from capital investment of capital in approved certificates, stocks, and bonds or from any permanent income derived outside the country (e.g., pension and Social Security). The minimum amount required is presently 400 times the daily minimum wage in Mexico City, plus half that per dependent. Figures fluctuate but figure on a little over $1000 USD per month, plus 50% per dependent.

Investors: For foreigners who make approved investments that are deemed to contribute to the economic and social development of the country to the tune of around $200,000 USD (or 40,000 times the daily minimum wage in Mexico City).

Professional: Must present valid professional credentials.

Positions of Confidence: This refers to foreigners who are asked to come and manage a company or other organization.

Scientist: For scientists engaged in research or other academic work.

Technician: Skilled technical workers coming to Mexico to perform specific work or research.

Family Members: For reuniting and being economically dependent on a family member or spouse.

Artists and Athletes: Just like it says.

Assimilated Persons: Those with spouses, children or other connections in Mexico

Permanent Resident/*Immigrado*: After five years legal residency on FM2, you are eligible to apply for permanent residency.

Citizenship: Anyone who has held an FM2 for five years can apply with the *Secretaria de Relaciones Exteriores* for citizenship. If you are under 60, be prepared to pass examinations in Mexican history and Spanish. If you are 60 or older, the only requirement is that you be able to speak Spanish. You can also apply for citizenship if you marry a Mexican national. If you are the father or mother of a child born in Mexico, are the descendent of a Mexican national, or if your accomplishments in science, technology, the arts, or sports have contributed greatly to Mexico, your residency requirements will be much reduced (around two years).

Cara Smiley

Oaxaca, Mexico

In December 2001, I decided to live permanently in Mexico. Even though it shares a several-thousand-mile border with the U.S. and is one of its principal trading partners, Mexico maintains an amazing sense of national and regional pride. Mexicans preserve and prefer local foods, music, language and culture over those across the border. This is impressive given the enormous economic pressures imposed on Mexico by the U.S.

For the first few years, I lived in Mexico City. You can find decent Japanese, Uruguayan, Italian, Chinese and Middle Eastern restaurants in Mexico City, but I can't find Thai or Indian food, two cuisines that I really love from back in the States. And world music—forget about it. I've seen more international music visiting Vermont than I've seen in four years in Mexico City.

In December 2006, my fiancé and I moved to Oaxaca City, Oaxaca. Although the principal reason that I moved to Oaxaca is because my husband is from here originally, there are several things that I have come to love about it:

1) An AMAZING Englishilanguage library that is run by an established group of (mostly) American retirees and which has over 30,000 books in English. The yearly membership is reasonable ($50.00 USD for a family) and they are always getting new books.

2) A large selection of restaurants with high quality and diverse menus and decent wine selections. At the luxury end (really creative ingredients, preparations, presentations, etc.), Eugenio and I spend around $120.00 USD for two appetizers, two entrees, two deserts, one bottle of wine, coffee, etc.

3) A local store that focuses on selling locally made/grown fruits, vegetables, foods, health and beauty products, etc.

4) The city is large enough that there is diversity in entertainment, shopping, etc. but small enough that it is easy to get from one place to another.

There is a large population of foreigners in Oaxaca City. Many of the foreigners are retirees who live either full-time or part-time here. Another large group works with the many NGOs established here. Because I am content working in my gardens and hanging out with my husband and dogs, I do not socialize much. Our best friends in Oaxaca are Mexicans.

While I love cooking, gardening, etc., I do not like housework. One of the wonderful things about living in Mexico is that it is affordable to hire a housecleaner. Our housecleaner, Vicki, is a single mother with three daughters who has worked with us for four years. Although most people in Oaxaca pay housecleaners $100.00 USD per week, we pay Vicki $160.00 per week. In addition, we give her fresh vegetables and herbs from the garden and we pay her and her children's dental care. Our relationship has improved both her and our quality of life.

Good quality clothes and laptops, printers and telephones are often more expensive in Mexico than in the U.S. I have purchased laptops and printers in the U.S., but regretted the purchase because American warranties aren't covered in Mexico. Health insurance, car insurance, house cleaning, car repair, physicians and food are less expensive in Mexico than in the U.S.

I continue to miss good infrastructure (roads, garbage, schools, telephones, government office efficiency, etc.). In general, Mexican government offices are understaffed and underequipped and are not as efficient as their counterparts in the USA. It took nine months just to get the title to my property.

Name Withheld by Request
San Miguel de Allende, Mexico

San Miguel was mentioned so many times by so many people I knew. I did a lot of searching and I found many helpful websites with message boards and made friends that I could talk to about details, who were extremely helpful. I could not have done this without them.

San Miguel is in the high central desert, nearly no humidity and is not too hot and not too cold. Another big reason was that it is an "artist's town." Very creative here, also a lot of writers and artisans of all kinds. It is also very up to date as far as high-speed Internet, has a Mac user group, and 15,000 Americans and Canadians. It is known as the "Beverly Hills" of Mexico.

My rent is $800, which includes utilities except for my own Internet line, which I wanted, otherwise it would have been included. I spoiled myself while working full-time in Chicago with a cleaning girl...cost $100 for four hours. Here, I have a maid once a week for four hours, included in the rent, which is standard in Mexico. She does my laundry as well and will do errands if asked.

Each day the weather is gorgeous, and I feel free to go out to a restaurant without worrying about every cent I spend. Local farmers come into town and sell fruit and vegetables at a fraction of what you'd pay in the U.S. I bought a huge bag of raspberries, and a huge bag of blackberries on the corner the other day, total cost 90 pesos... which is about 80 cents.

The restaurants here are wonderful, and since there are so many expats, decent restaurants are no problem as far as ice cubes, washing their vegetables correctly (they use a product called Microdyn)...I can go out to dinner and have filet mignon for about $15 USD, including a glass of wine. Beer is about $2.50. There are also many good less expensive places to eat, I have my list of favorites and it keeps growing.

It seems far easier to make friends here, but that may be because gringos recognize each other and want to know each others' "stories." About crime, it exists, but San Miguel is not a border town, so there is no drug-related crime that I know of. I feel very safe here as a single woman. If I'm coming home late at night from somewhere, I will most likely take a taxi though, as I would ANYWHERE, since they are only $2.50 USD.

314

James Young
Mexico City, Mexico

Since 2003, I've been renting a two-bedroom, two-bathroom, corner apartment in the stretch of centro between trendy Roma and the resplendent, but traffic-challenged, Historic Center. It has what my NYC friend described as "Juliet balconies" and overlooks a shady little park a quiet block from the Metrobus and Metro transit systems.

I only pay 3850 pesos (about US$330) a month in rent because I moved here when downtown was still considered the ghetto. (Don't get me wrong. Tepito is rough. Merced is crazy rougher, but they are on the other side of a very large neighborhood.) Nowadays, a place like mine might catch almost twice that rent.

All bills (Internet, electricity, gas AND rent) run to about $650 ($60), which I split with a roommate. That includes once-a-week housecleaning—I try to pay about U.S. minimum wage for that. In addition, I have a wash-and-fold laundry a block away that I pay about $1.60/kg. I live a block away from one of the city's finest fresh markets, and while nightlife and restaurants are still limited nearby, cabs are cheap. Not that I worry too much about that. My favorite place to down mezcal is only five blocks away, but like most of the places you fall in love with in this town, it's best discovered on your own.

Before that, I lived in the Zocalo. It was amazing and the landlords weren't overly concerned with paperwork, but as is often the case in that situation, they were jerks who'd barely lift a finger when anything went wrong with the place.

Probably the most important thing to know about renting your own place here is that you are most likely going to need what's known as a *fiador*, basically someone who co-signs your lease. They often have to own property in Mexico City and need to prove that they are up-to-date on paying their taxes.

But finding a fiador is probably the most harrowing aspect of moving here. The first time I needed one, my Mexican roommate convinced her dad to do it, but when she moved out, he went with her. I soon discovered that many parents will refuse even to do it for their own children.

The fiador agreement is basically some sort of demonic contract that will insure a hell on earth for any fiador, if and when the tenant can't pay the rent. In theory, the lessor can sell the fiador's property to pay for the debt if necessary. Keep in mind that with the agency I use (Lomelin—one of the most common ones here), they already ask you to put down at least a month of rent as deposit, sometimes two months or three, if they are really worried. They require you to pay for a private investigation service to confirm the details you submit on the contract. They also hate freelancers as a general rule.

I advise moving into a friend's place until you can line up your own fiador and get your bank records nice and pretty.

All this said, every year when I walk out of my meeting to turn in the new contract with the signatures of my fiador and myself on it, it is one of the best feelings in the world—a true sense of accomplishment. That can be said for the light contract, the phone contract, getting your work visa, your tax ID (oh, and your official receipts for work done). Each step of becoming official introduces its own unique set of pitfalls and challenges. Fortunately, as you begin to knock them off one by one, they all become a lot easier.

Plenty of expats come to Mexico City for a month or two, absolutely love the place, maybe even finagle a room here, but don't make it more than six months or a year. It is not easy to manage the countless little bureaucratic nightmares. You have to have boundless patience and, most importantly, be able to revel in the total absurdity of it all.

That said, things are way simpler for seniors drawing Social Security checks. Mexico makes it pretty easy to retire here. This is why you see all these little expat enclaves around the country—Lake Chapala, San Miguel de Allende, Puerto Escondido, etc. But Mexico City is a hard place, often too much for retirees just looking for a slice of peace and paradise.

I think that expats here must have something in common with people who move to New Orleans. You have to really love the magic of this city's chaos to set down roots. And this is just the starting point before you get to the business of finding a long-term place to live, a job, etc. More than anything, I think you have to find good friends here, who'll help you along the process, both practically and morally, and of course, that means you need to be a pretty damn good friend yourself.

I've seen jerks come and go, and money will only get you so far.

35. Morocco

Climate: Mediterranean, becoming more
    desert-like in the interior
Government: Constitutional Monarchy
Population: 31,285,174
Currency: Moroccan dirham (MAD):
    MAD = 0.12 USD
Language: Arabic (official), Berber dialects,
    French widely spoken and is language of business, government, and
    diplomacy
Religious Groups: Muslim (98.7%), Christian (1.1%), Jewish (0.2%)
Ethnic Groups: Arab-Berber (99.1%), other (0.7%), Jewish (0.2%)
Cost of Living compared to the U.S.: Very cheap

From Paul Bowles, William Burroughs, and company in Tangier to the hippies of Marrakech, Morocco has long beckoned American expats seeking an exotic destination. A stable monarchy that has so far managed to escape much of the political and religious turmoil of its neighbors, it once again beckons—this time to home buyers and surf (and more recently skater and BMX) bums, where the attraction of cheap living in sumptuous exotic surroundings is too compelling to resist. Moroccan people are friendly and hospitable—although the merchants in tourist areas sometimes get a bit aggressive, particularly with foreigners. The government is taking measures to curb this, with questionable success.

Living There

Governance: Moroccans don't have much opportunity to democratically get rid of a government they no longer like, since the monarch retains the ultimate power. Press freedom is limited; journalists can be jailed for treading too hard on certain touchy subjects, such as the royal family, Western Sahara, or Islam. Opposition parties are weak. Freedom of association is limited. Corruption is endemic, particularly in the judiciary.

Infrastructure: Modern freeways link the cities of Tangier, Rabat, Fez and Casablanca. Two-lane highways link other major cities. The train system has a good safety record. Secondary routes in rural areas are often narrow and poorly paved.

Internet: Morocco enjoys the third-highest number of Internet users in all of Africa; approximately one in three citizens are subscribers. Possibly Africa's most advanced broadband network.

Healthcare: Medical facilities are adequate for non-emergency matters, particularly in the urban areas, but most medical staff will have limited or no English skills. Most ordinary prescription and over-the-counter medicines are widely available.

However, specialized prescriptions may be difficult to fill and availability of all medicines in rural areas is unreliable. Emergency and specialized care outside the major cities is far below U.S. standards, and depending on where you are, may not be available at all.

GDP: $153.8 billion

GDP (Per Capita): $4,800 per capita

Sovereign Debt: 58.2% of GDP

Working There: Seasonal employment can be found in tourist areas although knowledge of French is usually required. English teaching is also possible.

Regulatory Environment: Efforts have been made to streamline the process of launching a new business but there are still some bureaucratic hassles.

Taxes: Corporate: 30%, Individual: 0–38%, VAT: 20%. Residents taxed on worldwide income.

Cannabis: Cannabis (hashish, really) may seem legal—many locals smoke it—but it isn't. Use caution.

Homosexuality: Technically illegal, with a maximum punishment of three years imprisonment, but the law is seldom enforced, and homosexual activity is fairly common. Same-sex unions are not recognized. No laws against discrimination. Discussion or overt displays are considered taboo.

Abortion: Allowed to save the woman's life and to preserve health. Spousal authorization required.

Women's Issues: Gender equality is the law but women still have fewer rights when it comes to marriage and divorce. Domestic violence is widespread, though new legal measures are attempting to address it, and polygamy is still practiced. Harassment of women, particularly Westerners, is hardly unknown.

Guns: Shotguns are the only firearms that can be legally owned. License and registration required.

Crime: Crimes tend to be property-related and are a serious problem in the major cities and tourist areas. Pickpocketing, purse-snatching and theft from vehicles are common.

Real Estate: Foreigners are allowed to purchase real estate. Mortgages available with one-third down payment. Expect to pay a total of 6% in notary fees, registration fees, stamp fees, and various other expenses. Profit on real estate sales is subject to a 20% tax.

Life Expectancy: 75.47 years

Moving There

There are no hard and fast requirements for an extended stay in Morocco. Simply ask nicely, present the required documents and don't make trouble.

Tourist Visa: U.S. citizens do not need a visa to stay in Morocco for up to 90 days but you may be asked to show that you have adequate funds during your stay.

Temporary Residency: To stay longer than 90 days, you must declare your intention to become a resident within 15 days of your arrival and apply for an alien registration card (*Carte d'immatriculation/Carte de Sejour*) at the Foreigner's

Office (*Service des Etrangers*) in the police station or Gendarmerie Royale where you plan to reside. The alien registration card is issued by the National Police (*Sûreté Nationale*) in Rabat and is valid for 10 years.

Residence Permit: If you are planning on a long-term stay in Morocco, you should apply for a residence permit. Applicants must provide evidence of adequate income (pension, annuity, social security, trust fund, bank statements, etc.). If you plan on working in Morocco, a contract signed by your employer and approved by the Ministry of Labor in Rabat is required. If you are self-employed or a professional, you must obtain and submit a work authorization from the Secretary General of the Government of Morocco. Permit is valid for ten years.

Student Visas available per the usual requirements.

36. The Netherlands (Holland)

Climate: Temperate; marine; cool summers and mild winters
Government: Parliamentary Democracy under a Constitutional Monarch
Population: 16,715,999
Currency: Euro (EUR): 1 EUR = 1.36 USD
Language: Dutch
Religious Groups: Roman Catholic (30%), Dutch Reformed (11%), Calvinist (6%), other Protestant (3%), Muslim (5.8%), other (2.2%), none (42%)
Ethnic Groups: Dutch (80.7%), E.U. (5%), Indonesian (2.4%), Turkish (2.2%), Surinamese (2%), Moroccan (2%), Netherlands Antilles and Aruba (0.8%), other (4.8%)
Cost of Living compared to the U.S.: Steep

In the popular imagination, Holland remains the undisputed liberal wet dream government and the ultimate nanny state. Free healthcare, over-the-counter cannabis, gay marriage, a sanctioned red-light district and every eco-friendly ordinance you can think of. On the other hand, government measures are driving the coffeeshops out of business and rent per square foot in Amsterdam is as expensive as anywhere you'll find in Europe. If you have some kind of independent hustle going, and don't need a work permit, the authorities don't make it too hard for you to stay. And if somehow you've managed to plant your feet here for a few years, the social entitlements can begin to accrue.

Living There

Governance: Free and fair elections (foreigners who reside in the country for at least five years can vote in local elections). The Netherlands has an independent judiciary, a thriving free press, and the government respects basic political and civil liberties. Transparency International, a non-profit that monitors corruption, considers the Netherlands one of the least corrupt countries in the world.

Infrastructure: Developed

Internet: Nearly nine in 10 Dutch residents have Internet access and for broadband penetration, the Netherlands is one of the leading countries in the world.

Healthcare: Dutch healthcare is generally good with all modern medical options available.

GDP: $680.4 billion

GDP (Per Capita): $40,500

Sovereign Debt: 64.6% of GDP

Working There: Some opportunities in factory production lines, casual harvesting between April and October, camping, au pairs.

Regulatory Environment: Overall, the Dutch regulatory system is transparent and compliance is easier than in many other European nations.

Taxes: Corporate: 20%–25%, Individual: 0–52%, VAT: 19% (6% for basic foods and selected items). Residents taxed on worldwide income.

Cannabis: The law does specify possession as an offense, but is not enforced, and criminal action is never pursued in cases of personal use of soft drugs. Pot, hash and other mental treats are still sold over-the-counter, though the famed coffeeshops are not as ubiquitous as they once were and even tighter restrictions have been proposed.

Homosexuality: Legal gay marriage and civil unions, laws against discrimination.

Abortion: Legal

Women's Issues: Very few problems for women in Holland

Guns: Only firearms for sporting purposes are legal to purchase. License and registration required. Owner must belong to legally sanctioned shooting or hunting club.

Crime: Petty theft common, however, violent crime extremely rare.

Real Estate: Foreigners can buy property in the Netherlands. Mortgages are generally available with approximately 15%–20% down payment. Interest payments on mortgages are tax deductible if the property is used as the primary residence. Legal transfer costs should amount to a tax of 6% of the property's market value or purchase price. Annual property tax varies by region and individuals pay no capital gains tax on real estate transactions.

Life Expectancy: 79.40 years

Moving There

If you're not a student or marrying Dutch (same sex or opposite), you need to start your own business. It's easy for Americans thanks to DAFT, the Dutch-American Friendship Treaty. To get the whole range of options, Dutch immigration authorities have set up a special English-language web page that even has a "visa wizard" that shows you what kind of residency permit you need and what the requirements are.

Schengen Visa: Maximum 90-day stay for 180-day period, no extensions.

Residence Permit: Applicants must possess adequate funds to live in the Netherlands, proof of health insurance, and stated purpose for stay must meet government requirements (study, work, self-employment, etc.) In some instances, a Dutch sponsor may be required. Newly arriving immigrants are advised to apply for residence within three days of entering the Netherlands. The initial residence permit is valid for one year, renewable and you can apply for permanent resident status after five years.

Self-Employment Visa: You must have health insurance with overseas coverage, possess sufficient funds to stay in the country, meet specific requirements for practicing a given profession, and the prospective business or self-employment work must serve a "Dutch economic purpose." The latter requirement is based on a three-part scoring system. You are awarded points for personal experience (education, work and freelance experience); business planning (financing, market analysis, organization etc.); and material economic purpose (job creation, investments, innovation etc.). Americans, by a special treaty, can obtain this visa with a minimum business investment of around €4500 (around $6500) for sole proprietors and around €11,200 ($16,000) for incorporated businesses.

Work Permit: A Dutch employer must apply for a work permit on your behalf should you wish to work in the Netherlands, and must apply at least six weeks before you begin employment. Your employer will not be given the work permit unless there is no one in the Netherlands or the European Union (excluding Bulgaria and Romania) who is available to fill the position. Valid for one year. When this period is up, the permit can be renewed for a period of three and a half years.

Permanent Resident: Foreigners can apply for permanent residency after five years of legal residency in Holland.

Citizenship: At least five years legal residency, proficiency in Dutch language (read, write, and speak). Applicants can either take written test or complete integration courses. No record of arrest or fine in previous four years.

Walter N.

Amsterdam, Holland

The quality of life in the Netherlands is much higher than anything in the United States. Cities are well managed and beautiful, the green belts around cities haven't been swallowed by uncontrollable suburban sprawl, and the public infrastructure is excellent. We are always reminded of how nice things are here when we visit my fair city of Los Angeles. The most important thing about life here is that it can be almost completely car-less. Almost all your transit needs can be handled by the bike, tram, or train. Also, if you need a car, there is a car-sharing program called Green Wheels, which is great and easy. For me, this is the single best thing about living in this country. There is more government intrusion but that is a small price to pay for the benefits.

The coffeeshop scene is most concentrated in central Amsterdam but you can find them in most neighborhoods throughout the city and most cities in the country. The wares offered in these places are excellent, varied, and well-priced. You can either smoke on location or take it to go.

Michael Luksetich
Amsterdam, Holland

Costs of living here may vary from what you are used to at home (wherever that may be). I can make some comparisons to New York as a general guide. Rents are far cheaper: a one-bedroom within the canal belt will cost between 900 and 1300 euros a month. If you're willing to bike another 10–15 minutes that same rent will get you a two-bedroom and so on. Eating out can be a bit more expensive but shopping and then cooking at home is less expensive. Health insurance costs are shared by the employer and employee. The employee pays (depending on the coverage they want) between 80 and 150 euros a month. This gets you full coverage, dental as well. And mass transportation costs for trams and buses around towns like Amsterdam, while being more expensive then New York (which is dirt cheap compared to pretty much everywhere else) can be easily avoided by riding a bike to and from work. After all, Amsterdam is a town of a little less than 800,000 people but more than 1,000,000 bikes so it is the only way to go for getting around the town or the country.

37. New Zealand

Climate: Temperate to subtropical
Government: Parliamentary
Population: 4,252,277
Currency: New Zealand Dollar (NZD):
   1 NZD = 0.84 USD
Language: English, Maori
Religious Groups: Anglican (13.8%), other Christian
   (13.8%), Catholic (12.6%), Presbyterian,
   Congregational, and Reformed (10%), Methodist
   (3%), Pentecostal (2%), Baptist (1.4%), Maori
   Christian (1.6%), Hindu (1.6%), Buddhist (1.3%),
   other religions (2.2%), none (32.2%), other or
   unidentified (9.9%)
Ethnic Groups: European (56.8%), Asian (8%), Maori (7.4%), Pacific Islander
   (4.6%), mixed (9.7%), other (13.5%)
Cost of Living compared to the U.S: Similar

Socially progressive, non-belligerent, the pair of islands that make up New Zealand boasts pristine beaches for surfing and snorkeling, snow-capped mountains and volcanoes, and acres of forests, vineyards and sheep. Best of all, with a population of a mere four million or so, the land of the kiwi looks kindly upon the immigrant. Not satisfied with the American immigration surge that occurred after *Lord of the Rings* advertised its spectacular beauty to the world, the country has launched its own marketing campaign to attract middle-class Americans looking for the stable comfortable life they can no longer find at home. They'll be happy to send you slick brochure packages touting the advantages and the how-to's of every possible avenue of immigration.

Living There

Governance: Free and fair elections, an outspoken free press, and an independent judiciary. The Kiwis reportedly run one of the least corrupt governments in the world. Human and political rights are respected.
Infrastructure: Developed
Internet: Individuals and companies wanting Internet access services have a range of options available from free dial-up to fee-based ISDN, cable and DSL broadband. Satellite provides an option in remote or rural areas.
Healthcare: Government-funded. Excellent. One of the best places in the world to get sick.
GDP: $119.2 billion
GDP (Per Capita): $28,000
Sovereign Debt: 25.5% of GDP

Working There: Opportunities in harvesting fruit, tourism sites like hotels, hostels, parks, bars, restaurants, ski resorts, au pairs, teaching, farming, construction and road work, architecture.

Regulatory Environment: One of the world's top locations for entrepreneurs. You can start up a company in just one day, costs are minimal, there is little red tape, and corruption is practically non-existent.

Taxes: Corporate: 30%, Individual: 12.5–39%, GST: 15%. Residents taxed on worldwide income.

Cannabis: Illegal, widely used. Short jail sentence for possession possible, but fines more likely, not just for marijuana or hashish but for a variety of other party drugs as well.

Homosexuality: Legal. Recognition of same-sex unions. Laws against discrimination.

Abortion: Legal in cases of incest and fetal impairment. Also allowed to save the woman's life, or to preserve mental or physical health.

Women's Issues: Laws prohibiting domestic violence, sexual harassment, and workplace sexual discrimination. Although equality of pay is a matter of law, women still earn slightly less than men.

Guns: Requires license from police.

Crime: Rare

Real Estate: Some government restrictions on purchases by non-residents, although these mainly have to do with large investments such as one that would result in 25 percent control or more of a business or property valued at more than $33 million or certain land deemed "sensitive" according to New Zealand's overseas investment legislation. Examples include land that exceeds 0.4 hectares that adjoins certain kinds of reserve or preservation areas, or property that exceeds 0.2 hectares that adjoins the foreshore. Consult New Zealand's Office of Overseas Investment for further information: **www.linz.govt.nz/overseas-investment**

Life Expectancy: 80.48 years

Moving There

The New Zealand Immigration website (**www.immigration.govt.nz**) can guide you through the myriad visa/residency/immigration schemes. Long and even permanent stays are within the reach of Americans of basic means, skills and education.

Tourist Visa/Visitor Visa: New Zealand considers the U.S. a "visa-waiver" country so American citizens can visit New Zealand for up to 90 days without a visa. Visitors must show proof of a return air ticket or valid ticket to another destination, and proof of sufficient funds (approximately $800 per month of stay). If you plan on staying longer, you can apply for a visitor visa which has the same requirements but visitors can stay in New Zealand for a maximum of nine months.

Temporary Retirement Visa: New Zealand offers a two-year visitor visa to retirees interested in investing in New Zealand. Applicants must be at least 66 years of age, in good health, and willing to invest approximately $630,000 in the NZ economy for a minimum of two years. To qualify you must also show proof of insurance, an annual income of $51,000 and at least $425,000 in "maintenance funds." So long as retirees meet the requirements, they are eligible to reapply for the visa after two years.

Working Holiday Visa: Applicants between the ages of 18–30 interested in working in agriculture, horticulture or viticulture (grape growing) can apply for a temporary three-month work visa. If you can show proof that you have worked at least three months in the horticulture or viticulture industries, you can apply for an additional three-month stay. Applicants must show proof of sufficient funds (approximately $3,500), health insurance, and a return ticket.

Business Visa: If you would like to own and operate your own business in New Zealand, the country offers a long-term business visa to qualified entrepreneurs. Applicants must submit a detailed plan to New Zealand's Business Migration Branch outlining previous business experience and how the prospective company will benefit New Zealand. Along with health, character, and English proficiency requirements, sufficient funds to live in the country and maintain business operations are also required. If approved, you will be granted a nine-month work permit that allows you time to get your business started. If you can provide evidence that your business plan has made significant progress, you will be given a permit to stay in the country for up to three years with the possibility of renewal and establishing permanent residency under the Entrepreneur program.

Entrepreneur Visa: New Zealand offers two schemes for individuals seeking to purchase or start up a business: Entrepreneur and Entrepreneur Plus. Those who already hold a long-term business visa and have successfully established a business that is considered beneficial to New Zealand can apply for residency under the Entrepreneur program. The Entrepreneur Plus scheme requires a minimum investment of at least $425,000 in a new or existing business that will create at least three full-time jobs. So long as basic criteria are met, applicants enjoy permanent residency status in New Zealand.

Work to Residence Visa: New Zealand offers a special visa program that allows you to parlay employment into residency and the possibility of a permanent stay. Applicants must be in good health and under 53 years of age, and certified if your profession requires registration in New Zealand. To qualify for the program you must possess a job offer from a New Zealand firm and your occupation needs to be listed on New Zealand's Long-Term Skills Shortage List (LTSSL). If you don't have a work offer but practice a profession or possess a skill that is on the LTSSL, you can still apply for the Work to Residence program. If you qualify you will be given a work permit/visa for up to 30 months. Visa holders can apply for permanent residency if they can show proof that they have been employed for two or more years.

Skilled Migrant: New Zealand offers immediate residency to skilled migrants. Applicants must be 55 years of age or under, in good health, of good character, and proficient in English. The process begins when you submit an Expression of Interest (EOI) to New Zealand immigration authorities outlining your background and claiming points based on employment history, professional qualifications, education etc. If you can claim 100 or more points, your EOI will go into a pool. Every two weeks, all EOIs above 140 points are selected and applicants are given an Invitation to Apply (ITA) for the program. If no one has scored above 140, other criteria like an existing employment background in a skilled trade needed in New Zealand will decide who is selected. If chosen, you will need to submit your application along with all the relevant documents pertaining to your employment background and other information provided in your EOI which will then be checked and verified. If you meet the relevant criteria and the government of New Zealand believes you will settle successfully, you will be offered a residence permit. If there is concern about your ability to successfully settle in the country, you may be given a work to residence visa or job search visa and if you secure employment within nine months you will be given permanent residence.

- **Permanent Residence:** Applicant must be a legal resident of New Zealand for at least two continuous years and meet all necessary requirements for current residence visa, e.g. maintain minimum investment, full-time employment, operate an existing business, etc.
- **Citizenship:** Applicant must reside in New Zealand as permanent resident for at least five years, speak and understand English, be of good character, understand the responsibilities and privileges of citizenship, and must express intent to continue to live in New Zealand.

Macaela

Wellington, New Zealand

I work in a retail clothing store. I get paid $12 an hour, work 9 to 6 selling clothes at a big NZ chain (think Gap), about 42 hours a week. I sort of had to swallow my pride when I took the job, but it pays the bills and I didn't come here originally to start a career—I came here to explore. I don't regret a thing. And when I get my two-year visa and start looking more closely into residency, then I'll worry about getting a job more suited to my education and skills.

In the States, the pay is often based on location. Here, the rates are basically the same throughout the country, but living in one of the country's biggest cities, I get paid the same as I would in the country and the cost of living is dramatically higher.

Things here are a lot more liberal, it's a huge refresher. People seem to just accept people as they are and get on with their lives. That said though, people do have a certain stigma toward Americans.

I would say people here are a lot less cliquish. People go out for a beer by themselves or with a few others and within a few moments will be chatting with the people at the next table. I would bring it down to people have less of that "don't talk to strangers" attitude. People are concerned with safety, but some of my best friends I've met here have just been from starting a conversation when I have been out in town. People are eager to talk to someone they don't know, share a coffee or a drink if they have anything in common, and it isn't about being attracted to them (not always, anyway).

I certainly hear of crime here, but on the whole I feel a lot safer than I did when I was living in Boston. In Wellington, there is a team called "Walk-Wise," hired by the town to be all around on any given night. They walked my friend home late one night without her even having to ask.

America definitely relies more heavily on the Internet, and I do miss having a need for something, ordering it online, and having it arrive in the mail two days later. The Internet is also more expensive and less accessible, and wireless is still relatively unheard of. Also, because so much has to be imported here, it takes longer to get what you need, and you often have to pay more for it. The upside of this, however, is that you find a lot less catalog and online shopping, which makes it possible for many little shops and boutiques to support themselves.

Noemi S.
Auckland, NZ

Some days living in NZ is great and other days I miss the States a lot. But all in all, it's a great, clean, safe, gorgeous country to live in and experience. One thing I don't like is the lack of variety in the stores. In NZ there are really only two clothing stores that have anything fashionable to choose from that's affordable. Chocolate here is wonderful, as is most anything dairy-related. Things are definitely more expensive here in NZ but the quality of life is better.

I find that since NZ is so far away, there are way fewer things to be tempted to buy and acquire here so even though I make less here than in the States, pay more for living expenses, I manage to save much more. I eat seasonally, buy sale items only or simply go without. I look forward to owning property here as there are no capital gains taxes!

38. Nicaragua

Climate: Tropical in lowlands; cooler in
   highlands
Government: Republic
Population: 5,995,928
Currency: Gold Cordoba (NIO):
   1 NIO = 0.04 USD
Language: Spanish (official), English and
   indigenous languages on Caribbean coast
Religious Groups: Roman Catholic (85%), other (15%)
Ethnic Groups: mestizo (69%), white (17%), black (9%), Amerindian (5%)
Cost of Living compared to the U.S: Cheap, even by Latin American
   standards

The devastations of the civil war between the U.S.-backed, right-wing Contras and the Marxist Sandinista government are finally receding into the past. Nicaragua is now catching the attention of the world's low-cost paradise-seekers, who are anxious to get in on the ground floor. The roads and utilities, and particularly Internet connections, are still quite iffy, but the government is actively courting investment and *residencias* and *pensionados* are available for a song. Those who don't mind roughing it to beat the crowds might find the move here appealing.

Living There

Governance: Although once ravaged by war, Nicaragua has made significant progress
   in recent years but elections are still plagued with allegations of corruption and
   vote-rigging. The Judiciary and any other state institutions are often directly
   controlled by political parties. Political violence and drug-related crime are also a
   recurring problem. The government is making efforts to curb human rights abuses
   by the police and military.
Infrastructure: There are a few roads near the coast, otherwise it is not a well-
   developed country, although more resorts and housing developments are in
   progress.
Internet: Pathetic. Worst-connected country in Latin America. Just one in 10 people
   has Internet.
Healthcare: Health insurance is available for around $100/month. Outpatient care is
   free.
GDP: $17.34 billion
GDP (Per Capita): $2,900
Sovereign Debt: 78% of GDP
Working There: Other than real estate, not a lot of jobs for expats. Conditions may
   improve as the expatriate community grows.

Regulatory Environment: Cumbersome, inconsistent, and often time-consuming

Taxes: Individual: 0–30%, Corporate: 30%, VAT: 15%. Residents taxed on Nicaragua-source income.

Cannabis: Illegal, but available in some of the larger cities and outlying areas. Penalties are severe.

Homosexuality: Legal but same-sex marriage and domestic partnerships not eligible for legal protections. Small gay scene. Culture tends to be homophobic and intolerant.

Abortion: Prohibited with no exceptions

Women's Issues: Violence against women, rape and harassment an ongoing concern.

Guns: Legal to own handguns, shotguns, rifles. Permit required.

Crime: Increasing street crime in Managua. Some gang activity, mostly in poor neighborhoods. Petty theft and occasional robberies occur in tourist areas.

Real Estate: U.S. citizens should be aware that the 1979–90 Sandinista government expropriated some 30,000 properties, many of which are still involved in disputes or claims. Hundreds of unresolved claims involving Americans are registered with the U.S. embassy. The judicial system offers little relief when the purchase of a property winds up in court. Once a property dispute enters the judicial arena, the outcome may be adjudicated on the bases of corruption, political pressure, and influence-peddling rather than the actual merits of the case.

Life Expectancy: 71.78 years

Moving There

Cheap and easy. They're happy you want to come.

Tourist Visa: U.S. citizens do not need a visa to stay up to 90 days (to stay longer you can apply for extensions).

Temporary Resident: Good for one year, renewable.

Pensionado or Rentista Visa: Provable income of at least $600 per month for pensioner visa and applicant must be at least 45 years of age. Rentista requires monthly income of $750/month. Both visas are valid for five years and renewable and equivalent to Permanent Residency.

Investor Visa: Applicant must invest over $30,000 in prospective business approved by Ministry of Development, Industry, and Trade. Investor Visa guarantees permanent resident status.

Work Permit: None needed.

Student Visas are available, per the usual requirements.

Permanent Resident: After three years of Temporary Residency, foreigners can apply for a Permanent Resident card, good for five years, renewable.

Citizenship: Foreigners can be naturalized after two to four years of Permanent Residency, two years for spouses of Nicaraguans. Must also pass a variety of language and culture tests. Nicaragua does not recognize dual citizenship.

39. Panama

Climate: Tropical maritime; hot, humid in the valleys and by the coasts, drier in the mountains, cloudy; prolonged rainy season (May to January), short dry season (January to May)
Government: Constitutional Democracy
Population: 3,360,474
Currency: Balboa (PAB), U.S. Dollar (USD): 1 PAB = 1.01 USD
Language: Spanish (official), English 14% (many Panamanians bilingual)
Religious Groups: Roman Catholic (85%), Protestant (15%)
Ethnic Groups: mestizo (70%), West Indian (14%), European (10%), Amerindian (6%)
Cost of Living compared to the U.S.: Very cheap

After many of the bargains in neighboring Costa Rica were snapped up by successive waves of retirees, civilization dropouts and beach bums, the action moved over to Panama ("the new Costa Rica"). Acres of tropical paradise can still be had on the cheap, and thanks to a century of U.S. colonialism, it also boasts the best infrastructure in Central America, allowing you to maintain yourself in something close to the lifestyle that you have grown accustomed to, though no amount of imperialism can purge the region's rampant mañana-ism. Giant retirement developments have sprung up among the coffee plantations in the volcanic highlands around Boquete, which Condé Nast has already dubbed "one of the six to-die-for second-home destinations in the Americas," but with two coasts, and miles of beautiful mountains, there is still plenty of country waiting to be discovered. Work is scarce, but residencies are available to anyone who can demonstrate an independent income of over $1,000 a month, even if you're not of retirement age. Though you don't pay much here in the way of taxes, a few shingles have come off the country's reputation as a tax shelter when Panama and the U.S. entered into a bilateral Tax Information Exchange Agreement at the end of 2010.

Living There

Governance: Free and fair elections but international observers worry that the judiciary is corrupt, inefficient, and subject to political pressures. Panama has an ostensibly free press, but the government has very strict penalties for libel and other offenses that make it difficult for journalists to work in Panama. Corruption remains a problem.
Infrastructure: First world. Roads are good.
Internet: DSL available. Internet cafés are common and inexpensive. Restaurants and coffee shops in urban and tourist areas have become wireless hotspots. Hi-speed widely available. Landline and mobile phone service easily acquired.

Healthcare: Facilities in the city are good but quality decreases toward outlying areas. Private care providers are very reasonably priced. Many doctors that speak excellent English and have degrees from the U.S.

GDP: $44.82 billion

GDP (Per Capita): $12,700

Sovereign Debt: 40% of GDP

Working There: Opportunities in the financial and banking sectors, as well as high-tech R&D. The real estate and tourism boom has resulted in a demand for construction professionals. Salaries, however, are nowhere near as high as you would fetch back home.

Regulatory Environment: Relatively efficient and easy to start a business, some corruption.

Taxes: No wealth or inheritance tax. VAT 5% (10%) for imports. Personal income taxes rates are based on a sliding scale ranging from 7% (up to $9,000) to 27% (maximum rate). Corporate tax rate is 30%.

Cannabis: Available but penalties are harsh. On the plus side, police don't really cruise the expat enclaves unless something major happens, and even then, it's iffy.

Homosexuality: Legal, no recognition of same-sex unions, no laws against discrimination. Though there is a fledgling gay scene, official and unofficial discrimination and harassment persists.

Abortion: Prohibited except to save the woman's life, rape, or fetal impairment.

Women's Issues: Violence against women a big problem. Women underrepresented in government and professional ranks.

Guns: Ownership of shotguns, rifles. Permit required. Owner must take urine test and provide DNA sample.

Crime: The U.S. State Department recently upgraded Panama's crime status to "high." Large cities like Colón and Panama City are experiencing a dangerous rise in narcotics-related violence. Credit card and ATM fraud are also becoming commonplace.

Real Estate: Non-citizens can buy property. The top areas for expatriates are Panama City (the Casco Viejo for true Colonial architecture and the rest of the cosmopolitan amenities), Bocas del Toro (beach people), and Boquette (fresh mountain air and coffee plantations). Real estate laws on the mainland can be quite different from those on islands, in coastal areas, and locations near national borders. If there is any sort of contract dispute, the contract must be translated into Spanish by a licensed translator. Property tax (for land value over U.S. $30,000): 2.1% yearly. Transfer Tax on Real Property: 2.1% of sales price or 5% of assessed value. The U.S. State Department has received a high number of complaints from expats relating to property disputes and urge American buyers to "exercise due diligence" when buying land in Panama. The website of the U.S. embassy in Panama offers some helpful tips for Americans who are considering buying property in Panama at **panama.usembassy.gov/purchasing_property.html**

Life Expectancy: 77.61 years

Moving There

A retirement mecca. If you look like you will behave yourself and spend money, you're in. Most visa-seekers let paid professionals push the paperwork for them and if the proper fees are paid, it's not likely anyone but the most obviously undesirable will be scrutinized too closely. There are a host of incentives for retirees of all ages—tax breaks on importing your household goods (up to $10,000), exemptions from automobile import duties and discounts on transportation, entertainment and medical care. For better or worse, the U.S. dollar is legal tender here.

Tourist Visa: Available to Americans planning to spend up to 30 days in Panama. The visa is extendable for up 90 days. **Short-Stay Visas** are also available for various categories—for instance, to start or conduct business, investigate investments, visit family/relatives, do research, volunteer. These are valid up to nine months.

Pensioner: Requires guaranteed income of $1,000 per month (plus $250 for each dependent) or $750 with a $100,000 property investment. Open to any "retiree" 18 years of age or older. Grants applicants right to reside in Panama indefinitely. You can also deposit enough money in a five-year interest-bearing CD with a designated (state) Panamanian bank. As long as the monthly interest exceeds around USD $850 (meaning a balance of around $260,000) you are considered a "retiree," as long as you keep fulfilling the requirements of the program.

Person of Means Visa: Minimum of $300,000 deposited in Panamanian Bank (house purchases can be applied toward this requirement up to a maximum of $80,000). Visa is valid for one year. After two annual renewals, permanent residency is granted. After five years, visa holder can apply for citizenship.

Agricultural Investor: Invest a minimum of $60,000 in a Panamanian agribusiness or aquaculture concern and you will be allowed six years of legal residency (you renew every two years).

Small Investor: Investment of at least $160,000 (plus $2000 per dependent) in a Panamanian business with at least five Panamanian employees. Valid for one year, renewable. After three renewals, you can receive permanent residency.

Reforestation: Investing $60,000 in an approved reforestation project used to qualify you for permanent residency status. However, it now entitles you to a six-year temporary resident visa. For an $80,000 investment, your visa CAN be converted into a permanent residency and eventually citizenship.

Work Permits: Work permits generally require an offer of employment and much paperwork (though the employer handles much of it) and must be approved by the Ministry of Labor. Experts, particularly in technology fields, have an easier time, especially under special rules that operate in the "City of Knowledge," Panama's public-private high-technology complex on an old U.S. military base in the Canal Zone. It's also possible to set up a shell company through which you can contract your services so you're not technically "employed." Panama has a "10% rule," which states that companies can hire one foreigner for every 10 Panamanian employees, under certain conditions.

Student visas are available per the usual requirements.

Citizenship: Five years legal residency (pensioner visa does not count toward citizenship), proof of economic self-sufficiency, testimonials from five witnesses attesting to good character and residence in Panama, proficiency in Spanish language and knowledge of Panamanian customs, geography, and history.

Name Withheld by Request, 49
David/Panama City, Panama

In San Antonio, TX, I lived in a small house in a gated community. It measured about 3500 ft. and was valued at about $150,000. My property taxes were $600 a month, my water $150, electric $350, insurance $300, common maintenance $100. The house was not paid off, but I would never have been able to own it outright due to costs and taxes...$1500 and not going down.

My place is 30 km up the hill from the town of David. For the same price as I was paying in San Antonio, I live in a 6500-ft. mansion. It is paid for. My property. Taxes are zero, my water is $3, my electric about $220, and my live-in gardener and maid $90. I have broadband, cellular, satellite TV, everything—but no gangs. If I can scare up $313 a month, I can live like a king.

The thing is I have a manufacturing business too so I got a place in Panama City. I just could not travel back and forth 550 km three to five times a week. My beautiful young wife who is from the hills up by David is just amazed you can call 30 restaurants (including McDonald's) that will deliver to your door, no charge. There are large stores. The car dealers have parts. And the dry cleaners work right. You can buy just about anything here you can get in Houston.

Back in the hills, of course, there's way cheaper property, electric and water, plus less crime and better climate. My place is at 3000 ft. In the tropics, you choose your climate by your elevation. Boquete, at 4000 ft, is a different climate.

I'm hoping to get the manufacturing thing straightened out within a year and move back home and start commuting here again. By then, we might be able to have a little company plane with some luck...not expensive here...liability insurance for private aviation does not apply.

Tom Bate
Boquete, Panama

The great thing about being here is that even a small community like Boquete has all the perks of the first world and all the benefits of the third. You have DirecTV and digital cable from Panama City, you have hi-speed Internet, and you have a city nearby where you can get anything you could want. But you also have very low healthcare costs, low food costs, low building costs, low labor costs, and low taxes. I pay $700 a month for a 2500-squareifoot, three-bedroom super deluxe place, with wireless Internet and satellite TV. It has a Jacuzzi, barbeque and awesome views. You also have very little crime here which is a big incentive for me, as I've had TWO armed robberies next to my house in a quiet neighborhood in New Orleans in the last year alone. Then you have the availability of the Pacific, Atlantic and all the jungle, rivers and mountains in between. Not to mention, this is the gateway for cheap travel to the rest of Central and South America.

I have met a lot of people that have moved to this area, and many are disgusted with the situation in America. The other main reason is the cost of living, which is a fraction of what it is in the States. Some are living on very small pensions that would never support you in the U.S., but here you can live relatively well.

40. Peru

Climate: Tropical in the east, dry and desert-like in the west. Temperate to frigid in Andean region.
Government: Constitutional republic
Population: 29,248,943
Currency: Peruvian Nuevo Sol (PEN):
   1 PEN = 0.35 USD
Language: Spanish [official] (84.1%), Quechua [official] (13%), other native languages (2.9%)
Religious Groups: Roman Catholic (81.3%), Evangelical (12.5%), other (3.3%), unspecified (2.9%)
Ethnic Groups: Amerindian (45%), mestizo (37%), white (15%), black, Japanese, Chinese and other (3%)
Cost of Living compared to the U.S: Reasonable

Inca-lovers and eco-entrepreneurs have flocked to the mountains and jungles around Cuzco, while retirees congregate near the coast around Arequipa, while anyone with any kind of real business to conduct will probably head to Lima. The living is cheap and slow and petty crime a constant nuisance, and the poverty a bit more squalid that what you might be used to.

Living There
Governance: Electoral democracy with generally free and fair elections. Basic freedoms are guaranteed by the government but the judiciary is notoriously

corrupt and abuses by police and state security forces are still a problem. Peru has an outspoken free press but intimidation of journalists is common. Corruption remains a problem.

Infrastructure: In the 1990s, Peru upgraded the country's highway system that connects the mountain and coastal regions but public transportation is very limited. In 1993, Peru privatized its telecommunications network which significantly improved both service and accessibility.

Internet: Roughly one in four Peruvians enjoy Internet access which is slightly higher than average in the region. Many log into what are called cabinas publicas which are public Internet sites that are sprouting up all over the country. Broadband penetration is at 2% but the government is pouring money into public initiatives to provide more access to hi-speed Internet.

Healthcare: Peru has one of the highest infant mortality rates in South America, but recent public initiatives have greatly improved the quality of care. Private insurance is generally the best option for expats.

GDP: $277.2 billion

GDP (Per Capita): $9,200

Sovereign Debt: 23.9% of GDP

Working There: Teach English, work for NGO.

Regulatory Environment: Recent reforms have made the process more user-friendly, but there is still a great deal of red tape and corruption is not uncommon.

Taxes: Corporate: 30%, Individual: 15–30%, VAT: 19%. Residents taxed on worldwide income.

Cannabis: Technically illegal but small amounts allowed for personal use. Police have been known to target tourists and Americans. Keep a low profile and be cautious.

Homosexuality: Legal, no laws against discrimination, same-sex unions not legally recognized.

Abortion: Allowed to save life and/or preserve health of mother

Women's Issues: There are existing laws prohibiting rape, spousal rape, and domestic violence but violence against women remains a concern. Women are granted equal rights and Peruvian women are making inroads in both politics and the business world.

Guns: Firearms legal to possess but must be non-military in nature, certain calibers are illegal. License required.

Crime: Violent crime is common in most major cities. Further from urban centers, Shining Path and other insurgent groups have been known to operate.

Real Estate: So long as the property isn't within 50 miles of the border, there are no restrictions on foreigners buying land in Peru. Transfer tax is 3% of purchase price and notary, title search, and deed registration usually comes to about $1,500. Despite the economic downturn, home prices in Peru have been surging. Homes in Miraflores, near Lima's Pacific coast are going for upwards of $300,000. You can still find bargains further inland.

Life Expectancy: 72.47 years.

Moving There

The Peruvians have lately tried to uncomplicate their visa process, but it's still a bit of a mess. Generally, you're looking at a few options outside the usual easy categories. Most opt for retirement-type visa which are issued to migrants of all ages. Anyway, you're seldom locked into a particular visa or migratory status and provided you meet the new qualifications and can come up with the documentation, you can usually trade up.

Tourist Visa: Can be obtained at the airport upon entry to Peru or at the border. Generally granted for a maximum of 183 days per calendar year, but length of stay is at the discretion of the immigration officer. Must show proof of sufficient funds for stay, visa cannot be extended. You must reenter country and reapply. You can however convert a tourist visa to a resident visa...or to a student visa, if you're enrolled in a Peruvian university.

Resident Visa: Recent changes to Peruvian immigration rules now allow holders of tourist visa to apply for temporary resident visas for work, family, business, etc. for around $200. Work visa requires letter from Peruvian employer. Freelancers must demonstrate the legitimacy of their professional standing and provide proof of financial stability. Students can get one if they are enrolled in an approved institution or program. Investors need only sink $25,000 or the equivalent into a business or stock or other fund. Visa is generally valid for one year. However, most apply for Foreign Resident Card (CE) after obtaining Resident Visa.

Rentista Visa: Applicant must provide certificate guaranteeing permanent income of at least $1,000/month ($500/month for each additional family member). The income must enter Peru via a banking institution and if funds are from outside the country, certificate must be legalized by Peruvian consulate and endorsed by the Ministry of Foreign Relations. Rentista Visa grants holder indefinite residence in Peru but any sort of work is prohibited.

Retirement Visa: Similar to Rentista visa with same financial requirements.

Foreign Resident Card (CE): To receive *Carne de Extranjeria* (CE) applicant must have valid Resident Visa (Work, Retirement, etc.). Valid for one year, renewable.

Citizenship: Immigrants can apply for naturalization two years after receiving CE. Applicants must also pass examination in Spanish language and history and culture of Peru.

41. Philippines

Climate: Tropical marine; high temperatures, sometimes excessive humidity and a great deal of rainfall during monsoon season (northeast occurs between November and April, and southwest tends to fall between May and October)

Government: Republic

Population: 101,833,938

Currency: Philippine peso (PHP): 1 PHP = 0.02 USD

Language: Filipino (official; based on Tagalog), English (official) and eight local dialects

Religious Groups: Catholic (80.9%), Muslim (5%), Evangelical or other Christian (9.6%), Agilpayan (2%) other (1.8%), unspecified (0.6%), none (0.1%)

Ethnic Groups: Tagalog (28.1%), Cebuano (13.1%), Bisaya/Binisaya (7.6%), Hiligaynon Illonggo (7.5%), Bikol (6%), Waray (3.4%), other (25.3%)

Cost of Living compared to the U.S: Cheap

The late great chess master, oddball and fugitive from U.S. justice Bobby Fischer moved here. So did weirdo late-night-talk-radio host Art Bell, as did plenty of old seamen who fondly recall their days around Subic Bay, and more than a few aging bachelors disillusioned about their romantic prospects back home. The cities can be a bit raunchy, but the jungle and wilderness are lush and green and the coast as aquamarine as anywhere in the tropics. The Sulu Archipelago and the island of Mindanao have problems with terrorism and an insurgency.

Living There

Governance: Although progress has been made since the days of the ruthless Marcos dictatorship, the Philippines' transition to a full-fledged democracy remains hampered by voting irregularities, political and religious violence, and corruption.

Infrastructure: Underdeveloped. The Philippine economy lags behind many neighboring countries because of inadequate investment in transportation, port facilities, telecommunications, etc.

Internet: Internet access in major cities but mostly dial-up and can be expensive. Less than 10% of the population owns computers so Internet cafés are the most common setting for web use. There is some broadband penetration but the rate is far below other countries in the region.

Healthcare: Because of more lucrative positions in the U.S., Saudi Arabia, and other locales, the country is currently experiencing a shortage of doctors and nurses (especially in rural areas). Still, the public/private healthcare system in the Philippines is considered affordable and provides quality care (many nurses and doctors were trained in the U.S.). However, many facilities may not be on par with developed countries.

GDP: $353.2 billion

GDP (Per Capita): $3,500

Sovereign Debt: 56.5% of GDP

Working There: Teach English, manage call centers, opportunities for healthcare practitioners due to recent doctor/nurse shortage.

Regulatory Environment: Cumbersome, corruption a problem.

Taxes: Individual: 5%–32%, Corporate: 30%, VAT: 12%. Non-citizen residents are only taxed on domestic income.

Cannabis: Strictly illegal; widely grown and smoked

Homosexuality: Legal, but public displays of affection between same-sex adults may be prosecuted under the country's "grave scandal" law. Currently no laws barring discrimination based on sexual orientation. The Philippines does have a growing and highly visible gay-rights movement and reform efforts are beginning to make some headway.

Abortion: Illegal

Women's Issues: Current laws prohibit sexual harassment and workplace discrimination but these measures often aren't strictly enforced. Still, Filipino women are highly visible and have been quite successful in both business and politics.

Guns: Legal to own firearms. License required.

Crime: Violent crime is on the rise in major cities but Americans generally aren't targeted. American tourists have reported instances of ATM fraud, pickpocketing, theft, and other related property crimes.

Real Estate: Foreigners are not allowed to purchase land but can buy apartment and condominium units so long as foreign ownership of a given building does not exceed 40%. Homes are available to buy but not the property where the building was constructed. There are also 50- and 25-year leases on land. Condo prices are highly affordable and can be purchased for as low as $20,000. Property rights are not as strongly enforced in the Philippines as in other countries; the court system can be cumbersome and prone to corruption.

Life Expectancy: 71.66 years

Moving There

Work, study, invest or retire. If you have something going, they don't ask for much else.

Tourist/Visitor/Non-Immigrant Visa: Applicants are advised to apply at least one month before departure date. There are three types of tourist visas: single entry (valid three months), multiple entry (valid six months), and multiple entry (valid for one year). U.S. citizens can stay up to 21 days without tourist visa. Temporary visas can be extended and exchanged for longer term non-immigrant visas by applying to the Bureau of Immigration.

Work Permit: All foreign nationals seeking to work in the Philippines must obtain an Alien Employment Permit (AEP) through the country's Department of Labor and Employment (DOLE) before applying for a work visa. In most cases, an employer will file the petition on your behalf. Once your AEP has been approved you can apply for a work visa at the nearest office of the Philippine Bureau of Immigration (BOI). www.dole.gov.ph.

Most **Immigrant Visas** (Permanent Residence) are only available to foreigners who marry Filipinos/Filipinas or have some other family or political claim to residing there. Outside of a small quota (per country) of such visas, the following visas are open to foreigners wishing to reside indefinitely in the Philippines:

Special Investor's Resident Visa (SIRV): Must be 21 years of age or older and invest a minimum of $75,000 in the Philippines. Visa holder can legally reside in the Philippines indefinitely so long as he or she continues to maintain required investment amount.

Special Resident's Retiree Visa (SRRV): Applicants must be in good health, at least 35 years of age, and able to deposit a specified amount in a government-designated bank account. Those between 35–49 years of age must deposit at least $50,000. Retirees who are over 50 must deposit a minimum of $20,000 (with pension) or $10,000 (without pension). Initial investment can be converted into "active" investment which includes condominium units. Holder of SRRV is entitled to stay in the Philippines indefinitely with multiple entry privileges. Along with this basic package, beginning in 2011, the Philippine government is offering new variations of this visa with differing benefits and privileges. Check the web page for the Philippine Retirement Authority (PRA) for more information. www.pra.gov.ph.

Special Visa for Employment Generation (SVEG): This new visa scheme grants a lifetime visa to any non-immigrant foreigner who operates a business that employs a minimum of 10 Filipinos in a "lawful and sustainable trade, business, or industry."

Student Visas available, per the usual requirements.

Citizenship: Naturalization of foreigners with no other claims to Philippine citizenship (birth, marriage, family, etc.) is possible after 10 years of legal residency with the additional requirement that the applicant possess either real estate holdings, or be engaged in a highly remunerative occupation, trade, business or profession.

42. Poland

Climate: Cold, cloudy, moderately severe winters with frequent precipitation; mild summers
Government: Republic
Population: 38,463,689
Currency: Zloty (PLN): 1 PLN = 0.34 USD
Language: Polish (97.8%), other (2.2%)
Religious Groups: Roman Catholic (95%), other [including Eastern Orthodox and Protestant] (5%)
Ethnic Groups: Polish (96.7%), German (.4%), other [including Byelorussian and Ukrainian] (2.9%)
Cost of Living compared to the U.S: Cheap

Few expats settle in Poland. This, however, may be changing. The economy is among the most robust of the former Eastern Bloc, so much so that even Polish emigrants have begun repatriating from the West. The English-teaching scene is booming and much less competitive than elsewhere in Europe and the country is keen on business investment. Time to cut out the jokes and start taking Poland seriously.

Living There

Governance: Poland has a thriving multiparty democracy. Human rights are generally respected although there are recurring problems with prison conditions, lengthy pretrial detention, and brutality by law enforcement. In post-communist Poland, respect for freedom of expression is widespread but there are incidents of the government using the charge of defamation (which can carry a two-year prison sentence) to silence critics.

Infrastructure: Market-based competition to the state-owned telephone monopoly has accelerated modernization of Poland's telecommunications infrastructure. Mobile cellular services widely available. Poland will be hosting the 2012 UEFA championships (European Soccer) and the country plans to improve the nation's slow-moving rail system, pave long-neglected roads, and upgrade airports and other transport hubs.

Internet: Nearly 60% of Polish citizens have Internet access. The growth of private sector ISPs is improving the quality of service but broadband penetration is still in its early stages. Only 13.2 people out of 100 have a broadband connection in Poland—almost the lowest in the E.U.

Healthcare: Persons covered by the general health insurance plan (on a compulsory or voluntary basis) are entitled to free health services in Poland. Quality of healthcare and facilities is good, though less so in rural areas.

GPD: $725.2 billion

GDP (Per Capita): $18,800

Sovereign Debt: 53.6% of GDP

Working There: Teaching English is the best work possibility, but there are increasing opportunities for IT professionals and those with business experience and skills.

Regulatory Environment: Bureaucratic and time-consuming. Some corruption.

Taxes: Corporate: 19%, Individual: 0%/18%/32% (optional 19% flat tax), VAT: 22% (7% on certain goods). Residents taxed on worldwide income.

Cannabis: Illegal. Polish government will prosecute even for small amounts. Despite the restrictions, you'll likely smell it everywhere the youth are gathered.

Homosexuality: Legal. No legal recognition of same-sex partnerships. Laws against discrimination.

Abortion: Legal to preserve physical health and to save a woman's life. Also in cases of rape, incest, and fetal impairment. Parental notification/authorization required.

Women's Issues: There are laws prohibiting sexual harassment but it is still a problem, as is domestic violence. Women are underrepresented in politics and business.

Guns: Some firearms legal to own with permit. These are often hard to obtain. Stringent storage requirements.

Crime: Low rate of violent crime. Petty crimes in major cities, particularly Gdansk. Some street crime around Warsaw, Krakow, and Gdansk. Car theft and carjacking are a problem. Occasional skinhead violence.

Real Estate: Americans must apply to the Ministry of the Interior for permission to buy property in Poland. Banks are starting to offer mortgages but many transactions are still done in cash. Prices are low. Two-bedroom apartments in Warsaw can go for as little as $80,000, while in rural areas, larger houses can be had for less.

Life Expectancy: 75.63 years

Moving There

If you're not coming on a work contact, bring your work with you and convince the Polish government you have a reason and means to stay. The OFF (Office for Foreigners; www.udsc.gov.pl) gives you in-depth info on how to make Poland your next home.

Schengen Visa: Maximum of 90 days per 180-day period, no extensions.

National Stay Visa: These visas are issued for one year and are not renewable, so they're of limited use if you're planning on staying long-term in Poland. Categories and requirements are similar to those for the Residence Permit.

Residence Permit: A (temporary) Residence Permit is usually granted if applicant can show that longer stay in Poland is warranted due to work, business, studies, marriage, religious duties, artistic endeavors (for established artists), scientific research, reuniting with family, etc. Proof of sufficient financial resources and medical insurance required in addition to documentation that establishes the nature of your stay (e.g., work contract/letter of employment, business records, letter of enrollment, etc.). Temporary residency permit cannot exceed two years but is renewable indefinitely and also issued to immediate family members.

Permanent Residency (Settlement Permit): Applicants must reside in Poland for at least 10 years continuously. Two years if married to a Polish citizen for minimum of three years.

Work Permit: Work visas are issued only by Polish Consul with the office appropriate for the applicant's legal permanent residence. An alien intending to work in Poland must enter the territory with a valid work visa as no visas can be delivered in Poland. English-language teachers planning to work in Poland at universities (colleges) must submit Certificate of Employment issued by President of that university/college.

Citizenship: Five years permanent residency required. Polish law allows for third- and even fourth-generation descendants of Polish citizens (going back to 1918) to reclaim their Polish citizenship if certain conditions are met.

Karen Dague
Lodz, Poland

Lodz is a fairly good-sized town with some nice areas to visit. You can walk or take a tram or city bus anywhere you want to go. I struggle to understand or speak Polish, but you can get along in most of the restaurants as a lot of the young people and waitresses speak English and most menus have an English version.

We haven't found the cost of living to be too bad here with the exception of the rent on the house we are living in—about $2000 a month. We did pick a larger house with a yard so we can have company over here, but even the small apartments seemed to be costly. Food items are generally comparable to the States...sometimes cheaper. The one surprise to me was the cost of soda over here. For the most part soda in the stores isn't too bad, but it can cost you $5 for a little bottle of Coke, while my husband gets beer in the restaurants for about $5 for a large glass.

Most of the Americans are located in big cities such as Warsaw where there is more of an English base of people. There are also English schools there. We don't have any children with us so we weren't concerned with this fact. There are probably some Americans living here, but locating them will be hard. We have not found any expat hangouts to date.

43. Portugal

Climate: Maritime temperate, average annual temperature is 16C (61°F)
Government: Republic
Population: 10,707,924
Currency: Euro (EUR): 1 EUR = 1.36 USD
Language: Portuguese
Religious Groups: Roman Catholic (84.5%), other Christian (2.2%), other (0.3%), unknown (9%), none (3.5%)
Ethnic Groups: Portuguese, African and Eastern European minorities
Cost of Living compared to the U.S.: Not too bad; the cheapest in Western Europe

Known for its charming tile-faced houses, windy streets and a drug policy that is approaching Holland's, Portugal is also facing a bailout and the inevitable "austerity" curse that follows. This hasn't diminished its buzz among expats and scene-seekers who congregate around Lisbon, while the southern coast (the Algarve) is Europe's biggest surf mecca, attracting expatriate beach bums and resort entrepreneurs.

Living There

Governance: A Western-style democracy with most of the freedoms and protections in place, Portugal does have a reputation for police brutality and poor prison conditions.
Infrastructure: Developed
Internet: Slow by Western European standards; only about one in 20 residents has broadband.
Healthcare: Portugal has an extensive state healthcare system, but overcrowding and inconsistent standards of treatment may make private care a preferred option.
GDP: $247 billion
GDP (Per Capita): $23,000
Sovereign Debt: 83.2% of GDP
Working There: Opportunities in tourism, teach English, au pairs.
Regulatory Environment: Inexpensive and relatively straightforward. Occasional delays.
Taxes: Corporate: 25%, Individual: 10.5–40%, VAT: 21%, non-resident corporations: 15%–40%. Residents of Portugal are subject to taxation on their worldwide incomes, capital gains and inheritances. Non-residents are generally only subject to taxation on their Portuguese-source income. Staying for 183 days in a given tax year in Portugal will make you a tax resident.

Cannabis: Portugal is one of the few countries in the E.U. that have decriminalized the use and possession of recreational drugs. While trafficking is still a felony offense, use and consumption of drugs is no longer under the jurisdiction of criminal courts.

Homosexuality: Portugal is one of the few nations that include a ban on discrimination based on sexual orientation in its constitution. Same-sex marriage legally recognized in 2010. Portugal is generally tolerant toward gays and lesbians and open communities exist all over the country.

Abortion: Legal to preserve mental health, to save the woman's life, and physical health; parental authorization/notification required. Also in cases of rape and fetal impairment.

Women's Issues: Outside of restrictive abortion laws, women's rights are protected and domestic violence is prosecuted.

Guns: Limited number of firearms allowed for civilian use. Must be for sporting purposes only. License and registration required.

Crime: Low violent crime rates. Car break-ins common.

Real Estate: Foreigners can own property in Portugal and many do, particularly in the southern Algarve region. Buyers must first apply for Portuguese tax number and must have representation by Portuguese resident. 6% transfer tax and legal fees for closing a purchase generally cost around €3,000. Prices are generally more reasonable than elsewhere on the continent.

Life Expectancy: 78.21 years

Moving There

Prepare and submit your paperwork for staying long-term in Portugal before you arrive. Anyone who wishes to stay in Portugal longer than six months must apply for a Residence Permit (*Autorização de Residência*). Portuguese residents must apply for a tax ID number or *Número de Indentificação Fiscal* (NIF), which is necessary for all major transactions, collecting wages or payments, and buying or selling vehicles.

Schengen Visa: Maximum of 90-day stay per 180-day period, no extensions.

Short Stay Visa: Of limited use since it often allows a maximum stay of six months, though academics and researchers can be issued a short-stay visa for as long as one year.

Residency Visa: Issued to immigrants interested in establishing residence in Portugal. Visa is valid for four months and allows holder to apply for a residence permit.

Resident Permit: Issued on various classifications and valid for one year, after which two-year renewals are possible. General conditions require that you are self-sufficient, haven't been convicted of a crime, have a residence, insurance and are in good health. Generally granted to holders of a valid work contract, those engaged in independent professional activity, or who operate a recognized business, conduct research, are enrolled in studies, as well as paid trainees or volunteers.

Permanent Resident: Can be granted after five years legal residency with Temporary Residence Permit. Must speak Portuguese. These permits still have to be renewed every five years.

Student Visa available, per the usual requirements.

Citizenship: Applicants must show proof of sufficient funds, proficiency in Portuguese language, and must have resided in Portugal with residence permit for a minimum of 10 years.

Jennifer (and Doug) St. Martin
Lisbon, Portugal

Lisbon is such a great place to live. The lifestyle is relaxed compared to most big cities I have been in. It has a "small town" feel to it, even though it is large. It feels personal to us, not cold like most cities do. People seem genuinely concerned about each other. After living here for two years, we have not had any negative experiences with people we come across in everyday life. It is like living among family.

The cost of living here is quite low compared to what one is used to in the U.S. If you live in the city, it is not necessary to have a car. There are many ways to get around on public transportation. You can eat really well on very little. You can go out and have a good time on a dime too, especially if you avoid the tourist traps.

As for language, English is very widely understood, and the Portuguese are helpful when it comes to language. We try our best to speak Portuguese, out of respect, but if we don't know a word, they are quick to help out in English. Some places I have visited in other countries get very snobby about language, but not here. Movies are not dubbed over, they typically have subtitles, even kids' movies are offered in both languages. We know people who have been living here for 20 years and still do not speak the language.

Lisbon is truly a beautiful city with so many sites and different areas. If you want old and historic, you have it. If you want modern and architecturally stimulating, you have that. If you want beach and mountains, you have it. It really has all the elements we love wrapped into one great city. This is truly the best place we have ever lived.

Our lifestyle here can be summed up in one word: peaceful. The stress of the American way of life was really bogging us down. Driving, driving, driving, bills, bills, bills, phone calls from random companies, organizations, campaigns, etc., stacks of junk mail every day, pressure for you to do this and that, pressure for your kids to do this and that—all wiped away when we moved here. Now we take the metro, bus, or train to get around, and occasionally borrow a car to go sightseeing with. We do have bills, but they are much smaller, much more basic, and simpler to keep track of.

We only get phone calls from people we know and love, which is so nice for the brain. There seemed to be always so much "noise" even when you were at home trying to get some peace and quiet. There is no pressure or expectations on us here. People get involved in things for fun, not because they are trying to keep up or save face. I particularly love how friendly strangers are here too. It shocked me that people take time to stop and say hi to strangers, men patting children on the head lovingly like a grandmother would do. Nice elderly ladies giving the children hugs and doting over them. Saying hello with kisses on the cheek, even when meeting the person for the first time. The camaraderie is just refreshing. Everyone seems like family that you just haven't met yet.

The disadvantages of living here are few:

We are not particularly fond that there is so much more smoking here than any town or city we have ever lived in (and we both come from Michigan factory towns, where smoking is the norm).

It can be difficult to find things you need when shopping, although I find this refreshing, and embrace the challenge. I can't just drive to the local megastore, going for one thing, and come back with 10 any more, and I love that. I also have to carry everything that I buy, so it helps us to save money and live more simply. In the case of food, if you want locally grown (which is so much better) you eat by the season. I don't buy grapes until the fall or strawberries until the spring.

Otherwise, it is truly like living on vacation!

€ric D. Clark
Lisbon, Portugal

Portugal is not expensive, but it does have class. Lisbon is EXTREMELY international: it reminds me of Paris or San Francisco. I am not wealthy or even close but my companion and I have an orange tree, a lemon tree, and a peach tree, with a small palm tree in the middle of our private garden on the second floor. What kind of people can afford this type of luxury in a capital city of this stature in the United States? I certainly could not live like this in Los Angeles for the same price, or try this in New York? I don't think so!

44. Russia

Climate: Subarctic in Siberia to tundra climate in the polar north; winters vary from cool along the Black Sea coast to frigid in Siberia; summers vary from warm in the steppes to cool along the Arctic coast

Government: Federation

Population: 140,041,247

Currency: Russian Ruble (RUB): 1 RUB = 0.03 USD

Language: Russian, many minority languages

Religious Groups: Russian Orthodox, Muslim, other

Ethnic Groups: Russian (79.8%), Tatar (3.8%), Ukrainian (2%), Bashkir (1.2%), Chuvash (1.1%), other or unspecified (12.1%)

Cost of Living compared to the U.S.: Reasonable outside of Moscow and St. Petersburg

Despite spinning off its imperial holdings after the dissolution of the Soviet Union, Russia or the Russian Federation still boasts the largest land mass of any country in the world. This gives you quite a bit of area to theoretically choose from, though much of it is bone-chillingly cold. Moscow and St. Petersburg are anything but low-budget destinations; nothing beats life among the gangsters and businessmen of Mother Russia. Crime can be a problem, the weather a challenge, and day-to-day life chaotic. Seat-of-the-pants capitalists and English teachers have the best shot at making a go of it, although all kinds of opportunities abound and salaries are high. Visa requirements are not as difficult as they are maddening, as the agencies in charge still seem to be staffed with the same kind of slow-minded apparatchiks who shuffled papers in Stalin's day.

Living There

Governance: Free and fair elections are a fantasy, state control of media is a fact of life, and opposition parties and independent journalists consider themselves lucky to be merely harassed and intimidated, as poisoning and other film-noirish methods of silencing haven't disappeared from the political playbook. The Kremlin is as powerful, lawless, and corrupt as it ever was, and the shortest joke in Russian is the words "human rights." While the Internet long remained the only unrestricted avenue of free speech, dissident bloggers have recently been carted off to jail, and the government has demanded that service providers retain evidence of each citizen's web-surfing habits, and block websites deemed "extremist." And let's not even get started on Chechnya.

Infrastructure: Russia is in the process of digitizing its telephone sector and rapid improvements are expected in the next few years.

Internet: Less than half of all Russian residents have Internet access but the number of users is expanding rapidly. Broadband penetration is at 26% and is expected to climb steadily over the next few years. Hi-speed Internet available in major cities.

Healthcare: Healthcare can vary tremendously depending on location, generally better in the major cities. Water quality also varies widely in Russia.

GDP: $2.229 trillion

GDP (Per Capita): $15,900

Sovereign Debt: 9.5% of GDP

Working There: Teach English. Many Western companies are developing joint ventures with Russian partners and there are opportunities for people from the U.S. to work in Russia.

Regulatory Environment: Stifling bureaucracy, lack of transparency, and corruption.

Taxes: Corporate: 13–20%, Individual: 13% (nonresidents 30%), VAT: 0–18% (reduced rate for certain goods and no VAT for small businesses except for import activities). Residents taxed on worldwide income.

Cannabis: Decriminalized. Possession of up to six grams of cannabis or two grams of hashish is now punishable only by a fine. Larger amounts can still result in a prison sentence. Note: foreigners are still subject to expulsion or denied re-entry into Russia even under new laws.

Homosexuality: Legal. No recognition of same-sex unions. No laws against discrimination. Strong cultural biases exist, and harassment of gays, including police raids of gay bars, still occur. There is a small but growing gay-rights movement in larger cities.

Abortion: No restriction as to reason

Women's Issues: Domestic violence is a recurring problem and women have few legal options. Women face considerable discrimination in the workplace with regard to pay and hiring.

Guns: Pistols illegal. Some firearms legal to own providing guns are of a non-military caliber. Licensing required.

Crime: Violent crime appears to be falling, although there are still several thousand murders each year. Ethnic-looking people can run into trouble with skinheads. Assaults, robbery, and pickpocketing are common in the larger cities. There is widespread corruption, and extortion and violence might as well be taught in business schools.

Real Estate: Russian law makes no distinction between citizens and expatriates when it comes to buying real estate. Mortgages are available, but rare, with 20–40% down payment. Terms usually 10–15 years at 15–20%. Even when mortgages are available, real estate transactions are usually conducted in cash and buyers often must reserve a sufficient number of bills at the bank. The proceeds of sale of any property, which was owned by the same person for five or more years, are tax exempt. Otherwise, the sale of real estate is subject to 13% tax for tax residents and to 30% tax for nonresidents.

Life Expectancy: 66.03 years

Moving There

Like almost everything else in official Russia, getting visas and permits for long-term stay is a pay-to-play affair, usually involving agencies specializing in these kinds of activities. In this racket, your acceptance or rejection may have more to do with their skill and connections than your own background, assets, etc. DIYers should be aware that all Russian visa applications submitted in the U.S. must be done online. Forms can be found at **www.evisa.kdmid.ru.**

Tourist Visa: One month. Requires "invitation" that can be ordered through a Russian travel agency.

Business Visa: Can be obtained with bona fide invitation of employment but can also be obtained via registered travel agencies. Student visa, humanitarian and religious visa are also available. Multiple entry visas valid up to one year, renewable, do get issued but there is a capriciously enforced 90-day rule and those with long-term aspirations try and apply for the three-year residence permit.

Temporary Residence Permit/Residence Permit: These permits put you on track toward unlimited residency and citizenship. In almost all cases, a temporary residence permit is first issued for at least six months before a Residence Permit is issued, valid for five years, after which one is eligible to apply for citizenship. Other than people who have a family connection or political connection to Russia, these permits are given out on a quota system. The reasons for acceptance or denial have even the most grizzled Kremlin-watchers scratching their heads.

Work Permit: Yearly quota of foreign employees allowed into the Russian workforce each year. Work permit required to work and is usually arranged via Russian employer. Teachers do not need a permit to work in Russia.

Student Visas also available per the usual requirements.

Citizenship: Five years of living in Russia as a Permanent Resident. Requirements are much reduced for former citizens of the USSR, and descendents, family and spouses of Russian nationals.

J.M.

Pushkin, Russia

We are able to live a much more relaxed, prosperous life than we would have in the U.S. Money goes much further here, and given the level of competition among providers of things like mobile phones, Internet, medicine and dental, food, etc., there's generally much higher quality easily available than what you could find in the States.

The laws in Russia can seem at some times much stricter than in the USA. The difference, of course, is that in the U.S. you are expected to actually follow them. In Russia, with the exception of major things like robbery or murder or political crimes, there's not much that you can't arrange to be able to do, or get okayed post-facto.

The legal system *is* different, and has some significantly different foundational assumptions from U.S. law. Some examples:

The biggest things you learn, living in Russia, are patience (traffic can be awful, and road qualities are pretty bad sometimes, too), and respect for procedure. There are certain boxes-that-need-checking and t's-that-need-crossing, and those simply must be done. It can be frustrating, being able to resolve a speeding ticket on the spot with the police, but then having to spend four hours waiting for them to write up their report—longhand, in triplicate—after your car has been hit on the road. The other major issue can be the availability of big Western consumer infrastructure, like malls and mega-grocery stores. At the moment, those are far and few between outside the major cities, although there are several Russian chains that are making fast inroads all over the country.

To be honest, we tend to avoid Americans in Russia. Most of the American expats we've encountered are incurious, insular government or NGO types. Russians are so sociable that there's really no need to have enclaves of foreigners, unless those foreigners for some reason *want* to avoid Russians. The expats we do know in Russia all speak the language and have gone just as native as we have.

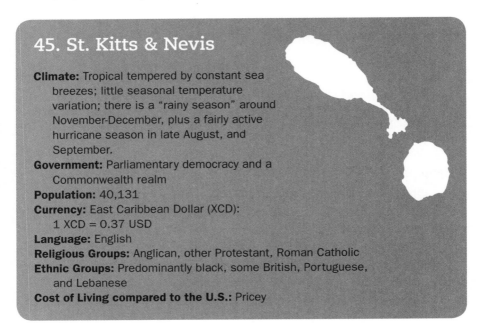

45. St. Kitts & Nevis

Climate: Tropical tempered by constant sea breezes; little seasonal temperature variation; there is a "rainy season" around November-December, plus a fairly active hurricane season in late August, and September.
Government: Parliamentary democracy and a Commonwealth realm
Population: 40,131
Currency: East Caribbean Dollar (XCD):
  1 XCD = 0.37 USD
Language: English
Religious Groups: Anglican, other Protestant, Roman Catholic
Ethnic Groups: Predominantly black, some British, Portuguese, and Lebanese
Cost of Living compared to the U.S.: Pricey

Famous among expats for having the longest-running passport-for-sale program (despite determined efforts by the U.S., in particular, to get these nations to stop the practice), so if you're keen on getting citizenship, have $250K–$350K to spare and want to while away your years in a tropical tax-shelter paradise, then this place might be for you. In fact, once you're in, you don't really even have to live here. On the other hand, there are worse places to exile yourself than a tropical island.

Living There

Governance: Free and fair elections. Independent judiciary. Constitutional guarantees of freedom of religion, free expression and the right to organize are respected. Unfettered access to the Internet.

Infrastructure/Internet: Telephone and hi-speed Internet available

Healthcare: Medical care is limited. There are three general hospitals on St. Kitts, and one on Nevis. Both islands have several health clinics. Neither island has a hyperbaric chamber. Divers suffering decompression illness are transported to the island of Saba, in the Netherlands Antilles. Serious medical problems requiring hospitalization and/or medical evacuation to the U.S. can cost thousands of dollars. Doctors and hospitals expect immediate cash payment for health services.

GDP: $719.5 million

GDP (Per Capita): $14,400

Sovereign Debt: 185% of GDP

Working There: Work in tourist industry or live off your money.

Regulatory Environment: Less efficient than other countries in the region; lots of red tape but reform efforts are underway to make it easier for businesses.

Taxes: No personal income tax. There is a capital gains tax of 20% on profits or gains derived from a transaction relating to assets located in the Federation which are disposed of within one year of the date of their acquisition. Individuals and ordinary companies remitting payments to persons outside the Federation are required to deduct a 10% withholding tax from profits, administration, management or head office expenses, technical service fees, accounting and audit expenses, royalties, non-life insurance premiums and rent.

Cannabis: Illegal, but available

Homosexuality: Illegal (males only), no recognition of same-sex unions. No laws against discrimination. Pervasive anti-gay sentiment.

Abortion: Only to preserve mental or physical health

Women's Issues: Violence against women is not uncommon, though criminalized in specific legislation. A measure passed in 2008 bars sexual harassment.

Crime: Since 2008, crime has been on the rise. Although most murders involve locals and are primarily gang-related, U.S. residents have experienced incidents of burglary, armed robbery, and other property crimes.

Real Estate: Since 1984, as part of the Citizenship by Investment program, if you invest in a property (minimum $350,000) you will be granted instant citizenship.

Life Expectancy: 74.37 years

Moving There

Show them the money.

Tourist Visa: For Americans, stays of up to three months are granted at Immigration. Anyone requiring an extension must apply to the Ministry of National Security. Residence visa requires proof of income.

Work Permit: Requires offer or contract from local company. Don't count on it.

Student Visas are available, though it's doubtful anyone would head here to enroll in a formal course of education.

Citizenship by Investment: This is the reason foreigners are interested in St. Kitts & Nevis. To quality for citizenship, applicants must make a minimum investment of $350,000 or more in government-approved project or $200,000 or more to Sugar Industry Diversification Foundation.

---

46. Saudi Arabia

Climate: Saudi Arabia has a dry, hot desert climate, with very low humidity. All regions have very little rainfall, with the exception of the extreme southwest which is close to the monsoon belt.

Government: Monarchy

Population: 28,686,633 (note: includes over 5.5 million non-nationals)

Currency: Saudi Riyal (SAR): 1 SAR = 0.26 USD

Language: Arabic

Religious Groups: Muslim (100%)

Ethnic Groups: Arab (90%), Afro-Asian (10%)

Cost of Living compared to the U.S.: Comparable (most expats live in Saudi Arabia on all-inclusive packages and because common entertainments like bars, clubs and movies don't exist, tend to spend very little).

Fat contracts are offered in Saudi Arabia to attract skilled workers. Most Americans live in gated "Stepford Communities," cut off from the daily life in the country. Terrorism has been on the upswing, causing many Westerners to leave. Salaries and incentives have therefore increased to get them and their replacements to stay. The wave of reformist protest and revolution has threatened to disrupt the Kingdom, but at press time, the monarchy was not only holding firm, but had enough muscle to spare to squelch protest in neighboring Bahrain. The other cloud on the horizon is a quota-like system called *Nitaqat*. Employees whose companies violate the Nitaqat system may see their visas revoked after six years.

Living There

Governance: Saudi Arabia is an absolute monarchy that held its first-ever elections (just municipal posts with women excluded from the polls) in 2005. It is considered one of the least free nations on the planet, though the faintest whiff of reform is in the air.

Infrastructure: Because of the vast distances that separate Saudi Arabia's main cities, air travel has long since replaced the camel as the most efficient means of transportation across large distances. There are three major airports complemented by some two dozen local and regional ones. There are also extensive, well-kept highways. Saudi Arabia has good telephone service.

Internet: There are several Internet Service Providers (ISPs) and Internet cafés can be found in the main cities. Hi-speed DSL Internet is available. Government censors filter content from international sites.

Healthcare: Most employers provide healthcare insurance for their expatriate employees and sometimes for their dependents. If this is not provided, the cost of hospitalization and treatment can be very high. It is therefore advisable, and will soon be mandatory, to take out private health insurance, either under a local hospital contract, or with an international health insurance provider. Saudi Arabia has excellent medical facilities, and it is seldom necessary to travel overseas for treatment.

GDP: $622.5 billion

GDP (Per Capita): $24,200

Sovereign Debt: 16.7% of GDP

Working There: English teachers, engineers, administration and healthcare professionals are all offered large incentives to work there.

Regulatory Environment: Efficient and easy to negotiate: Saudi Arabia is ranked 11th in the World Bank's Doing Business Index.

Taxes: Corporate 25–45%, Individual: none (non-residents who earn income from investment in a Saudi business or professional activities are taxed at rates of 5–30% depending on income).

Cannabis: You gotta be joking...

Homosexuality: Probably no worse place on earth to be gay. Whipping is commonly used as an "alternative" to long prison sentences or the death penalty.

Abortion: Legal to preserve physical health, spousal and parental approval required.

Women's Issues: Women have received some benefits of recent reforms, but for the most part are excluded from male society. Women can own businesses but cannot drive automobiles, and marriage laws decidedly favor the husband.

Guns: License required. Carry is legal.

Crime: Low crime index perhaps due to severe penalties. Some terror attacks targeting Westerners.

Real Estate: Not impossible, but very difficult. Property values are high, few banks lend to foreigners and not enough of them can or intend to live in the country long enough to make purchasing worthwhile.

Life Expectancy: 76.30 years

Moving There

If you're not here for work, business or hajj, you won't make it out of the airport.
Outside of those reuniting with families or spouses who can apply for residency on those grounds, employment is coupled with a residency permit/booklet (*iqama*). Families of employees are allowed to reside in the Kingdom, as well.

Business Visa: Issued to employees of American companies who are sponsored by a Saudi company. Valid only three months .

Employment Block Visa: Issued to employees sponsored by a Saudi company. The sponsor (usually the employer) obtains work and residence permits for the employee and for any family members.

Scott

Riyadh, Saudi Arabia

I prefer the lifestyle here overall as it provides many things for me. First is a good income which is stable and guaranteed by my employment contract.

Second is it allows me to take paid vacations with airfare (my previous employment allowed only one week off per year until three years of employment). Most contracts in KSA allow one month per year with airfare plus various local time off for Ramadan and Hajj.

Third is the ability to support my family due to the money I am earning and lack of significant expenses here (no taxes, no utilities, cheap gas for my car).

I can earn and save more here than I could possibly do back home. Even if the salary in the kingdom is less than what I could potentially earn back home, the tax benefit and absence of utilities makes up the difference. In Saudi, our salaries are based on equivalent salaries in the U.S., but with the tax exemptions, absence of basic bills, annual bonus and end of contract bonus—it adds up to being more than what I could expect in the States.

As for life on a Western compound, it is probably the best situation for most Westerners for numerous reasons. The primary reason is that the companies employing them provide the compound housing and services. If a person/family lived on the economy, the social network for the person (or wife and kids) would be more difficult to establish. That is a huge benefit for compound living: the built-in English speaking neighbors!

Other aspects are compound functions and bus transportation for the school kids and for shopping. This is from my experience at least—some compounds may be no-frills type of affairs and only provide housing and security (or maybe just housing).

The compounds which I have lived on in Riyadh have all had swimming pools, gym of some extent or another, a library of contributed books, videos and magazines. Most have a restaurant, some serve excellent quality and selection of meals.

Our company just recently left the Jadawel compound. It had an excellent restaurant, one formal dining area (for special occasions or ladies coffees). The Jadawel also had a full gym, racquetball and squash courts, swimming pool and part-time theatre (very part-time).

Other compounds offer similar, more or less. Some smaller ones are open for rental. One man in Riyadh that I know of specializes in smaller compounds for small companies or individuals. The features vary from place to place but the price generally starts at about U.S. $23,000 per year furnished. Villas outside have a broad spectrum of prices—from U.S. $13,000/yr to huge numbers (well above my counting range).

I am currently in the process of bringing my Mom here to experience life in the "sandbox" for herself. We will rent an apartment as my company doesn't allow families ('as per the contract').

Dating is a compound thing as it is illegal to be alone in a car or alone in the company of the opposite sex without being related (marriage, blood relative) or without a married couple along.

Deportation can happen quickly as can jail detention. Everyone knows the risk and consequences for being with your girlfriend or boyfriend out on the town. Often, people are never asked by the Mutawa (religious police) and go their entire stay in Saudi without a problem. Sometimes, however, people do get caught, get taken to the police station (until the company comes and gets them out) or get deported quickly.

That is why compounds are desired as well: protection from getting busted for something normal.

Dating local girls or guys can be risky—but especially dating Saudi girls. If caught, she can be beaten and suffer greatly at the wrath of their family.

Best advice: stay away from that temptation—it can mean the death of the girl if discovered.

47. Singapore

Climate: Tropical; warm, humid, lots of rain. Singapore has two monsoon seasons: northeastern from December to March and southwestern from June to September. Between seasons thunderstorms are common.

Government: Parliamentary republic
Population: 4,740,737
Currency: Singapore dollar (SGD): 1 SGD = 0.77 USD
Language: Mandarin [official] (35%), English [official] (23%), Malay [official] (14.1%), Hokkien (11.4%), Cantonese (5.7%), Teochew (4.9%), Tamil [official] (3.2%), other Chinese dialects (1.8%), other (0.9%)
Religious Groups: Buddhist (42%), Muslim (14.9%), Taoist (8.5%), Hindu (4%), Catholic (4.8%), other Christian (9.8%), other (0.7%), none (14.8%)
Ethnic Groups: Chinese (76.8%), Malay (13.9%), Indian (7.9%), other (other 1.4%)
Cost of Living compared to the U.S: High (especially Real Estate)

This literal island of cleanliness and efficiency at the southern tip of the Malay Peninsula is open for business, attracting economic libertarians from all over the world with their laissez-faire business environment and degree-toting foreigners chasing the highest per-capita expat salaries in the world. Libertines, stoners and slackers, however, should probably look elsewhere.

Living There

Governance: If you live in Singapore you can look forward to top-notch healthcare, a well-developed infrastructure, a thriving business sector, and spotlessly clean streets. In exchange, you'll have to rethink how much you value your freedoms. The media is tightly regulated, some Internet sites are blocked, elections are largely controlled by the ruling party, and the country's criminal laws are notoriously harsh.

Infrastructure: Well-developed: completely digital telecommunications system, extensive road and modern mass transit system (bus, light rail, train), air and sea ports are well-maintained and efficiently run.

Internet: Nearly 80% of Singapore residents enjoy Internet access and the country is one of the world leaders in broadband penetration.

Healthcare: The healthcare system in Singapore has been rated one of the best in the world. Medical facilities are state-of-the-art and healthcare practitioners are well-qualified (many are trained abroad). The country currently has one of the world's lowest infant mortality rates and longest average life expectancy. Singapore's healthcare plan is available to citizens, permanent residents, and non-residents.

GDP: $292.4 billion

GDP (Per Capita): $57,200

Sovereign Debt: 102.4% of GDP

Working There: Construction, digital media, finance, healthcare, sales and tourism.

Regulatory Environment: A prime location for new businesses; Singapore is ranked first in the World Bank Doing Business Index. The average time to start a business is three days, there is minimal red tape, and corruption isn't an issue.

Taxes: Individual: 0–20% (non-residents taxed at 15%), Corporate: 17%, VAT: 7%. Singapore does not tax foreign-sourced income.

Cannabis: Bad idea: prison for possession/use. Death penalty for large amounts. The fortunate get off with just a caning.

Homosexuality: Illegal between men (generally not enforced) but can result in two years imprisonment. No legal recognition of same-sex partnerships. No laws against discrimination. Small but growing gay rights movement.

Abortion: No restrictions (gestational limit of 24 weeks)

Women's Issues: Laws against rape but no laws against sexual harassment. Women enjoy the same legal rights as men but are underrepresented in politics and business management.

Guns: Some shotguns may be legally owned. License required and weapon must be stored at gun club-type facility.

Crime: Rare. Occasional petty theft in tourist areas, some credit card fraud.

Real Estate: Foreigners are allowed to purchase apartments but houses, bungalows, or vacant lots require permission of Singapore Land Authority (SLA). Financing is available for up to 70% of purchase price at competitive rates but proof of income required. Prices are some of the highest in Asia—a two-bedroom apartment can easily cost you a cool million.

Life Expectancy: 82.14 years

Moving There

Work or business. And be prepared to show your stuff. If you want fun in the sun, try Thailand.

Tourist Visa: Visa not required for U.S. citizens. Length of stay is determined by immigration officer at Singapore Changi Airport (usually 14–30 days). Visitors can request an extension of stay by applying in person at Immigration and Checkpoints Authority before duration of stay expires.

Employment Pass (EP): The standard EP is the most common type of work visa for foreign workers. Applicants must show proof of qualifications (work history, experience, education, etc.), have an offer from a Singapore employer (company must apply on your behalf) and expect to earn a minimum of around (effective January 2012) $2,300 per month (S$3000) to be eligible for the most basic of the three varieties (Q-1). There is also a P-2 (monthly salary above S$4500) and

P-1 (monthly salary above S$8000). Passes are renewable after two years for first-time applicants and every three years after initial renewal. Job seekers are advised to research available positions and work visa options at the Singapore Ministry of Manpower site (MOM): **www.mom.gov.sg**

Entrepass: Available to entrepreneurs. Applicant must show proof of experience in successful business ventures and submit plan that involves hiring at least two Singapore citizens. Minimum of $50,000 in operating capital deposited in Singapore-based bank required. Company must be registered as a Private Limited Company with Singapore Accounting and Corporate Regulatory Authority: **www.acra.gov.sg.**

Permanent Residency: Singapore offers four different schemes to immigrants seeking permanent residency. The Global Investor Program Scheme (GIPS) is available to recent arrivals seeking to invest a substantial sum in the local economy (approx. $800,000) or launch a well-funded startup. The Financial Investor Scheme (FIS) is for "high net worth" individuals (minimum assets approx. $15 million) willing to invest approx. $8 million. The most common route to a permanent stay is the Professional, Technical Personnel and Skilled Worker scheme (PTS). Applicants who hold most work passes are eligible to apply after six months, though one and two years (depending on the visa) is more the rule. The Foreign Artists Talent Scheme (FA) is a new program available to distinguished foreign artists in the fine arts, photography, dance, music, theater, literature, and film.

Citizenship: If you are gainfully employed or married to a Singapore citizen, you can register for citizenship after two years of permanent residency. Dual citizenship is not recognized by the government of Singapore so applicants must renounce U.S. citizenship. Citizens of Singapore are also considered Commonwealth citizens and are afforded certain rights and privileges in the U.K. and other Commonwealth countries.

Paul Tenney

Singapore

Singapore is a very expensive place, and some things like housing costs have simply exploded over the past year. I arrived in Singapore in January of 2010, at a low point in the housing market. That said, it depends on your lifestyle. I enjoy dining, drinking, and smoking cigarettes, which are all quite pricy here. However, it is also entirely possible to live quite cheaply here as well if you aren't trying to pretend your life is an episode of *Lifestyles of the Rich and Famous*. In any case, despite the high cost of living (I'd put it on par with Manhattan), I remarkably find that I in fact do have quite a bit more money and do enjoy a much better style and quality of life.

48. Slovenia

Climate: Mediterranean climate on the coast, continental climate with mild to hot summers and cold winters in the plateaus and valleys to the east

Government: Parliamentary Democratic Republic

Population: 2,005,692

Currency: Euro (EUR): 1 EUR = 1.36 USD

Language: Slovenian (91.1%), Serbo-Croatian (4.5%), other or unspecified (4.4%)

Religious Groups: Catholic (57.8%), Muslim (2.4%), Orthodox (2.3%), other Christian (0.9%), unaffiliated (3.5%), other or unspecified (23%), none (10.1%)

Ethnic Groups: Slovene (83.1%), Serb (2%), Croat (1.8%), Bosniak (1.1%), other or unspecified (12%)

Cost of Living compared to the U.S.: A cut below, though a plummeting dollar can quickly change that

The tiny nation of Slovenia was the first to break with the former Yugoslavia and did it with a minimum of bombing and bloodshed as well. Its capital, Ljubljana, offers plenty of well-preserved European architectural beauty as well as a thriving avant-garde scene. Prices remain lower than its Western European neighbors. A poor man's version of Vienna and a bit more exciting and exotic.

Living There

Governance: Slovenia embraces all the tenets of liberal Western-style democracy and its citizens suffer the least amount of corruption of all the newly admitted E.U. states. Oddly, it is against the law to insult a public official.

Infrastructure: Developed

Internet: Hi-speed widely available

Healthcare: Adequate medical care readily available

GDP: $56.81 billion

GDP (Per Capita): $28,400

Sovereign Debt: 35.5% of GDP

Working There: English teachers are needed in private schools in Slovenia. There are specially-trained EURES advisors in all E.U./EEA countries, whose job it is to support those seeking employment in another E.U./EEA country.

Regulatory Environment: Efficient, minimal red tape

Taxes: Corporate: 21%, Individual: 16–41%, VAT: 20%.

Cannabis: Illegal. Punishable by fine. Fairly ubiquitous.

Homosexuality: Legal. Recognition of same-sex unions pending. Laws against discrimination. Slovenes are generally tolerant of gays and lesbians and open communities can be found in cities and resorts.

Abortion: No restriction as to reason; however, parental authorization is required.

Women's Issues: Gender equality is a matter of law. Slovenia has the smallest male-to-female wage disparity in the E.U.; women earn 93.1% of what their male counterparts are paid.

Guns: Strictly licensed but legal for hunting providing one has valid membership in hunting club. Can be owned for self-defense but must show proof that life is in danger. Permit required as well as medical exam and must show knowledge of firearm use and safety.

Crime: Overall crime is low and violent crimes are relatively uncommon.

Real Estate: Slovenia's E.U. status has made purchasing property far less complicated. American citizens can now purchase property without having to apply directly to the government. 10% down payment is required and mortgages can be obtained via SKB Banka in Slovenia.

Life Expectancy: 76.92 years

Moving There

Non-E.U. citizens (e.g. Americans) don't have too many categories to choose from. You can study, do research, somehow swing a job offer or get married. Slovenia does offer some allowances for students who study here to seek employment after graduation and apply for a work and residence permit.

Schengen Visa: Maximum of 90 days per 180-day period, no extensions.

Temporary Residence Permit: Valid for up to one year stay and renewable. Applicants are required to possess valid passport, proof of sufficient monthly income (roughly equivalent to what a typical worker earns in Slovenia), and adequate health insurance. They must have a valid reason for wanting to stay in Slovenia.

Work Permit: The Ministry of Labour, Family and Social Affairs (www.mddsz.gov.si) posts complicated regulations and legislation relating to labor laws. More detailed information can be found on the Employment Services of Slovenia website (www.ess.gov.si) though, sadly, in Slovenian. If you are hired by a Slovenian company, the employer will handle the bulk of the paperwork. Corporate transfers (people working in Slovenia for a foreign firm) can also receive a permit. Under very limited circumstances where your skill set is actively sought, a permit can be issued without a job offer, allowing you to surf the Slovenian employment market. As a rule, work permits are narrowly defined and are issued for one year (occasionally up to three), renewable.

Permanent Residence: Requirements are similar to a Temporary Residence permit and applicants must live for five years in Slovenia uninterrupted.

Citizenship: Ten years legal residency (at least five years continuous prior to application), evidence of good character, proficiency in Slovenian language, and proof of self-sufficiency required.

49. South Africa

Climate: Desert; hot, dry summers with moderate winters. The climate on the east coast is subtropical. Rainfall occurs mainly during late spring and summer and during this time daily late-afternoon thunderstorms are the norm.

Government: Republic

Population: 49,052,489

Currency: South Africa Rand (ZAR): 1 ZAR = 0.14 USD

Language: IsiZulu (23.8%), IsiXhosa (17.6%), Afrikaans (13.3%), Sepedi (9.4%), English (8.2%), Setswana (8.2%), Sesotho (7.9%), Xitsonga (4.4%), other (7.2%)

Religious Groups: Christian (79.7%), Muslim (1.5%), other (2.3%), unspecified (1.4%), none (15.1%)

Ethnic Groups: Black African (79%), white (9.6%), colored (8.9%), Indian/Asian (2.5%)

Cost of Living compared to the U.S.: Reasonable

Though things have decayed a bit in recent years, post-apartheid South Africa still boasts the best infrastructure on the continent. It also has a spectacular landscape, great beaches and abundant resources. It also boasts the worst crime problem in all of Africa, if not the world (which it leads in homicides and rapes). Things have improved following its hosting of the 2010 World Cup and for those willing to take some risks, opportunity knocks.

Living There

Governance: South Africa enjoys all the trappings of a Western-style democracy with free and fair elections, independent press and judiciary, etc.

Infrastructure: The 2010 World Cup was held in South Africa and to meet the exacting standards of FIFA, the world's most influential soccer organization, significant upgrades were made to the country's public transportation, roads, and telecommunications system.

Internet: Despite advances over the past few years, Internet use among the general population remains sluggish with just a little over 10% of the population connected. Broadband is mostly available in urban areas and resorts and can be expensive as can dial-up due to telephone call charges. Mobile cellular remains the most popular communications medium and is widely available.

Healthcare: Both public and private systems. Private medical facilities are good in urban areas and in the vicinity of game parks, but they may be limited elsewhere. Pharmacies are well-stocked and equivalents to most American medicines are available. Public facilities tend to be lower quality.

GPD: $527.5 billion

GDP (Per Capita): $10,700

Sovereign Debt: 33.2% of GDP

Working There: Shortage of skilled labor, managerial and technical personnel.

Regulatory Environment: Recent reforms have made it easier to launch a business, but the regulatory process still has a great deal of red tape.

Taxes: Corporate: 28%, Individual: 18–40%, VAT: 14%. South African residents are taxed on all income sources. Temporary residents living in South Africa more than 183 days per year are only taxed on income earned in the country. Capital gains are taxed at 15% for individuals, 30% for corporations.

Cannabis: Illegal but widely available

Homosexuality: Legal. Same-sex marriage legally recognized. Laws against discrimination. There are disturbing cases of "corrective rape" in which lesbians are targeted for rape in order to "cure" them of homosexuality.

Abortion: Unrestricted

Women's Issues: Domestic violence and violence against women are a longstanding concern.

Guns: Gun ownership legal for pistol, shotgun, rifle with permit.

Crime: South Africa ranks first in the world in rape and murder. Carjacking, assaults, and robberies are very common. There has been a small decline in violent crime, offering a glimmer of hope for those yearning to venture out of their secure compounds.

Real Estate: Non-citizens are allowed to purchase property. Properties over $71,000 are subject to a transfer tax of R7,000 ($1,010) plus between 5–8% of the value of the property over $71,000. Attorney fees for transferring property can be as much as an additional 2%. Full mortgages are available for permanent residents or those in the process of becoming residents. Non-residents can finance up to half the cost.

Life Expectancy: 48.98 years

Moving There

Generally open to people of adequate means. South Africa is eager to attract people who can help economically (via labor or capital) rebuild their country. Skilled workers are in demand and investors are golden, and recent college grads are invited to apply for all-inclusive work/visa/accommodation packages. Very detailed information is posted on the South African Government services website: **www.services.gov.za**.

Tourist Visa: A visa is not required for U.S. citizens wishing to stay in South Africa for up to 90 days.

Visitor Permit: Available to foreigners seeking to reside in South Africa on sabbatical, for voluntary or charitable activities, or research. Applicants must provide documentation from institution confirming mission in South Africa and letter from host organization. A deposit in the amount equivalent to the cost of a round-trip plane ticket is required as is proof of valid medical insurance and adequate funds. Visa is valid for three months to three years.

Temporary Residence Permit: Over a dozen categories of these permits exist. They are available to foreigners seeking to work, study, retire, or operate a business in South Africa. Requirements are similar to visitor permit (proof of funds, insurance etc.) and valid for up to three years. General work permit requires contract signed by employer and proof of experience and/or qualifications. There are also permits for workers with exceptional skills and those who fulfill quota needs, as well as corporate transfers. Retiree permit requires proof of income (approx. $2,877/month). Business Permit requires capital outlay of 2.5 million Rand (around $375,000) plus it must employ five locals. There is also an Exchange Permit program allowing applicants under 25 to come to South Africa for one year and work in a program where all lodging and other needs are taken care of by the employer.

Five years temporary residency with work permit allows immigrant to apply for **Permanent Residency**. Also offered to anyone who has received a permanent offer of employment.

Student Visas available per the usual requirements.

Citizenship: Four years residence required in eight-year period prior to application. Must be proficient in each of South Africa's official languages, be of good character, and possess knowledge of rights and responsibilities of South African citizenship.

50. South Korea

Climate: Temperate, with rainfall heavier in summer than in winter. Winters are very cold with frequent frost and snow.
Government: Republic
Population: 48,636,068
Currency: South Korean Won (KRW): 1 KRW = 0.0009 USD
Language: Korean, English widely taught in middle and high school
Religious Groups: No affiliation (46%), Christian (26%), Buddhist (26%), Confucianist (1%), other (1%)
Ethnic Groups: Korean
Cost of Living compared to the U.S.: Similar

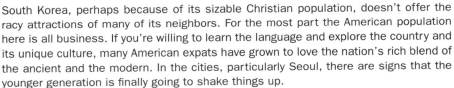

South Korea, perhaps because of its sizable Christian population, doesn't offer the racy attractions of many of its neighbors. For the most part the American population here is all business. If you're willing to learn the language and explore the country and its unique culture, many American expats have grown to love the nation's rich blend of the ancient and the modern. In the cities, particularly Seoul, there are signs that the younger generation is finally going to shake things up.

As one of the most prosperous and well-developed countries in Asia, South Korea allows you to enjoy all the conveniences of modern life with the added plus of being able to step back in time as this ancient land is studded with rich archaeological ruins and beautiful, centuries-old Buddhist temples and monasteries. If you love beautiful scenery and like to go hiking, Korea offers a number of natural wonders and picturesque landscapes that range from eye-catching mountain ranges to Hawaii-like sandy beaches, subtropical vegetation, and dazzling waterfalls. Many foodies rank Korean cuisine among the world's tastiest.

Living There

Governance: South Korea is a Western-style constitutional democracy governed by a president and unicameral legislature. The country holds free and fair elections and the government shows an overall respect for human rights. Korea has a very independent media and freedom of speech is allowed although the state can restrict speech deemed Communist or pro-North Korea. Korea's National Police Agency, particularly the Combat Police Division, have been known for cracking a few heads, particularly during protests.
Infrastructure: Up to Western standards
Internet: 100% broadband penetration, most of it blazing fast. Ranked first in the world.

Healthcare: State-of-the-art.

GPD: $1.467 trillion

GDP (Per Capita): $30,200

Sovereign Debt: 23.7% of GDP

Working There: Large demand for English teachers for which attractive packages are offered. Technical and business skills are also in demand.

Regulatory Environment: Regulatory framework designed to foster new businesses and innovation; efficient and easy to negotiate.

Taxes: Corporate: 24.2%, Individual: 35%, VAT: 10%. Residents taxed on worldwide income (some exemptions available).

Cannabis: Strictly illegal, but not unheard of around the alternative youth scene. An American English teacher spent three months in a detention facility then was fined and deported for showing traces of hashish in his bloodstream.

Homosexuality: Legal. No recognition of same-sex unions. Laws against discrimination.

Abortion: To preserve a woman's health and in cases of rape, incest, and fetal impairment.

Women's Issues: Women enjoy the same legal rights as men and there are laws prohibiting sexual harassment but Korea has a strong patriarchal culture. Korean women have very low workforce participation rates, there are substantial wage disparities between men and women, and sexual discrimination in the workplace is common. Domestic violence remains a problem.

Guns: Majority of guns are strictly illegal. Some firearms can be owned by hunters and sport shooters with special government approval.

Crime: Low violent crime

Real Estate: A foreigner who resides in Korea can purchase property. The process for non-resident foreigners is a bit more complicated, but still possible. Be warned: South Korea has notoriously steep transaction costs (approximately 22% of the property's value).

Life Expectancy: 78.81 years

Moving There

Visas operate on a complicated letter system:

- **A** = Official government business
- **C** = Short-term visas (e.g., tourist)
- **D** = For students, trainees, investors, corporate transfers, artist/performers and journalists. Validity periods vary but are generally renewable as long as conditions of issuance still apply.
- **E** = Longer-term but finite (non-immigrant), usually work-related (e.g. English teacher) visas. Generally issued for one year, renewable.
- **F** = Immigrant class visa. For those who wish to stay for very long or indefinite terms. Generally for families and spouses but also open to other residents under certain conditions.

Most Americans who come here, however, hardly need to delve into the minutiae, since they have job offers (particularly English teaching) and most of the details are taken care of by the hiring company. Unless you're reuniting with a family or mate, few people come here just to hang out or retire anyway.

Tourist Visa: Visa is not required for U.S. citizens who wish to stay in Korea for up to 90 days (extension of stay is not permitted).

Investor Visa (D-8): Korea has stiffened requirements for those wishing to set up a company and conduct business in the country. Investment should be around $95,000 (100m KRW). Visas are issued for one year and renewable as long as conditions still apply.

Work Visa: The Republic of Korea offers over a dozen different kinds of work visas that cover a wide range of professions. An in-person interview at an overseas consulate or embassy is usually required to apply. Foreign Language Instructor (E-2) is the most common among American transplants. To be employed as a language instructor in Korea, applicants must provide employment contract, résumé/CV, copy of official academic transcript and proof of college degree, job description, and a notarized letter of reference. Most employers will assist new hires in filing for visa and providing the appropriate documents and paperwork. All work visas are usually valid for one year, renewable.

Residence (F-2): Those who belong to select professions (foreign language instructors, professors, individuals working in specialized trades, etc.) can apply for residence status through a point system established by the Ministry of Justice. If you reside in Korea for one year or more, you can apply for F-2 status, and after three years, apply for **Permanent Resident status (F-5)**. The primary criteria are age, academic or professional background, work or study experience in Korea, and/or whether applicant has completed a Korean social integration program. Applicants scoring 80 out of a possible 120 points qualify for the visa upgrade. Investors of $500,000 (or others who are deemed to be special contributors to the Korean economy) are also welcome.

Citizenship: Applicant must have legally resided in Republic of Korea for more than five consecutive years, be of good character, show proof of economic self-sufficiency, be proficient in Korean language, and possess knowledge of Korean customs and culture.

Rob York
Seoul, South Korea

When I arrived here many things were different, particularly as most of my bills, for housing/electricity/water, were covered by the institute I taught for. Because I am a native English-speaker I am asked for favors that I never would have been in America, usually to tutor, and all the more so because I have experience doing things, like writing articles and speaking publicly, that not all English-speakers have. In essence, living here has made me feel a lot more valuable, but at the same time creates a lot more demands on my time.

Having a Korean family has its own advantages and disadvantages. They are particularly tight-knit, and therefore my mother-in-law has provided most of the care for our son, and my brother-in-law has helped us out financially when we needed it. However, living with one's mother-in-law is not always convenient, and my brother-in-law has had hard times of his own that we have been obliged to help him with. Since the financial crisis he has had great difficulty in keeping a job, and we have at times had to take him in.

Outside of Seoul Americans are not common, and those that live there receive a good deal of attention. In Seoul, they're all over the place. They are easy to find at Itaewon and a few other districts, but a few Internet searches would reveal many more nascent foreign communities in Seoul and other parts of Korea.

Leslie Reed
Incheon, South Korea

Culture shock takes at least three months to get over, or at least make peace with. Everything is unfamiliar, and the smallest tasks require great effort due to the language barrier. Korean apartments have a thermometer that can be set to heat the floors, and there's a separate button that must be pressed to turn on hot water for showering. No one will tell you about these things at first, Koreans don't think about it, and other Westerners are proud to have figured it out and want you to learn it the hard way. Another word of wisdom is to bring sheets and soft pillows. Neither are readily available, and are grossly expensive. Another huge expense is coffee, $30 for a mid-sized bag of beans. Everyone drinks tea or instant coffee packs.

One lesson to learn fast is that the most important social skill here is to keep face. This means that you do not get anywhere in this country by being emotional in any way. You need to be forceful and resolute in negotiations, but getting angry gets you nowhere, and you instantly lose the respect of the other person.

Incheon is the third largest city, but has a very suburban feel. For art and culture and non-Korean food you have to travel the hour and a half to Seoul. Being a lesbian, I was very curious about the gay scene and have been to every gay bar in Seoul. Most are located in Itaewon near the army base. The neighborhood is famously seedy, and is where most Westerners and GIs go to party on the weekends. The gay area is called "homo hill" and is a little off the main drag. The first time I looked for it I took the wrong street and ended up on "hooker hill" a block over. Behind me were two army guys and all the women leaned out of dark doorways beckoning to them in lingerie. Quickly made my way over to the other hill and found a vibrant strip of bars, drag queens, and dancing. The vibe is very fresh and fun because Koreans are coming out of the closet and going through a rapid social transformation, especially after the very famous actor, Hong Suk Chon, came out.

Turner Wright
Bugu, South Korea
I am in the small town of Bugu, on the east coast of Uljin City, in the Gyeongsangbukdo region of South Korea. I have a Korean apartment, which was included in my teaching contract (some are, some aren't). I don't need much space and this place is perfect for lounging and the occasional couchsurfer. For the most part, apartments in Korea are smaller than those in the U.S.; there's a threshold at the door for removing your shoes; the toilet, sink, and bathing area are all in one space, not separated by a curtain or different flooring; there is no oven; there is no dryer—clothes are hung in a "room" between inner and outer windows; carpeting is rare—usually the floors are soft wood or a veneer; air conditioning is not central, if you even have it—a small unit can be turned off and on as needed; closets aren't too common either, as wardrobes are available; during winter, the floors can be heated.

51. Spain

Climate: Temperate. Summers are hot in the interior and more moderate and cloudy along the coast; winters are cold in the interior and partly cloudy and cool along the coast.
Government: Constitutional monarchy
Population: 40,525,002
Currency: Euro (EUR): 1 EUR = 1.36 USD
Language: Castilian Spanish [official] (74%), Catalan (17%), Galician (7%), Basque (2%)
Religious Groups: Roman Catholic (94%), other (6%)
Ethnic Groups: Mediterranean and Nordic
Cost of Living compared to the U.S.: Far from the most expensive country in the Eurozone, but don't expect any bargains. Rents, particularly in Madrid, are stiff.

Once upon a time, life in Spain was affordable. Then came the Euro. Undaunted Americans still flock here, congregating in Barcelona and Madrid, while students head for the medieval city of Salamanca. Nightlife is excellent and tends to go late. The siesta breaks during the afternoon haven't disappeared but the jobs have. Unemployment has soared to 20%, the real estate bubble that previously supported the economy has collapsed, and the conventional wisdom marks this country as the next bailout case and rumbles of Athens-like social unrest have begun to be felt. For all that, people for the most part seem boisterously happy. Must be the Sangria.

Living There

Governance: Spain is a Western-style democracy, with free and fair elections, independent judiciary and media, with freedom of speech and assembly guaranteed.

Infrastructure: It's no Switzerland but still OK.

Internet: Overall Internet use slightly above European average. Broadband penetration considered average compared to rest of Europe.

Healthcare: Medical care and facilities are good throughout the country.

GDP: $1.376 trillion

GDP (Per Capita): $29,500

Sovereign Debt: 63.4% of GDP

Working There: Teach English or translate, if you can. Some opportunities in the tourist trade.

Regulatory Environment: Spain recently eased its regulatory guidelines and licensing requirements to make it easier for new businesses. Spain still averages over a month to launch a business.

Taxes: Corporate: 25–30%, Individual: 0–42%, VAT: 18%. Residents are taxed on worldwide income.

Cannabis: Decriminalized; possession and home cultivation for personal use allowed but you can still be fined if you light up in public. Judging by the odor that wafts through many a Spanish street, this hasn't discouraged many people.

Homosexuality: Same-sex marriage legal, laws against discrimination. Spain is tolerant toward gays and lesbians and open communities exist all over the country.

Abortion: To preserve mental health, to save the woman's life and physical health. Also in cases of rape or fetal impairment.

Women's Issues: Women's rights are protected by the government, though cultural habits mean that violence and harassment are still problematic. Nonetheless, women are well presented in all levels of business and government.

Guns: Some pistols, rifles, shotguns legal to own with permit.

Crime: Some violent crime in Madrid and Barcelona. Pickpocketing and other petty crime common in tourist areas.

Real Estate: Purchase of property is legal for Americans. Buyer inherits all unpaid debts on the property.

Life Expectancy: 80.05 years

Moving There

Spain's tough. Visas are not handed out willy-nilly unless they're for students, family, retirees or spouses. Jobs are scarce and the government is not eager to see them go to foreigners, particularly those from outside the E.U. Freelance writers (or those who can produce documentation that make them appear that way), however, have an in. The wealthy, as usual, have it easy, too.

Note: Requirements for Spanish visas often vary according to applicant's nationality, purpose of stay and other variables (e.g., having Spanish family members). Unless you are renewing or upgrading a residence permit, you must apply at the Spanish consulate here in the U.S. for the proper entry visa unless you fancy making a return trip. A Schengen (tourist) visa cannot be extended or converted in Spain. Once you arrive, you still must take your visa and apply for a Residency Permit/Card (*Tarjeta de Residencia*) within 30 days of arriving in the country at the Foreigner's Office (*Oficina de Extranjeros*) or local police station.

Schengen Visa: Maximum 90-day stay per 180-day period, no extensions.

Resident Visas/Permits are generally valid for one to five years and are renewable up to five years.

Residence Visa for Retirement: Must prove pension of a minimum of $10,000 per year and $1700 for each additional dependent.

Residence Visa/Work: Requires formal offer of work and not easy to come by in E.U., particularly in Spain, with skyrocketing unemployment.

Non-Lucrative Resident Visa: This means you have your own source of income and don't require doing anything gainful in Spain except eat and sunbathe. Requires a minimum demonstrated income (pension, annuity, investment dividend, etc.) of $75,000 (plus $15,000 per dependent) annually.

Freelancer or Collaborator's Resident Visa: Because Spain is an E.U. country, unless you have a direct connection with a Spanish employer, it may be hard to get permission to work in Spain. If you have a writing background, some American expats recommend you pursue this visa which is specifically designed to give legal residency to media professionals. You will need to provide documentation that you are representing an American publication (but you don't need an actual contract, so just getting an editor or publisher to writer this on your behalf is enough) and that only you can carry out the duties you are assigned.

Student's Visa: Per the usual requirements. Good for as long as you're enrolled in an approved program of study or research.

Permanent Resident: Foreigners are generally eligible to apply after five years.

Citizenship: All legal residents of Spain can apply for citizenship after 10 years. Nationals of Latin American countries, Andorra, Philippines or Jews who can show proof of Sephardic ancestry are eligible to apply after two years. Descendents of exiles from the Spanish Civil War or those with Spanish family or spouse are also eligible to apply.

Colleen Terry
Madrid, Spain

I live in a major city here with everything you need within a couple square blocks, whereas in the U.S. you have to depend on your car to get anywhere. Gas prices used to be much higher in Spain than in the States, but they are beginning to even out. Right now I'm paying €1.32/liter for diesel ($7.22/gallon).

I pay around €200 / year for property tax, €150 for vehicle tax and €50 for garbage tax. Three property tax references I have for the States are €3000/year, €7000/year and €30,000 year (two in California and one in Chicago), so here it is clearly a lot more affordable.

Drug prices are often less here. For example, back in the '90s I was getting Depo-Provera birth control shots (don't think that even exists anymore), which cost me $40 in the States and about $3 in Spain.

Years ago, it was really hard (if not impossible) to find things like peanut butter, flour tortillas, cranberry juice and all the other American comfort food we've grown up with, so I had my Mom send care packages so I could "survive." Now you can get practically anything you are looking for—with the exception of sour cream—at reasonable prices. At this point, though, I no longer feel the need for most of that stuff anyway.

It took me a while to get used to the food here, especially all the canned seafood like cockles and mussels, clams and barnacles, plus a bajillion other things that were just plain weird. Meal times can be a bit tricky as well. I have no problem eating dinner at 10:00 or even 11:00 on weekends, but during the week I try to sneak a quick dinner closer to 8:00 or 8:30, which is unheard of here. I've tried all the things that people seem to love here—blood sausage, heart, kidney, lung, liver, brains, pig trotters, snout, sweetbreads and other assorted animal parts which I would never have considered food, and I just cannot seem to develop a taste for them. Well, blood sausage is actually pretty yummy if done right, but I just can't do the other stuff.

Public transport in Madrid is very likely the best in Europe. The number of Metro stations has probably increased fivefold in the past 20 years, and the facilities and installations are state-of-the-art. Roads are generally good and plentiful, but a lot of local streets are full of potholes that get patched up occasionally, but then just turn to rubble a couple of months later.

Bureaucracy is no different from in the U.S.—it's a lot of running around in circles, calling phone numbers that nobody ever answers, standing in long lines (only to find out it was the wrong one)...although it seems that things are getting a little better.

52. Sweden

Climate: Temperate in south with cold, cloudy winters and cool, cloudy summers; subarctic in north

Government: Constitutional monarchy

Population: 9,088,728

Currency: Swedish Krona (SEK): 1 SEK = 0.15 USD

Language: Swedish (official), Sami- and Finnish-speaking minorities.

Religious Groups: Lutheran (87%), other (13%) [includes Roman Catholic, Orthodox, Baptist, Muslim, Jewish, and Buddhist]

Ethnic Groups: Swedes with Finnish and Sami minority; some Yugoslavs, Danes, Norwegians, Greeks, Turks

Cost of Living compared to the U.S: Pricey

Daunting though it is in reality, many people dream of moving to Sweden. Some seek the ultimate social-democratic paradise. Others like the fact that everybody's blonde. The weather can be a bit dreary, and the culture perhaps a bit unexciting to some, but everything works, there's very little crime and the state sees to it that everybody's basic needs are met. And unlike most of Europe, it's not that crowded and still retains ample swaths of reasonably pristine nature. The downside to all this is that Sweden is not really that excited about having non-Swedes cutting themselves in on the deal. The major industries here tend to be technology-intensive (automotive, energy, telecommunications and pharma) and multinational (Volvo, Ericsson, Electrolux), and that's good news for the highly skilled, since they have opportunities to come over, either on a job offer or by transferring over after securing a positing in the American branch first. Those with knowledge and credentials can fill posts at universities and technical institutes. Otherwise, marrying usually works and even having a Swedish boyfriend or girlfriend can be considered grounds to issue a residence permit. Self-employment permits are not easy. Established freelance journalists can swing it, but typically you need to present something that is documentable and sustainable—basically, a real business plan. Expect it to be examined with the same intensity as it would receive from a venture capitalist. Once you're in, however, it doesn't take long to establish yourself permanently.

Living There

Governance: Free and fair elections, independent judiciary, and a government strongly committed to respecting human rights and political liberties. Sweden has some of the strongest freedom of information laws in Europe and a thriving free press. According to Transparency International, a non-profit that monitors corruption, the Swedish government is one of the least corrupt in the world.

Infrastructure: Developed

Internet: Widely available; over 90% of Swedish residents have Internet access. Sweden enjoys one of the highest broadband penetration rates in Europe; hi-speed Internet widely available.

Healthcare: Sweden has a world-renowned public healthcare system that is considered one of the best in the world. Healthcare is available to immigrants who possess a residence visa. Small co-pays are required for some services. Private pay insurance is also available but most prefer the national healthcare system.

GDP: $354 billion

GDP (Per Capita): $39,000

Sovereign Debt: 40.8% of GDP

Working There: Some demand for advanced IT, banking and accounting, sales, marketing.

Regulatory Environment: Efficient, transparent, and designed to encourage small businesses and innovation. The World Bank Doing Business Index ranks Sweden the 14th best location in the world to start a business.

Taxes: Corporate: 26.3%, Individual: 54–61%, VAT: 25%. Residents taxed on worldwide income.

Cannabis: Illegal, somewhat available and usually discreetly consumed. Fines for small amounts, prison for large quantities. Note: consumption of cannabis is a crime in Sweden and police can make suspected users take a drug test.

Homosexuality: Legal; Sweden is considered one of the most gay-tolerant countries in the world. Laws prohibit discrimination, and same-sex unions (registered couples) and same-sex marriages are legally recognized.

Abortion: Legal without restriction as to reason (gestational limit 18 weeks)

Women's Issues: Thanks to the strange case of Julian Assange, few people are unaware that Sweden has some of the world's strictest laws regarding rape, domestic abuse, sexual harassment and gender discrimination in the world. Women are well represented in both business and politics. Small wage gap between men and women.

Guns: Legal to own some firearms. Strict licensing and storing requirements.

Crime: Crime rates are low in Sweden and violent crime is rare. Some petty theft in larger cities and on public transportation.

Real Estate: There are no restrictions on foreigners buying property in Sweden. Buyer must pay stamp fee that comes to 1% of purchase price. Financing is available from local lenders for up to 75% of purchase price. The average price for a one- or two- building building property is approx. $285,000. Prices are significantly lower in central Sweden.

Life Expectancy: 81.07 years

Moving There

Sweden is not open to new residents and most Americans living there do so by dint of family or marriage. Failing that, bring some heavy skills, wads of cash or you're likely to be disappointed.

Schengen Visa: Maximum 90-day stay per 180-day period, no extensions.

Residence Permit: Foreign nationals wishing to reside in Sweden for more than 90 days must apply for a residence permit. Applications must be submitted to Swedish embassy in country of origin. If you are already in Sweden, you must apply with the Swedish Migration board. Documents showing proof of employment, self-employment, or reason for remaining in Sweden (family, relationship, study, retire, etc.). If you are unemployed or retired, you must show proof of income (at least $1,100/month) and have a pretty compelling reason as to why they should let you hang around.

Work Permit: Offer of employment from Swedish firm required and earnings must be sufficient to support yourself. Employer must also provide information to Swedish Migration Board that position could not be filled by E.U. resident and other relevant data. Permit is valid for two years and in four years you can apply for permanent residency. Applications for work permits can be made online via Swedish Migration Board (see below).

Permanent Resident: Non-E.U. citizens are eligible for a permanent resident card (known as a PUT) after four years (not counting student years).

Citizenship: Minimum of five years continuous legal residency (not counting student years) and record of good conduct while living in Sweden.

Your official portal into the process of moving to Sweden and remaining there can be found here: www.migrationsverket.se

53. Switzerland

Climate: Temperate, but varies with altitude; cold, cloudy, rainy/snowy winters; cool to warm, cloudy, humid summers with occasional showers
Government: A confederation similar in structure to a Federal Republic.
Population: 7,604,467
Currency: Swiss Franc (CHF): 1 CHF = 1.04 USD
Language: German [official] (63.7%), French [official] (20.4%), Italian [official] (6.5%), Serbo-Croatian (1.5%), Albanian (1.3%), Portuguese (1.2%), Spanish (1.2%), English (1%), Romansch (0.5%), other (2.8%)
Religious Groups: Roman Catholic (41.8%), Protestant (35.3%), Muslim (4.3%), Orthodox (1.8%), other Christian (0.4%), other (1%), unspecified (4.3%), none (11.1%)
Ethnic Groups: German (65%), French (18%), Italian (10%), Romansch (1%), other (6%)
Cost of Living compared to the U.S.: Ouch!

With its unbeatable standard of living and a sovereign currency that holds its own while surrounded on all sides by the mighty Euro, it's not easy getting in on the world's most neutral country. But if you've got plenty of money or an "in" at the U.N., a life of ski slopes and fine chocolates could be yours. Recent treaties and modifications have tarnished the country's once-gleaming reputation for banking discretion, but as long as you're not hiding your money, there are few safer places to keep it. For the young and brainy: the country boasts world-class higher education and research institutions (including the most badass atomic particle accelerator in the world) and while standards are high, tuitions, unlike almost everything else here, are a bargain by U.S. standards.

Living There
Governance: As free, democratic, and squeaky clean as they come.
Infrastructure: Developed
Internet: Hi-speed widely available
Healthcare: There is no state-run public healthcare service in Switzerland, and no reciprocal arrangements for healthcare with other countries, so health insurance is essential. Although all medical provision is private, it is heavily regulated by government, as is the health insurance system. All Swiss residents are required to take out basic health insurance within three months of arrival in Switzerland, the cost of which varies between cantons and insurance companies. All of which makes the Swiss healthcare system one of the best, and most expensive, in the world.

GPD: $326.5 billion
GDP (Per Capita): $42,900
Sovereign Debt: 38.2% of GDP
Working There: It is difficult to find a job in Switzerland unless you are employed by the United Nations, are posted there by an overseas employer or have specialist or technical skills that might be in demand in Switzerland, such as IT. Salaries are well above European averages.
Regulatory Climate: Efficient, transparent, and relatively easy to negotiate. You can start a business in Switzerland in under three weeks.
Taxes: Corporate 13–25%, Individual: 0–13.2% (federal), VAT: between 3.6% and 7.6%. Residents taxed on worldwide income (earnings from foreign permanent establishments and real estate are exempted).
Cannabis: Technically illegal, but enforcement is spotty
Homosexuality: Legal. Legally-recognized domestic partnerships. Some laws against anti-gay discrimination. Although the Swiss tend to be culturally conservative, there is nevertheless no real harassment or intimidation of gays and lesbians.
Abortion: Legal without restriction as to reason
Women's Issues: Despite Switzerland's sterling international reputation, the country is dogged by concerns about domestic violence. One in five women in Switzerland (especially immigrants) will likely experience sexual or domestic abuse. Despite laws against employment discrimination, advocacy groups contend that Swiss women are still underpaid compared to men.
Guns: No permit required for single-shot or semi-auto long gun. Most other firearms require Weapons Acquisition Permit. Permit required to carry concealed weapon.
Crime: There have been rumors that such a thing exists, but most Swiss have yet to witness any.
Real Estate: Legal residents with a Permit C have few restrictions on their ability to buy property. Other foreign nationals are restricted to holiday homes or designated investment properties and must receive approval from their local canton. Mortgages are available to residents usually with a 20%–40% down payment. Interest rates are below 5%. In some cases, property may not be sold for five years.
Life Expectancy: 80.85 years

Moving There

Have a job, and offer to study at a university or a few mil in the bank. Otherwise, your stay will not exceed 90 days on their precisely-calibrated chronometers.
Schengen Visa: Maximum 90-day stay over 180-day period.
Residence/Work Permit: If you would like to prolong your stay or establish residency in Switzerland, you must apply with the cantonal immigration and labor market authorities where you hope to stay. Each canton has jurisdiction over immigration and labor policy. Permits are issued for short-term residence (less than one year), annual residence permits, and permanent residence permits (unlimited stay).

If you have a specific part of Switzerland where you would like to work or settle, consult the web page for cantonal immigration and labor market authorities: **www.bfm.admin.ch**

Student Visas are available, requirements are somewhat cumbersome, but if you've been accepted and enrolled at a Swiss university, you should be able to swing it, provided you promise to leave when your schooling ends.

Citizenship: Twelve years legal residency required and must have lived in Switzerland as resident at least three of previous five years prior to application. Depending on residence, you must be proficient in German, French, Swiss German, Italian, or Romansch. You must also possess sufficient knowledge of Swiss history, customs, and traditions. Note: In Switzerland, citizenship is not granted by the central government but by the authorities in the canton where you reside.

Bryn Martin
Lausanne, Switzerland

Life in Lausanne is incredibly beautiful and balanced. Great weather, refreshing lake, majestic mountains, flowery parks, cobblestone streets, authentic bars, efficient transportation, fresh food, authentic dining, super street musicians, tasty street markets, crunchy baguettes. The shops close on weekdays at 7 p.m. and on Sundays every dad goes to the park to play games with their children and all you can hear are bells.

The most difficult part of establishing residency in Switzerland is finding an apartment. You must be accepted by the agencies who control the apartment rentals, all of whom have dozens and dozens of other candidates. There are a lot of steps you need to take before you can even start to apply, and even after you apply it can take many months to be accepted. In many ways, the whole process can be a bit of a Catch-22. The best way to make the transition is to sublease an apartment for the first three to six months after arriving and while you are living there get your forms (housing permit, etc.) and start applying for apartments. This is nearly a full-time job and I have met people who took more than six months to find an apartment. It took us three months, while renting a one-room flat without a kitchen for $2000/month. The best place to find a sublet is the Swiss website anibis.ch. Craigslist-switzerland and petitesannonces.ch are full of scams. Don't use them.

Everything is about as expensive as it was in Chicago. A two-bedroom apartment costs about $1300–2000+/month. Some things are much more expensive, such as meat which can be 10 to 20 times the cost in the USA. Eating out at a "sit-down" type of place will cost at least $50 for two people. If you have a drink, it can easily be more than $100. Public transportation is super and costs about $70/month. Owning a car requires a job that pays at least $100k/year unless you are very frugal.

54. Thailand

Climate: Warm and tropical monsoon with temperatures averaging between 75 and 82 degrees. Three seasons: the cool season (November to January), hot season (April to May), and the rainy season (June to October).

Government: Constitutional monarchy

Population: 67,089,500

Currency: Baht (THB): 1 THB = 0.03 USD

Language: Thai (official language), English is second language of elites, regional dialects

Religious Groups: Buddhist (95%), Muslim (3.8%), other (1.2%)

Ethnic Groups: Thai (75%), Chinese (14%), other (11%)

Cost of Living compared to the U.S.: Very cheap

The land of a thousand smiles, scuba fanatics and sex tourists has seen its fair share of political turmoil in recent years, though it doesn't seem to have scared much of the expat community away. Not when a modern one-bedroom beachfront condo in Pattaya can be had for under $100,000 and $20 will buy you a nice dinner for two with plenty of change left over. Outside of late winter/early spring monsoon season and the occasional visit to a local temple, t-shirts and shorts are all you need.

Living There

Governance: The ousting of Prime Minister Thaksin Shinawatra in a military coup in 2006 plunged the previously stable democracy into political turmoil. Due to the political unrest, Internet and press censorship are becoming common, and clashes between protesters and police are a frequent occurrence.

Infrastructure: Needs improvement

Internet: Broadband expanding out of cities and developed tourist areas. Connection speed slightly slower than in the West. Many Thai users still rely on dial-up access.

Healthcare: Adequate in most parts of the country

GDP: $580.3 billion

GDP (Per Capita): $8,700

Sovereign Debt: 42.3% of GDP

Working There: Teach English, volunteer.

Regulatory Environment: Overall, Thailand's regulatory requirements are less costly and time-consuming than many countries in the region. Some corruption.

Taxes: Corporate: 30%, Individual: 5–37%, VAT: 7%. Residents of Thailand are taxed on worldwide income if money was derived during period of residency.

Cannabis: Strict laws but widely available

Homosexuality: Legal. No legal recognition of same-sex unions, No laws prohibiting discrimination. Thais in general are very tolerant toward gays and lesbians and there is a thriving gay scene in some of Thailand's larger cities.

Abortion: Legal to save a woman's life or to preserve mental or physical health. Allowed in cases of rape or fetal impairment.

Women's Issues: Sexual harassment strictly illegal in both public and private sector and laws are enforced. There is a significant wage disparity between men and women. Domestic violence, human trafficking, and child prostitution are problems.

Guns: Pistols, rifles, and shotguns legal to own. License required. Strict limits on ammunition.

Crime: Low, except for the typical petty crime nuisances

Real Estate: Foreigners cannot own land in Thailand unless they invest an additional $1.3 million for five years in Thai government-authorized investments (such as government bonds). This restriction only applies to land and foreigners frequently and legally buy, sell, and invest in condos, especially in resort areas. Condo building must be over half Thai-owned and the money to pay for the condo cannot have been earned in Thailand. None of these restrictions apply to permanent residents and they are also commonly circumvented by forming a holding company. The transferring fee is 2% the registered value of the property and there is a .5% Duty Stamp from either the appraised value of the property or actual purchasing price, whichever is higher. These taxes can be paid by either the seller or buyer, depending on the agreement. If you are selling a property after fewer than five years, the tax rate is 3.3% of the selling or assessed price of an asset (whichever is higher).

Life Expectancy: 75.02 years

Moving There

Very open to retirees. Investment visa requirements can be steep but if you're starting a business the bar drops appreciably, though that's more than made up for in your tax liability. Most freelancers get by on regular border runs.

Tourist Visa: Copy of round-trip ticket and proof of adequate finances for stay (approximately $500) required for one that's valid for 60 days (one extension between 7–30 days allowed; most expats who don't advance beyond this visa opt for a border run). Visa enables three entries into Thailand. For shorter visits, citizens of most Western countries are given a 30-day entry stamp upon arrival to Thailand via airline. Your return ticket must show that you will leave prior to 30 days to get this visa.

Investment Visa: Requires investment of 10,000,000 baht (approx. $330,000) in Thai bank. Valid one year, renewable.

Non-Immigrant Visa for Retirees: Must be 50 years or older and show proof of Thai bank assets of at least 800,000 baht (approx. $26,000) or monthly income of 65,000 baht (approx. $2,100). Valid one year, renewable, though retirees must report to immigration every three months to verify their address.

Non-Immigrant Visa: These come in many familiar flavors—employment, study, teach, conduct business, unite with family, etc. Documentation, such as letter of invitation from a sponsor, nature of the business you will conduct and business license, company profile, number of employees, shareholders, etc. Those coming with a letter of employment will still need to apply for a work permit, as well. Applicants must show proof of adequate finances (at least 20,000 baht, or approx. $667). Work permit and letter of approval from Ministry of Labor are also required (this is usually arranged through employer). Prospective business owners must provide evidence of financial status (if self-employed), and company information if planning on working with Thai firm. Valid for one year, renewable, but you must exit the country (simply crossing the border and returning will do) every 90 days.

Immigrant Visa (Permanent Residency):

Must have a total of at least three years on a Non-Immigrant Visa with three extensions.

Permanent Residency is granted on the basis of business (judged on the size and nature of the business), employment (three years valid work permit); investment (between $100,000–300,000 in property, government or state enterprise bonds, as a deposit in one or more Thai banks, and other investments in accordance with the specification of the Immigration Commission), expert or academic purpose (must have annual income above $10,000); supporting a family who are Thai citizens; being a dependent of a husband or father who is a Thai citizen; being accompanied by a husband, father or son/daughter who already has a residence permit.

Thai citizenship is seldom granted to those outside family and spouses of Thai citizens and most citizen functions and activities are open to Permanent Residents.

David Herrick

Phuket, Thailand

I moved to Thailand around 8½ years ago. I came first on vacation and fell in love with the place and wanted to spend time here long-term.

People aren't running scared here like they are in the States. There is not a sense of impending doom that I feel when I am in the U.S. Politicians are generally not trusted or liked here, but the Thai people don't rely on government to the extent that Americans do. Social services are minimal, and there is no Social Security after retirement. Family is the cornerstone of Thai society, and that's where financial support is expected. Contrary to the States though, the children (specifically, the daughters) are obliged to support their parents and brothers.

Laws in Thailand are only applied if the police choose to do so. For instance, prostitution is illegal but you'd never know it walking into any one of thousands of bars where the bar girls make it abundantly clear that the customer can go with them for a fee.

Cost of living is significantly less here in Thailand. The only thing that's about the same as in the States is gasoline. I drive a motorcycle most of the time, which is far more economical than the vehicles I drove in the U.S.

I speak enough Thai to get what I want, although not well enough to have a conversation. Here in Phuket, one has less motivation to learn Thai because it is a tourist area and many Thais speak varying degrees of English. The same goes for Bangkok. There are many places where understanding Thai is not necessary.

I have both an account in the U.S. that I can withdraw from using an ATM, and a Thai bank account. To establish my Thai account, I had to show a passport and address of residence.

Making a living locally is difficult (Thailand pays very poor wages), and dealing with cultural, political and religious differences can sometimes be a problem. Foreigners cannot "own" land in Thailand, but I do have investments in several properties. I have built and sold two homes.

Public transportation is adequate, affordable, and reliable. Stores are not always well-stocked, and customer service can either be very good or almost non-existent. Also consider quality of healthcare and sanitation (I am more tolerant of bacteria here after a few high fevers).

The Thai people are generally very friendly to Americans (as well as all foreigners) and accept us being there. The ladies and men are open to conversation and smiles are abundant. I believe that there is far less crime here, and I feel quite safe. I love it here, even with the frustrations of not always being understood and sometimes getting something different than what I'd expected. If you are impatient, demanding or short-tempered, Thailand is not the country for you.

Ken Bower

Bangkok, Thailand

After living there for 3½ years, I can say I'm a big fan of Bangkok. Once my friend showed me how easy it was to navigate Bangkok using the subway, skytrain and taxis (and how economical it was to use any combination of the three transportation venues) Bangkok became my favorite city in the world, replacing Singapore, which had been my favorite city since 1955.

Because I moved into the Lumpinee area, close to JUSMAG, the military compound where I received my U.S. Mail privileges (I am a retired military person), and also changed my lifetime VFW membership from Udon Thani to Bangkok, I attended their monthly VFW meetings, occasionally had lunch there and almost always attended their "Steak Night" function on the last Friday of each month. My furnished one-bedroom apartment only cost $270/mo, and had several acceptable restaurants within walking distance, as well as Internet cafés, a flea market, etc.

I've visited all the new super huge shopping malls, favoriting Paragon, Central World, Emporium, Esplanade, or MBK, and saw over 200 movies each year in the huge, clean, inexpensive movie complexes. There are over 200 restaurants, serving American or Continental food, as well as many serving Thai and Asian entrees.

I've become close friends with so very many Thais and *farangs* (including Americans) that owned businesses in Bangkok and more importantly befriended so many staff members that worked in restaurants, shops, stores within the malls and other Bangkok locations.

55. Turkey

Climate: Northern coastal region (Black Sea): cooler, more rain; southern and western coastal regions (Mediterranean and Marmara Sea), mild; central interior region (Anatolian plateau); cold winters, hot, dry summers.
Government: Republican Parliamentary Democracy
Population: 76,805,524
Currency: Turkish Lira (TRY): 1 TRY = 0.66 USD
Language: Turkish (official), Kurdish, Arabic, Armenian, Greek
Religious Groups: Muslim [mostly Sunni] (99.8%), other (0.2%)
Ethnic Groups: Turkish (official), Kurdish, Arabic, Armenian, Greek
Cost of Living compared to the U.S.: Generally cheaper; more so outside Istanbul and a few resorts

Fascinating, exotic, ancient but quickly modernizing, Turkey has plenty to offer those with the means to live there—and outside of Istanbul, it doesn't take all that much. Technically part of Europe, its Islamic/Ottoman feel gives the place an aura more in line with what you find in the Middle East. Nonetheless, it's a secular nation, and there is strict separation between mosque and state, though outside the cities, particularly Istanbul, and the resort areas along the Aegean and the Mediterranean (the "Turkish Riviera"), conservative cultural values prevail. The country's desire to enter the E.U. means the government has great incentives to keep things chill. Though the law generally protects them, women and gays might still find the cultural milieu less than optimal.

Living There

Governance: Turkey's candidacy for full membership status in the E.U. has been a catalyst for many reforms that have broadened democracy here. Recent elections have been judged to be free and fair, the military's role in civilian affairs has been reduced, and torture and other forms of judicial brutality are decreasing. Government and judicial corruption is still widespread, stifling of media and free expression still goes on, and while freedom of religion and expression are matters of law, the treatment of the minority Kurdish population leaves much to be desired

Infrastructure: Developing rapidly. The Turkish government is giving high priority to infrastructure projects in the hopes of expanding the economy and achieving E.U. membership by 2014.

Internet: Approximately 44% of the Turkish public enjoys regular Internet access. Broadband penetration expected to reach 19% by 2012.

Healthcare: Turkey's healthcare system is not as advanced as those in many Western European countries. Although the situation is improving, the funds allotted for medical and healthcare resources are insufficient considering the need.

GPD: $958.3 billion

GDP (Per Capita): $12,300

Sovereign Debt: 48.1% of GDP

Working There: Teach English, summer tourism jobs, au pairs. By law, foreigners cannot practice as: medical doctor, dentist, midwife, sick-attendant, pharmacist, optician, veterinarian and chemist, judge and public prosecutor, attorney, notary public, director at newspapers, or a member, representative, assistant or commissioner at the Stock Exchange. Foreigners are also forbidden from selling monopoly products. Recent unemployment is spurring calls for a further crackdown and more laws restricting the number of foreign workers in the country.

Regulatory Environment: Despite recent changes, regulatory procedures are still bureaucratic and inefficient.

Taxes: Corporate: 20%, Individual: 15–35%, VAT: 18%. Foreign residents are considered full taxpayers and are taxed on their worldwide income. Nonresidents are viewed as limited taxpayers and are only required to pay taxes on their Turkish sources of income. Professional tax advice is an essential requirement for every expat.

Cannabis: Illegal. Individuals found in possession of small amounts are fined, forced to attend rehab and undergo drug screenings. Additional offenses merit harsher penalties. That said, the stuff is everywhere.

Homosexuality: Legal. No recognition of same-sex unions. No laws against discrimination. There are open homosexual communities in Istanbul, along the Aegean coast, and in Ankara, though cultural biases are strong and homosexuals are often persecuted under vague morals laws. Tops need not worry; Turks only consider "passive" homosexuality as taboo.

Abortion: Legal up to 10 weeks, requires spousal notification, parental notification/authorization.

Women's Issues: Women are guaranteed equal rights but culturally they are often treated as second-class citizens. Half the women under 15 do not attend school and there is large-scale discrimination in the workplace. Sexual harassment and domestic violence are not uncommon.

Guns: Rifles are illegal but shotguns permitted. A permit is required to own or carry a pistol.

Crime: Low

Real Estate: Americans can buy property in Turkey, as long as it is outside of village boundaries and other designated off-limits areas. These laws do not affect most city housing and those in resort areas such as Antalya where most expats choose to live. Although mortgages were once unavailable to foreign buyers seeking to purchase Turkish property, recent legislation has allowed local brokers to provide 30-year loans at varying rates (4–7%). Purchase tax of 1.65% is due upon the sale and a yearly property tax of between 0.1 and 0.3% is assessed. Individuals do not have to pay capital gains if they own the property for at least one year. Laws are slightly different for corporate owners and income property.

Life Expectancy: 71.96 years

Moving There

Best chances of getting legal residency are to demonstrate that you're there for business or cultural reasons. Retirees on a livable pension are also generally welcomed. Only those with a valid work permit or who are retired can bring an automobile permanently into Turkey. You can apply for a visa at your local Turkish consulate and then apply for a residence permit at the local police station during your first month in Turkey. Foreigners in Turkey on a tourist visa may apply for residency while in Turkey under certain conditions. Work permits are scarce (slightly more common in tourist-related industries) and there are many complicated criteria and certain types of employment (particularly medical, legal and financial positions) are off limits to foreigners. Academics, on the other hand, can work without a permit.

Tourist Visa: Can be issued at port of entry. Valid for 90 days.

Residence Permit: Foreigners who wish to stay in Turkey for more than three months are required to apply for a Residence Permit by filling out a Declaration of Intent form with the police. Applicants must have proof of financial capacity to meet basic standard of living. Preference is given to those who already hold a work permit or are the relative or spouse of someone who does. Residence

Permits are issued by the Ministry of Internal Affairs and valid one to five years, renewable.

Student Visa: Valid one year. Get it before you arrive. The usual rigmarole prevails.

Work Permits: For applicants with an offer of work. Employee applies at a Turkish mission, submits an application form and a letter from the employer, and that employer files the rest of the paperwork to the Ministry of Labour and Social Security. The procedure is very complicated and must be carefully coordinated between employer and employees. Academics who come to Turkey to teach at a university, conduct research or other scholarly activities are generally exempt. Those who come to Turkey to conduct business are also eligible but here, too, criteria are numerous and complicated. Generally, you're expected to own a minimum of 20% of a company and generate sufficient income so it's clear that the business is actually viable. Detailed requirements can be found on the Turkish Investment Support and Promotional Agency website: **www.invest.gov.tr.**

Citizenship: For those without family ties to Turkey, anyone wishing to apply for citizenship must have five years of legal residency, be self-sufficient, speak decent Turkish and be of satisfactory physical and moral health.

56. United Arab Emirates (UAE)

Climate: Desert; cooler in eastern mountains

Government: Federated with specified powers delegated to the UAE federal government and other powers reserved to member emirates

Population: 4,798,491

Currency: Dirham (AED): 1 AED = 0.27 USD

Language: Arabic (official); English is also spoken, along with Hindi, Farsi, Tagalog, Urdu, Malayalam, Russian, Tamil and others

Religious Groups: Muslim (96%) [16% Shia], other [includes Christian and Hindu] (4%)

Ethnic Groups: Emirati (19%), other Arab and Iranian (23%), South Asian (50%), other expatriates [includes Westerners and East Asians] (8%)

Cost of Living compared to the U.S.: About the same

To maintain its status as the playground of the Muslim world, ultra-modern Dubai, in the oil-rich United Arab Emirates (which also includes Abu Dhabi, Ajman, Fujairah, Ras al-Khaimah, Sharjah, and Umm al-Quwain), imports 80% of its labor. That means Americans can earn living wages in various skilled industries such as IT, engineering, architecture, construction, business and teaching English. Although Dubai's debt melt-down in 2009 may have put any future skyline-altering megaprojects on temporary hold, there's still a lot of high-powered oil money oozing into the UAE. There is also booze, the largest shopping mall on earth, planned residential communities that come complete with canals, waterfalls, and nearly as much swimming pool area as living space. Next door in the more low-key Abu Dhabi, the Sheikhs have poured massive amounts of money into English-language publishing, often raiding large (but downsizing) U.S./U.K. media institutions for talent. Oh, and taxes? They don't need no stinking taxes.

Living There

Governance: The UAE has the distinction of being one of the few countries never to have held an election in its entire history. They have no political parties. All power emanates from a band of sheikhs known as the Supreme Council of Rulers. Laws prohibit criticism of the government and other institutions by the media and individuals; large political gatherings are out of the question, as are labor unions. The government is run as efficiently as a corporation with a minimum of corruption. "Morally objectionable" Internet sites are often blocked. Just go about your business and let the government go about theirs and everything will be jake.

Infrastructure: Excellent

Internet: Hi-speed widely available

Healthcare: First-world

GDP: $199.8 billion

GDP (Per Capita): $40,200

Sovereign Debt: 44.6% of GDP

Working There: Opportunities in many skilled areas, from programming to graphic design, business, editing and publishing, marketing, architecture and teaching.

Regulatory Environment: Overall, the process of starting a business and obtaining the necessary licenses is straightforward and efficient. The UAE is dotted with dozens of Free Trade Zones that are laissez-faire capitalist utopias with no corporate taxes (for 15 years, renewable), no income taxes, no import/export taxes, no restrictions on foreign ownership and 100% repatriation of capital and profits. If you can't make it here, you can't make it anywhere.

Taxes: Almost none

Cannabis: Forget about it.

Homosexuality: Illegal; prison sentences common, death penalty possible.

Abortion: Only to save a woman's life. Spousal and/or parental approval required.

Women's Issues: Gender discrimination is widespread.

Crime: Very little

Real Estate: The emirates have relaxed laws restricting the purchase of property by foreigners. Property values are coming down in the aftermath of Dubai's recent debt crisis, but prices are still quite high. Mortgages available from both international and local lenders.

Life Expectancy: 76.11 years

Moving There

More than likely, you're here to work, in which case most matters are taken care of on your behalf. Preference also seems to be given to disgraced icons of the Western capitalist oligarchy.

Other than tourists, visas/residence permits need to be applied for in advance (though again, this will likely not be your concern).

Note: In 2011 the UAE government shortened the validity period of Residence Permits from three years to two, though there has been talk of reversing this.

Tourist Visa: American citizens do not need a visa for stays up to 30 days. Round-trip airline ticket required.

Residence Permits for Partner/Investors: Issued to a foreign investor in partnership with a local. Minimum stake: around $20,000.

Residence Permits for Employment: There are versions for private sector and public sector employees. Employer must sponsor the visa and file the paperwork.

Student Visas are available, per the usual requirements (the University is basically your "sponsor"), but few pursue this path.

U.S. Citizens (tourist and business people) may apply to the UAE embassies in the U.S. for one-to-10-year multiple entry visas. A sponsor is required and the visa will be granted free of charge. Each stay, however, limited to six months, so it's only good for snowbirds and those who go in and out on business.

Name Withheld by Request

Dubai, UAE

Dubai is really an expat haven. I think there must be more expats here than any other place in the world. The work environment is exciting and people are extremely friendly. Since everyone is an expat, it's an easy place to meet people and learn about different cultures. I have friends from Moldova, Turkey, Canada, Slovakia, Hungary, and England—a pretty diverse group.

Dubai is indeed the Las Vegas of the Middle East. Alcohol, clubs, bars are everywhere and parties are common. There are some restrictions that might seem odd. Like the fact that I have to get a permission letter from my company to actually purchase liquor at one of the state-owned liquor stores. However, there are no restrictions in the bars. Anyone can drink there. It's almost like London or L.A.

Dating and relationships is taboo as a subject. In practice, everybody does it and it's easy to meet people of the opposite sex. Most people who live in Dubai are not natives and are from many other countries. I met my wife here, through work. She's not American which of course adds spice to the relationship. FYI, condoms and birth control are readily available.

We all travel a lot. Dubai is in the middle of Europe and Asia. I racked up 130,000 frequent-flier miles last year.

The summer is too hot. There is not much to do. But in winter things really pick up. The city has grown so much that traffic is a nightmare. The salaries for someone entry-level or mid-career-level might be low compared to the U.S., but everything is tax-free, so it usually equals out. People who are sent out here on expat packages really rake in serious cash. Once you have experience in the Middle East, most employers tend to try to keep you and pay a solid salary. The most expensive part about living in Dubai is housing. There is an extreme shortage of affordable housing, so most people share. I lucked out and secured a one-bedroom apartment.

Life has changed in Dubai over the past seven years. The housing bubble finally burst and the biggest expense in Dubai was halved in about three months' time. This also meant a lot of friends were forced out of the country, because their construction jobs disappeared. A crisis makes you really learn a lot of things about expat life. It's important one lives within their means or they could get caught out. I still live here, and we are still enjoying the tax-free lifestyle. I don't know if we will be here forever, but it was definitely a good place to ride out the economic crisis. Our jobs are stable and we survived, all the while by still being able to travel and enjoy the great weather. The government has placed reforms here for business and UAE is really open for business. I have been seeing a lot more Americans here, especially the younger generation. I believe if anyone is looking for a really interesting place, UAE is definitely a place to come for a couple of years to get some experience. You will find that companies will be very open to hiring young energetic Americans and they will in turn find they will be able to quickly move up the corporate ladder which might be slower if based in the USA.

57. United Kingdom

Climate: Generally mild and temperate, though often dreary; weather frequently changes but extremes of temperature are rare
Government: Constitutional monarchy
Population: 61,113,205
Currency: British Pound (GBP): 1 GBP = 1.63 USD
Language: English, Welsh (about 26% of the population of Wales), Scottish form of Gaelic (about 60,000 in Scotland)
Religious Groups: Christian (71.6%), Muslim (2.7%), Hindu (1%), other (1.6%), none (23.1%)
Ethnic Groups: English (82%), Scottish (10%), Irish (2%), Welsh (2%), other [includes Indian and Pakistani] (4%)
Cost of Living compared to the U.S.: Steep

Despite the hurdles and dreary weather, the U.K. (England, Scotland, Wales, Northern Ireland, Isle of Man, and the Guernsey Islands) is still a top destination for American refugees. Most head for London, one of the most expensive cities in the Western hemisphere, where you'd be lucky to score a single-room flat on the city's periphery for $1,500 a month. Costs go down in the minor cities and in Scotland and Wales. Obtaining residency and work permits can be daunting but not impossible. Working under the table is hardly unheard of. Previously, Her Majesty's Government did not tax income earned outside the U.K. and whatever island nuggets remain of the Empire, but that's fallen by the wayside as the government desperately seeks to recoup revenue lost in the financial mania of the previous decade or so. And, with a bit of effort, the language spoken here is comprehensible to those raised speaking American.

Living There

Governance: United Kingdom is a Western-style democracy with a high level of political, religious and cultural freedom. Muslim minorities do complain of discrimination. There are also privacy concerns about the proliferation of security cameras—now numbering in the millions—that conduct constant surveillance on the population.
Infrastructure: Fully developed nation
Internet: Ranked 5th in the world for total number of broadband subscribers (18 million). 12th highest number of broadband subscribers per 100 inhabitants (29.5).
Healthcare: The National Health Service (NHS), funded through taxation, provides free or relatively low-cost medical care to U.K. residents. Overseas visitors from

non-E.U. countries are eligible for free emergency treatment at NHS hospitals, but have to pay for inpatient treatment and other medical services.

GDP: $2.189 trillion

GDP (Per Capita): $35,100

Sovereign Debt: 76.5% of GDP

Working There: Difficult but there are some opportunities. If you have a background in healthcare, the National Health Service often needs administrators, social workers, physical therapists, nurses and other medical staff. Recent shortages in electronics, engineering, IT, and education. Americans also land jobs in media and advertising.

Regulatory Environment: Another top location to start a business. The British regulatory system is streamlined, efficient, and transparent; you can start a business in less than two weeks. The World Bank Doing Business Index ranks England the 4th best location in the world for setting up shop.

Taxes: Corporate 21%–28%, Individual: 0–50%, VAT: 20%. Residents who are domiciled in the U.K. are subject to taxation on worldwide income.

Cannabis: Although you may not be arrested for small amounts, you will get a "cannabis warning" and your name will be entered into the government's Criminal Records Bureau (CRB) database. If arrested more than once, you may face a fine and possible jail time if arrested again.

Homosexuality: Discrimination based on sexual orientation illegal in housing and employment. Same-sex couples permitted to adopt children. Same-sex civil partnerships legally recognized since 2005.

Abortion: Legal on the basis of socioeconomic grounds, to save a woman's life, physical health and mental health

Women's Issues: Women are guaranteed equal treatment, though they could be better represented in the upper strata of business and government.

Guns: All firearms must be licensed (Firearm Certificate or Shotgun Certificate). Owner must provide valid reason for purchasing weapon (self-defense is not accepted). Extensive background check and strict storage requirements.

Crime: England's violent crime rate is currently one of the highest in the European Union. Armed robberies, muggings, and other violent crimes have been on the increase (especially in London), despite strict gun control laws.

Real Estate: Foreigners are allowed to own real estate and mortgage financing is available. Property in the U.K. is outrageously expensive and with the pound's relative strength vs. the dollar, few can afford it. Even with plummeting home prices in the aftermath of the 2008 financial crisis, the average home price still exceeds $300,000 nationwide. In London, it's closer to $600,000. Property (in England and Wales) can be classified as only leasehold, which means that instead of owning it outright, you lease it for up to 99 years.

Life Expectancy: 79.92 years

Moving There

Unless you're one of those people with a natural ability to negotiate through government paperwork and bureaucratic language, the U.K. immigration system is considered one of the most complicated in the world. If you'd like to get a work permit, for example, there are 22 different "schemes" offered to would-be immigrants. On the plus side, the government has a very user-friendly website that walks you through each step of the process and explains the different types of visas and requirements (**www.ukvisas.gov.uk**). U.K. visas have a "visa enquiry form" on the official website which can be used to determine whether you need entry clearance as well as providing details of the nearest British post where you can make your application. Some of the schemes require work permits while others do not. For brevity's sake we've included information about a couple of basic visa types below. Don't expect an easy time of it but on the plus side, regardless of your status, if you can evade deportation for 14 years, there's a chance you can stay for good. Oh, and be aware that you will need to submit to a biometric scan to get a any kind of long-term visitor visa. Then again, if privacy concerns are paramount, you should probably avoid the U.K. altogether since its denizens are some of the most surveilled people in the world.

Visit Visas: Americans are permitted to visit the U.K. for up to 180 days over a 12-month period without a visa. You have the option of extending your stay, but you must secure the approval of British immigration officials. Avoid extending your stay beyond the allotted six-month period. If you are discovered and British immigration authorities suspect that you are attempting to get a foothold toward legal residency as opposed to visiting, you may be permanently banned from the country for up to 10 years.

There is also a long-term visit visa than can be valid for one, two, five or ten years and allows multiple unlimited entries for up to six months for the duration of the visa. You must show a "frequent and sustained need" to come to the U.K. such as a business-related concern or family links. You must also provide evidence that you can support yourself while in the U.K.

Work/Investor Visa: If a British firm is willing to employ and sponsor you and you have all your paperwork in order, getting a permit to work and live in England shouldn't be too hard. If not, you may find the process difficult but not impossible. For example, there is a program called "Tier 1 (General)" that allows highly skilled workers, professionals, and entrepreneurs to settle in the U.K. to look for work or develop possible business prospects. A points-based system is used to determine eligibility based on your age, work and financial history, education, knowledge of English, and other criteria.

If your application is accepted, you can live in the U.K. for a maximum period of two years while looking for work or trying to start a business and you can apply for an extension if needed. Unfortunately, sometimes the British government will cease issuing these Tier 1 visas for a period of time, so if you're thinking about applying, check the webpage mentioned above to make sure the government is accepting applications. If you don't think you would fit in this category of visa, there are several other work permit categories that offer work visas to individuals trained in occupations that are needed by the British economy so be sure and investigate all your options.

Passive investors (i.e., those who just write a check and leave the day-to-day operations to others) can score an Investor Visa with at least a million pounds "at your disposal" and three-fourths of this amount must be invested in a British company or various approved funds (known as "unit trusts"). Active investors can do the same for a mere 200,000 GBP invested in a U.K. business. The visa is good for three and one-third years and so long as your initial investments meet the minimum requirements you can apply for renewal. If your investment falls below the minimum amount due to market fluctuations you can still apply for renewal. Then again, if you've even read this far, you can probably afford the kind of professional assistance that would make this information superfluous.

Student Visa: For many Americans, their U.K. experience starts as a student. Acceptance at a university means a fairly simplified (relatively speaking) visa experience and even the possibility of part-time employment, internships, etc.

Permanent Residence: Known technically as Indefinite Leave to Remain (ILR), this is available to spouses and domestic partners after two years, most legal residencies after five years, ANY legal residency after 10 years and any residency at all after 14 years.

Citizenship: There are various forms of British nationality (much of it a result of Britannia's far-flung territorial possessions) and a slew of different contingencies but generally speaking, after five years of legal residency, the door to citizenship (at least the ability to apply, anyway) is open.

Ellin Stein,
London, U.K.

To live here, you should consider how long you can live without seeing the sun. Are you willing to pay an enormous amount for, well, everything? If you're planning on driving, can you deal with narrow tortuous roads, going the opposite direction that you are used to, and tons of traffic? Does irreverence bother you? Are you willing to accept a smaller range of available food and produce? Technology that's five years behind?

I'm happy I moved to London even if everything costs about 10 times as much and the weather can be dispiriting. The U.K. is attractive because it's English-speaking, you get lots of U.S. music, films, books, TV shows, and news so you don't feel that cut off, there are lots of Americans here, and, in London at any rate, it's very cosmopolitan. The media climate is much better though—TV, though not what it was, is still better and we get all the best U.S. TV shows. Plus you can still get actual news. And there's the theater of course. I feel more on the same wavelength and continue to meet people I like. Also, people here tend to have a more international outlook than people in the U.S. And the National Health Service is a big plus. For all its problems it's great, plus it keeps private insurance prices down because there's an alternative. A great pleasure is being able to get to France or Italy within two hours, or, even better, take a train to France.

As for minuses, it's difficult to find workers who do things right instead of half-assedly. But there's been a big influx of Eastern Europeans with a fierce work ethic, fortunately. Also there's enormous amounts of litter and general dirtiness.

Americans here tend to fall into three categories: The corporate types sent over to do a tour of duty tend to congregate in St. John's Wood, near the American school. If they're corporate but childless, they tend to live in South Kensington, Chelsea, Belgravia—all very wealthy parts of London. There are the academics/media/creative who tend to live in not-so-affluent parts of London or in university towns. Often self-employed, they tend to be here for the longer haul. Then there are the expats who married a native or are independently wealthy.

Tim
London, U.K.

Because of the sheer number of colleges and cultural institutions, London is in many ways the intellectual and artistic hub of Europe. On any given week, philosophers, film-makers, scientists, politicians, historians, musicians, and artists are stopping through town, many giving free talks, cheap concerts, and world-class seminars for the general public. In London, I swear you could get a master's level education just by showing up. I feel like my brain would atrophy living anywhere else.

A large chunk of your money will be spent on rent, but cheap housing is possible if you are flexible and have some time to look around, and tons of money can be saved on transport by getting used to riding a bike. London is trying hard to be a bike-friendly city, although it's still a daily battle with buses and taxis. Cheap food is terrible but this only inspires one to cook, and farmers' markets are a great way to get your produce and get to know British food culture.

The first apartment we rented was in a neighbourhood called Dalston. Despite its relative distance from the centre of London and scrappy appearance, we were living four people in a two-bedroom apartment to make it work, splitting a £360 per week rent four ways. The local area was amazing, with one of our favourite street markets on Ridley Road (with costermongers yelling 'havalook! havalook!'), Turkish and Jamaican food on every corner, and a burgeoning constellation of small cafés and music venues. With one of the best venues for experimental music (Café Oto) and one of the trendiest summer parks just down the road (London Fields), it was just a matter of time before Dalston became the next Williamsburg. We now live in Islington, which is usually more expensive, but we found a great deal, off the books, through a friend. This is the key to finding cheap accommodation in London: never use an agent. You think they have a monopoly on housing in the city, but there is always a way around them. Although there is not so much to do or see in our little pocket of Islington, surrounded by mostly million-dollar flats, we are actually closer to school and paying about £600 (£300 each)—per month—to rent our room. That's less than I paid in Los Angeles! Alas, the dream is over this fall, when the house gets renovated and we are chucked back out on the street looking for more of those mystical word-of-mouth opportunities.

58. Uruguay

Climate: Warm, temperate
Government: Constitutional republic
Population: 3,308,535
Currency: Uruguayan New Peso (UYU):
    1 UYU = 0.05 USD
Language: Spanish (official), Portunol, Brazilero
    (mixture of Spanish and Portuguese spoken on
    Brazilian frontier)
Religious Groups: Roman Catholic (47.1%), non-Catholic Christian (11.1%),
    nondenominational (23.2%), Jewish (0.3%), atheist or agnostic (17.2%),
    other (1.1%)
Ethnic Groups: White (88%), Mestizo (8%), Black (4%)
Cost of Living compared to the U.S: Cheap

It doesn't offer the excitement of its neighbor Argentina, but little Uruguay has recently been catching the attention of bargain-hungry expats thanks to its fairly mild taxation system (with numerous areas designated Free Trade Zones), stable and democratic government and decent quality of life. Montevideo, Uruguay's capital and largest city, was recently ranked as one of the most livable cities in Latin America, while along the coast, cheap beachfront property can still be yours. You'll certainly be getting in before the rush. Not much in the way of work here, but if you can scare up a few hundred bucks a week, you can probably stay as long as you like. Oh yeah, retirees looking for a second passport can find one here, along with lots of other perks.

Living There
Governance: Free and fair elections. Constitutional guarantees of basic human rights and freedom of speech are generally respected. The judiciary is independent but the courts are often clogged leading to sometimes lengthy pretrial detentions. Although there have been abuses in the past, the country's Transparency

Law punishes a wide range of abuses by officeholders and has led to Uruguay becoming one of the least corrupt countries in Latin America.

Infrastructure: Semi-developed. Uruguay has made great strides in digitizing its telecommunications network. The country's highway and rail centers are adequate but in need of investment. The current government is planning a variety of infrastructure projects.

Internet: Roughly 40% of residents in Uruguay enjoy Internet access but this number has been climbing in recent years. Uruguay ranks third in Latin America for broadband penetration behind Argentina and Chile. Hi-speed Internet is available mainly in the larger cities.

Healthcare: Uruguay provides healthcare to all its residents. Hospitals and clinics are available through the country and the quality of care is quite good. There are also private insurance options available that are far from expensive.

GDP: $48.43 billion

GDP (Per Capita): $14,300

Working There: Some IT, tourism, teach English.

Sovereign Debt: 56% of GDP

Regulatory Environment: Bureaucratic and time-consuming; compared to most other countries in Latin America, it takes longer to start a business and fulfill all necessary requirements.

Taxes: Corporate: 25%, Individual 10–25%, VAT: 22%. Residents not taxed on worldwide income. Non-residents must pay 2% net worth tax.

Cannabis: Possession of small amounts for personal use legally permitted

Homosexuality: Legal. Laws against discrimination, same-sex unions legally recognized.

Abortion: Allowed to preserve physical health or save life of mother. Permitted in cases of rape.

Women's Issues: Laws against rape (including spousal rape), domestic violence, and sexual harassment. Women enjoy the same legal rights but Uruguayan courts have yet to litigate a gender discrimination case. Income disparities; on average men earn 30% more than women.

Guns: Permit required for all firearms. Concealed weapon allowed with permit.

Crime: Property crime is prevalent in Montevideo and other large cities. Recently, violent crime has increased, especially "Express Kidnappings" where a victim will be kidnapped at gunpoint and led to an ATM to withdraw funds.

Real Estate: Foreigners are allowed to buy property in Uruguay. Transaction costs generally average about 9% of purchase price. In Punta del Este, a beachside resort area popular among foreigners, apartments can be had for under $100,000. Smaller homes begin in the high $100,000s. Homes and apartments are significantly more affordable away from the fashionable areas and resorts.

Life Expectancy: 76.21 years

Moving There

Uruguay has not experienced any kind of immigration rush and hasn't erected many hurdles to those seeking a new life there. So unless you come across as a mooch or troublemaker, you'll likely not encounter much resistance. The retiree package offers tax-free import of household goods and an automobile, and a passport to those who qualify.

Tourist Visa: U.S. citizens do not need a visa to stay in Uruguay for up to 90 days (extensions are available).

Residence Permit: There are many categories of temporary residence permits but the process is essentially the same. Applications must be filed with the Dirección Nacional de Migración (DNM). For example, if you plan on working in Uruguay, you must show a notarized letter from employer. Students must provide an acceptance letter from a university prior to arrival. The DNM will request proof of sufficient funds to stay in Uruguay. This is generally considered to be about $6000 a year but a little extra doesn't hurt since applications are considered on a case-by-case basis. Applicants who wish to stay permanently can apply for a permanent residency within six months of arriving in Uruguay.

Retiree Second Passport: Uruguayan law allows retirees to receive permanent residence and a Uruguayan passport as long as they can prove they receive a permanent fixed pension of over $18,000 a year, plus a $100,000 investment in real estate or other approved securities (or combination of the two). This is not technically citizenship and under the program, retirees cannot seek or take employment.

Citizenship: Citizenship available to legal residents after five years (three years, for families), with proof of self-sufficiency (if you don't have a Uruguayan spouse, that is).

59. Vanuatu

Climate: Tropical
Government: Parliamentary Democracy
Population: 221,552
Currency: Vatu (VUV): 1 VUV = 0.01 USD
Language: Bislama (Pidgin), English, French (over 100 tribal languages)
Religious Groups: Presbyterian (36.7%), Anglican (15%), Roman Catholic (15%), Indigenous Beliefs (7.6%), Seventh-Day Adventist (6.2%), Church of Christ (3.8%), other (15.7%)
Ethnic Groups: Melanesian (98%), other [including French, Vietnamese, and Chinese] (2%)
Cost of Living compared to the U.S: Similar. Most manufactured goods including food are imported and expensive. Rented accommodation is also expensive.

Unless you're part of Hollywood royalty and earning seven digits a picture, chances are chucking it all and putting down roots in Tahiti à la Marlon Brando might be out of your price range. That doesn't mean life in a South Pacific paradise is beyond your means. A similar dream can be lived out on the equally charming island of Vanuatu at a slightly lower price tag and with more manageable entry hassles.

Living There
Governance: Free and fair elections, an independent media, and a government which shows a general respect for human and political rights. Critics complain that the judicial process is far too slow and prison conditions are poor.
Infrastructure: Typical developing nation
Internet: Less than 10% of residents enjoy Internet access. Wi-FI and DSL available primarily in developed urban areas.
Healthcare: Hospital accommodations are inadequate throughout the country and advanced technology is lacking.
GDP: $1.216 billion
GDP (Per Capita): $5,500
Sovereign Debt: N/A
Working There: Probably not
Regulatory Environment: Despite recent changes, the regulatory process remains complicated, somewhat costly, and burdensome.
Taxes: No income tax, no withholding tax, no capital gains tax, no inheritance taxes, or exchange controls. VAT: 12.5%.
Cannabis: Illegal; use and cultivation on the rise

Homosexuality: Legal. No recognition of same-sex unions. No laws against discrimination.

Abortion: Legal to preserve physical health and to save the woman's life

Women's Issues: Women enjoy equal rights under the law but still suffer discrimination in employment, credit, and wages. Laws against domestic violence.

Guns: Civilians can only purchase shotguns and .22 caliber rifles. License required.

Crime: Low

Real Estate: You do not have to be a resident of Vanuatu to purchase property and there is no capital gains tax on the sale of any real estate. All property in Vanuatu is leasehold. Most leases are for 75 years.

Life Expectancy: 64.33 years

Moving There

Retire if you're old, start a business if you're young. Immigration policies are fairly liberal but don't expect much in the way of work.

Tourist Visa: Residents of the United States with valid passport, return ticket home, and proof of sufficient funds do not require a visa for a short-term stay. Visitors are allowed to stay for 30 days with the possibility of extending a visit for up to four months.

The government of Vanuatu limits residency permits to investors, retirees, and employees:

Investor Visa: Vanuatu is interested in immigrants who will contribute financially to the country's economy. If you invest anywhere from $60,000 to $1.2 million, you can apply for a residence permit ranging from one to 15 years. Renewal may be dependent on investment status and other considerations. Applicants must first obtain approval from Vanuatu Investment Promotion Authority (VIPA). Consult: **www.investvanuatu.org**

Retirement Visa: Retirement permits are available to immigrants providing they can show proof of a monthly income of at least $3,500 per month that will be transferred to a financial institution in Vanuatu. Applicants must provide medical certificate, letter of authorization from Vanuatu Investment Promotion Authority (VIPA), and document from local bank showing proof of monthly revenue transfer of approximately $3,500. Once awarded, retirement permits are good for a lifetime.

Work Permit: Permit required for all non-citizen employees to work in Vanuatu. Employer and Employee must apply to Department of Labour with copy of work contract and supporting documents showing employee experience and/or qualifications. The permit is renewable each year by Commissioner of Labour. Persons employed in Vanuatu qualify for one-year residency permit, renewable annually.

Student Visa is available, per the usual requirements.

Tracy Bailey
Vanuatu

Our story is a bit strange. We met a man a few years back when we used to go boating. At the time he owned a boutique resort in Vanuatu and was in the process of buying a small island. We got to know him and started investing. After a year of nothing really happening, my husband (Doug) went to visit Vanuatu. He was impressed with the country but thought that there really needed to be somebody on the ground here to get things going. So we packed up our life, Doug quit his high-paying engineering job and we headed on down. It took about six months to prepare for the journey, which I think is record time. We leased out our house, sold off most things and packed a 40-foot container with a Ford Excursion and furniture.

I think it is very difficult living outside the States but we have adjusted pretty well. We live on the island of Efate and it has everything we need. I had a really hard time getting used to shopping, Aussie slang among other things, and just being away from the real world. The majority of expats here are from Australia and New Zealand. There is quite a large community of Chinese and some Americans; mostly Peace Corps, Bible translators and pastors. My kids are learning to speak French, Bislama (local language), and of course a little Aussie, mixed with some Kiwi.

I really didn't know what to expect but it has been an interesting journey. We have never done anything like this before but we don't regret the decision. We also have two children, ages six and eight. It has been great for them.

There are banks here that are based out of Australia that we use for local bills. We also do online banking for U.S. stuff. I pay credit cards, mortgage etc. online.

We buy insurance that is good here but not in the States. It also includes medevac so if something serious arises they will fly you out. We have no U.S. health insurance so when we do come back for a visit we pay out of pocket. OUCH! We do our taxes every year since we do own property in the States.

About the only thing that is helpful to us is the Internet. We stay in touch with people and try to keep up with the current events.

60. Venezuela

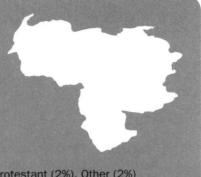

Climate: Tropical; hot, humid, more moderate in highlands
Government: Federal Republic
Population: 28,814,843
Currency: Bolivar Fuerte (VEF):
  1 VEF = 0.23 USD
Language: Spanish (official), numerous indigenous dialects
Religious Groups: Roman Catholic (96%), Protestant (2%), Other (2%)
Ethnic Groups: Spanish, Italian, Portuguese, Arab, German, African, indigenous people
Cost of Living compared to the U.S.: Cheap

Venezuela is home to the cheapest gas in the world, miles of beaches and lush rainforests. Getting behind the Chavez revolution is much facilitated by the fact that the professional and business classes have been fleeing the country and their jobs, leaving a vacuum to be filled by expat labor. So come thumb your nose at the Yanqui imperialistas from the safety of these distant shores, but keep in mind that "safety" in this case is relative: Crimewise, the rate, even by urban U.S. standards, is downright murderous.

Living There

Governance: Free and fair elections. Economy heavily regulated by government. Judiciary and other key institutions are strongly influenced by the Hugo Chavez-led Unified Socialist Party of Venezuela (PSUV). Some censorship and government intimidation of journalists and independent media. Freedom of expression and academic freedom protected by law but in practice, threats and attacks by pro-government groups are not uncommon. Venezuela routinely ranks as one of the most corrupt countries in Latin America but let's not forget who's doing the ranking.

Infrastructure: Telecommunications good. Highways good. Rural roads unreliable.

Internet: Internet and broadband penetration lower when compared to other countries in the region. DSL is provided by CANTV, a state-owned subsidiary, which is slower and more expensive than other Latin American providers. You may need to rely on wireless or satellite.

Healthcare: Medical care at private hospitals and clinics in Caracas and other major cities is generally good. Public hospitals and clinics generally provide a lower level of care, and basic supplies at public facilities may be in short supply or unavailable.

GDP: $344.2 billion
GDP (Per Capita): $12,600

Sovereign Debt: 25.5% of GDP

Working There: The post-Chavez brain drain of the professional and business class makes for more opportunities for people with skills than you're apt to find in most of Central and South America.

Regulatory Environment: Stifling, bureaucratic, and lacking transparency; it takes over four months to start a business and fulfill all regulatory requirements.

Taxes: Venezuela relies on a progressive income for both personal and corporate income. Corporate taxes range from 15%–34% and personal income taxes range from 6% to 34% depending on income. Venezuela recently raised its VAT from 9% to 12%. Capital gains earned by non-residents are taxed at a flat rate of 34%. Residents of Venezuela are taxed on worldwide income.

Cannabis: In January 2004, Hugo Chavez decriminalized the possession of any "euphoric substance" for personal use; under 20 grams allowed.

Homosexuality: Legal. No nationwide recognition of same-sex unions. There are laws prohibiting workplace discrimination based on sexual orientation but no nationwide laws upholding gay rights. Despite great gains made by activists in Venezuela, culturally, many of the old taboos remain; police harassment and discrimination are common.

Abortion: Prohibited except to save a woman's life

Women's Issues: Women are well represented in business and politics. Cultural prejudices do exist; domestic violence, rape, and sexual harassment are not uncommon.

Guns: Under 2002 Disarmament Law, most firearms outlawed. Only non-military calibers, some shotguns. Strict registration and limits on ammunition and number of guns.

Crime: Venezuela has one of the world's highest murder rates. There are parts of Caracas that police only dare enter in force. Political demonstrations often descend into violence. Property theft, armed criminal gangs, muggings, and "express kidnappings" in which individuals are taken at gunpoint to withdraw funds from ATMs are a problem. Narcoterrorism has rendered the Venezuela/ Colombia border a no-go area.

Real Estate: Non-residents can buy property with a valid passport, tourist visa, and a Registro de Informacion Fiscal (RIF). These can be obtained from government tax authorities or through a local attorney. Buyers must pay a tax of 5% on purchase price.

Life Expectancy: 73.77 years

Moving There

Piece of cake, although you might be suspected of being a spy or agent provocateur.

Tourist Visa: Tourist visas can be issued for up to one year, with multiple entries, though only up to 90 days per entry. Applicant must demonstrate they don't intend to immigrate (proof of foreign address, bank account and employment).

Work Permit: Work permits are issued to individuals who are looking to work or conduct business in Venezuela. A company letter stating that the firm will pay expenses while in Venezuela is required. If you own your own business you will need to provide financial documentation showing that you have sufficient funds. The work permit is usually granted for one year with multiple entries. Renewable. Note: Artists, foreign correspondents of a news service, and professional athletes are exempt from Work Permit requirements, though they must register with the Ministry of the Interior and Justice which will establish requirements on a case-by-case basis.

Investor Visa: To be granted this type of visa, you must provide to immigration authorities a legally-attested document that you have made an investment that was approved by the government of Venezuela. This visa is granted for three years with multiple entries. After three years you must apply for a two-year visitor extension, and, if this is granted, you can apply for Resident status providing you meet the requirements of the Ministry of the Interior and Justice.

Fixed Income Visa: You must show proof of a permanent monthly income of more than $1,200 per month (plus $500 per dependent) from interest income, retirement benefits, or investments from outside Venezuela. This visa is granted for one year and can be renewed multiple times.

Student Visas are available for students attending university or technical schools in Venezuela. The typical requirements prevail. Valid for one year with multiple renewals allowed so long as you are pursuing your studies. **Religious visas** (one year, renewable) are also available. Venezuela also offers **Business and Entrepreneur visas** but these are of limited use since they don't allow more than a six-month stay in the country at a time. Those with Venezuelan spouses or family can obtain one-year visas with unlimited extensions upon valid documentation.

Resident Card (*Cédula*): Foreigners with a valid visa can apply at the Ministry of the Interior and Justice for a separate Resident Card (Cédula). These are valid for five years and renewable. Holders receive a tax ID number and are eligible for social services.

Citizenship: Foreigners can apply for citizenship after 10 years legal residency. Spouses of Venezuelans are eligible after five years of residency and marriage. Spouses and dependents of visa holders are generally issued visas whose terms match those of the original visa holder.

61. Vietnam

Climate: Tropical monsoon
Government: Communist party-dominated
    constitutional republic
Population: 89,571,130
Currency: Liberation Dong (VND): 1 VND = 0.00001 USD
Language: Vietnamese (official), English (increasingly
    favored as a second language), some French,
    Chinese, and Khmer, mountain-area languages
    (Mon-Khmer and Malayo-Polynesian)
Religious Groups: Buddhist, Christian, Hoa Hao, Cao Dai,
    indigenous beliefs, Muslim
Ethnic Groups: Vietnamese (85–90%), other [including
    Chinese, Muong, Tay, Meo, Khmer, and Cham] (10–15%)
Cost of Living compared to the U.S: Cheap

Vietnam has forgiven all that napalming. In fact, the sons of some of America's Vietnam vets are now slacking in Saigon (Ho Chi Minh City), working in Hanoi, or teaching English in the jungle. The living is cheap, the sun ever-present (except during monsoon season) and thanks to the French colonization of the 19th and 20th centuries, the cuisine and architecture are outstanding. Pollution and urban traffic (the two not unrelated) are high on the list of hazards. Most expats find life there ridiculously cheap, but if you're locked into the local currency (the VND), you'll suffer the consequences of the highest inflation rate in Asia.

Living There

Governance: While most American expats speak highly of their experience living in Vietnam, recent reforms have not scaled back the prevalence of big brother-style Communist rule. Many types of free speech (particularly criticism of the government) can result in arrest, the judiciary is often a rubber-stamp for the whims of party officials, and censorship is quite common.

Infrastructure: Developing

Internet: Approximately 10–12% of the population enjoys regular Internet access, a number the Vietnamese government would like to increase to 35% in the next year or so. Hi-speed Internet mainly in major cities.

Healthcare: Lacking. Facilities often do not meet Western standards, especially in rural areas. Although adequate for most minor injuries and illnesses, evacuation may be required for more serious conditions. Most physicians and facilities require immediate cash payment for treatment.

GDP: $278.1 billion

GDP (Per Capita): $3,100

Sovereign Debt: 56.7% of GDP

Working There: Teach English. Some IT and business positions.

Regulatory Environment: The Communist bureaucracy has initiated reforms to stimulate private sector business, but the regulatory process is often opaque and can be time-consuming. Some corruption.

Taxes: Corporate: 25%, Individual: 0–35%, VAT: 10%. Worldwide income is subject to taxation (real estate transactions involving family members, remittances, and scholarships are exempt).

Cannabis: Marijuana is illegal in Vietnam, as well as most other social vices, though you could hardly guess that from walking the streets. Penalties are technically stiff, but the police seem to look the other way or will negotiate an informal "fine" paid on the spot. The big problem in this country is opium and heroin, so marijuana hardly registers on the law enforcement radar.

Homosexuality: Legal. No recognition of same-sex unions. No laws against discrimination. In 2002, homosexual behavior was deemed a "social evil" by one of the government's media organs.

Abortion: No restriction as to reason

Women's Issues: Laws prohibiting sexual harassment and domestic violence. Although there are laws granting women equal rights to men, women aren't always given equal treatment and domestic violence remains a problem.

Guns: Illegal to own firearms

Crime: Low. Some petty crime in the cities.

Real Estate: Non-citizens cannot own land in Vietnam but can take out 50-year leases on plots of land and build their own home, or in some instances, purchase apartments in specifically designated developments. Mortgages are rare and most purchases are done in cash or gold.

Life Expectancy: 71.94 years

Moving There

Vietnamese immigration have begun cracking down on the layabout expatriate class and restricting visas to people whom they feel have some connection to Vietnam or will otherwise contribute to the economy. Their ability to enforce that is another matter. Also, like everything else in this so-called "Communist" country, there is an industry built around pushing your paperwork.

Tourist Visa: Up to three months. Applicant must either apply by mail or go to nearest Vietnamese Consulate. You have the option of extending your stay once you arrive in Vietnam or make regular border runs.

Business Visa: This has been the easiest and most popular option but recently the government has cut back the maximum stay from six months to three months. Once approval has been granted, you can then apply online or through the Vietnamese embassy. The visa can be renewed three times before you have to leave and start the whole process again.

Work Permit: Takes a bona fide job offer and documentation that this job could not be filled by a Vietnamese national. Generally, the employer handles most of the details.

Temporary Residence Cards: After a one-year legal stay in Vietnam, you can apply for a Temporary Residence Card (TRC), valid for up to three years. Those without family here and/or without a work permit, functioning business or a substantial amount of money in a local bank and a Vietnamese sponsor, will find these hard to come by.

Five-Year Visa: American spouses and children of Vietnamese nationals can return to Vietnam and receive a five-year visa (technically, a visa exemption).

Student Visas are available and do not have to be applied for before arriving in-country. Even enrolling in a Vietnamese language school will make you eligible.

Tyler Watts
Ho Chi Minh City (Saigon), Vietnam

The cost of living compared to America is quite low. If you really want to you can eat hearty meals for about $1 and household items are consistently cheaper. The only deviation from the rule is typically with electronic items. This is changing however with a devalued VN dong and rising inflation. For example gas prices just increased by 24% and electricity by 15%.

In terms of infrastructure, roads linking cities are not up to good standard but slowly improving. Within the cities, traffic is a problem and the streets just aren't made for the population they now handle. Coming from the L.A. area it's no more a hassle here than it is there except if you are on a motorbike you are outside with all the exhaust and pollution. Internet is usually decent and no problems with access. You can go just about everywhere in the country and find a café with an open wi-fi network and particularly in the cities you are hard-pressed not to find wi-fi networks nearby you. Facebook is about the only issue expats rail against as Vietnam performs a "we don't, but we do" type blocking. There are plenty of workarounds that get passed between blogs and Twitter so most people still access it. Unless you are keen on reading overseas Vietnamese anti-Communist websites there's very little you can't access. Cellphone service is great and the three major phone companies (Vinaphone, Mobifone, Viettel) operate on SIM card-style service where you can buy cards when you run low on funds. There is also 3G service here but it's spotty and not as nice as it sounds when advertised from what I hear.

By product availability I would clarify that big supermarket chains like Metro provide nearly every imported item you could hope to find and smaller places in the big cities provide hard-to-find goods that they don't.

There are most definitely English-speaking enclaves. District 2 has developed as a kind of expatriate hub. There is a range of speakers from basic to quite fluent in terms of speaking the local language. I would say the average is on the lower side in the cities with Vietnamese being a difficult language and city life not a good environment for learning it. There is a significant population of Americans.

District 1 offers lots of restaurants, cafés and bars catering to the international scene and this is where most people congregate but as mentioned above District 2 is slowly becoming an international enclave unto its own. Most Americans are here working and I believe primarily in business but there are still plenty of opportunities to be had for the traveler turned English teacher. I know some retired Americans who have come here because of family connections or historical connections (i.e. veterans) and have stayed.

If you live in Saigon or Hanoi then you can get by quite easily without Vietnamese (particularly in certain downtown areas). Even in areas with large tourist flow there is sufficient English ability among local Vietnamese (Hue, Nha Trang, Dalat, Can Tho).

Vietnam operates outside all the time. My neighbors are always sitting in front of their gates. We know each other's names and about each other's children and there is a sense of looking after one another too. I believe it's easy to make friends but perhaps due to cultural limitations and language it is nice to have international friends to complement the Vietnamese friendships. On the other hand, my Vietnamese friends and the Vietnamese in general are some of the kindest people ever, going out of their way to assist in the little things.

Living in Saigon there is definitely a presence of crime like any big city, but I feel safer at night here than I would in, say, Los Angeles.

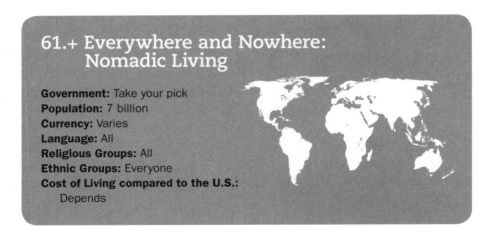

61.+ Everywhere and Nowhere: Nomadic Living

Government: Take your pick
Population: 7 billion
Currency: Varies
Language: All
Religious Groups: All
Ethnic Groups: Everyone
Cost of Living compared to the U.S.:
  Depends

Getting Out doesn't necessarily mean settling down somewhere else. If the journey is more important than the destination, or you feel like you need to always stay one step ahead of a cascading global collapse, or you simply don't want to hassle with establishing long-term foreign residency, you can drop down, hook up your Internet connection, and hang out wherever as long as the hanging is good and your visa lasts. Some people chase the next scene, others opportunity and still others flee the crowds who have once again "discovered" the little gem you once had practically to yourself. There are dozens of networks of Permanent Travelers, Mobile Bohemians, Digital Nomads and other fellow Americans afflicted with wanderlust and dedicated to a life that is constantly on the move.

Moving There
Just go.
Tourist Visa: All you need, if that.

For more information on nomadic living consult:
www.digitalnomad.org, www.ptclub.com, www.howsthewifi.com, www.almostfearless.com, www.exilelifestyle.com

Cap'n Mike
Somewhere in the Caribbean
There are a whole bunch of us who live aboard our boats which are in "foreign" lands, er, waters. We "boat people" fall into two groups:

1) Retired geezers. They have homes in the States (or Canada) and who spend the winter in the Bahamas (or the Caribbean). Think of them as floating snowbirds.

2) Boat bums. Me, for instance. People of all ages, from 18 to 90-something. Some work, some are trust fund babies, some just hustle. A lot of people hustle jobs off the books, as work visas are scarce. Boat deliveries, carpentry, diesel repair and fiberglass repair are all available jobs for boat bums with a skill set.

Some marry locals and can then enter the local economy. Others, me again, exploit loopholes in the laws. I write software for a company in California. There is a work exemption in almost all the islands for "writers." The point is, I'm not competing for jobs with locals, so no one cares what I do.

Clusters of these folks can be found in the Bahamas (Abaco), St. Maarten (world headquarters of boat bums), St. Lucia, and Grenada. The French bums cluster in St. Martin, Guadeloupe, Martinique.

And yes, we all have our own boats. These can be surprisingly cheap. I almost picked up a 30-foot sloop for my son for $4000. That's with Bahamian duty already paid! A friend just had a boat given to him by a fellow who has a new boat and didn't want the hassle of dealing with the old one.

People without boats are suspect.

Most folks just rely on the standard tourist visa. When time's up (usually three months), you just sail to another island.

As for living expenses, it's a wash. When I visit the States, I find myself out spending money just to pass the time. This does not happen in the out islands! Food is a little more expensive, but manageable. I don't eat out much. Fish are, of course, free.

You usually pay a permit fee for the boat. This ranges from free (the French, God bless 'em) to $300 a year in the Bahamas. Anchoring is generally free, although St. Maarten is now charging a slight fee for anchoring in the Lagoon. Moorings are the next step up. More secure in a blow, but not free. These range from $10 a night in most places, up to $25 a night in the British Virgin Islands (ouch!). Needless to say, the BVI are not on my list of places to hang out.

Most of this community do not park at a dock. I do, at the moment, but it's a special deal with a buddy. Marinas are expensive pretty much everywhere. Besides, marinas are like trailer parks (not this one, I'm usually the only boat here).

I try to make myself agreeable and entertaining, and find myself dining aboard yachts and in finer homes and restaurants. I'm not poor, nor am I a hustler, but I also will not turn down good food and company.

Supplies are not a big deal. Any island of more than 100 people has SOME kind of grocery/general store. Special boat parts can be a problem in the Bahamas. But a local will probably have a friend flying in or boating in from the States, and they'll carry it in for ya.

Support networks consist mainly of the "dock bar telegraph." I don't do Facebook. I don't think many here do. We just yak, and if somebody needs a hand or advice, it is offered willingly. Quid pro quo, but nobody keeps score.

Josh Plotkin, 20
Last seen in Vitoria, Brazil

During my senior year of high school I started getting interested in politics and Austrian economics, and the more I learned the more worried I became about the future of the United States. Back then the debt was only 11 trillion dollars, but it was enough to scare the shit out of me. For the next two years I was constantly thinking about the deteriorating state of the economy, the increasing debt, the rising prices of commodities, the continuing war on our civil liberties, the increasingly totalitarian laws being passed and that things would only be worse when I graduated. I needed to take action. After assessing my options I did what any sane individual in my position would do: I bought a one-way ticket to Mexico.

It's also true that I wanted to see the world, experience new things and speak different languages. I joined an organization called WWOOF (World Wide Opportunities on Organic Farms: www.WWOOF.org), which connects volunteers with organic farms, and went to work on a farm a few miles south of Cancún. Since I was in the area I decided to go to Cuba, and I symbolically chose Nov 2, 2010, election day in the U.S. as the day to go. After a month working on the farm, I realized that by teaching English I would be able to go almost anywhere in the world and find work, so I took a TESOL class in Oaxaca, Mexico. After the course was finished I returned home for the holidays and began thinking about where I would go next. I chose Colombia because it seemed dangerous and exciting, though I would later learn that most of the reports about Colombia being dangerous were just media hype. I wanted to leave right after the New Year.

I landed in Bogotá with the idea of staying there for a few months and teaching English. After two days of nonstop rain and cold weather I realized the flaw in this plan and moved on to Cartagena. I stayed there for a few days enjoying the beaches, but I couldn't stand the heat and humidity so I left for Medellín.

I came to Brazil because my brother was visiting his friends here, and since we were on the same continent, I figured I would come and visit him. I would like to stay in Brazil for a while, but without citizenship or a special visa the longest I can stay in a year is six months. If I can't figure out a way to stay here longer then I will start looking into the next country that I will go to. I like learning languages and immersing myself in other cultures, so I like to live in places where English isn't widely spoken and there aren't too many gringos around to ruin the experience. The next country I go to will either be somewhere in Eastern Europe, Southeast Asia or Southern Africa.

I've been heavily influenced by Simon Black of SovereignMan.com and Grandpa of ByeByeBigBrother.com who write about the PT or Permanent Traveler lifestyle. If you haven't already heard of Six Flags theory, this article explains it. (www.byebyebig-brother.com/pt_six_flags_theory.php). I think PT lifestyle is not only a way to escape the tyranny of the American government, but it is the best way to maximize freedom in this life.

The two flags that I am pursuing right now are the Citizenship flag and the Internet business flag. I've been living off of my savings for a while, but they won't last forever and I need to find a way of making money that is consistent with the lifestyle that I want to live. I tried teaching English but ultimately I gave up on it because I realized that the income I could earn from teaching would never be enough to pay for immigration lawyers and the other things I want in life. So now I'm focusing my energy on building an online business that will provide me with passive income and free up my time to pursue my other projects.

I love the Toward because of the way it has revolutionized the way we can connect to each other. I can find people with whom I share a very specific common interest. For example, www.rooshv.com. His writing on Colombian and Brazilian women influenced my decisions to travel there, and now that he's in Poland, he's got me thinking about going there as well. Another expat nomad I follow is www.exilelifestyle.com.

Failed States: 10 Countries You Don't Want To Move To

Unless you're a mercenary, dedicated humanitarian aid worker, or hardcore journalist, you can easily scratch these 10 names off your list of countries to consider:

Somalia
The country has been without a central government for over two decades, been ravaged by civil war, separatist schisms, drought, famine and more than a few issues with an international piracy industry. Generally considered the "most failed state" by international experts.

Chad
If political violence, corruption and the worst poverty on planet Earth suits your taste, this sunny, dusty land is for you.

Sudan
Poverty, periodic outbreaks of brutal bloodshed, and famine land this country year after year on the failed state list. The recent secession of South Sudan has international observers talking about an entirely new concept: the pre-failed state.

Democratic Republic of the Congo (Congo-Kinshasa)
Rich on paper (thanks to abundant resources) but abjectly poor in practice, the people of Africa's most populous country have been living a nightmare of war and human rights abuses, not to mention disease, famine and the usual blights, killing as estimated 45,000 people or so per month.

Haiti
Already an international basket case, thanks to U.S. meddling, internal corruption and the worst poverty in the Western hemisphere, a devastating earthquake in 2010 delivered a knockout punch from which the country has still to recover.

Zimbabwe
Poverty, unemployment, medieval human rights abuses and AIDS. There is some optimism that the 2009 unity government can pull the former colony of Rhodesia out of its tailspin, but you'd probably want to give this place a few years of wait-and-see.

Afghanistan
The traditional graveyard of empires has a few thorny problems to work out between NATO, the resurgent Taliban and various warlord/druglord factions before its stunning natural beauty and ancient culture can be appreciated.

Central African Republic
Poverty, political instability and widespread violence and torture add up to your typical post-colonial horror.

Iraq
Though President Barack Obama announced the end of all combat operations in Iraq in 2011, the killing continues apace.

Ivory Coast
If intractable civil war is your thing, this is the place for you.

Part III: Doing It

ADIOS USA

Getting Real: The Transition and Beyond

Don't pack your bags just yet. The devil, as everyone knows, is in the details. Here are the major issues that you'll most likely confront when transitioning to a new life. Of course, it's impossible to anticipate every eventuality, but with a positive attitude and a bit of flexibility, and a little help from a network of resources, you should be able to join the millions of Americans already enjoying a rewarding life somewhere outside of the U.S.A.

Driving

 Most people have heard of the International Driving Permit, which valid is 150 countries. These permits can be obtained in the United States from two organizations—the American Automobile Association (AAA) and the American Automobile Touring Alliance (AATA). For around $10. What most people don't realize is that while the permit is valid as long as your driver's license is, most countries will require that you get a local license within a year of residency. Depending on the country, and even what U.S. state has issued your license, you might only have to take a written test and pay a small fee. Otherwise, you might have to start all over from Driver's Ed. In Europe, for instance, this process can cost you over $1,500.

Frank
Orosi, Costa Rica
If you come here with a valid driver's license and you go to the driver's license facility and you show them that license, they give you a physical, an eye exam and all that stuff, and then they just issue another license.

Ex-pets

Moving a pet to another country involves all the hassles that go along with moving humans, plus a few more. Usually, a dog or cat (and other rabies-carrying animals such as a ferret) is required to have its own immigration paperwork. A veterinary certificate of health, which includes rabies vaccinations, deworming, and other measures, is usually required and often the pet must be microchipped, too. Some countries require a lengthy quarantine. Island nations in particular, such as the U.K., Australia, the Philippines, New Zealand, and Indonesia have completely eradicated rabies and don't need a new case coming through customs, are most likely to quarantine pets, though the U.K. has recently waived the requirement if the owner follows a program which must be undertaken a full six months before the pet is scheduled to arrive. For detailed information, you'll need to consult the embassy or consulate of the country you're planning on moving to and get their detailed instruction. A good source for pet entry requirements internationally can be found at **www.letsgopets.com.**

Gadget Power

When you consider what appliances to bring, be aware that there are 13 varieties of electrical outlet configurations in the world, many of them not compatible with others. In most cases, it's better to purchase adapters in the country where they will be used. Voltage is usually delivered in 110v or 220v–230v AC doses. If your device is not made for that standard, you will also need a voltage converter. Laptop cords have converters built in and the plug cord is removable from the power pack. These are easily available in computer shops in major cities, but if you're heading into the outback, you'll need to order it from the computer manufacturer in advance. Other digital devices (camcorders, etc.) are similarly adaptable. Since many of our beloved consumer electronics are chargeable via USB, simply sort out your computer's power source and the rest of the process connects the same anywhere in the world you go. You'll find a comprehensive breakdown of the electrical systems and sockets or adapters required at **www.kropla.com.** The site also covers international television standards, telephone compatibility (hardware and software, mobile and landline), and much more.

With the exception of parts of Asia and a few other "special economic zones" scattered around the world, brand-name consumer goods, particularly electronics, are far cheaper in the United States, often to the extent that you could pretty much cover your plane fare back to the States for particularly high-ticket items.

Also worth keeping in mind is that QWERTY is not the international language of keyboards. While any operation system can "read" a foreign keyboard as if it was a U.S. English type (though a few odd characters and functions might not work right), the actual letters and symbols you see on the keys will be different, often resulting in a frustrating typing experience. This is particularly important with laptops, where U.S.-style replacement keyboards are harder to come by. As for your cell phone, assuming it's unblocked or jailbroken and of fairly recent vintage, it's likely tri or quad band and will work with any local SIM card. If it's any older, it won't do you any good beyond Canada.

Insurance and Health

 If the laws of probability hold, you'll be moving (or have already moved) to a place where a saner healthcare system prevails. As for finding an English-speaking practitioner close to you, the International Association for Medical Assistance to Travelers (**www.iamat.org**) provides members with a searchable database of English-speaking doctors in 90 countries.

You can also find a list of healthcare practitioners, facilities and even air ambulance services at your local U.S. Embassy's website (**www.usembassy.gov**).

Uninsured Americans who require hospitalization overseas run the same risk of being driven bankrupt as they do at home. Medicare is severely limited when it comes to healthcare services or supplies obtained outside the U.S.. Private insurance companies aren't much better, unless you requested a specific option that covers you overseas, particularly once you've been there longer than a typical vacationer. In many countries, proof of insurance is required before they'll let you live there. If you settle in for the long haul, and are comfortable enough to entrust yourself to the medical care of your new country, you can look into buying into an insurance plan and probably for a lot less. If you're lucky enough, you might even be able to sign up with your new country's national health plan. Until then, you may need a special policy to tide you over. While it's not advisable to go anywhere without adequate coverage, many countries have decent medical care that's affordable out of pocket and you find many expats from Southeast Asia to South America paying for their healthcare on an as-needed basis.

Most (but not all) of the firms that will assist you with international coverage are based in the U.K. They include:

Aetna Global Benefits: **www.goodhealthworldwide.com**
Bupa: **www.bupa.com**
Clements International: **www.clements.com**
eGlobalHealth Insurers Agency, LLC **www.eGlobalHealth.com**
Expatriate Health Ins. Protection Plans: **www.expatriateinsurance.com**
IMG: **www.expathealthcentre.com**

NOTE: While insurance policies geared to expatriates and long-term travelers will cover you if you're sick or hospitalized, some E.U. countries require coverage from a domestically-approved insurance company before they will issue you a residency permit. Be sure to check the health insurance requirement before you commit to any policy or company.

Derek Patterson
eGlobalHealth Insurers Agency, LLC – www.eGlobalHealth.com

For those that require illness/accident/emergency evacuation health and life insurance needs for months as opposed to many years, a Short/Intermediate Term health plan with medical evacuation and accident life insurance is a great option. These plans can be written from as little as five days to a total of two years or more. They are automatic, guaranteed-issue plans—which means "you apply for it, and you get it," regardless of your medical history. (There are limited coverages, though, for pre-existing conditions.) Prices for a 30–39-year- old male/female are priced anywhere from $0.93 to $1.74 per day, approximately $28 to $52 per month depending on the level of coverage you choose. Those of Medicare/Retirement ages (65–69) range from $3.41 to $6.47 per day or approximately $102 to $194 per month. This type of plan is typically utilized for a Schengen, Work or Long-Stay Visa or other Consulate-required Visa application, but can be used in the long term, being rewritten every two or three years.

Worldwide Annual Insurance plans exist for those residing outside their country of citizenship for at least 50% of a policy year. Limits of coverage are $5 million per person per lifetime. The plans are designed to allow U.S. citizens to come back to the U.S. for up to six months per policy year. We have options as well for unlimited return to the USA without the six-month restrictions and are priced a bit higher. The insured can use a PPO network when in the U.S. and when outside the U.S. they are able to visit any licensed provider of their choosing regardless of network provider affiliation. They come in a "basic version" and a more "comprehensive-style" worldwide plan. These basic plans are lower in premium and have more streamlined benefits for the Expat that doesn't need the "bells and whistles" of the more comprehensive plans. Prices below reflect including coverage back in the USA or Canada. Premiums are typically about 20% less if you were to exclude USA/Canadian coverage.

Annual premiums for a comprehensive plan are as follows (prices as of December '10):

- 30–34-year-old male, $500 deductible=$1179
- 30–34-year-old female, $500 deductible=$2108
- 60–64-year-old male, $500 deductible=$5758
- 60–64-year-old female, $500 deductible=$5288

Annual Basic plan premiums as follows:

- 30–34-year-old male, $500 deductible=$1009
- 30–34-year-old female, $500 deductible=$1804
- 60–64-year-old male, $500 deductible=$4929
- 60–64-year-old female, $500 deductible=$4527

Coverage includes: Hospitalization, ICU, Surgery, Emergencies, Transplants, Medicines, Outpatient Services, Maternity, Newborn Care, Adult and Child Wellness, Complementary Medicine, Dental Emergency, Mental/Nervous Care, among others. Coverage for many pre-existing health conditions is also available, but most insurance companies require up to a 24-month waiting period.

In the unfortunate circumstances when death occurs during your trip, have you thought about where your bones will go? The average costs associated with repatriation of mortal remains is around $7,000 but can be as high as $20,000 if you happen to die in a far-off corner of the world. The plans include accidental death and dismemberment coverage, as well.

Optional Equipment

In most nations with a well-developed sense of commerce, a local plan might be available. But what if you plan to travel back and forth to the States? And what if standards of medicine in your adopted land don't live up to the standards that you feel comfortable with? Costs associated with international evacuations from Europe to the U.S. average more than $40,000, and can well exceed $100,000 in Asia, Africa or South America!

Emergency medical evacuation programs can give you peace of mind. There are even programs available that will guarantee transport to your hospital of choice (worldwide), waive any limits to covering pre-existing conditions and also have no restrictions to the monetary limits of the program benefits. Some even cover both international and domestic transports. It is "door-to-door" medical care. These programs are not insurance but rather a membership program—no additional fees or co-pays required.

Rates can run from as low as about $200 per year to over $500 per year for an individual, depending on whether they spend most of their time domestically or internationally. There are also plans available for short-term trips that cost from $70 to $150. All ages are eligible, even up to age 85 with certain restrictions.

For Extreme Expats Only

Traveling to Iraq, Rwanda or the Gaza Strip? If you don't currently have life insurance, it may be harder than you think to acquire a conventional life insurance policy. As of December 2010 there are over 60 countries that are recognized "underwriting hotspots" for war and terrorism—that equates to 31% of all countries around the globe!

Hot Spots: Afghanistan, Algeria, Angola, Azerbaijan, Burundi, Central African Rep., Chad, Colombia, Congo Republic, Cote D'Ivoire, Dem. Republic of Congo, Egypt, Eritrea, Ethiopia, Georgia, Guatemala, Guinea, Haiti, Indonesia, Iran, Iraq, Israel, West Bank (Israel), Gaza Strip (Israel), Jammu (India), Jordan, Kashmir (India), Kenya, Kosovo, Kuwait, Kyrgyzstan, Lebanon, Liberia, Madagascar, Malaysia, Morocco, Nepal, Nigeria, Pakistan, Philippines, Qatar, Russia, Chechnya, Rwanda, Saudi Arabia, Senegal, Sierra Leone, Somalia, Sri Lanka—North and Eastern Provinces, Sudan, Syria, Tajikistan, Thailand, Togo, Turkey, Uganda, Uzbekistan, Venezuela, Yemen, Zimbabwe.

The solution is high-limit accidental death insurance, referred to as AD&D. It can also have a dismemberment clause added and a special rider for travel to those 60 "hotspots" around the globe. These can be written for durations as short as two weeks to one-year terms or longer.

Worried about terrorism? Get a terrorism medical insurance rider on the policy. This has become commonplace since 2001. If an insured person is injured as a result of an act of terrorism, and the insured person has no active participation in the act, the plan will reimburse eligible medical claims subject to a $500,000 lifetime maximum. Pricing can be as high as 25% over the normal premium. Claims incurred as a result of nuclear, chemical or biological weapons or events are never covered.

There are also terrorism life insurance riders. The limitations of coverage are very similar (not covering nuclear, chemical or biological weapons or events), and it will additionally not cover those individuals who are "actively participating" in acts of war or terrorism (obviously).

One last thing to consider strongly when traveling to say, Mexico, Colombia, or Middle East, where it's not unusual for people of affluence to be abducted on the street and held for ransom, is a policy they call Kidnap, Ransom and Extortion. These types of policies provide not only ransom benefits but also informant money, crisis management services, accidental death, legal liabilities, rehabilitation, personal security consultation, negotiation services, family counseling and more, depending on how extensive you'd like your coverage to be. Costs for a K&R plan are dependent on many factors including net worth, business activities, travel itinerary and previous threats or incidents, etc. The average K&R policy limit of coverage is usually around $1 million and for one year of coverage for an average case starts at about $1000 and goes up from there.

International Shipping: Take It or Leave It?

Do you want to bring along your desktop computer, your wardrobe, your grand piano or your Prius? Depending on how long you're going away for, and your attachments to the material aspect of your world, you can choose to sell it, store it, or give it away. And whatever's left has to fit in your suitcases or it must be boxed and shipped. You can find international movers in your local yellow pages or at hundreds of sites on the Internet. But beware. It's a minefield out there, and moving scams make up a hefty portion of the complaints filed with various consumer protection organizations. One solution is to only deal locally, with a mover whose place of business you can verify. There are also a number of organizations that certify movers in the United States. These are:

American Moving and Storage Association (AMSA) **www.moving.org**
International Association of Movers (ISM) **www.iamovers.org**
International Shippers Association (ISA) **www.isaship.org**
Florida Movers and Warehouseman's Association (FMWA)
    www.fmwa.org (Florida only)

There are many ways to move your stuff, none of them cheap. Depending on how much you're willing to shell out, you can have a bunch of burly movers show up with packing material, and inventory, pack and ship your goods while you sit on the last remaining chair and sip tea, and the same in reverse can be had at the other end. The more work you're willing to do yourself (short of actually loading it onto a container and sailing the vessel to where it's going) the more you'll save.

Regardless, unless items are particularly valuable or indispensable, you're probably better off letting them go and re-accumulating once you're settled.

Remember, while your basic personal and household items can be brought over without any flags being raised, import taxes may apply to unused items, very valuable items or items in excess of what that country deems sufficient for personal use. Cars can be problematic—in Costa Rica, for instance, imported automobiles are levied a tax equal to the value of the car itself. Firearms, if you own any, probably will be banned. For a list of import rules, you can contact the embassy or consulate. A fairly comprehensive list can also be found at **www.world-widemovers.com**. The site also has a database of international movers searchable by location, a packing checklist, and many other moving-related resources.

Art F.
Sihanoukville, Cambodia
When I came here, I had sold almost everything I owned. Everything else got packed into two suitcases or stored in my kid's attic. Shipping to Cambodia is expensive and undependable. Things seem to get "lost" easily. You may also have to pay "duty" or "tax" to the local post office—again nothing more than extortion.

Minor Details: Your Children

Leaving the country with children adds a few new dimensions to the process, nor does having them overseas make it less complicated. How will the move affect them? Certainly, the younger they are, the easier it will be to adapt to life in another culture. As for their education, this presents a problem, particularly in places where English is not the spoken language, or in less-developed countries where the standards are simply not up to par. You can always home-school, of course, or do what most expats do and educate your kids at an American or international school. If the location you're moving to has any kind of American expat population, then more than likely there is a school for the children. The U.S. Department of State Office of Overseas Schools supports hundreds of schools around the world so that overseas government employees can have a place to send their children. A list can be found at **www.state.gov**.

For more choices check out: Worldwide Classroom: **www.worldwide.edu**

Because of an alarming uptick in international abductions, families where the child is not in the company of both biological parents may be subject to more intense official scrutiny, and often consent letters from either parent, divorce decrees, death certificates and other documentation of legal guardianship will be required.

Bruce Epstein
Orsay, France

Those parents with the means send their kids to one of the International schools; the rest of us have to tough it out. Our daughter, who was in second grade and spoke no French when we arrived, went to a Catholic elementary school (even though we're not Catholic) because the local public school didn't want "another immigrant." For junior high, a nearby school was starting a bilingual section. By high school our daughter spoke fluent French. But she still had a very rough time. One of her teachers was so prejudiced that she refused to give any extra help, saying "ask your parents," knowing full well that we wouldn't be able to help. In the end, she was so turned off by the French education system that she didn't even consider staying here for university; she went to Canada (Toronto) where she received a bilingual bachelor's degree and is now happily living and working.

Money Matters:
Deposits, Withdrawals, Currency and Cash

Many places allow foreigners to open bank accounts and some even allow you to keep your balance in U.S. dollars (this can be good or bad depending on where you think the exchange rate is headed). In other cases, some level of residency is required, which means you'll have to run your financial life from an account in the States. If you're paid from the U.S., try to set up a direct deposit arrangement, otherwise you'll have to arrange for someone to deposit your checks for you. Most banks offer online bill pay, allowing you to pay bills over the Internet. Credit card companies are happy to bill you that way, too, and their exchange rate fees are usually better than changing the dollars yourself, so using them wherever possible solves a few problems. PayPal is another way international payments are made and collected. For the rest of your legal tender needs, ATMs have reached most corners of the world. Some U.S. banks have signed ATM-sharing deals with overseas banks, meaning you can use them without paying the often exorbitant fees per each use. If you need to know what your money is worth, you can find out the current value of any currency against the dollar or any other currency at **www.xe.com**. Many former Americans choose to keep two accounts—one locally, and the one they had in the U.S. Expect banks to charge a fee for wire-transferring money between accounts (around $25) as well as a percentage on the currency conversions when the money is received (usually around 3%, the difference between their "buy" and "sell" rate). If you are moving large sums of money and often, it pays to open an account with a currency broker, who will generally charge less both in transactions and in conversion fees. They are many out there and their deals vary from company to company, as do their reputations. You can find an online directory and reviews at **www.forexfraud.com**.

NOTE: Because of the prevalence of money-laundering, a host of U.S. and international agencies keep a close watch on money moving across borders and some countries place limits on how much currency can be imported or exported. Also, be aware that the IRS requires U.S. citizens to declare on every tax return their holding in a foreign account if it exceeded $10,000 at any time during that year. Stiff penalties are levied for those who don't comply.

Marshall Creamer
Hong Kong

I have a local bank account in Hong Kong, and I also have an account in the U.S.

Setting up the account here in Hong Kong wasn't a very hard process. I did a lot of research on this before I left the U.S. so I was able to have a copy of some bills with my U.S. address on them, and then I just needed my U.S. passport and housing contract in Hong Kong. (My company put me up in a Serviced Apartment for one month; I just used that address, and then changed it to my work address later.)

I kept my U.S. account because I have some investments set up through them, and I have a credit card there that I have a small remaining balance on, as well as a few monthly re-occurring bills that are automatically deducted from my checking account.

I just send money back to my U.S. bank account so that I have enough money to pay the bills I still have. I save most of my money in a regular bank account here in Hong Kong then make transfers back to the U.S. every few months.

Real Estate: The Ownership Society Abroad

The overseas real estate game offers opportunities to purchase property at a fraction of what you might pay even in the collapsing U.S. market. For some, this means they can afford a dream home or condo. Profit-minded Americans can look to healthier markets abroad where they can buy properties and rent them out and/or flip them for a profit.

Before Getting Into the Game:

Know the Ground Rules: As in America, the real estate business in any country is likely to be more complicated than any layman can sort out. But you should get a handle on a few basics. Many countries require that all property be at least 51% locally owned, though Free Trade agreements have been slowly rolling back those requirements. Often, foreigners resort to forming a holding company with a local citizen named as shareholder to purchase their property. Some countries, like Mexico, have Eminent Domain laws wherein property is not technically sold, but given over in 99-year renewable leases. Centralized real estate listing databases are not the norm outside of the developed world, which means finding your dream property can involve a lot of shoe leather on your part or hiring an agent (reputable or recommended, preferably), who has his/her ear to the ground in the area you're interested in.

If you feel confident enough to go it alone, you can probably save money even if you hire legal help with the contract work. In some countries, Germany for instance, the government will make you hire a notary, who is essentially an attorney, at a fixed fee to oversee the contract from creation to signing and take care of land registry placement and other technicalities. While they will not advocate on your behalf, they will make sure that the sale itself is legal and above-board, that funds are secured before the property changes hands, and answer any legal questions you may have.

Mortgage: Mortgage lending overseas seldom comes near the freewheeling extravaganza it was in the heyday of the U.S. real estate bubble and is rarely an option to newly-arrived foreigners, though it is an option in many countries for established residents with an appropriate and documented work and income history. Most Americans of modest means who buy property overseas usually use the equity from selling their current home in the States. Condos and houses can sell for as little as $50,000 or less in parts of Eastern Europe, Latin America and Southeast Asia, and a lot of people simply pay cash.

Beware of Scams: Nothing attracts grifters like real estate. The Internet is cluttered with "Buy Property Overseas" come-ons of dubious merit. Local listings and sites are a better source but nothing can replace a personal visit and asking a lot of questions to get a clear idea of what properties are worth and how much people are generally paying for them. These will likely be far less than what you might gather surfing the 'net.

J.M.
Pushkin, Russia

We own a 1500-sq-meter plot of land on which we have built a 300-sq-meter paid-as-we-went house. Russian property titles are actual ownership, not long-term leaseholderships. And there's no regularly-recurring property taxes on your residence—so unlike in the U.S., you don't have to pay rent to the government for the privilege of getting to claim that you "own" your house.

Kelly Kittel
Tamarindo, Costa Rica

We own one lot on a large finca that we used to cooperatively own with others but sold our share and just have that left. It's for sale. Bought it years ago because of a family connection. You have to have a corporation here so that is one of the machinations of owning anything, even a car. Love the part of the country where our land is (S. Pacific) and hoped to build eventually but there are no schools near there for the older kids. Not as big of an expat community there as here because the main highway to there wasn't paved until just recently. Now I expect it will grow. Much more lush and rainforesty there than here in the north Pacific where it is dry, savannah-like. So more birds and other wildlife there.

I would NOT recommend buying anything (no matter where you are going in the world) until you have lived there for a year. The seasons here change dramatically and you might buy in the dry season only to find out your lovely home is inaccessible in the rainy season! Roads are a big issue and most folks don't see them in their full rainy-season glory when you can be up to your doors in mud. In general, it is best to rent and get a realistic feel for the area before buying, and there are lots of rentals here. Now it might be true that you would never visit in rainy season anyway, but still, you should know what it is like. There is always the concern of leaving any place unattended for any amount of time that you will have to reckon with. So it may be that your caretaker or property manager can't get there though the mud either.

I have friends who have retired, bought their dream condo during their first or second visit here (in the dry season), and now regret buying. After spending a year or two getting it all fixed up the way they like it and getting a feel for chilling out there, they wish they had the freedom to rent here and there around the country and beyond instead of being tied to their condo. And condo life is not always for everyone, so best to rent one and see what it feels like being stacked on top of each other and attending an owner's meeting to see if everyone can agree on anything from paint colors to community grills.

Another issue in CR is that you can't own in the maritime zone. I don't know all the particulars on how many feet from sea, etc. but usually to "own" a house like the one I am in means you are only leasing the land from the govt. for an extended time.

Ande Wanderer
Buenos Aires, Argentina

I was going to rent an apartment but I discovered that the rental market is saturated and it is practically impossible to find a reasonably priced apartment without a "guarantee" that says you already own property in the city. Believe it or not, it is much easier to buy if you have the money. So I bought property for the first time in my life (and I've never even bought a car worth more than $1000).

I found the apartment on a website called soloduenos.com ("Only Owners"). I bought my place directly from the owners in 2004, which at that point was still challenging as I spoke Spanish like a five-year-old on tranquilizers.

It is a 61-square-meter, two-bedroom walk-up apartment in San Telmo, the Greenwich Village of Buenos Aires. The most complicated part was the actual financial transaction because, like most owners, the people wanted to be paid in cash. I didn't want to use Western Union, pay a 3% fee and have to walk the streets with $29,000—someone I know here was robbed doing just that. Instead I wired the money into their bank account. The bank's policy was that the money had to be converted money into pesos, and then back to dollars, with heavy fees. No one wanted to lose so much money in the currency conversion. In the end we decided to split the bank fee but I had to play a little hardball at the office of the *escribana* doing the paperwork.

David Morrill, Partner: Cuenca Real Estate
Cuenca, Ecuador

Buying property in Ecuador is relatively straightforward. Foreigners have the same rights as locals to own property and you don't need be a resident to buy. Ownership is simple and outright. It's important, however, to have an attorney guide the foreign buyer through the process, do a title search and handle the money.

There are of course many downsides to buying here. There is no MLS (multiple listing service) system so price comparisons are harder to make. Many real estate agents are not licensed although there is a licensing process. There are often wide spreads between asking and selling price.

A buyer who does his or her due diligence and uses an attorney recommended by other foreigners will do fine.

Staying in Touch

Unless your travels take you somewhere truly primitive, you'll never be too far from an Internet café. These places tend to be ubiquitous, not only in tourist centers, but even in poor Third World communities, where few have the luxury of a connection at home and thus must gather there to email friends, surf the web and run their escrow fortune and lonelyhearts scams.

If it's just you and your laptop, wireless is available at over 296,000 locations in 145 different countries around the world.

The United States is still the leader with China in second place, but the rest of the world is catching up quickly. Searchable directories of Wi-Fi spots can be found at:

www.jiwire.com
www.hotspothaven.com
www.wefi.com
www.wi-fihotspotlist.com

The most exciting development for expatriates is the advent of VoIP (Voice-over Internet Protocol) which allows telephone-like conversation over the Internet, anywhere, often for free. These are bundled along with many Internet messaging services like AOL, MSN or Yahoo! For an overwhelming majority of 21st- century expatriates, Skype is part of their vocabulary, their hard drive (and mobile device applications) and their life. This free, downloadable program (**www.skype.com**) works from any computer with a high-speed connection and a microphone (though a headset or USB telephone is recommended). Like any Internet messaging program, calls between Skype members are free. Skype also allows you to call any phone number at a reduced rate or on a variety of unlimited monthly plans, usually with voicemail, call forwarding, call-waiting, caller ID, email and SMS notification and more. They'll even rent you a dedicated phone number so you can receive calls from outside phone numbers like any other telephone—a great way for those running a U.S.-based business from abroad to have a U.S. presence by having a U.S.-based number. The phone will actually ring at your computer wherever you are, as long as you're connected to the Internet.

Depending on how much you depend on your computer to be your telephone, you could venture into the slightly-techie world of VoIP beyond Skype (and even Vonage, the other, more business-upscale, well-known VoIP brand), and find far better deals and often far better and more reliable connections. For an up-to-date list of what companies are offering and where, you can check out **www.voip-info.org** where they keep a wiki page that continually tries to stay abreast of the VoIP scene internationally.

Except for the purposes of delivering high-speed Internet to your residence, you will probably make do overseas, like most people who live there do, with a mobile phone. Indeed, the poorer a country is, the more cell phones they seem to have. The situation varies around the world, but generally, if you have established some kind of residency, you can usually buy a discounted monthly plan. Otherwise, you'll have to go prepay. This can be cheap in Eastern Europe and Southeast Asia, but can easily run you hundreds of Euros a month in a place like France. Leave your plan back in the U.S. Your worldwide roaming plan is useless unless you truly do roam the world. The costs are much steeper than a local prepay and few people in your host country are going to pay to call a U.S. phone number (particularly from their mobile phone where typical plans would charge exorbitant per-minute fees) just to invite you to dinner.

If you insist on going low-tech, every country has a bewildering variety of cheap international phone cards for sale. Rates to the States run as low as .04 a minute for parts of Europe and Mexico, and even calls from as far as the Asian steppes rarely run more than 0.35 a minute. Another solution is "international callback." When you register with an international callback company, you get a phone number to dial from anywhere in the world. The computer on the other end doesn't answer the phone (so you pay no local phone charges), but immediately calls you back and gives you an open dial tone. Most international calls done that way are charged at pennies a minute. Calling the U.S. from Beirut on GlobalTel (**www.globaltel.com**), for instance, runs about 0.15 a minute and one from Paris would come to roughly .07. Before you sign on the dotted line, keep in mind that many countries have banned international callback due to concerns that the service is not licensed or regulated—which is to say, it cuts into telecom profits.

The lowest of low-tech is of course snail mail. The post office doesn't mess with forwarding mail overseas, so you'll need to turn to more privatized entities—i.e. the mail forwarder. The private mailbox service at your local shopping mall might offer overseas forwarding. Otherwise, you can try Access U.S.A. (**www.myus.com**) or U.S. Global Mail (**www.usglobalmail.com**). Whichever method you choose, you will receive a U.S. street mailing address, which you can give to the post office so all your mail can be forwarded there. You can also use it as your "permanent" U.S. address. All mail is then forwarded to your overseas address. Depending on what level of service and speed you prefer, rates run from $35–$50 per kilogram of mail. Most mail forwarding companies have repackaging services so you can have all of your packages sent at once to save money.

Name Withheld by Request
San Miguel de Allende, Mexico

Gringos who move here get a Texas mailing service address. This is so that you can buy things online etc., and the mail is forwarded from Texas. There are many services that do this. Mine charges 17% of the value of whatever I purchase online, and one dollar per pound. I pick up my mail and packages. They will deliver if requested. This Texas address is on my credit cards and bank accounts now. This is how it's done here.

Vina Rathbone
Buenos Aires, Argentina

Thank God for Skype and online banking. Skype keeps me connected to my friends and family for free, and my online banking helps me manage my U.S. bank account while I am here. I also purchased a Blackberry while I was here, only for the Blackberry chat function, which allows me to text for free with friends internationally.

Marshall Creamer
Hong Kong

The Internet is the number one tool for helping people living abroad. I can manage my finances back in the U.S. with online banking, I can call my parents using Skype and other similar services, I can translate Chinese websites using Google...I'm pretty sure I talk to my parents more living in Hong Kong than when I was in Chicago...I think making a big move like this really helped to motivate them to get a little more tech-savvy, my parents are talking about getting smartphones and Skype on their cell phones so we can chat...

Also, Facebook allows me to keep up with what's going on with my friends, and I'm able to share pictures and what's going on with me to my friends and family.

Bob Hand
Rio Grande do Sul, Brazil

The Internet has been available in every city, large or small, which I visited in Brazil. I stay in touch with people in the USA via e-mail and Skype. I have high-speed service here and use Skype regularly with both audio and video. I purchase items via the Internet, both from the USA and Brazil. In my work, I communicate via e-mail with companies in China. I posted my résumé on a local website and that was how I obtained my consulting work. So the Internet is a key factor in successful living in Brazil.

Taxes: The IRS and You

Even if you're hell-bent on renouncing your citizenship and escaping the clutches of the U.S. Internal Revenue Service, paying taxes (or at least filing returns) is going to be a reality for the next couple of years, if not the rest of your life. You can choose to do their tax returns yourself. Those with adjusted gross incomes less than $58,000 annually can also e-file for free using 'freefile' on the IRS' (www.irs.gov) website. Those with higher incomes can use commercial software, but be sure to verify that they can be used with foreign addresses, since not all of them can. But as it is Stateside, many choose to use a professional accountant or tax preparer whose knowledge of the system and all available deductions are often worth more than the nominal fees they charge for their services. Your former accountant may arrange with you to do your taxes even after you've left the country, but be aware that a fellow expat tax professional is likely to have more experience with your kind of return. Obviously, referrals are the best way to choose one. You can also find them advertised on expat bulletin boards, and often the U.S. embassy or consulate abroad provides a list of local tax professionals on their website.

Mike Schiop, CPA MST, CPA Abroad LLC
London, U.K.

Americans move abroad for various reasons; some are entrepreneurs, some are artists, some are teachers, some are students and some retired. They are rich, poor and everything in between. And regardless of how they feel about the United States, most of them are not ready to renounce their citizenship.

For all those people, the overwhelming majority of Americans abroad actually, your tax situation, at least as far as the IRS is concerned, is pretty straightforward—well, as straightforward as tax-related matters go, anyway. And of course there is also the question of your tax liability to the country where you currently live, but that obviously varies considerably, depending on the country, and for that, you'll have to seek competent tax assistance locally.

The general 'American abroad' tax situation

As far as the IRS is concerned, Americans abroad are under certain obligations, such as filing a tax return reporting their worldwide income every year. This is not too much different than what you would do if you still lived in the U.S. If your income exceeds your Federal standard deduction and exemption amounts for the year, you must file a tax return.

In addition, April 15 is the tax deadline, no matter where you live. While the paper filing (or e-filing) deadline of June 15th is true for those whose tax home is outside of the U.S., the tax payment deadline is still April 15th, after which you incur interest and penalties for any tax owed. But if you're not going to owe any tax, then June 15th is fine.

If you cannot file your tax return by April 15th, or by June 15th, respectively, you can apply for an extension by filling out Form 4868, in which case, you'll have till

October 15th. You must file this form and pay any tax that you owe by April 15th. For those who live abroad, you can check the box 'out of the country' on the form itself and if you owe no tax, you can file it by June 15th.

Even if you owe no tax for whatever reason(s), you still must file a return!

Some taxpayers living abroad cannot reasonably file their tax return by October 15th—for example, high-net-worth individuals who have interests in partnerships and need to receive schedules K-1. As the partnerships have an extended deadline to September 15th, the taxpayers may not have enough time to gather all of their documents before October 15th. Thus an additional two-month extension can be applied for by writing to the IRS to extend their filing deadline until December 15th. Again, please note that these extension deadlines apply to the filing of your tax return, not paying the tax that you owe, which is due by April 15th. When the tax return is filed, it is advisable to have a statement attached that reads "Extension of Time to File Tax Return Pursuant to Treasury Regulation 1.6081-5(a)", which notifies the IRS that you are a taxpayer living abroad.

For those who own a foreign business either wholly, or via an interest in a foreign corporation or partnership, they must report them on certain Information Forms, such as 8858, 5471, or 8865.

Americans living abroad may file their tax returns by claiming the Foreign Earned Income Exclusion, Foreign Tax Credits for taxes paid in the foreign jurisdiction, or a combination of both.

The Foreign Income Exclusion excludes $91,500 of income earned abroad and it remains in effect for that year and all later years until you revoke it. If your income is below that number and you file under this claim, you will pay no tax. In addition to the Foreign Earned Income Exclusion, you can exclude or deduct a portion of your housing costs, if they are more than the U.S. Government allowance of $14,640 per year, but less than the yearly limit for the location in which you incurred them. The standard limit of housing expenses is $27,450 for 2010, but depending on your location, it may be greater. If you live in Berlin, your limit is $56,300 instead of the $27,450, so you can exclude a greater amount of housing costs if you qualify.

The Foreign Tax Credit can be advantageous to high income-earners abroad, since it credits you for the amount of tax you pay to a foreign jurisdiction against your overall tax bill in the U.S. So, in a "plain vanilla" example (a situation that does not include any kind of reductions in your foreign tax paid, because this can also happen for various reasons), if your tax obligation to the IRS comes to $11,500 but you've already paid the equivalent of $9,500 in local income tax, then your payment to the IRS would only be $11,500 minus $9,500, or $2,000. If the foreign tax rate is higher than in the U.S., you build foreign tax credits. As a CPA familiar with the U.K. and Romanian tax systems, I see both sides of the coin.

U.K. example: John lives in the U.K., earns 200,000 GBP from his employment, and has no other sources of income. He pays a graduated U.K. tax of 20% and 40% on income up to 150,000 GBP, then 50% on the rest. Clearly he pays more U.K. tax than the highest U.S. tax rate of 35%, but he can only claim credit for tax that he owes to Uncle Sam. The rest of the tax paid becomes a credit that he can either carry back or carry forward, depending on his circumstance.

Romania example: Dorothy lives in Romania and earns the equivalent of $150,000, but only pays 16% tax on her salary. Her best choice would be to exclude $91,000 worth of income, then calculate the tax owed on the remaining amount after taking into account the Foreign Tax paid in Romania.

If you choose the Foreign Earned Income Exclusion one year and only the Foreign Tax Credits in the next year, you will not be able to claim the Foreign Earned income exclusion for the next five years, as it is deemed revoked. Careful planning is imperative to get through the myriad rules and regulations, especially if your income exceeds $100k. As mentioned above, tax planning is very important, as you want to maximize your foreign tax credits and improve your tax position. It is not easy, and it may be a good idea to consult a tax advisor who is familiar with international tax.

OK, let's talk about your assets.

Americans who have foreign bank accounts, which exceed $10,000 in the aggregate, must report them on Form TDF 90-22.1, Report of Foreign Bank and Financial Accounts (FBAR). The FBAR form must be received by the Treasury by June 30th, and this deadline cannot be extended. The FBAR seems simple, but extended regulations have added additional filing requirements, so read the instructions carefully.

In recent years the IRS has made efforts to bring taxpayers that have used undisclosed foreign accounts and undisclosed foreign entities to avoid or evade tax into compliance with United States tax laws. The IRS created the Voluntary Disclosure program, whereas taxpayers with undisclosed income from offshore accounts, such as foreign banks, could come forward and get current with their tax affairs.

Renouncing your citizenship.

For those who do want to renounce their citizenship, they must know that they will renounce all of their rights and privileges and the renunciation is irrevocable. There is a legal step, wherein you need to formally renounce your citizenship, and a tax step, wherein you need to comply with the IRS requirements.

You must file a dual status return for the year during which you expatriate, which means that you file a resident return up to the date that you expatriate and a non-resident return for the rest of the year after that date. You also need to file Form 8854 with the IRS and satisfy their tax requirements. The expatriation rules apply (with certain exceptions) if you expatriate after June 16, 2008 and:

1. Your average annual net income tax for the five tax years ending before the date of expatriation is more than $147,000 (if you expatriate in 2011).
2. Your net worth was $2 million or more on the date of your expatriation.
3. You fail to certify on Form 8854 that you have complied with all federal tax obligations for the five tax years preceding the date of your expatriation (Certification Test).

If the above rules are met, you are considered a covered expatriate and will fall under the rules of section 877A, which imposes income tax on the net unrealized gain in your property as if the property had been sold for its fair market value on the day before your expatriation date ("mark-to-market tax"). This applies to most types of property interests you held on the date of your expatriation, with a few exceptions. The net gain from the deemed sales that you otherwise must include in your income is reduced in 2011 by $636,000, but not below zero.

However, just because you do not meet the above income tax liability and net worth threshold, you must still pass the Certification Test in #3.

I personally do not advise my clients to renounce their citizenship. But if this is what you want to do, and your net worth is such that it would make any kind of financial sense to even contemplate it, then it is best to consult a law firm specializing in these matters before to get a precise picture of how it would affect your particular circumstances.

The Long Arm of U.S. Law:
A Short Course in Extradition

ex·tra·di·tion (eks´ trə dish´ ən)
n. Legal surrender of a fugitive to the jurisdiction of another state, country, or government for trial.

A note to would-be fugitives: before you get any ideas, be aware that nobody pursues extradition with greater zeal than Uncle Sam. The United States currently has more bilateral extradition treaties than any other nation, over 112 at last count. We negotiated our first in 1794, with, surprisingly enough, our then-enemy, Great Britain. Most recently, Antigua and Barbuda, Barbados, Grenada, India, the Philippines, Sri Lanka, St. Kitts and Nevis, St. Lucia, St. Vincent and the Grenadines, Trinidad and Tobago and Zimbabwe all signed on to America's "Nowhere to Hide" doctrine. Older treaties are constantly being re-ratified to close any possible loopholes.

For the United States to have one of its citizens (not only citizens, but anyone who's committed a crime within its borders) delivered back to the bosom of the homeland, numerous conditions must apply, most notably that the crime is severe enough to warrant the hassle (what constitutes "severe" is open to interpretation), that there is clear-cut evidence of guilt, and that the act committed is considered a crime in both countries (Vietnam-era draft dodgers weren't extradited because Canada had no mandatory conscription, but anyone ducking out of their military service in Iraq or Afghanistan is extraditable because both countries have laws against desertion).

Mexico, Canada, and most European nations will not allow extradition to nations with capital punishment unless they are assured that the death penalty will not subsequently be imposed. Usually, the United States simply agrees not to fry the perps should they be found guilty, and back they go to face life imprisonment in America.

In any case, it's standard operating procedure in most of the world to require that you present your police record before they'll issue any kind of residency permit. Not surprisingly, most governments feel they have enough criminals of their own and aren't eager to import any from the United States, or anywhere else for that matter. And you may have also noticed that if the U.S. wants someone bad enough, they don't bother themselves with the legal niceties.

Lands Beyond Justice:
Countries with No Extradition Treaties with the U.S.

Afghanistan

Algeria

Andorra

Angola

Armenia

Bahrain

Bangladesh

Bantu Homelands

Benin

Bhutan

Bophuthatswana

Bosnia

Botswana

Brunei

Burkina Faso

Burundi

Cambodia

Cameroon

Cape Verde

Central African Republic

Chad

China (People's
    Republic of China)

Ciskei

Comoros

Côte d'Ivoire

Djibouti

Equatorial Guinea

Ethiopia

Gabon

Guinea

Guinea-Bissau

Indonesia

Iran

Korea (North)

Kosovo

Kuwait

Laos

Lebanon

Libya

Madagascar

Maldives

Mali

Marshall Islands

Mauritania

Federated States of
    Micronesia

Moldova

Mongolia

Mozambique

Myanmar

Nepal

Niger

Oman

Qatar

Russian Federation

Samoa

São Tomé & Principe

Saudi Arabia

Senegal

Serbia

Sudan

Syria

Taiwan

Togo

Transkei

Tunisia

Senegal

Uganda

United Arab Emirates

Vanuatu

Vietnam

Yemen

Vanuatu

Web Resources

A World Wide Web of Resources

Still have questions? Well, that's not surprising. There is only so much information that can be packed into one book. This one has given you the lay of the land (actually, many lands) so that you can understand what is easy, difficult or impossible for you, what appeals to you and what doesn't and what you might have to sacrifice along the way. You have an idea about your best options and dealbreakers. In other words, you know how to THINK about Getting Out.

As you put your plan into action, we encourage you to branch out further —find the mother lode of information for the exact country and topic that most interests you. There is a world of resources out there—informal networks of like-minded individuals, websites, organizations, agencies, as well as a host of books and other publications—to help you succeed. The trick is in knowing where to search.

Bottom line: this is a uniquely advantageous time to be living abroad. Thanks to the Internet, there is a wealth of information at your fingertips. There are countless blogs, websites, and other resources available to answer your questions or point you in the right direction. We've amassed some quality websites below which we hope you find helpful. Even more resources can be found at **gettingoutofamerica.com**.

And don't forget that, ultimately, your most valuable resources are made of flesh and blood, not 1s and 0s. Many of the websites below offer user forums and other functions where you can connect with actual people who are already living where you want to live and doing what you want to do. And don't forget your social network. Facebook (**facebook.com**), Twitter (**twitter.com**) and other social networking platforms can be indispensible in building a network that will help you get to where you're going and make your life easier once you get there.

General Information and Data on Countries Worldwide

Ironically, two of the most helpful resources for Americans planning their escape are funded and operated by the same country you're leaving behind— the CIA and the State Department. At **www.state.gov** and **travel.state.gov**, you'll find a world of information regarding travel to and living in every country on the planet—courtesy of the government you're saying goodbye to. Even more information and local resources can be found at the website of the U.S. Embassy in that country, a list of which (along with addresses, URLs, etc.) can be found at **www.usembassy.gov**.

For a detailed lowdown about any aspect of any country, check out the *CIA World Factbook*. Updated annually, you get the latest on the balance of trade, miles of coastline, incidence of AIDS, number of paved runways and any other wonky question you might have. It costs a little over 10 bucks on Amazon, and there is also a Kindle edition for a dollar less, but you can simply peruse it online and even download the book for free at **www.cia.gov/library**. We recommend the Central Intelligence Agency's fine work to anyone who is planning to escape the U.S. You'll never get a better chance to appreciate your tax dollars at work.

Also indispensable is the Portals to the World site which gives a country resource list compiled by the subject experts at the Library of Congress: **www.loc.gov**.

To obtain a country's official immigration and visa policies and requirements beyond those of a casual tourist, navigate your way to its Ministry of Foreign Affairs website, though you may find they lead you to other, more dedicated, immigration sites. Most these days have an English version and generally provide a full list of that country's embassies and consulates around the world, whose individual websites (particularly foreign embassies/consulates in the U.S. and other English-speaking countries) are also sources of similar, though often not identical, information. Look for the tab marked "consular affairs." You can find a comprehensive list of official government websites at **www.govspot.com** and a specific embassy and consulate list at **www.embassyworld.com**.

You'll also find that many of the most comprehensive reports and data compiled on countries are done by banks and other corporate institutions and associations. Generally, these focus on business and economics, but since there's hardly an aspect of life in a nation that doesn't impact the overall economy, the information collected tends to be pretty comprehensive.

Organization for Economic Co-operation and Development: An international organization dedicated to studying the interaction between policy and quality of life, compiles numerous in-depth reports, databases and statistics of a variety of variables affecting the quality of life in their member countries, comprising most of the developed world. **www.oecd.org**

New Economics Foundation: A refreshing antidote to the point of view of rapacious capitalism, this anti-globalism foundation publishes reports and compiles economic and other data "as if people and the planet matter." www.neweconomics.org

World Bank: Data, resources, and publications about the performance of governments around the world. www.worldbank.org

World Economic Forum: WEF provides a wealth of economic data, reports, and analysis on countries around the world. www.weforum.org

And of course, if a country flies a U.N.-recognized flag, there's plenty of info on it on the U.N.'s website (www.un.org). Navigating through it and those of its affiliated organizations, however, is not always easy, though the search engine should take you right to where you want to go.

Other good general sites include...

Convert It: A handy site to bookmark since it offers measurement, time zone and currency conversion plus international phone codes and a whole lot else. www.convertit.com

Countries of the World: A massive and searchable database compiling histories, data and other facts about every country in the world. www.theodora.com/wfb

General Expat Resources

The following sites are primarily geared toward people moving or living abroad:

Alliance of Business Immigration Lawyers: Primarily geared toward the business crowd, this website represents a worldwide network of immigration lawyers and provides a wealth of practical information and resources regarding work, immigration, citzenship and doing business in many countries around the world.

@llo Expat Worldwide: Resources and discussion forums focusing mainly on Asia, the Middle East and South America. www.alloexpat.com

Association of Americans Resident Overseas (AARO): An advocacy group for American expatriates (particularly tax policy). The site also provides some useful data and news. www.aaro.org

AngloINFO Worldwide: Full service guide to 20 countries, and growing. Site keeps an excellent list of English-language media outlets around the world. www.angloinfo.com

BlogExpat.com: A directory for expat blogs, travels and blogs abroad, open to any personal blog of an individual living abroad and sharing their expat experience. www.blogexpat.com

CraigsList: Established in over 80 cities (not including those in the U.S.) in 50 different countries, with more being added all the time, this unique web resource offers bulletin boards for buying, selling, renting, jobs, activities and personals. Not specifically designed for expatriates, but most of the posts are by English speakers even in non-English-speaking countries. www.craigslist.org

Easy Expat: Focus mainly on Australia, Belgium, Canada, France, Germany, Italy, Spain, Switzerland, U.K. www.easyexpat.com

Expat-Blog: Active expat forums, searchable user databases (by name, nationality, current residence, etc.) with active links to users' offsite blogs. www.expat-blog.com

Expat Focus: Although geared slightly toward British expats, this general resource site covers around 40 countries, with more added frequently. www.expatfocus.com

Expat Exchange: Another general expat website, geared more toward the upscale traveler and corporate transfers. www.expatexchange.com

ExpatFinder.com: Comprehensive country-by-country guides to moving, living and working abroad. www.expatfinder.com

Expat Forums: People helping people. Expat Forums offers a number of active online forums to ask, share and receive questions and information and opinions. www.expatforums.org

Expatica.com: Plenty of detailed information aimed at the business and professional set. Limited to: Belgium, France, Germany, Luxembourg, Portugal, Russia, Spain, South Africa, and Switzerland. Well-researched news, information, forums, and employment opportunities for expats. www.expatica.com

Expatify.com: "Inspiring expatriatism"; information, resources, destination guides, etc. www.expatify.com

Globe Dweller: General expat site with country guides, forums, job boards, etc. Membership consists of those "wishing to integrate into their host country and immerse themselves into its culture and help others do the same." www.globedweller.com

Just Landed: Offers excellent coverage of Spain, Germany, Netherlands, France, Switzerland, Austria, U.K., Canada, Belgium, Luxembourg, Australia, Italy, Ireland, Portugal, New Zealand, Greece, Cyprus, and South Africa. www.justlanded.com

Living Abroad: Membership site geared toward business transfers. www.livingabroad.com

Meetup: This site lists group meetings in cities around the world and has extensive listings in the "Expat American" category. www.meetup.com

Overseas Digest: This site provides resources for living, studying and working abroad; also publishes a weekly online newsletter. Geared toward business and bureaucratic types. www.overseasdigest.com

Tales from a Small Planet: This excellent webzine provides news, stories, links, active message boards, and other resources for travelers and expatriates: www.talesmag.com. The mag also maintains the discussion group "Small Planet" at: groups.yahoo.com/group/smallplanet

Transitions Abroad: One of the best expat resources on the web. Transitions Abroad offers an online gateway to hundreds of articles, books, and resources about every aspect of moving, living, studying, and working abroad. www.transitionsabroad.com

Resources by Topic:

Alternative Accommodation

CouchSurfing: An International non-profit that connects travelers with locals willing to share couch space and hospitality in over 230 countries. www.couchsurfing.org

Squatter City: Blog covers squatting and squatter cities across the globe. squattercity.blogspot.com

Worldwide Opportunities on Organic Farms (WWOOF): Links volunteers with organic farmers. www.wwoof.org

Workaway: Work exchange for room and board abroad. www.workaway.info

Currency

The following websites allow you to convert the value of any amount of any currency into any other currency (and offer currency broker services):

The Currency Site: www.oanda.com

XE: www.xe.com

Currency, Brokers

Forex Fraud: Offers a directory of currency brokers with reviews as well as general articles and how-to on safely navigating the foreign exchange market. www.forexfraud.com

Cost of Living

Mercer Human Resource Consulting: Catering to the corporate transfer and per diem set, this outsourcing/consulting firm keeps data on various costs associated with living in cities around the world. www.mercer.com

Numbeo: Free Internet database about cost of living and housing indicators worldwide wiki-type database of various types of cost of living data plus averages and rankings by city and country. www.numbeo.com

Xpatulator: This website charges a fee for in-depth reports, but you can certainly make do on what is provided free—information on cost-of-living indicators for various goods and services around the world, plus other articles on relocating and expatriation. www.xpatulator.com

Drugs and Drug Policy

Drug Policy Alliance: A non-profit dedicated to progressive, harm-reduction strategies to combat addiction and facilitate debate about current drug policies in a number of countries around the world. www.drugpolicy.org

Erowid: Global drug policy, information, and resources. www.erowid.org

International Harm Reduction Association: Non-profit devoted to pursuing more enlightened drug policies. Monitors drug laws and legislation around the world. www.ihra.net

Media Awareness Project: Searchable directory of news articles relating to drug policy around the world. Updated daily. www.mapinc.org

Webehigh.com: Worldwide marijuana traveler guide with dispatches by local, er, "correspondents." Laws, prices, where to go, etc.. Not always completely reliable, but that's stoner culture for you. www.webehigh.com

Ecology and Sustainability

Environmental Performance Index: Yale Center for Environmental Policy and Law conducts an annual study that ranks the environmental policies of 163 countries based on 25 performance indicators. www.epi.yale.edu

Happy Planet Index: Information and ranking on countries and their ecological footprint. www.happyplanet.index.org

Electricity, Adapters, Etc.

World Electric Guide: Country-by-country guide to the voltage, frequency and plug and outlet types used in every country in the world. www.kropla.com

Families/Children

Associates of the American Foreign Service Worldwide: Geared toward diplomatic families, this site provides helpful resources for any family living overseas, including information on education, finances, and domestic issues. www.aafsw.org

Families in Global Transition: Resources and information for expatriate parents. www.figt.org

Family Life Abroad: For and by expatriates on family life outside the U.S. www.familylifeabroad.com

Ori & Ricki: Cartoon couple Ori and Ricki star in this website that was actually created for expat children. Games, stories, links and more than a few resources for Mom and Dad as well. www.ori-and-ricki.net

TCK World: Essays, resources and articles devoted to "Third Culture Kids" including military brats, preachers' kids, Foreign Service and corporate kids, and others who have lived as children in foreign cultures. www.tckworld.com

Travel with Your Kids: With particular emphasis on parents traveling or moving abroad with children. www.travelwithyourkids.com

Gay and Lesbian

Gay Times: Well-researched listings give the legal as well as cultural situation for gays and lesbians worldwide. Website contains a searchable database of the rules and customs of every country as well as links to other resources. www.gaytimes.co.uk

International Lesbian and Gay Association: Reports on gay and lesbian issues around the world. www.ilga.org

International Gay and Lesbian Human Rights Commission: Information about government policies pertaining to gay and lesbian communities around the world. www.iglhrc.org

International Gay and Lesbian Travel Association: Website of trade association focusing on travel options for gays and lesbians. www.iglta.org

OutTraveler: Provides city guides, travel basics, information about events, and guides to clubs, bars, and nightlife in a number of different countries. www.outtraveler.com

SodomyLaws.org: Worldwide monitor of sodomy laws, gay rights, etc. www.sodomylaws.org

Guns, Crime and Safety

Freeexistence.org: Everything you want to know about gun rights anywhere in the world. www.freeexistence.org

European Institute for Crime Prevention and Control: U.N.-affiliated organization focused on crime and justice issues. www.heuni.fi

Maplecroft: This global risk management company assesses, rates and ranks risks of everything from terrorism to climate change. www.maplecroft.com

Small Arms Survey: Keeps track of small arms proliferation worldwide. www.smallarmssurvey.org

United Nations Office on Drugs and Crime: Publishes reports and surveys on crime around the world. www.unodc.org

Governance, Regulatory Environment, Human Rights

Amnesty International: Worldwide watchdog of human rights. Offers country-by-country human rights reports. www.amnesty.org

Doing Business Project: The World Bank's Doing Business Index measures and rates the business and regulatory climate in over 183 countries. www.doingbusiness.org

Freedom House: Nonprofit watchdog groups that monitors human rights and the growth of democracy and freedom across the world. Country profiles on webpage. www.freedomhouse.org

Human Rights Watch: Publishes annual human rights report covering the human rights situation in 90 countries around the world. www.hrw.org

Transparency International: Global organization that monitors corruption in government. www.transparency.org

World Bank: Data, resources, and publications about the performance of governments around the world. www.worldbank.org

Health

English-Speaking Doctors: The International Association for Medical Assistance to Travelers provides a searchable database of English-speaking physicians around the world. iamat.org

The following sites list up-to-date information regarding recommended vaccines, infectious disease outbreaks and other health issues worldwide:

U.S. Department of Health and Human Services, Centers for Disease Control and Prevention: www.cdc.gov/travel

U.N. World Health Organization: www.who.int
The following sites provide information and up-to-date information on food safety and outbreaks of food-borne illnesses.

Bites: bites.ksu.edu

World Health Organization (WHO) Food Safety Division: www.who.int

Insurance: Overseas Providers

Aetna Global Benefits: www.goodhealthworldwide.com

Bupa: www.bupa.com

Clements International: www.clements.com

eGlobalHealth Insurers Agency, LLC: www.eGlobalHealth.com

Expatriate Health Ins. Protection Plans: www.expatriateinsurance.com

IMG: www.expathealthcentre.com

International Calling

GlobalTel: International callback numbers. globaltel.com

Kallback: Low-cost international calling service operates from anywhere to anywhere. Internet or VoIP not required. www.kallback.com

Satel Call: Offers low-cost long distance from anywhere to anywhere via a "callback" number. Internet or VoIP not required. www.satelcall.com

International Embassies

Embassy World: This site lists embassy/consulate locations, phone numbers and websites for most countries. www.embassyworld.com

International Mail Forwarding

U.S. Global Mail: Offers a dedicated U.S.-based address where you can have your mail delivered or forwarded. Mail can then be forwarded to anywhere in the world. www.usglobalmail.com

My U.S.: Offers a dedicated U.S.-based address where you can have your mail delivered or forwarded. Mail can then be forwarded to anywhere in the world. www.myus.com

International Moving

American Moving and Storage Association (AMSA): Offers advice, information and helpful hints about international moving, and posts listings of AMSA-certified companies. www.moving.org

Household Goods Forwarders Association of America (HHGFAA): Offers searchable directory of HHGFAA-certified members. www.moverworldwide.com

International Association of Movers: (ISM): Professional association of movers and forwarders. Database of global movers and online shipping guide. www.iamovers.org

International Shippers Association (ISA): www.isaship.org

Mover Worldwide Directory: Offers searchable database of moving companies based on the location you are moving to and/or from. www.moversworldwide.com

Internet Cafés

The following sites offer searchable databases to find Internet Cafés worldwide:
Cyber Captive: www.cybercaptive.com
CyberCafes.com: www.cybercafes.com
Travel Island: www.travel-island.com/internetcafes

Internet ISPs

Internet Access Providers Meta-List: www.herbison.com

The List: www.thelist.com

Internet Penetration

The Bandwidth Report: News, statistics and technical information regarding Internet usage worldwide. www.websiteoptimization.com/bw

Internet World Stats: Offers news, statistics and technical information regarding Internet usage around the world. www.internetworldstats.com

Speedtest.net: Compiles user-supplied stats on various countries and Internet providers, particularly average upload and download speed. www.speedtest.net

Internet VoIP

Skype: Free downloadable software allows free unlimited VoIP calls to any other Skype user and low-cost calls to other landlines and cellular phones. Also available for a small fee are voicemail and "Skype In" which allows incoming calls from cellular phones and landlines. www.skype.com

Vonage: Fee-based VoIP provider, requires yearly contract. Allows incoming calls from all phones. Calls are free within the U.S. and Canada and are billed at discounted rates to the rest of the world. **www.vonage.com**

Voip-info.org: A global reference source for "all things VoIP." **www.voip-info.org**

Internet Wi-Fi

The following websites offer searchable directories of Wi-Fi spots worldwide:

JiWire: www.jiwire.com
Hotspot Haven: hotspothaven.com
WeFi: www.wefi.com
WiFinder: www.wifinder.com
Wi-Fi Hotspot List:
www.wi-fihotspotlist.com

Jobs

Anywork, Anywhere: Seasonal, temporary and permanent job listings and resources. anyworkanywhere.com

BUNAC USA: Provides temporary work permits for students and recent graduates for Britain, Ireland, Canada, Australia and New Zealand. **bunac.com**

InterExchange: Hooking up Americans with cultural/work/volunteer opportunities abroad. www.interexchange.org

Manpower Group: Corporate employment firm provides quarterly labor market outlook reports showing where the jobs are. **www.manpowergroup.com**

Relocate Magazine: For HR Global Managers and Relocation Professionals, this site is packed with articles and resources covering every aspect of corporate relocation and labor migration. **www.relocatemagazine.com**

Workpermit.com: Information and assistance with immigration/work permits in U.K., Australia, and Canada. **www.workpermit.com**

The following sites offer job listings for international jobs:

Career Builder: www.careerbuilder.com
Careers Without Borders:
www.careeerswithoutborders.com
Craigslist: www.craigslist.org
Eurojobs.com: www.eurojobs.com
ExpatCareers.com: expatcareers.com
International Herald Tribune (classifieds): www.iht.com
International Job Center:
www.internationaljobs.org
Jobs.com: www.jobs.com
Monster.com: www.monster.com
Overseas Jobs: www.overseasjobs.com
Stepstone: www.stepstone.com
Wall Street Journal Online:
www.careers.wsj.com

Jobs, Au Pair/Nanny

The following sites match au pairs and families worldwide (unless otherwise indicated) and offer discussion forums, resources and other advice for au pairs and host families.

Au Pair Box (Austria, Canada, Czech Republic, France, Germany, Ireland, Italy, Spain, Switzerland, USA, U.K.)
www.au-pair-box.com

Au Pair Connect: aupairconnect.com

Almondbury Au Pair & Nanny Agency: (Europe Only): www.aupair-agency.com

Great Au Pair: www.greataupair.com

E-Au Pair: www.eaupair.com

Au Pair World: www.aupair-world.net

The Au Pair Company: www.theaupaircompany.com

Find Au Pair: www.findaupair.com

International Au Pair Association at www.iapa.org where you'll find a searchable database of au pair agencies around the world.

Jobs, English Teaching

Aeon: Japan-based firm that specializes in English instruction with branches in every prefecture in Japan. aeonet.com

Dave's ESL Café: The top resource for English teachers Includes articles, job boards, discussion forum and links. www.daveseslcafe.com

ESL Directory: Directory of ESL lessons and programs around the world. www.eslinternational.com

ESL Guide: Guide to English-language schools and ESL programs worldwide. www.esl-guide.com

ESL Junction: Job listings, resources, TEFL/TESL courses and forums worldwide, particularly Asia. www.esljunction.com

ESL Worldwide: General information and listings for English-teaching jobs, TEFL/TESL programs and schools worldwide. www.eslworldwide.com

English International: Information and advice on TEFL/TESL training, certification, job market, publications, etc. www.english-international.com

Europa Pages, International Language Job Center: Free service for both English-teaching job seekers and employers. europa-pages.co.uk.jobs

Expat Teaching Recruitment: Specialist recruitment agency that places English teachers in foreign countries. www.expatteaching.com

The International Educator: A nonprofit publication listing hundreds of English-language teaching jobs. Also provides information on salaries, benefits, and how to secure an overseas position. www.tieonline.com

JET Program

The JET program was started with the purpose of increasing mutual understanding between the people of Japan and the people of other nations. It aims to promote internationalization in Japan's local communities by helping to improve foreign-language education and developing international exchange at the community level. jetprogramme.org

Jobs, Journalism/Writing/Media

Journalism Jobs: Has listings of journalism jobs worldwide. www.journalismjobs.com

mediabistro: Media website offers forums and (occasionally international) job listings. www.mediabistro.com

Editor and Publisher: Leading journalism trade magazine has extensive job listings. www.editorandpublisher.com

Society of Professional Journalists (SPJ): Along with protecting the rights of journalists worldwide, SPJ offer fellowships to working writers seeking time away "for study and research." www.spj.org

Jobs, Private Military Contractor

The Exchange: Provider of a lot of "like at home" goods and services to U.S. military personnel overseas. Their job board offers exciting overseas careers in retail store-stocking and food service work on bases around the world. odin.aafes.com

University of Maryland, University College: Job board lists openings for administrative and academic positions all over Europe and the ("downrange," they say) Middle East. ed.umuc.edu

University of Phoenix: Another education contractor, they operate in Europe and Asia-Pacific. Their website keeps a standing call for graduate-degree-level talent to apply to work as an instructor. www.phoenix.edu

Pets

ASPCA: Includes basic information for traveling with pets. www.aspca.org
Independent Pet and Animal Transportation Association: Links and resources concerning moving pets overseas. www.ipata.com

Let's Go Pets: A comprehensive and informative site covering all aspects of pet travel. Contains quarantine rules for over 40 countries. www.letsgopets.com

Pet Travel: All around pet and travel resource site, with quarantine rules for every country. www.pettravel.com

Permanent Traveler/Digital Nomads

Almost Fearless: Website for the permanent travel lifestyle. www.almostfearless.com

Digital Nomad: Information and resources for the digital nomad. www.digitalnomad.org

Exile Lifestyle: Kind of like "Zen and the Art of the Permanent Traveler" in blog form. www.exilelifestyle.com

How's the Wi-Fi? Website with articles about being a digital nomad. www.howsthewifi.com

Nomadtopia: Articles and resources for living "your ideal travel-centric life" edited by "location independent" Amy L. Scott, currently in Buenos Aires, Argentina: www.nomadtopia.com

PT Club: The privacy and sovereignty site contains lots of useful information for digital nomads. www.ptclub.com

Religion

Adherents.com: An A—Z guide to religions around the world. www.adherents.com

Schools, American and International (Primary and Secondary)

Association of American Schools in South America (AASSA): AASSA is a nonprofit membership association currently serving 43 International schools throughout South America and offshore islands. www.aassa.com

Association of Boarding Schools: Searchable database of boarding schools in Austria, Canada, England, Ireland, Italy, Switzerland, and Tanzania (and U.S.A.). www.schools.com

U.S. Department of State Office of Overseas Schools: The State Department supports hundreds of schools around the world so that overseas government employees can have a place to send their children. www.state.gov

Worldwide Classroom: Any program, any country, any school, this massive database complete with handy icons helps you find what you are looking for. www.worldwide.edu

Study Abroad

Study Abroad Universities: Information, links, and resources for students interested in taking courses abroad. www.studyabroaduniversities.com

Student Network: Up-to-date news for students and recent graduates regarding Internships, Scholarships, Summer Schools, Masters and Ph.D. programs. www.scholarshipandphd.blogspot.com

Scholarships 4 Development: Locate overseas scholarships in developing countries. www.scholars4dev.com

Taxes

Internal Revenue Service: All the information, forms and latest news and updates from your friendly IRS can be accessed at www.irs.gov

Tax Articles International Articles Directory: Country-by-country business and taxation articles and information. www.taxarticles.info

Worldwide Tax: Information about taxation worldwide. worldwide-tax.com

Publications, Blogs and Websites of Some of Our Contributors

Adam Lederer
Berlin, Germany
www.elmada.com

Ande Wanderer
Buenos Aires, Argentina
www.wander-argentina.com
www.wander-argentina.org

Bob Hand
Rio Grande do Sul, Brazil
www.mybasicprinciples.com

Bryn Martin
Lausanne, Switzerland
www.bryyn.com

Cara Smiley
Oaxaca, México
www.integratedorganic.com

Camille Moreno
Berlin, Germany
www.berlininart.com

David Morrill
Cuenca, Ecuador
www.cuencahighlife.com

€ric D. Clark
Lisbon, Portugal
soundcloud.com/eric-d-clark
mixcloud.com/EricDClark
subcurrent.net

Easton West
Berlin, Germany
www.highculturelowclass.com
www.sonofcataclysm.com

Jennifer Ashley
Chengdu, China
www.gochengdoo.com
www.chengdoo-magazine.com

James Lindzey
Medellín, Portugal
www.ParadiseRealtyMedellín.com
www.ColombiaVisas.com
www.MedellínTours.net

Jennifer and Douglas St. Martin
Lisbon, Portugal
www.centroquiropratico.com
fenixwellness.wordpress.com
www.livingclean.mionegroup.com

Jonathan Lukacek
Osaka, Japan
www.bandanna-almanac.com

Josh Plotkin
Permanent traveler
www.JoshPlotkin.com

Kelly Kittel
Tamarindo, Costa Rica
www.kittelposse.blogspot.com

Marlane O'Neill
Narbonne, France
www.narbonnegites.com
author of *Living the Dream on the Canals of England* (PublishAmerica, 2003)

Michael Schiop, CPA MST
London, U.K.
www.cpaabroad.com

Michael Luksetich
Amsterdam, Holland
www.mikesbiketoursamsterdam.com

Noemi S.
Auckland, New Zealand
www.Noemi.co.nz
www.thehousesitter.co.nz

Paul Schuble
Hyogo, Japan
www.jadij.com

Paul Tenney
Singapore
www.the-pffl.com

Sharon Hiebing
San Ignacio Town, Belize
www.wealthships.com
www.redroofpropertymanagement.com
author of *The Anti-Love at First Sight Expat Relocation Guide, Phase 1, Research*
(ebook available on Amazon.com).

Tinuola
Prague, Czech Republic
blackgirlinprague.blogspot.com

Turner Wright
Bugu, South Korea
onceatraveler.com
www.keepingpaceinjapan.com

Vina Rathbone
Buenos Aires, Argentina
mybeautifulair.wordpress.com

www.gettingoutofamerica.com

www.processmediainc.com